Native Title in Australia

An Ethnographic Perspective

Native title continues to be one of the most controversial political, legal and indeed moral issues in contemporary Australia. Ever since the High Court's Mabo decision of 1992, the attempt to understand and adapt native title to different contexts and claims has been an ongoing concern for that broad range of people involved with claims. In this book, Peter Sutton sets out fundamental anthropological issues to do with customary rights, kinship, identity, spirituality and so on that are highly relevant for lawyers and others working on title claims. Sutton offers a critical discussion of anthropological findings in the field of Aboriginal traditional interests in land and waters, focusing on the kinds of customary rights that are 'held' in Aboriginal 'countries', the types of groups whose members have been found to enjoy those rights, and how such groups have fared over the last 200 years of Australian history.

Peter Sutton is a distinguished anthropologist and linguist, and is widely regarded as one of Australia's foremost consultant anthropologists. He has worked with Aboriginal people in remote and rural areas since 1969 and he speaks languages from western and eastern Cape York Peninsula. He has written or edited eleven books, including *Languages of Cape York*; *Art and Land: Aboriginal Sculptures of the Lake Eyre Region*; *This is What Happened: Historical Narratives by Aborigines*; *Dreamings: The Art of Aboriginal Australia*; *Wik-Ngathan Dictionary* and *Country: Aboriginal Boundaries and Land Ownership in Australia*.

Native Title in Australia

An Ethnographic Perspective

Native Title in Australia

An Ethnographic Perspective

Peter Sutton

CAMBRIDGE
UNIVERSITY PRESS

PUBLISHED BY THE PRESS SYNDICATE OF THE UNIVERSITY OF CAMBRIDGE
The Pitt Building, Trumpington Street, Cambridge, United Kingdom

CAMBRIDGE UNIVERSITY PRESS
The Edinburgh Building, Cambridge CB2 2RU, UK
40 West 20th Street, New York, NY 10011–4211, USA
477 Williamstown Road, Port Melbourne, VIC 3207, Australia
Ruiz de Alarcón 13, 28014 Madrid, Spain
Dock House, The Waterfront, Cape Town 8001, South Africa

http://www.cambridge.org

First published 2003

Printed in Australia by BPA Print Group

Typeface Garamond (Adobe) 10/12 pt.   System QuarkXPress®   [PH]

A catalogue record for this book is available from the British Library

National Library of Australia Cataloguing in Publication data

Sutton, Peter, 1946– .
Native title in Australia: an ethnographic perspective.
Bibliography.
Includes index.
ISBN 0 521 81258 5.
1. Native title (Australia). 2. Aborigines, Australian –
Land tenure. 3. Torres Strait Islanders – Land tenure.
4. Land tenure – Law and legislation – Australia. I. Title.
346.940432

ISBN 0 521 81258 5 hardback

Contents

Figures

Acknowledgements

FOR WHAT I HAVE learned first-hand in over four years of field-work in Aboriginal Australia since 1969 I am grateful to all those Aboriginal people who have had the patience and drive to act as my mentors on the topics of this book. There have been so many that I cannot list them by name, but I am particularly indebted to the people of Cape York Peninsula, Daly River, Darwin, Western Arnhem Land, Tennant Creek, Murranji Track, Simpson Desert, Lake Eyre and Ayers Rock regions.

John von Sturmer and Athol Chase first aroused my interest in systematic ethnographic mapping during several months of joint fieldwork in Cape York Peninsula in the years 1974–76. Peter Ucko, then Principal of what is now the Australian Institute of Aboriginal and Torres Strait Islander Studies, provided inexhaustible (and exhausting) intellectual stimulation, and encouragement to look further into anthropology, when he was my boss 1973–75. My colleague, friend and former postgraduate supervisor, Bruce Rigsby, has been a constant mentor and support, and a generous sharer of his anthropological knowledge, since that same period. He read the penultimate draft of this book and made many valuable suggestions. Jamie Dalziel also generously read the draft and made numerous suggestions from a legal point of view which have been enormously helpful. Over the years many other colleagues have discussed and debated with me the issues addressed here, but I also particularly thank John Avery, Geoffrey Bagshaw, Ian Keen, Francesca Merlan, Nicolas Peterson, John von Sturmer and Nancy Williams.

The following colleagues generously provided me with helpful comments on earlier drafts of various parts of the book, or supplied me with unpublished field data of their own, or both: Barry Alpher, Robert Amery, Christopher Anderson, John Avery, Geoffrey Bagshaw, Brett Baker, Richard Baker, Kim Barber, Jeremy Beckett, Diane Bell, Christina Birdsall, Robert Blowes, Valda Blundell, John Bradley, David Brooks, Karin Calley, Kerstin Calley, Scott Campbell-Smith, Andrew Chalk, Christopher Charles, Athol Chase, Kim Doohan, Britta Duelke,

Derek Elias, Nicholas Evans, Katie Glaskin, Jenny Green, Diane Hafner, Kenneth Hale, Mark Harvey, Jeffrey Heath, Luise Hercus, Komei Hosokawa, Ian Keen, Patricia Lane, Marcia Langton, Robert Layton, Gaynor Macdonald, David Martin, Howard Morphy, John Morton, Julia Munster, David Nash, Graeme Neate, Kingsley Palmer, Noel Pearson, Nicolas Peterson, Sylvie Poirier, Fiona Powell, Marina Rigney, Bruce Rigsby, Gary Robinson, Deborah Bird Rose, Alan Rumsey, Jerry Schwab, Diane Smith, Patricia Stanner, W.E.H. Stanner, John von Sturmer, John C. Taylor, David Trigger, Petronella Vaarzon-Morel, Daniel Vachon, Michael Walsh, James Weiner, Nancy Williams, Susan Woenne-Green, Guy Wright; and those who participated in those National Native Title Tribunal workshops which I conducted in various cities 1996–98, and those who attended the 1997 and 1999 Summer Schools in Native Title and the Anthropology of Aboriginal Land Tenure at the University of Adelaide. I am particularly grateful for the suggestions for improvements to the present volume made by two anonymous referees appointed by Cambridge University Press. For research assistance I thank Marian Thompson, Vicki Humphrey and Kaylene Leopold.

Funding for the writing of this book has come from many sources, the principal one being the National Native Title Tribunal which engaged me 1996–98 to conduct a series of seminars at the Tribunal in Perth, but also in Brisbane and Sydney, on the topics represented in most of the chapters that follow. Many chapters began as notes for those events. Funds raised by teaching these topics in summer schools at the University of Adelaide were combined with university funding to enable me to teach an undergraduate course in Aboriginal land tenure and sacred sites at Adelaide's Anthropology Department. Parts of those lectures have also found their way into this book. Some sections of the book were funded by consultancies with the Cape York Land Council, Northern Land Council, Central Land Council, New South Wales Aboriginal Land Council and the Australian Anthropological Society. A visiting fellowship in 2000 at the Humanities Research Centre, Australian National University, gave me the opportunity to put together the first draft of the book. Its revision, and the writing of a number of original sections, were done in my own time.

Although there is much previously unpublished material in this book, the greater part of it has appeared in some form elsewhere, as discussion papers and as articles in academic books and journals. Their contents have been revised and in some cases thoroughly rearranged for this book. I thank the following publishers for allowing me to reproduce relevant papers or passages in various chapters as follows: the National Native Title Tribunal (Chapters 2, 3, 7, 8); Australian Anthropological Society (Chapters 1, 4); *Oceania* (Chapter 5); Centre for Aboriginal Economic Policy Research, Australian National University (Chapter 6); Australian Institute of Aboriginal and Torres Strait Islander Studies (Chapter 4). Notes identify chapters that have had earlier published versions.

Finally, I wish to thank text editor Jean Cooney, and Cambridge University Press staff Kim Armitage, Karen Hildebrandt, Jane O'Donnell, Phillipa McGuinness and Amanda Pinches, for their patience and support during the book's production.

Introduction

THROUGH MUCH OF THEIR history, anthropological studies of Aboriginal land and marine tenure have been focused on contemporary groups with strongly surviving classical traditions, or on reconstructing those traditions for people whose social and cultural lives have been even more greatly changed since Australia's colonisation by Britain in the eighteenth and nineteenth centuries. Following the arrival of legislative schemes for recognising customary Aboriginal land rights, beginning in the 1970s but reaching a high level of activity since the passage of the *Native Title Act 1993 (Commonwealth)*, more anthropological attention has been given to current relationships between 'country' and Aboriginal people of a wide range of cultural backgrounds, including those who live in urban and rural circumstances as well as those in remoter areas where older traditions have better survived.

This book attempts to take into account this wide range of information in order to discuss the major issues confronting Aboriginal native title claimants and title holders and those who seek or hold recognised rights under state and territory land and marine rights legislation. The emphasis, however, is on the native title context. Readers unfamiliar with the bewilderingly complex Australian native title legal and bureaucratic apparatus should familiarise themselves with the basic relevant literature if they want further background on the state of the law and its interpretation and implementation.[1] The issues covered in this book are currently faced by legal, bureaucratic and anthropological practitioners, whether the context is one of native title determinations by consent or by litigation. A number of them are also pertinent to indigenous land use agreements.

My orientation is necessarily both to present practices and to the classical 'baseline' situation reconstructible for the early contact period, which varied from the seventeenth century to the 1980s depending on location. This necessity arises in part from legal requirements, especially the need, under certain circumstances, to prove the continuity of present traditions with those held at the time when British sovereignty was established in Australia. But it also arises because it is important to apply insights gained from earlier land tenure systems when trying to understand how contemporary systems function and may be analysed, and how they might or might not have their roots in the classical or in innovations. Furthermore, knowledge of present systems can shed light on the frequently fragmentary records of the deeper past.

The legislative background

In 1969 and 1970 members of land-holding groups in north-east Arnhem Land, in the Northern Territory of Australia, brought action against the mining company Nabalco and the Commonwealth of Australia in an attempt to gain recognition of their own traditional rights over the land of the Gove Peninsula.[2] This led to the famous Gove case of 1971, which resulted in a reaffirmation of the doctrine of *terra nullius* which had long been the basis for official non-recognition of customary and pre-existing indigenous rights in land and waters in Australia.[3] A form of statutory Aboriginal title was introduced by the Commonwealth government for the Northern Territory in the *Aboriginal Land Rights (Northern Territory) Act 1976 (Commonwealth)*, section 3(1) of which reads:

> 'traditional Aboriginal owners', in relation to land, means a local descent group of Aboriginals who –
> (a) have common spiritual affiliations to a site on the land, being affiliations that place the group under a primary spiritual responsibility for that site and for the land; and
> (b) are entitled by Aboriginal tradition to forage as of right over that land;

This definition, which rested on anthropological ideas and advice of the time, inevitably drew many anthropologists into researching and providing evidence in the many claims heard under this Act, claims which at the time of writing were coming to a close. The State land rights scheme created for Queensland in 1991 has similarly drawn many anthropologists into the application of the legislation to the claims process, which recognises three bases of claim: traditional affiliation, historical association and economic viability.[4] Other state legislative schemes which deal with Aboriginal land interests (other than native title, see below) have not required the same kind of anthropological involvement.

In 1982 three Murray Islanders, Eddie Mabo, David Passi and James Rice, on their own behalf and on behalf of their families, commenced proceedings in the High Court of Australia seeking, *inter alia*, a declaration that they were the holders of traditional native title and that the Crown's sovereignty over the Murray Islands (Torres Strait) was subject to their rights according to local custom and traditional native title. In 1992 the High Court delivered its historic *Mabo* judgment in which a majority (6:1) held that native title could be recognised by the common law of Australia.[5] By the end of 1993 the Australian government had passed the *Native Title Act* which created a statutory scheme for the recognition and protection of native title and, among other things, provided (i) a mechanism for determining claims to native title (ii) ways of dealing with future acts affecting native title and (iii) in certain circumstances, compensation for its extinguishment.[6] Although the

Act was subject to far-reaching amendments in 1998, attaining a complexity found daunting even by lawyers, it retained its essential definition of what constitutes 'native title' or 'native title rights and interests'. Section 223(1), reads in part:

> The expression **native title** or **native title rights and interests** means the communal, group or individual rights and interests of Aboriginal peoples or Torres Strait Islanders in relation to land or waters, where:
> (a) the rights and interests are possessed under the traditional laws acknowledged, and the traditional customs observed, by the Aboriginal peoples or Torres Strait Islanders; and
> (b) the Aboriginal peoples or Torres Strait Islanders, by those laws and customs, have a connection with the land or waters; and
> (c) the rights and interests are recognised by the common law of Australia.

A series of High Court decisions have gradually refined the proper construction and meaning of these words, although there will undoubtedly be more to come. It is now clear that claimants need to establish that the traditional laws they acknowledge and the traditional customs they observe, and on which their rights in land and waters are based, are substantially the same as those of their predecessors in the same area prior to the imposition of British sovereignty. Those laws and customs must have normative content. The chain of transmission of these traditions also must be shown to be substantially unbroken, and traditions reconstituted in recent times will be of no avail.[7] Many are of the view that this decision effectively removes the possibility of succeeding in having native title recognised except in remote regions where classical traditions have persisted most appreciably. It is also clear now that the High Court has rejected broad traditional claims of an essentially proprietary kind, preferring instead the 'bundle of rights' approach.[8] These decisions have pushed the emphasis of anthropological research on native title cases into greater historical depth of detail and into a greater focus on particular rights or traditional 'activities'.

It is conceivable that a native title scheme that did not encourage or require work to be done by anthropologists might have been created, and it is notable that the definition of native title rights and interests in the Act, unlike the Northern Territory Land Rights Act and similar legislation, owes little of a direct nature to anthropological models. There is variable opinion on the extent to which anthropologists are necessary, even in the evidentiary testing process, given that claimants are typically called, in contested cases, to give evidence about themselves. But there are good reasons why expert evidence is normally called as well, and may be relied upon by a court.

Anthropologists working on native title cases record claimants' and other informants' statements about how one may rightfully belong to a place, what rights flow from one's traditional connection to a place, how one should behave according to customary rules to do with interests in sites and areas of country, and so on. These statements are highly important guides as to how people consciously formulate relevant principles. Those statements, however, do not alone account for or predict how people relate systematically to places or how they in practice allocate rights and interests in them. They are 'folk models' – and usually only fragments of them – that contribute important subjective knowledge to the record. An anthropological model, on the other hand, has to take into account what we can learn from people's actual behaviours, including other statements, as well. A senior man may say, for example, that strong interests in a country can only come from having a birthplace there or a father from that place, but it may become fully apparent that there are many cases which do not conform to this 'rule', yet which are so patterned as to clearly be manifestations of a regular customary system. Furthermore, a scholar who has good archival or other older historical records of the relevant ethnographic area can reach longitudinal conclusions spanning as much as a couple of centuries, well beyond living memory or even oral history. Do patterns which people do not recognise, or do not wish to recognise, fall outside the normative?

In non-legal and anthropological terms the 'normative' covers not only explicit rules but may also include the behavioural reflection of the *assumption* of a norm,[9] and *average* or *typical behaviour* as well as ideal norms.[10] In classical Aboriginal cultural traditions it would be abnormal, perhaps even inconceivable, that people would produce explicit, full and objective articulations of how their social order works, comparing ideals with action, and extracting underlying patterns of typical behaviour. Anthropologists rely on combined informant verbal and behavioural evidence together with documentary evidence in order to gradually form a systematic picture of topics such as customary ways of recognising rights in country and how they might have changed over time. For these reasons it would be both unsophisticated and counterproductive to reduce the category of evidence for traditional 'laws and customs,' for example, entirely to verbal formulations that might be elicited from particular Aboriginal informants or witnesses. One cannot put the weight of responsibility for such central probative matters on brief statements given in what is often a culturally alien context, and sometimes in a person's third or fourth language. If one takes a narrow view of how traditional rights are 'acknowledged' by claimants, restricting it merely to their verbalisations and omitting what may be abundant other evidence for their possession of a complexly patterned cultural logic, an ingrained system, of recognising rights, one may miss important evidence. Patterned behaviour is not merely a statistical norm when it comes to human social behaviour: such behaviour is informed by often deeply submerged cultural presuppositions, of which the people concerned may be only partly aware. There may also be presuppositions and rules of which people are aware but which they may be constrained, by customary law, from articulating, especially in public. Without the analysis of an external observer, they may not be able to do justice to their cases in a context where a negotiation or court hearing simply can never offer claimants and their assessors the kind of direct exposure to significant periods of everyday life and to multiple sources of evidence that an anthropologist necessarily engages with during fieldwork. Further, contemporary statements by claimants may be of little assistance in articulating the normative content of relevant laws and customs which applied before sovereignty was established, or in articulating transformative and other relationships between past and present.

The approach

In this book I have endeavoured to maintain a focus on the ethnographic rather than on the legal and bureaucratic dimensions of native title, about which in any case I know little. Theoretical issues of the discipline of anthropology are also only in the background here. This book is aimed not only at my anthropological colleagues and their students but also at people other than anthropologists, especially those legal and administrative practitioners concerned with the processing of claims, whether mediated, directly negotiated or litigated. For this reason, specialist terminology and many anthropological concepts are introduced without an assumption of anthropological training on the part of the reader. I do not go into questions of territorial boundaries in any detail in this volume, as my views on that subject are contained in another publication.[11]

Throughout the text I employ a distinction between 'classical' and 'post-classical' social and cultural formations and practices. The term 'classical' has begun to replace 'traditional' in Australianist writing since the late 1980s.[12] The main reason for this is that the former customary distinction between 'traditional' and 'contemporary' (or 'urban/rural') tended to suppress the fact that contemporary urban and rural Aboriginal people also have traditions. I prefer to use it as a distinction, not between kinds of society but between particular socio-cultural institutions. By 'classical' principles and practices I mean those which may be considered to take substantially the same form as can be reconstructed for the early colonial contact period and the era immediately before it. Many classical elements, such as classificatory kinship *per se*, belief in Dreamings (Ancestral Beings), totemic identities, or the inalienability of land, are widespread and share many underlying similarities across Australia. When taken in conjunction with the archaeological record, which reveals only very gradual and modest transformations in the hunter-gatherer economy and material culture kit over millennia before colonisation, many of these underlying features must be considered of ancient provenance. The classical practices and institutions persist to a significant degree in the remoter parts of the continent, and there are important elements of them that also at times persist in rural and urban Australia as well.

By the 'post-classical' I mean those cultural practices and social institutions that have developed distinctively since colonisation. It is useful to distinguish classical and post-classical whole systems (such as kinship) or underlying principles from specific classical and post-classical activities, social rules, artefact types and so on. Thus a specific rule for reckoning membership of a kin group which holds land may be post-classical in form, but the fact that an appeal to common ancestry remains the cornerstone of landed group identity in a particular region may be a classical principle that has come down more or less intact from pre-colonial times. One often finds that Aboriginal people in urban or rural areas have regular post-classical social practices which can be sourced back to older classical forms but they do not necessarily articulate those practices as 'laws'. However, where they are regular and to some degree regulating of behaviour I would regard them as having a jural component. That is, they attract a negative sanction in the breach. Matters jural are not simply a matter of individual preference or choice.

Some colleagues, however, may find my approach too much influenced by the 'jural paradigm' of mid-twentieth-century anthropology, and too little influenced by certain recent theoretical developments in the social sciences.[13] While that may be so, and I acknowledge a jural orientation in this aspect of my work, it is important to recognise that much of the existing anthropological literature dealing with Aboriginal land tenure has been oriented in a similar way, and familiarity with the ideas and language of that literature is important to grasping its ethnographic content in a way that takes account of its theoretical background (for example, Chapters 1 and 4), whether or not one takes a very different approach oneself. I hope that my introductions to technical terminology and concepts of kinship and social organisation (Chapters 7 and 8), for example, are useful to those who wish to understand the literature of the past and a good deal of that of the present. They are not intended as an encouragement to return to a past variety of structuralism, although I do argue for a persisting interest in structure and the need for anthropologists working in the native title arena to have the training to be able to perform a structural analysis of a body of data (Chapter 6). The kind of anthropological evidence that tends to be emphasised in the native title context is that which is relevant to legal questions of proof. This inevitably skews attention towards that which is collectively patterned, normative and rooted in old traditions (for example, Chapters 2 and 3). The application of methodological individualism may result in some rather different views of the same ethnographic base material, without necessarily contradicting observations made while paying greater attention to collective forms. Aboriginal people themselves, in most regions, traditionally pay a great deal of attention to collective formations such as named groups. It would be reductionist, in a comprehensive academic study, to examine such traditions purely through the lens of the collective objectifications of one's informants, just as it would be to examine them purely through the lens of egocentric kindreds, for example. But native title research only occasionally enjoys the luxury of being grounded in a comprehensive academic study, as when researchers return to places where they have carried out long-term fieldwork (for example, 12–20 months or more). In fact most native title anthropological research is carried out by consultants or staff who have much tighter time-frames.

This book is largely concerned with mainland Aboriginal Australia. Although there is some reference to the Torres Strait Islands in the text, a region usually regarded as part of Melanesia, I cannot claim any expertise in the anthropology of land and sea relationships there, and there is a book by Nonie Sharp which deals specifically with native title issues and historical developments for that region.[14]

Themes

Given that the focus of native title in Australia is on the translation of customary and traditional rights in country into legal 'rights and interests', Chapter 1 enters in some detail into various conceptual schemes which have been put forward for characterising and categorising the various recorded types of rights. In particular, I advance a model in which 'core' rights are distinguished from those that are 'contingent'. The initial motivation for this hypothesis was that I had seen a number of native title applications in which the rights claimed were listed in such a way that even people with only rather ambient interests in the claimed area might have been lumped together with those for whom the area was their primary country. It remains to be seen whether or not such a distinction, which I believe commonly reflects the ethnographic facts, is too problematic to survive in this rather skeletal form.

By way of background, especially for those new to the subject, Chapter 2 offers the reader a brief history of ideas about Aboriginal 'local organisation' (basically, land tenure and land use) from the late nineteenth century to the mid-1960s, just before the land rights era proper. While being necessarily selective, I trace the evolution of models of relationships between social organisation and customary interests in and rights over land, waters and their economic, religious and other content. In that period these ideas moved from a framework of historicism to one of ahistorical structural-functionalism and then, especially in the case of W.E.H. Stanner, to a more processual kind of modelling that also encompassed ecological considerations.

Although native title rights may be those of individuals (see above), they are most often put forward in terms of a group of some kind. Some claimant groups have been based on a common linguistic territory identity, as they have been in other jurisdictions, such as cases heard under the Aboriginal Land Rights Act or the Queensland Aboriginal Land Act. As in the case of some other developments in the field, I have been closely involved in several such cases.

The pitfalls of this domain of 'groupness', especially for those new to the topic, are perhaps greater than those of any other discussed in the volume. For this reason I digress a little in Chapter 3 into the thorny subject of relationships between sets and groups, and groups and labels for groups, before setting out what seem to me to be the main issues to do with how groups of people and the relevant areas of country are conceptualized in relation to each other. This discussion is extended in Chapter 4, where I discuss some practicalities and conceptual issues concerned with how widely or narrowly the net may be cast when sets of people are collectively identified as having links to and rights in areas of different relative sizes. Here again I revisit the history of ideas, looking at concepts of Aboriginal 'nations' and 'communities' between the late nineteenth century and the land rights era.

I argue for a model of local Aboriginal country relationships which takes account of regional tenure systems and regional populations as well, but in a particular way (Chapter 5). This model suggests a two-layered conception whereby those who are alive and have rights in local countries have 'proximate' entitlements which are pendant on a less labile, more widespread regional system of underlying title. Although this hypothesis resembles the radical title/ beneficial title scheme of English legal tradition, it is not based on it and it is not the same, although some of the similarities between the two are striking. A consequence of such a model might be that, even where there are for a time no living holders of proximate title over an area, native title might still be found to exist there, albeit held in a kind of wider or neighbouring regency arrangement, so long as keepers of the regional system maintain that system.

Note: Aboriginal norms which have customary force, especially those underpinned by religious belief, and bodies of relevant belief and ritual practice, are here distinguished in spelling as 'Law'. This is also the common English term for such norms and bodies of belief and practice among Aboriginal people.

In line with the convention in legal texts, I have adopted the use of italics in referring to land claim or native title cases: for example, *'Mabo', 'Lake Amadeus', 'Jawoyn'* and *'Kenbi'*.

Places and regions referred to in the text.

1 Kinds of rights in country[1]

NATIVE TITLE RIGHTS are rights recognised by Australian law, not customary law rights *per se*. They are attempts to recognise customary rights by translating them into legal terms. Native title is in this sense a 'recognition space'.[2] The terms of this recognition are those of the *Native Title Act* of 1993. Native title rights are products of a process in which evidence about indigenous cultural understandings and practices comes under legal scrutiny and is tested, usually by non-indigenous professionals. It is common for that body of information to be presented in the form of written and oral anthropological evidence, or anthropological evidence combined with that obtained directly from those whose native title application is being determined.

This chapter discusses from an anthropological perspective the kinds of rights and interests in country which people hold under Aboriginal traditions. In doing this it is also necessary to address the problem of terminology, as we are confronted with at least the following distinctions in the literature on Aboriginal rights in country:

- local individual or family rights versus tribal overrights and rights granted through intertribal territorial comity;
- rights versus privileges;
- primary versus secondary rights;
- unmediated versus mediated rights;
- presumptive versus subsidiary rights;
- actual versus inchoate versus potential rights;
- generic versus specific rights; and, more recently,
- core versus contingent rights.

In his review of much of the existing literature on tribes and intertribal relations in 1910, Gerald Wheeler found that Aboriginal tribal territory was subdivided generally among undivided families, but there was some evidence also of private or personal ownership of land, especially in areas where fishing rights were important. There was some evidence of a 'tribal overright' such that rights of local groups, families or individuals over smaller areas were not entirely exclusive, as certain products of the country may be free of access to members of the same tribe generally. While Wheeler had described such privileges of vicinage as widely held rights to which those of individuals and local groups were subject, he was lacking 'clear information' on this point. 'Absolute rights' were acknowledged and maintained over 'the tribal' territory and all its products, but this 'territorial sovereignty' was qualified by 'certain customs of intertribal comity' whereby members of other tribes were invited or permitted to share in the benefits of a tribe's country at certain times and under certain conditions.[3] That is, the capacity to exercise 'overrights', if not their abstract formulation, could depend critically on the state of relationships.

Mervyn Meggitt, who worked with the Warlpiri and others in the Tanami Desert area in the 1950s, distinguished between 'rights' to country and 'privileges' in it, the former being held basically as of birth, the latter being held as a consequence of marriage and co-residence.

> Apparently, residence in itself gave only economic and ritual privileges (rather than rights) to immigrants, including spouses of existing [i.e. natal] members. These people were free to share in the available food and to participate in many ceremonies, but they had no real authority in these situations – they could not legitimately command the actions of true members of the community.[4]

It is common to hear life-long and even second and third generation Aboriginal 'immigrants', including incoming spouses, deferring to the local landowners even when exercising a perfectly customary right to use the 'host' country which has long been their home. Christopher Anderson records that at Wujalwujal in Cape York Peninsula

> [o]ne man ... who was on the settlement council, and who was having trouble making any decisions go his way, said to me with a resigned sigh: 'No one listen to me. I'm only stranger here' (despite 35 years' residence in the area). What he meant was that he had no real right to speak. It was not his country. This is one of the most powerful principles governing politics in Aboriginal settlements across much of Australia.[5]

It is not so much 'immigrant' status as 'non-core rights-holder' status that more broadly underlies this kind of deference, as it can also apply between people with contiguous countries and a history of close co-residence, when one defers to the other on the other's land. In such cases nobody is an 'immigrant' in the ordinary sense because they are both just continuing the ancient practice of owners of neighbouring estates making relatively free use of each other's countries. But it is possible for those who lack core rights over an area where they live to describe themselves as 'only tourists' while staying there. The joke has a serious undertow. The same kind of deference can even apply where a person's relationship to a country is based on indirect descent rather than a contractual relationship such as marriage, or a history of long association, or the fact of holding a neighbouring estate. Such people will usually defer to those with more direct links to the country, at least in contexts where primary proprietary kinds of relationships are the focus of discussion.

While indirect links such as shared distant ancestry, or the sharing of totemic identities, may offer people more solid life-long presumptive rights in others' countries than links based on a history of co-residence, at least in non-Western Desert regions, it is people who commonly reside together who tend to share use rights over each other's countries most readily. People with direct traditional links to a country but little or no history of a social relationship with those who live on or near it may find it difficult to put into action the rights they hold in principle, especially where their descent link, for example, is rather oblique. Thus there are times when people with ancient 'rights' may defer to the knowledge and authority of those with more recently entrenched 'privileges', yet without blurring the principle of the distinction between the kinds of rights involved. There is often a disjunction between authoritative knowledge of country and the holding of primary proprietary interests in it. Thus the right to speak *for* a country will usually rest on somewhat different criteria from the right to speak *about* a country, although in the Western Desert region the blurring of this distinction, where it occurs, seems to be at its greatest.

The character of a right over a country or its resources cannot be determined in any depth merely by observing behaviour. In 1974, at Bathurst Heads in Cape York Peninsula, Johnny Flinders, whose clan estate was nearby at the other end of the same bay, was taking and eating rock oysters. The site which had the oysters was in his mother's mother's clan estate, not his own. At one point he turned to me and said, in his own language: 'I'm eating my mother's mother's oysters'.[6] His was a non-primary relationship to the country and its resources, given that his genealogical tie to it was non-patrifilial, but the link rested on a specific and quite close family connection. Johnny Flinders's right to eat the Bathurst Heads oysters was in an important way contingent on his mother's mother's own core proprietary rights over the clan estate (*Alpirr*) into which the oyster site fell. At the level of clan groups, the relationship between Johnny Flinders's estate and that of his mother's mother was one of relative proximity in space, relative unity of language, and participation in overlapping networks of marriage alliances and other connections. It is generally the case that ordinary kinds of mundane use-rights over each other's countries are shared among owners of neighbouring countries, even in the absence of a close genealogical connection, so long as the relevant neighbours remain on reasonable terms.[7] But from an individual's point of view, factors like estate proximity are generally of less significance than genealogical ties in conferring a sense of rightfulness about entering and using adjacent estates, unless genealogical ties are absent.

It is perhaps somewhat misleading to speak of 'use rights over countries' when traditional patterns of occupational use of land and waters were not aligned at all neatly with the geographic extent of such countries. Countries, in the sense of clan estates, Dreaming track segments or language group areas, are units of tenure, not units of economic use. There is no evidence that a classical band's range – a camping group's normal area of dwelling and resource exploitation – was the same area as a single clan estate, and it is usually described as much larger. Nor is there any evidence that a band's range was confined to a particular clan estate, or that it was a very fixed kind of constant as compared with the relative stability and definability of the geographic scope of estates. Use rights are usually rights in the use of regions that include a variety of estates or parts of them. There are often parts of estates which are not open to use by all-comers. For that reason alone it is not helpful to speak of 'use rights' being over estates *per se*. Rights based on spiritual or other deeper forms of identification are usually rights in estates as wholes, which are specific sets of sites usually considered to be relatively stable in composition.

DEGREES OF CONNECTION VERSUS KINDS OF RIGHTS
Primary and secondary rights; unmediated and mediated rights

A distinction between 'primary' and 'secondary' rights in countries has been around in the anthropological literature on Aboriginal land rights for many years. In an important early paper on the question of succession to Aboriginal countries, Peterson, Keen and Sansom said:

> A traditional owner of a clan estate gains primary rights in his territory by patrilineal descent. Secondary rights are a product of recognised social relationship(s) that link non-members of a clan, either to an estate owned by members of another clan or to one or more members of such a clan. Primary rights are thus direct rights while secondary rights are mediated rights. Six kinds of secondary rights can be distinguished ...[8]

They then discussed the six ways by which the acquisition of secondary rights were mediated: place of conception; place of birth; place of death/burial of an important relative; kinship ties, especially the relationship through the mother's mother; company for ceremony (sharing totemic and ceremonial links to other estates); and being the child of a female 'clan owner'.[9]

With the advantage of current knowledge such a statement would have to be revised in several ways, but these are not our concern here.[10] The relevant point is that regional Aboriginal land tenure systems tend to recognise that these ongoing 'secondary' forms of connection to an estate may become activated as acceptable bases for claims of succession to estates whose owners have died out. Those who succeed in this way, a process which often takes many years or even decades, convert their interest in the relevant estate from a secondary one to a primary one, or at least ensure that the interests of certain of their descendants in that estate are recognised as primary ones in due course. That is, in the terms of Peterson *et al.*, a person with 'mediated' rights to an estate and who succeeds to core rights in it, once they become the relevant primary predecessor in title for certain of their own descendants, will retrospectively be seen to have passed on those rights in a 'direct' or unmediated way. It may be said, then, that the full process of succession in such cases is not complete until a 'normal' situation has been restored whereby at least some people again enjoy unmediated rights in the country, and their precise origin is forgotten.

Many of these processes of succession are driven by one person or by just a close-knit set of siblings, for example, who hope to succeed to the estate concerned. These are cases of individual succession, but they normally have implications for the re-establishment of a group with interests in the country. In other cases it is apparent that the elders of an area 'appoint' an individual successor, who may be a newborn child, but again the succession starts with an individual who newly instantiates the group.[11] In time, such acts of individual succession would usually become the basis of the emergence of a replacement group holding the country. It is because of this, and because of the way the individual's relationship to the country is conceptualised, that it is usual to recognise that the tenure of an Aboriginal group over its country remains communal even when the group lacks more than a single member, or even any members, for a time.

Group succession: from neighbourly interests to insider rights?

Group succession occurs when, for example, the territories of extinct groups are subsumed by one or more extant groups. This is said to have been the case when people of the Ganggalida language group subsumed country of the defunct Min.ginda in the Burketown area, the Waanyi subsumed the country of the erstwhile Injilarija in the Lawn Hill region, and the Pangkala subsumed at least part of the territory of the much depleted Nauo (Nyawu) of Eyre Peninsula.[12] There are other cases where physical and cultural occupation of lands whose former occupants had shifted elsewhere, and/or became locally depleted, have turned into controversial bases for legal claims by members of the historically incoming groups. These are not readily categorisable as cases of succession, nor can they be likened to conquest, since they involve the assertion or assumption of rights which in some cases are recognised by descendants of the original inhabitants and in others are not, but there is no conclusive evidence of a formal handover of title nor of forcible occupation. These include the situations which form the backgrounds to the Northern Territory claims of *Finniss River, Lake Amadeus* and *Kenbi,* and native title claims by Yankunytjatjara, Pitjantjatjara, Ngaliya and Kukatha people in the *Far West Coast* region of South Australia, for example.[13]

These are cases of sudden population collapse due to colonisation, combined with the assumption of new rights or extension of old rights by groups moving into depopulated areas, with or without any recorded processes of the ceding of rights or the handing over of sacra from the former inhabitants. While such cases may in the long-term past have led to a relatively fast replacement of rights-holding groups for a particular area, over perhaps only three generations, under modern conditions the persistence of records plays a powerful role in preventing the ready extinguishment of consciousness of how things were before.

Under similar catastrophic conditions members of the surviving subgroups of a single language group or other wider regional identity group have at times jointly assumed responsibility for all the untenanted estates of their wider group as well as maintaining or amalgamating their own local estate interests. Details of these processes are not often available but the cases of *Malak Malak*, *Jawoyn*, *Cape Melville* and *Lakefield* provide a range of relevant examples.[14] These are clearly not cases where existing 'normal' succession pathways are engaged in by one or two individuals or a small genealogical subgroup. Whole language groups or similar-sized regional groups may be involved. For this reason I refer to such processes as instances of conjoint succession. These cases do not involve the extinguishment of pre-colonial rights of surviving groups so much as their transformation – usually involving considerable simplification – and their generalisation to wider 'tribal' areas. One cannot exclude the possibility that similar catastrophic population losses may have occurred before the colonial era, where epidemics could have wiped out large numbers of people from time to time.

It is often the case that a person has a primary relationship to one parent's estate and a range of other ties to, for example, their other parent's estate, their mother's mother's estate, the site or country on which they were born, neighbouring estates on the same main Dreaming track as their own, the country where their mother was buried, and so on, depending on region. People may rank their connections to these various estates in terms of importance. In a succession context this kind of ranking is an attribute of an individual rather than of a group *per se*, even though some of the secondary interests may also be those shared among classes of kin standing in common ritual or genealogical relationships to the country; for example the *jungkayi* (who include people whose mothers are in a primary relationship to the country) and *dalnyin* (who include people whose mothers' mothers are in a primary relationship to the country) of the Roper River region.[15]

Group succession in a strict sense seems to rely on territorial proximity and pre-existing systemic grounds for territorial amalgamation. Such systemic grounds include commonality of language, shared rights in Dreamings, geographic unity (e.g. 'We all one river'), and shared kin-class standing, rather than specific genealogical links. In many regions a group or person succeeding to an estate should ideally be of the same kin-class membership as the defining sites and Dreamings of the estate concerned. This may include being of the same subsection patricouple, the same patrimoiety, or the same semimoiety, as the country and its original (or rather erstwhile) owners. This is another reflection of the principle that, while rights may in some senses be 'achieved', the classical Aboriginal systems were very much geared to corralling such achievements within structural constraints which worked counter to a strongly meritocratic approach. In Nancy

Williams's terms (see below), it seems that group succession may be based on potential rights, the setting for which is various proximities and commonalities between erstwhile neighbours, while individual succession is usually based on already existent but inchoate rights which become upgraded or augmented.

People whose countries are contiguous or which intersect or overlap in a number of 'company' areas may express a higher-order unity at any time, not just in situations of potential succession, by saying 'We are from one valley', or 'We are the same mob, same country, but we've got our own areas'. The current state of relations between two such groups may determine whether or not they prefer to present themselves as one group with common rights over a single larger country, or as two groups with a high degree of shared rights in each other's distinct countries. At times there may not be unanimity on this very question itself. During such times of negotiation or conflict it would be misleading to assert either that there is one group with one country or two groups with reciprocal rights in each other's countries. The anthropologist's job in such a case is to describe the group dynamics as far as necessary for the purpose at hand, not to stress a collectivist or atomist reading for the purpose of neatening the case to suit the demands of litigation.[16]

A group's members may have a strong secondary relationship to an adjacent country based on the paths taken by particular Dreaming tracks through both countries, and on their active ceremonial knowledge of both sets of sites. A group whose Dreaming track responsibilities run up close to another group's major site, but do not extend right into the site, can say of the place and its surrounds: 'We come in there too', or 'We go halfway to there'. These expressions are typically oblique references to the placement of song verse handover points at particular stages in the recounting of the progression of a Dreaming through a set of sites. The next group 'picks up' the authoritative relationship to the singing of verses from a certain geographical point onwards. This is the kind of ethnographic fine grain which gives substance to generalisations, still at least partly true for many areas, to the effect that land tenure 'depends on' ceremony.

To 'come in' to a place is not the same as to 'belong to' it in the fuller sense. People may often express such non-primary connections by the use of the terms 'just' or 'only'. For example: 'We are not traditional owners, we are just custodians', or: 'That's not main place for us, we only half owner'. By contrast, I have never heard anyone say: 'We are only the traditional owners of that area'. As a vernacular English expression, often constituting a not completely happy translation of some indigenous expressions, 'traditional owner' is a term of first rank when specifying who has rights and interests in country. On the other hand, many people with some traditional rights in a country, even some very strong rights, will normally deny that they are 'traditional owners' of it if they lack a primary connection to it based on identity.

A person or group or kin class would never have both a primary and a secondary relationship to the same country, except perhaps in the rare case of someone with parents who were both from the same country, in which case they could trace a primary connection to it through one parent and a secondary connection to it through the other. In terms of small land-owning groups, estate group exogamy (out-marriage) was the predominant classical pattern. In terms of language groups, linguistic endogamy (in-marriage) varied widely, from predominant to partial to rare. In recent times and in rural and urban regions one occasionally comes across the view that language group endogamy is to be avoided on the grounds that those marrying would be 'too close'. For various reasons, including post-colonial mobility and the decline of arranged marriages, more Aboriginal people than ever come from parentage of diverse and widely separated country origins. Someone from near Darwin may marry someone from near Adelaide, for example, and they bring up their children in Darwin. In such cases long residence in or near one parent's country rather than the other's can mean that the other's country is one in which one only has rather inchoate secondary rights unless they are activated by visitation.

In the classical systems, a man who came from a distant area and who had no ancestral connections to the country of his wife would not, for that reason, be in a 'secondary' (or 'tertiary', etc.) relationship to the country in the sense usually understood, but would still have every right, and typically also an obligation under bride-service traditions, to make normal day-to-day economic use of the land and its products as a hunter and forager.[17] Today he may be more likely to have some obligation to take up employment in his wife's residential community and enjoy (and share) the fruits of local wages. This is a thought based on anecdotal evidence rather than systematic research, but it could be explored in the first place using community employment statistics.

These usufructuary rights are rights contingent on those of having a spouse's standing, and they could be removed in the event of a separation. They would also, potentially at least, be the same rights whether the individual was on country to which his wife had primary claims or on country to which her claims were of a secondary kind. That is, she would be just as free to live on her primary (e.g. father's) country, as on her secondary (e.g. mother's) country, and it is improbable that her spouse's freedom to make ordinary use of the two areas would be any different.

When we speak of primary and secondary connections to countries, we are usually speaking of ties which belong to individuals or to sets of close siblings, for example, rather than referring to features of groups such as clans or ritual groupings. It can sometimes be the case, however, that an entire group such as a clan does have a range of formal connections to one or more estates other than its own. An example is North East Arnhem Land where sets of clans with estates connected by ancestral Dreaming travels are linked in what anthropologists have at different times called 'phratries', sets of 'sister clans', or 'strings' of patrifilial groups.[18] The focus of anthropological analyses has been on the composition of such sets as units made up of sub-units, or as egocentric 'strings' whose composition varies considerably depending on context, but the relevant ethnography at least suggests that a patrifilial group or clan might be said to have differentially ranked connections with a set of several different estates in something like the way persons do.

Presumptive and subsidiary rights; potential, actual and inchoate rights

Nancy Williams prefers to avoid the implications of 'an automatic or fixed hierarchy of rights in land that numeric terms may convey' and thus prefers 'presumptive rights' to 'primary rights' and prefers 'subsidiary rights' to 'secondary rights'. In the *Yolngu* case,

> [i]ndividuals acquire certain rights in a direct way determined by patrifiliation; that is, each one succeeds to certain rights by virtue of membership in a patrilineal clan. Some subsidiary rights are inchoate rights[19] and some are potential rights. Inchoate rights exist and need only to be activated in a specific way. Potential rights are rights that may or may not come into existence.[20]

Inchoate rights would include, for example, a Western Desert person's rights in the countries of that person's father, the person's mother, and the person's birthplace, all of which would be established at birth:

> Thus a child may belong to two or even three estates. He does so actually, not potentially. But the rights are inchoate; more is required before they can be exercised in respect of any one estate.[21]

Here we have an operational distinction between actual rights, inchoate rights, and potential rights. A major practical difficulty in any one case, in a native title context, is that of carrying out 'ethnography' on who holds what kinds of rights, and therefore of writing a report which will be used to decide whose case for the assertion of native title rights is likely to be sustainable. Such anthropological investigations are often carried out in an already charged atmosphere, especially if there is a financial agreement in the offing, and cannot be represented as some kind of context-free scientific pursuit of 'the facts'.

Although it is one fraught with difficulties, this situation is one in which I suggest that the anthropologist should present as clear an account as possible as to who holds what kinds of rights and in the eyes of whom, and avoid intermingling the ethnographic process with that of negotiations as to whose names will be on what lists for whatever purposes. It may be that people associated unambiguously with a particular area will seek to limit the dimensions of the claimant or beneficiary group to those with activated rights, and may seek to exclude from the legal process those with inchoate and merely potential rights. Those with inchoate rights may seek to activate them in the native title context, thus distinguishing themselves from people who have merely potential rights or no rights, and may compete with core people for standing. They may have arguably valid reasons as to how their inchoate rights would have been actualised were it not for the intervention of forces beyond their control, such as the removal of themselves or their antecedents to mission dormitories.

In such a situation, from whom do the lawyers take their instructions? This may not be such an issue when the core of people with primary connections is large and the active penumbra of those with lesser rights is small or politically weak, but if the reverse applies then the pressures from people with non-primary interests may be great. And who decides who will give instructions? A short answer to this is that such things are usually hammered out in meetings. But some organisation usually calls the meetings and funds aspects of attendance, which must have an effect on who is present to give instructions or to decide who the instruction-givers should be. Furthermore, those with weaker cases for traditional connection to the area in question may attend a meeting under the auspices, or at least with the support, of kin who have strong cases. Such kin are normally under a customary obligation to provide that kind of support, especially in a public context. They may seek the inclusion of their own distant kin while rejecting the distant kin of others, or may support their distant kin in public, while privately denying them.

In examining the question of who holds strong traditional connections and the rights that flow from them, one will often observe a tug of war between collectivist and atomist forces. These forces are likely to exist in the relevant Aboriginal community as well as among anthropologists, lawyers and administrators. In the Aboriginal community, it may be those with potential, inchoate or contingent rights only who are most active in pressing for a minimal definition of who is a holder of native title rights. The people with strong rights and primary connections may seek a more substantial definition so as to reflect their values and also contain the number of claimants or beneficiaries. Within indigenous organis-ations there can be a struggle between those who want to maximise the manage-ability of a group by keeping it small and tightly defined, and those who want to do the greatest good for the greatest number, perhaps reflecting a communalist and egalitarian ideology.

As Williams has said, 'primary' and 'secondary' are perhaps over-neat and restrictive as a way of classifying interests in country, even if we restrict their application to kinds of connection rather than kinds of rights. 'Primary' is also a legal term in at least one other relevant jurisdiction. The *Aboriginal Land Rights (Northern Territory) Act 1976 (Commonwealth)* in Section 3(1) in part defines 'traditional Aboriginal owners' as 'a local descent group of Aboriginals who ... have common spiritual affiliations to a site on the land, being affiliations that place the group under a *primary* spiritual responsibility for that site and for the land' (emphasis added). This has usually been taken to mean that the group's enjoyment of spiritual responsibility for the land is first among others, rather than merely basic or fundamental, although the point is arguable.

It may be better to distinguish 'primary' connections simply from 'non-primary' ones, given that the latter may present a range of variation from substantial to quite insubstantial links to countries, and there may be times when the same links are ranked differently, depending on the demands of context.

Ranking of connections and rights

Although the term 'primary' is in this instance a part of anthropologists' usage, the concept has common equivalents in Aboriginal English and Aboriginal languages.

Among the various English expressions referring to a primary country connection are 'main-place', 'number-one country', and the statement that certain people are 'boss for', 'come in front for' or are 'longa [in the] lead for' a certain country. Expressions of these concepts in Aboriginal languages may be semantically similar, although very much more varied in actual wording. In the *Milirrpum* case of North East Arnhem Land, for example, Nancy Williams recorded that 'it was clear in every case that Yolngu witnesses regarded one group as owners, holders of radical title; they were said to be *ngurrungu* ("first"), or *bunggawa* ("boss"), for the land in question'.[22]

Quite often there is an expression in Aboriginal languages which people translate as 'traditional owner of country' or 'person who really belongs to the country', and it may be an idiomatic expression using 'country' as its stem (as in the Western Desert varieties which employ *ngurraritja*, *ngurrara*, etc., or in Mudbura's use of *ngurramarla*); or it may be a semantically opaque term, such as a word referring to patrifilial totems and those who hold the relevant country patrifilially (for example, *mangaya* in Warumungu).[23] In the same languages or other languages there is often a suffix denoting 'native of' or 'person who really belongs to', which is added to a name for a major site or area, as in the following: *-wardingki* (Warlpiri), *-wartingi* (Warlmanpa), *-warinyi* (Warumungu), and *-ngarna* (Mudbura).[24]

One may also hear people asserting that a certain area is their 'number two country', that they 'come into' it 'halfway', that it is 'part of my run too, you know', or is an area for which 'we come behind that main mob'. These expressions usually refer to a non-primary but significant form of connection. Without further research, however, such terminological categorisation of individuals should not be assigned exclusive weight and certainly should not be the only considerations driving an anthropologist's analysis of relations between groups and countries.

This is because claims of a non-primary kind may be described in similar ways in a limited conversation but may include a wide range of degrees of connection in actual practice. One of the jobs of anthropologists in native title cases is to provide independent and detailed evidence which can flesh out such broad-brush statements. Clearly, in the absence of field mapping of Dreaming track sites or analysis of songline sequences, it would be difficult to compare the foundations of the claims of several different groups who stated that they 'came into' the relevant parcel of land or waters on the basis of Dreaming stories or songlines. Sometimes a tenuous thread of connection is used as the basis for a person's claims, claims which may have been publicly confirmed by the claimant group. Tenuousness of connection is not in and of itself fatal to the recognition of rights, within the practices of a certain group, although some parties to a native title case might argue this position from an outsider perspective. An anthropologist or lawyer who goes into court ignorant of the different bases and strengths of claimant connections, and the reasons why some tenuous claims have been found acceptable by the group, may find it more difficult to engage with such evidence.

I suggest that the terms 'primary' and 'secondary' or (preferably) 'non-primary' be reserved, in native title anthropological contexts, for *forms of connection or affiliation* between people and places, rather than used to speak of types of rights and interests as such, and that kinds of rights be differentiated in other ways. One axis along which I suggest rights be differentiated is that of core rights versus contingent ones.

CORE AND CONTINGENT RIGHTS

Applications for the determination of native title include listings of native title rights and interests asserted by the claimants. Some listed rights are very broad, such as:

- the right to possession of the land and waters to the exclusion of all others;
- the right to occupation, use and enjoyment of the land and waters to the exclusion of all others;
- the right to inherit and bestow native title rights and interests;
- the right to resolve as amongst themselves disputes about land tenure;

Most listed rights, however, are more specific, and include such phrases as:

- the right to hunt and fish on the land or in the waters;
- the right to take natural resources from the land and waters, including digging and using minerals, and quarry materials such as flints, clays, soil, sand, gravel rock and all other resources;
- the right to dispose of such resources by trade or exchange;
- the right to move about on the land or waters, or live on and erect dwellings on the land;
- the right to conduct ceremonies on the land;
- the right to grant or refuse permission to any other person to do any of the above;
- and so on.

Such listings often make no distinctions of type among such 'rights', although the order in which they are given may indicate that some are more fundamental than others. But they are not all of the same order or character. It is, of course, a matter for investigation in each case whether or not certain rights are held by certain people over the country at issue, but 'country' – in the sense of units of customary tenure – is not necessarily the only framework or structure in which such rights may be held.

It is common for there to be a distinction between rights over countries, rights over sites or areas within countries, and rights over features that are part of countries. A site within a country may be one over which certain people belonging to neighbouring countries have rights, while they assert no similar rights over the country of that site as a whole, or even over the ground on which the site itself is located. That is, pre-eminent rights to control a site, and obligations to protect it, may belong to people who say it is not a part of their country. For example, there is a Two Euros (Maraji) site south of Tennant Creek, for whom the principal ritual custodians are particular Kaytetye people of the Neutral Junction area who live far to the south. The Dreaming links those distant people to local Warlpiri, Warlmanpa and Warumungu people of the Tennant Creek area, but it is the latter, not the former, who hold the 'soil' at the site and are locally responsible for the site's wellbeing.[25] To simply define such people as 'native title rights holders' in a way which fails to distinguish them from the country's owning group members may be to sow the seeds of conflict, especially once these relationships become bureaucratised or are brought into play in competition for resources.

Rights in 'things' in this context may range from access to specific natural resources, rights to use traditional trackways or 'easements' through countries,[26] and other 'material' kinds of interests, to seemingly more 'abstract' rights in sacred stories, objects, designs, songs or ritual performances associated with sites and countries. There is also a widespread but not universal pattern by which traditional rights in the country where a modern residential settlement is located have been extended to privileged rights, not only over the receipt of community services such as housing, but also in having a corner on the supply of service delivery itself.[27] Given that service delivery is the main or only economic activity other than transfer payments in many settlements, this can be important. An even greater emphasis on native title holder status in the allocation of benefits and job opportunities provided by native title corporate bodies is to be expected.

Listings of native title rights also frequently fail to make distinctions between culturally logical relations between different kinds of rights. Clearly many of these rights flow from certain others within the same list, and might therefore be distinguished as *contingent rights,* which flow from *core rights.* I mean 'contingent', not in the sense of 'accidental' or 'uncertain', but in the sense of 'dependent upon something else', 'consequential' or 'conditional'.[28]

The right to use someone else's country is usually contingent, for example, on the nature and state of relationships with those other people. It is arguable also that even the right to make economic use of one's own primary country flows from deeper rights to identify with and make proprietary claims over that country. On the other hand, some would argue that economic use rights over one's own estate are just as elemental and 'core' in nature as those others.[29]

Rights which flow from others are often the kind of rights held over an area by non-claimants to that area in native title cases. A right to fish and hunt, for example, may be one held under a standing licence on the grounds that one is married to a 'traditional owner', or is a long-term resident on the land, or on some other contractual or historical grounds. It might also flow from being a primary landholder under customary law, that is, from being a holder of core rights. In all cases, however, the right to fish, or hunt, or live on the country, is a contingent one, because use rights are not self-sustaining. For a 'traditional owner', hunting rights may be asserted to flow from being an 'owner' of the country. For that person's brother-in-law, hunting rights over the same area may be asserted to flow from being married to an owner of the country. For a next door neighbour in a settlement street, someone whose own traditional country is 300km away, hunting rights over the area where they live might be asserted to flow from fifty years of family residence on the country concerned and at least acquiescence in this state of affairs by the area's 'traditional owners'. But it does not arise directly from the cultural landed-group identity of the next door neighbour him- or herself.

An elementary core right is that which enables a person to claim a certain area as their own 'main place', their own 'proper' or 'real' country, and thus to assert a fundamental proprietary relationship to it. Some of the other core rights asserted by native title claimants are concerned with the bestowal or recognition of specific other rights, and might be described in particular as meta-rights (rights about rights), or rights-generating rights. These include the right to transmit further transmissible rights to make proprietary claims on the country, and the right to pass on certain aspects of group identity through the assignment of names, languages or totems to children, for example, as well as through the handing on of knowledge, including designs and songs, which may symbolise the relationship between a group and its country.

If those who hold only contingent rights for an area are excluded totally from determinations of native title over that area, they may justifiably fear that they could lose the security and predictability of their present situations. Such people may seek recognition during the native title process, even if the case is not started by them. In the case of the *Hopevale* consent Determination, after establishing that native title rights and interests existed and noting that members of thirteen clans with estates in the determination area held those rights and interests, the Determination then set out the rights in some detail. This was followed by a special section called 'Recognition of other Aboriginal People's Rights', part of which reads:

16.1 The native title holders recognise: …

16.2 the rights of Aboriginal historical residents of the dogit [Deed of Grant in Trust] land to travel over, hunt, camp, fish and gather on the native title land in accordance with the traditional laws and customs of each of the native title holders[30]

As cases unfold, the way determinations or agreements recognise the legitimate interests of those who do not hold core native title rights may put the legal–administrative system to considerable test. Are non-core rights held by non-claimants native title rights, for example?

Transmission of rights

Transmission of such core rights may be described as either active or by default. In systems where serial patrifiliation is a principal means of acquiring primary land rights, for example, a person does not have to make deliberate decisions about handing on country rights, or even be mentally competent, in order to be someone through whom primary rights pass to lower generations. The system is sufficiently prescriptive for cases of such a descent of rights to be regarded as the default situation. Here a person as ancestor is in a sense a conduit for rights rather than a particularly active bestower of them. In many regions of Australia the passing on of primary rights in country through men to their offspring was, and in some regions remains, the preferred mechanism by which core rights in country descend. The process is not the only means by which rights descend through time, nor is it completely automatic, but it is often the one to which members of the group subscribe, perhaps doing so even after its practice has diminished or has come to an end among younger members of the same community.

The active aspect of this kind of transmission may lie in the decision to accept this default transmission of rights to oneself as descendant, but very often this is again merely the 'understood' normal practice. In fact most assignments of people to country, or at least to a primary country affiliation, begin at birth or in childhood, when they are in no position to make such decisions for themselves. In any case, such a system is not personally voluntary in character and in general an individual could not – and in most regions still cannot – make a unilateral decision about which ancestor's country is their own primary country. The views of others are an essential ingredient in the assignment of rights so long as these rights are communal in nature, even when, due to recent cultural change, identification with a country group has become much more voluntary than it was before.[31]

As they grow up, some individuals may take an active decision to shift the emphasis of their country affiliations to a usually less preferred option such as the assertion of a controlling interest over a mother's mother's or father's mother's country. Such shifts are often due to the making of succession claims over unpeopled estates, or may arise from shifts of place of primary residence, for example. But in these cases the person concerned still has to work to muster support and recognition for such non-default claims. These kinds of situations, although made more frequent by depopulation and migration as a result of colonisation, cannot in my view be argued to be recent in origin.

In areas where there is not now, or never was, a single heavily dominant default mechanism for the transmission of rights in country, people have to more actively pursue their or their group's case for rights in a country and may have their claims more frequently questioned by their peers. In these circumstances a wide variety of people may be able to mount claims of some kind or other on a multiplicity of different bases, and unanimity as to who among these contenders has a primary connection to a place or country may never occur. In these cases, and others as well, it can be impossible for the outside observer to come to 'certainty' as to 'who exactly' holds which rights in what areas.[32] Expectations of simple certainty in these cases are naïve and unrealistic, and rest on the kind of legal and corporate rigidities that are far more realistically desired and achieved in industrial societies. In an industrial society the rules for dealing with rights in property are geared more to transactions between strangers rather than to transactions between kin. Objective records, stable agreements and fixed and codified rights are a necessity where the social fabric has to cope with transactions between unrelated persons.

Kin have many claims on each other apart from relationships to do with rights in property. Kin relations have a wide range of emotional colouration, can alternate quite quickly between solidarity and conflict, and are often the focus of feelings of jealousy, rivalry and rage as well as of loyalty and amity. Where property interests in country are those principally of groups of kin, they are also likely to be subject to similar dynamics. Writing of the Lozi of southern Africa, Max Gluckman said:

> We say that a person or a group 'owns' a piece of land or some item of property. We are speaking loosely when we use this sort of phrasing: what is owned in fact is a claim to have power to do certain things with the land or property, to possess immunities against the encroachments of others on one's rights in them, and to exercise certain privileges in respect of them. But in addition other persons may have certain rights, claims, powers, privileges and immunities in respect of the same land or property. ... land ... may be subject to a cluster of rights held by different persons in terms of their relationship within the network of kinship ties.[33]

To demand of a kin-based society that it produce simple, stable and definitive lists of rights and rights-holders in land and waters is ethnocentric. It can also be counterproductive, in the sense that attempts to arrive at definitive lists of which living persons hold which rights in what country may engender the very kind of conflict between claimants which certainty-seekers fear. There is no certainty in a false simplicity. It is usually the complexity of claims over country, not some allegedly vague indeterminacy or inherent rubberiness of the claimancy situation, that prevents their reduction to fixed formulae. It is for the convenience of the bureaucracy and industry that such demands for fixity are likely to be made upon native title claimants. But codification, at least for many such groups, is itself contrary to their own laws and customs. As Aboriginal people say so often, 'We've got it in our heads. You put it on paper'. It will be interesting to see whether the statutory process for the recognition of native title results in the codification of native title rights and interests and ultimately succeeds in imposing itself on custom in the Australian experience. It is already clear that there are legal pressures to frame anthropological reports within the categories and even the language of the law and the High Court. While reports have to be germane to the task, they may encourage codification by too narrowly taking a 'tick all the right boxes' approach. On the other hand, for some, at least, codification may come as a relief from negotiation and conflict, whether they are native title holders or staff administering the bureaucratic system. For others, codification is likely to be read as yet another ingestion of the indigenous by the exogenous.

Earlier I discussed 'default' mechanisms by which rights may be transmitted, and the active way in which claimants may pursue different bases of claim in the same country. There is, however, also a practice of active transmission of primary (and further transmissible) rights to country which has been documented in different forms in different places. It occurs, for example, when senior men in the Borroloola region decide to incorporate a young person into a certain country group by means of a ceremony and the making of certain objects.[34] It occurs when a defunct land-holding group is restored through the divination of a newborn's conception site in its country, and the person so conceived may establish a new lineage of primary landholders for that country.[35] It occurs when a grandmother, in a cognatic descent group system, decides that certain of her grandchildren will be 'under her' for purposes of landed and tribal identity and is able to get others to accept this.[36] It occurs when people decide that a child born to a non-Aboriginal father and an Aboriginal mother is to belong to its mother's country, or that of the mother's husband, or that of the child's place of birth, and so on.[37] And it occurs when a couple who have no children of their own are 'given' a child from another family so that the child may be 'grown up' in such as way as to inherit country rights through one or both of the adoptive parents.

Distinct from this kind of right to assign core rights flowing from identity is the capacity to bestow rights that are *not* readily transmissible by the recipient to third parties. These are rights to use the country of others, or usufructuary rights. Non-transmissible rights received in this way are not of the same character as the same rights received by birthright or incorporation into a group, even though the concrete enactment of the rights will appear to take much the same form in both cases.

A common occurrence in the bush, in my experience, is that when landholders and others go fishing, for example, and the latter do not have much success, the difference may be attributed to the fact that the country is favouring its own people and recognising that the others are different. In the Wik region of Cape York Peninsula the difference between landholders and others is perceived by the ancestral spirits in the water as a difference of smell, in particular the smell of underarm sweat. That is, the ability to exploit fish licitly may be held in common between both kinds of person, but the relationship of landholders to the right is conceived of as an essential one, one of essence, arising from their inner nature, which rests both on bodily and spiritual descent. By contrast, the relationship of non-landholders to the same right to catch fish is non-essential and contractual or historical in origin, or based on less intimate forms of kinship.

This does not mean, by the way, that all people who smell familiar to the spirits are therefore landholders, because anyone with a history of living in the area will have been already perceived by the Old People and thus their sweat is already familiar to the country. I have seen people 'give smell to' (anoint with armpit sweat) newcomers to sites which the 'baptisers' themselves would not dream of claiming as their own, although there is a general preference in Cape York Peninsula for this 'baptising' or 'anointing' (Cape York English), where possible, to be done by senior landholders. A landholder has the right 'smell' for their country as a matter of birth. A non-landowner may acquire a recognisable 'smell' through residence. Each may regard the other as 'countrymen', but they do not blur the distinction between those to whom the country belongs and those of its familiars to whom it does not belong.

Generic and specific rights

The core/contingent and primary/non-primary distinctions are different in turn from the generic/specific distinction.[38] A generic right would be, for example, the right to use the vegetation in an area, and under such a head might be specific rights, such as to take timber for making shelters, to use dead wood for fuel, to use live wood for making artefacts, and so on.

One of the pitfalls of codification, especially when it comes down to the level of cementing into legal documents people's rights to specific natural resources, is that the more specific the rights codified, the more unwieldy the consequences. On the other hand, the vaguer the specification of rights, the greater the difficulty with which the listing of rights can be matched to daily situations and thus provide the kind of 'certainty' so desired by bureaucracy and industry.

For example, members of a traditional 'community' of rights-holders may have the right to catch marine species.[39] But, actually, certain species at certain stages, such as mature barramundi or dugong, may be prohibited prey for any-one but older men in some groups. In some regions women may be restricted to catching fish only by line, net or hand, and may be prohibited from spearing fish at all. In at least one region (Wik) women may spear fish so long as they do not employ a spearthrower at the same time. There may be times when a person's temporary condition (for example, when menstruating, pregnant, recently bereaved, newly initiated) prohibits them from entering certain foraging places or from killing certain species even in their own country. The basic point here is that one can specify very generic kinds of rights as native title rights, adding that they may be trammelled and qualified in various ways according to local customary law, but one can never go on unravelling the nature of specific rights to some mythical point of 'completeness' where every right, and all conditions under which it might properly be exercised, can be exhaustively described and enshrined on paper.

Rights of 'traditional owners' versus those of 'historical people'

The possession of one or other of these two differently-founded kinds of right – core and contingent – marks the primary line of cleavage between 'traditional owners' and 'historical people' in many places. These expressions are both now widespread in Aboriginal English. The term 'traditional owner' comes from the *Aboriginal Land Rights (Northern Territory) Act 1976 (Commonwealth)*, where it has a legal definition. It has a reasonably stable vernacular sense. The phrase 'historical people' seems to have arisen in Queensland soon after the passing of the *Aboriginal Land Act 1991 (Queensland)*, and derives from the fact that under that Act it is possible to make a claim to certain lands on the basis of historical association as well as, or instead of, traditional affiliation. It took nearly twenty years for the English phrase 'traditional owner' to become common usage in Cape York Peninsula, where the possibility of legal recognition of land rights for so long seemed a lost cause, but it took a far shorter time for the term 'historical people' to spread west and south from Queensland to much of the rest of Australia during the 1990s. This seems to have been a distinction waiting for a tag.

In common Aboriginal usage, 'traditional owners' are deemed to have rights to assert a relationship with their country as a matter of their origin there, whether they live there or not. They 'really come from' or 'properly belong to' their country in an intrinsic sense. The 'traditional owners' are those with proprietary relationships to the country, possessors of core rights as well as contingent ones. 'Historical people' are living where they are because of historical factors such as migration and deportation, and do not 'really come from' their current location. They are not without country as they usually assert themselves to be 'traditional owners' of places elsewhere, and assert only contingent rights in the country of current residence. This is putting it somewhat crudely, and there are cases where people whose historical ancestors were immigrants reject the second-grade standing this may impose upon them in the eyes of others, but as a heuristic distinction it is useful and it is one that is commonly important in the way groups are identified by Aboriginal native title claimants themselves.

The rights of 'historical people' in the resources and sites of the area where they currently reside are not necessarily geographically circumscribed along the lines of traditional land tenure units. The members of a 'community' – in the sense of a township's residential population, for example – may enjoy a common foraging right within a certain radius of the township, or along certain routes between settlements, but this does not mean that all the members of the community are in customary-lawful occupation of the land in a *uniform* sense. This is one more reason why a residential community is a poor candidate for being described as a group holding native title.[40] Such a description would combine all locally resident rights-holders regardless of the different bases on which they hold certain common rights. This is a recipe for bitter conflict.

Definitions of 'incidents' or rights that merely describe the capacity to perform a particular kind of action on or in relation to land and water are of little use or value if they stand alone. Ideally they should be located, placed in context, in terms of customary law. This means they should be located in terms of local cultural meaning. When I cut a tree it is not necessarily the 'same action' as when you cut a tree – even if it is the same tree and the same axe. The deeper jural facets of actions, not just their immediate permissibility, are an integral part of their rights-based status, and not just a nebulous 'cultural background' outside them. That is, we need to know how such actions flow from which kinds of standing the actors have, in order for descriptions of rightful actions (e.g. 'to dig clays from the ground') to be made relevant to the task of understanding what local practices might amount to in any particular case in terms of translation into native title rights based on traditional laws and customs.

Do you need to know and enact a right in order to have it?

The capacity to understand and exercise such rights is not uniformly distributed among native title claimants, many of whom will be small children and some of whom may be intellectually disabled, for example. This raises the question of whether membership of a claimant group depends on a person's capacity to understand and/or exercise their listed rights.

A short answer to this question is that the nature of their entitlement is communal in its foundation. That is, the holding of a customary right is typically a characteristic of membership of an identifiable group, or of mutual recognition by others asserting similar rights, and therefore proof of its enjoyment by an individual usually entails showing that it derives from the person's membership of or recognition by that group or network, not from a certain form of personal consciousness or ability. Such rights are enjoyed and enacted by individuals as far as they choose, and as far as their capacity is not hindered by mental or physical incapacity or some other form of hindrance such as distance, terrain, or human obstruction, or some form of prohibition such as the nature of a sacred site, a temporary state of closure due – for example – to a death, or a temporary state of a person who is in mourning, menstruating, pregnant, ill, or recently initiated. Indeed, observing these limitations on use of country for foraging or other pursuits is typically an obligation that is part of the Law of the country concerned.

It is the policing of land-based obligations, more than the obligations themselves – which in many cases are incumbent on anyone who goes there – that tends to be a right particularly associated with landholders. But landholders acquire the foundations of such policing rights through affiliation to a collective property-holding and identity group or kin network, not through individual realisation alone. On the other hand, policing is a function of senior people. Individual abilities and structural positions, not only age and group membership or kin connections, underlie the attainment of this status.

Evidence that claimants have physically exercised customary rights in country is useful in making concrete their claims before an outside audience. But to demand such evidence as an absolute necessity of proof of the existence of all of the rights claimed would be onerous and illegitimate, nor is this what the law requires, as I understand it. For example, I may have the right to use my freehold land for the harvesting of trees, or pasturing stock, or for growing crops. I do not have to cut down my trees in order to prove I have the right to do so. Were I to do so, proving the existence of the same right the next day might be difficult. What is necessary, should I want to activate such rights, is that they come to me as an incident of my title, that is, that they flow from the nature of my legal relationship with the land.

Can one have rights of which one is ignorant? In short, yes, and most citizens of any nation state have rights of which they are only partially or even dimly aware. Some people nevertheless seem to hold the view that unless each native title claimant, as an individual, can spell out their customary rights in country, they cannot claim title. I reject this.

Briefly, to deny the proposition is to confuse affiliations with knowledge. One does not have to know anything about cricket in order to be recognised as a member of the Melbourne Cricket Club – one merely has to meet its criteria for membership and pay the dues. It may be necessary for the players, at least, to know something about the game, and to be able to play it, if 'cricket club' is to be an apt description for the MCC. That is a matter for the laws and customs of the club concerned, and also for those of the wider public who police the accurate use of terms like 'cricket club'. If a cricket club by definition must contain at least some members who understand and play cricket, then a reasonable sample of players and officials could establish this by their evidence.

It is normal for infants and disabled people to be regarded by senior and knowledgeable Aboriginal people in their country-based groupings as fellow members of such groupings in spite of their lack of consciousness of the content of their affiliations to the country concerned. The idea that children of traditional landowners are to be excluded from positive determinations of native title on the grounds that they cannot enact their rights or recount how the group is connected to the country is tantamount to the state telling indigenous people that their children are without country because they are children. This is normally contrary to Aboriginal customary law.

THE BASIC CHARACTERISTICS OF ABORIGINAL COUNTRY AS PROPERTY

In recent years there has been a renewal of anthropological interest in questions of property.[41] The anthropological perspective on property tends to be dominated by the idea that it is 'not a thing, but a network of social relations that governs the conduct of people with respect to the use and disposition of things'.[42]

This idea has been prominent in the discipline since Radcliffe-Brown published it in 1935, when he said that a right is a measure of control that people have over others such that the latter are, as a consequence, liable to the performance of a duty. Rights over things, as against persons, impose duties on other persons in relation to that thing.[43]

By tradition, Aboriginal country is inalienable. This, of course, is to focus on country as a thing rather than as a medium of transactions between people. A different way to put it is to say that Aboriginal country does not normally enter into relationships between people, other people and things that could be described as exchanging, giving to or stealing from.

It is not at all common for the record to suggest that territorial conquest has occurred in Aboriginal Australia or is even admitted as a possibility. Indeed, the ethnographic record commonly contains statements to the effect that territorial aggrandisement is alien to Aboriginal thought and practice. But in a relevant sense a person or group of people may be alienable from their birth country, but only very gradually over time, perhaps involving two or more generations of 'forgetting' about their former origins. For example, Hiatt reports some originally inland descent groups in north-central Arnhem Land which by 1958 had become attached to, and then integrated with, groups holding coastal country.[44] This process would presumably have involved some kind of gradual self-divestment of their inland country rights and interests.

Far more common than such incorporation into other groups are cases of succession to the countries of extinct groups. Those succeeding to untenanted countries may in their own lifetimes maintain at least an equivalent interest in their original country while taking up new rights and interests but, in time, they, or more likely their descendants, cannot maintain both sets of interests equally and their rights in the original country will diminish or disappear. This may, however, more often be a case of the descendants of successors simply not taking up rights in the original country of the original successors.

A second fundamental characteristic of rights and interests in Aboriginal country is that they are held communally. In a sense, Aboriginal country is thus defined more by inclusion than by exclusion, although both are present. Sometimes only one person is left who claims a country but this does not establish individual tenure in principle. Countries remain collective possessions in their basic construction.

Third, while it is true that physical contact with and knowledge of the geography of a country plays a role in the maintenance of rights in it, as Bruce Rigsby points out, following Stanner, customary Aboriginal rights *in rem* [in things] in this case flow ultimately from rights *in animam* [in the spiritual].[45] Another way of putting that is to say that these kinds of rights flow from aspects of identity. Among some Aboriginal groups, the spiritual basis of one's country identity no longer consists of a complex combination of Dreaming-based ritual and other relationships and relationships to ancestral human spirits, but has been simplified largely to the latter. For some people the identity basis of interests in a traditional country may have shifted emphasis from the spiritual to an historically-, politically- and racially-grounded ethnic identity. However, it is also important to note that these identities still usually have their roots in the classical past of the families concerned.

The extent to which these simplified, or more secularised, bases of interests represent a rupturing of tradition, or an attenuation of it to the point where there is no longer an observance of traditional laws and customs, is a somewhat subjective question. In a native title case, claimants may establish that their group asserts and practises certain rights in a country, and neighbouring indigenous groups may agree with them, but if the basis of such rights is no longer one of 'traditional law and custom', and is something quite different or is a resurrection of past practices which have fallen into desuetude, they will have a hard time having their case accepted. Establishing this is not, however, strictly a matter for anthropological opinion. There is no technical anthropological standard for 'measuring' such changes. The whole idea of an anthropologist, or for that matter the judiciary, opining or deciding when it is that a group's traditional laws and customs have been 'washed away by the tide of history' is highly problematic. Even more problematic would be the spectacle of a courtroom in which a number of non-indigenous persons, who might typically include some secular humanists and atheists, sit arguing whether or not a claimant group's members have maintained sufficient spiritual connection to their country for it to count as an element in their proof of continuing connection. It is not a concept with a history as a term of art in the social sciences, nor is it, as far as I can ascertain, a concept with a history in Australian law and its predecessors. Presumably, the concept will gradually attain an operational definition as determinations of native title accumulate. But there are already clear inconsistencies between the ways the concept is being applied on different occasions.

Traditional Aboriginal rights in country do not exist in isolation from obligations. These obligations include the observance of restrictions and taboos. In fact, the emphasis of the native title process on 'rights' obscures the fact that stewardship roles, even more than rights, lie at the heart of holding country in Aboriginal tradition. By stewardship I mean the care for and maintenance of different aspects of the country, including its supernatural powers, knowledge of it, religious enactments or objects that relate to it, and physical care as well.

One might think of obligations as being dependent on rights in the sense that the state of being obliged to care for a country rests on the prior right to claim 'traditional ownership' of it (that is, having both core and contingent rights) or to claim to be a licit user of it (that is, having contingent rights only). But both rights and obligations in this context flow from country-based identities of persons and rest on relationships between persons.

Fred Myers makes the important point in the Pintupi context (Western Desert) that co-ownership of country is *a sign of transactions in shared identity*.[46] The other side of this coin is that distinguishing one's own country from that of others is an exercise in *autonomy*, manifested in the right to be asked, for example, about visiting the country.[47] These two principles, which exist in tension with each other, are highly general across Aboriginal Australia. This is not to say that Aboriginal land tenure is 'just grist for the mill' of symbolic activity, because the land and waters of one's own region were also, until recently, the only source of the basic necessities of life. Under new conditions they may continue to have economic importance, not only because of bush tucker but also because of royalties and rents received as owners, or because of compensation arrangements. If we make no distinction between economies of meaning and economies of economics we have lost an important distinction.

USE OF COUNTRY, ACCESS TO COUNTRY

Native title determination applications typically assert the claimants' right to have access to and use of the country concerned. It is important, however, to keep in mind the distinction between the minimal rights enjoyed by bona fide Aboriginal travellers who may sustain themselves with water, shade, fruit, wallabies or other resources while temporarily travelling on other people's countries, and those rights of access and use enjoyed either by those with core rights in the country, or those enjoyed by others who may have contiguous countries or a long history of regular residential use of the country concerned. Particularly since the introduction of motor vehicles and roads and large regional centres, but even earlier during the movement of stock between pastoral leases, for example, modern conditions have greatly freed up the extent to which Aboriginal people might move over each other's countries. *Pax Britannica* has also played its role in relaxing physical territorial constraints.

Rights to access and make use of country that are based on the right-holder's own connections to the country may be usefully distinguished from those that are essentially contractual in nature. This is something of a simplification, as there is often a negotiable element in a right-holder's connection itself.

Holders of contingent rights often have them by a standing permission or customary licence rather than by specific permissions. A customary licence to make use of neighbouring countries usually obtains between owners of them so long as they remain on reasonable terms, or so long as a country is not 'closed' due to a death or ceremonies, or some other factor is not adduced. Lauriston Sharp's description of the situation on the lower Mitchell River in Cape York Peninsula in 1933 probably applies widely in Aboriginal Australia:

> The right of exclusive use of the land, which is distinguished from ownership [by patrilineal clans], is extended to the children of clan women and to members of clans associated in the same patrilineal line. The right of exclusion is exercised only in exceptional cases, in which there is an actual or pretended drain on the resources of the land, indicating that one of the chief functions of clan ownership is the apportionment and conservation of natural resources. The natives state that a clan may even forbid a man crossing clan territory to get from one of his own clan territories to another, but no example of such extreme clan action could be cited. People gather and hunt, ordinarily, in whatever country they will. Thus there is practically a standing permission which opens a clan's countries to all, but this permission may be withdrawn by the clan for those who are *persona non grata*.[48]

Nancy Williams has written more about the question of territorial permissions than any other anthropologist of Aboriginal Australia.[49] I will not attempt to summarise her work here but will draw a few salient points from it and from my own knowledge of the subject.

People do seek permission to enter or use each others' countries in many instances, but they may not always or even normally do so in the form of an overt request. A proposed visit to someone else's area may be informally mentioned as an intention rather than put in the form of a request, and to see if there might be any objections. People will not normally attempt to seek such permission if relationships with the owners are so bad that they could expect a refusal. In any case, it can be after the visit that things are 'squared' with the owners in what amounts to a debriefing session, sometimes in the form of the recounting of aspects of the visit, or the making of observations on how the country is faring, or the sharing of game or other products taken from the country. An unusually distant visit through countries of people not well known to the visitor would normally have required far more elaborate or formal permission-seeking and perhaps formal gift-giving for rights of transit, for example to visit a quarry or pituri (narcotic) stand or to conduct a revenge expedition. Hosts, however, also have obligations to guests, and there is a tendency for reciprocity and balance, rather than an asymmetry between privileged permission-giver and importuning permission-requester, to be the preferred tone of interactions on the subject of intervisitation.

THE RIGHT TO EXCLUDE

If there is an Aboriginal customary–legal concept relatable to the common law notion of 'possession', it is first and foremost a proprietary relationship with a country, not something closely based upon patterns of physical residence. It is consonant with this that Aboriginal assertions of rights to exclude others in relation to country emphasise above all excluding those others from misappropriating country, or its symbols, or the identity which grows out of it. Although there is a right to exclude physically, and the notion of trespass is well developed, the exclusionary right is one that is often qualified in complex ways.

For example, a man has little right, under classical Aboriginal principles, to exclude, say, his parents-in-law from coming onto the land of the man their daughter has married. Indeed, under classical laws the young husband typically was *obliged* to feed his parents-in-law, either by staying with them and hunting for them in the area where they lived, or, if they visited him where he was living, hunting on his own range area and feeding them all the same. If at some stage he and his wife were living on his own estate then his in-laws, or indeed his wife, could not normally be sent away from it purely on the grounds that it was his country and not theirs.

So while the man could assert rightfully that his possession or occupation-as-of-right of his own country was itself exclusive of his in-laws, it does not follow that he could tell them to leave his land whenever he liked. In fact there was a general understanding that people of the same general area with cross-cutting kin ties, could – when there was no particular serious dispute occurring – make use of at least the common and renewable resources of each other's countries as they moved about.[50] As countries in the richer areas may be crossed in as little as an hour's walking, one can see how it would have been ridiculously inconvenient to have to track down an authoritative member of the group owning each estate every time people wanted, or needed, to shift camp.

Compared with rights of physical exclusion, under Aboriginal customary law one has a far less limited power, and culturally a very much more important power, to exclude others from the exercise of rights which are at the core of customary entitlements. These core rights have far greater historical durability and continuity than rights to classical forms of land use, such as foraging, which are sanctioned by custom but subject to sometimes rapid transformations.

Core exclusive rights typically include, but are not necessarily limited to:

- the right to state 'proper' (customary–lawful) proprietary claims over land;
- the right to speak for, on behalf of, or with unconstrained authority *about* the country and its content as cultural property (that is, to *represent* it, in both senses);
- the right to transmit proprietary rights in country to one's descendants, such that those receiving the rights may in turn pass them on to others, such as their own descendants;
- the right to be asked for permission to access the country by non-owners who lack existing access rights;

- the right to be asked about granting any serious country-changing interest (such as, in present conditions, the right of non-owners to authorise the building of a Club Med complex);
- certain ceremonial rights in sites;
- the threefold right to hold, assert and concretely exercise the fullest level of responsibility for the welfare of the country, for example to burn off country as of untrammelled right, in some places to ritually activate increase centres for desired species, or in recent times to authorise dealing with noxious weeds or feral animals.

This domain of rights and powers, not that of concrete residence, is the key location of the exclusionary aspects of Aboriginal customary law concerning country. If concrete residence were a major focus of exclusionary rights under Aboriginal tradition, then one would expect territorial boundaries to have been both much more precisely defined and much more obviously defended than in fact they have been. The areas in which boundaries are recorded as fairly precise are largely restricted to the richest ecological zones, but even so they are not as precise as those of cadastral maps. There is no record of the deliberate visual marking of country boundaries in classical cultures of Aboriginal Australia as far as I am aware.

In remote areas local traditional owners may have been initially reluctant to host too many people from elsewhere at the time when missions or settlements were being set up on their estates, but after a time, perhaps when it all seemed such a *fait accompli,* these resentments did not surface easily or they may actually have withered away, the town area becoming essentially a non-Aboriginal domain for many purposes. But traditional ownership of a township site is not usually forgotten, and can be vigorously reasserted – in some cases resulting in a deal in which the 'historical people' who live in the township are to be granted explicitly and in writing a long-term right to reside. It is thus possible for long-term residence of non-owners to be recognised by customary owners and for this arrangement to be codified under an agreement or determination.

I do not suggest that there is always a single, fixed domain of exclusionary rights. Some 'exclusive rights' may be nested such that group A's exclude those of group B, but at a higher or geographically wider level the rights and interests of groups A and B may combine to exclude those of groups M, N and O. This is determined by context.

WHAT ARE RIGHTS?

Rights are more than the mere capacity to act, or the ability to control. They are social and cultural phenomena. As we have seen above, not all rights-holders in Aboriginal tradition have the physical or mental capacity to enact their inchoate rights in country, but they nevertheless remain identified as members of land-holding groups. Furthermore, there are times when people have the power to act to use or occupy or control land in a way regarded by their peers as unlawful, or at least as being outside the bounds of acceptability. It would be stretching the language to describe such powers as rights. If a right is a power, it is only a power to act in accordance with a system of values and principles acceptable to a particular society or group. This can raise problems of proof for rights about which consensus is lacking.

The *Macquarie Dictionary* says a right is, among other things:

- a just claim or title, whether legal, prescriptive, or moral;
- that which is due to anyone by just claim.[51]

The Western cultural orientation of such definitions is revealed mainly in the use of the appeal to a notion of the 'just'. An Aboriginal approach to such a definition would be more likely in terms of the authorisation of such claims on grounds of ancestral precedent and the stated knowledge of contemporary elders regarding the traditional Law or customary dispute resolution procedures concerned. The underlying common feature of such approaches is that possession of a right implies a correlative duty between persons. The assertion and protection of rights in classical Aboriginal traditions was generally based on self-help and mutuality between kin, in the absence of a higher office or group which held a monopoly on the use of violence to enforce those rights.

Individual and collective rights

Examples of individual connections to and interests in sites or countries include:

- birthplace (of self, of a parent, sometimes of one's own child)
- conception place
- burial place of parent
- initiation site
- personal Dreaming tree[52]
- place or area of main habitation
- etc.

Some of these may give rise to proprietary claims over the country concerned, while others do not. This is a matter of local tradition. In the southern Western Desert, birthplace is a major pathway to rights, not merely in the birthplace, but in the wider district to which the birthplace or a nearby Dreaming track belongs. In some regions a personal relationship, especially a spiritual one, may give a person the right to be consulted about a place or a country, or to be compensated for damage to it, but not to assert it is their own. In the Western Desert a personal spiritual connection to a place, may by contrast, be a dominant form of pro-prietary relationship to the country concerned, even though the shared, hence communal, nature of such interests is recognised.

There was an argument put forward by Daniel Vachon and Sandra Pannell that needs to be given consideration.[53] It suggested basically that native title research should focus on the individual's relationship to communal title, rather than on any particular kind of mediation of that relationship via locally-defined collectivities such as clans or tribes. I cannot see how dealing with both can be avoided, given the way in which most native title claimants will put their assertions of the basis of customary entitlements during their evidence. An anthropological account would normally be expected to offer an analysis of the way claimants conceive of and describe the sets of persons who hold interests in country, among other things. In most regions this discourse will tend to be dominated by reference to various kinds of groups.

In classical Aboriginal traditions, use of the material resources of the country is not neatly separable into an 'economic' domain. I once asked a senior Mudbura man if a certain kind of seed was edible (it was a Currajong). His answer was: 'Yes! Old People [ancestors] used to *live* on Dreaming!' This species was, as it turned out, a major matrilineal social totem in the region. But it was also very much a major food prior to the arrival of wheaten flour. In similar vein, a number of claimant witnesses in land claims over the years have given hunting and gathering of bush tucker as their first answer to questions from counsel as to how they 'look after' and 'care for' the country under claim. This may arise from the fact that custodial actions such as burning off undergrowth, talking to ancestral spirits near camp sites, cleaning out fouled wells or checking recent tracks near sacred sites were typically part and parcel of days spent foraging on the move, but it can also derive from a perception that to live off the land is to exchange substance with it. People will sometimes say that eating bush tucker from their own country makes them feel well, fresh and happy. The country is in such ways looking after its own, reciprocally.

Traditions of conception Dreamings often involve the expectant mother consuming a particular species of animal or plant, or the father successfully hunting a particular species, for example. The spirit of the species then animates the foetus and links the identity of the future child with the location of the special event. These are cases of 'economic activity' which are themselves inseparable from the maintenance or creation of spiritual connections to country, connections from which certain rights flow. But where most conceptions are now taking place in and around townships, the potential for the link between conception and place to play a role in the assignment of rights in a variety of countries has declined. With the decline of a decentralised bush economy there has also, correspondingly, been a decline in the role of birthplace as conferring rights in country. This has not necessarily meant a decline in the possession of rights in country, as descent principles and other factors such as knowledge and long residence may rise in importance when conception and birthplace decline as bases for assigning rights. Some might argue that descent is a less religious form of connection than conception or birth near a certain kind of Dreaming site, but it depends on the facts of the case.

From an analytical point of view it is possible to identify 'economic' as opposed to other kinds of rights, but as we have just seen it can be the case that economic rights shade into ritual ones, for example. Economic use rights might nevertheless be broadly broken up into:

- harvesting of renewable resources (plants, animals, firewood, water etc.)
- extraction of non-renewable resources (stone, ochres, clays etc.)
- exchange of products of the country (often highly ritualised)
- maintenance of species (both ritual and pragmatic means recorded)
- application of knowledge of species' properties (e.g., medicinal, technological).

It is important to distinguish such economic use rights from economic decision-making rights. Although present-day economic decision-making about Aboriginal land may have considerable continuities with the pre-colonial past, many of the decisions with which people are faced today are on a very different scale compared with those of the past. It is one thing to decide to burn off a grass plain, but it is another thing to decide to lease the grass plain for the car park of a Club Med complex which will bring in 2,000 strangers as a body of new residents.

Under modern conditions, economic decisions can lead to the rapid recasting of the local or even regional political, cultural and racial mix. If, 150 years ago, only five people had any real say in when and how a particular grass plain might be burned off, it is unlikely that a similar group of five senior people would today bear the burden of deciding about establishing a new Club Med complex on the same grass plain. The scale of the event would make it necessary to exercise a 'right' of new dimensions and one which would have new kinds of consequences, even though it is a 'right' built on old foundations. It should be no surprise that financial, bureaucratic and political decision-making, involving unprecedented issues and their repercussions, has put a strain on the notion of the 'exercising of traditional rights' among Aboriginal people. There can be conceptual difficulties in defining what constitutes a 'right to consent' when 'informed consent' may require those with traditional authority to grapple with matters they do not always claim to understand.

Hunting, fishing, gathering?

When trying to explore the nature of contemporary rights asserted by native title claimants it is useful to look at the principles revealed in some of the older, better recorded ways rights in country have been exercised. Part of the value of looking at hunting, fishing and food-gathering lies in what they reveal of these principles.

For example, hunting and foraging in the bush with tradition-oriented people often impresses on one the extent to which economic use rights are hedged about with what appear to an outsider as a massive complex of restrictions and obligations. Restrictions of this kind are often called taboos. Jon Altman, in an economic study carried out in north-central Arnhem Land, usefully distinguished between 'producer taboos, consumer taboos, and miscellaneous taboos'.[54]

In the 1970s senior Wik people would say, for example, that flying fox carcasses, after a meal, should be left lined up neatly on a sheet of bark, with respect, not merely thrown into the fire or the bush. Such an obligation matched the way newly killed species were often spoken to in tones of compassion and unavoidable regret by hunters, and it formed an integrated part of the whole process of foraging properly and as of right. Saltwater stingray flesh could be washed only with salt water, not with fresh. I am not sure whether a reverse rule applied to the freshwater stingrays. These saltwater/freshwater taboos are clearly related to the major social, cultural and political distinction between coastal and inland people which is common right around Aboriginal Australia. For freshwater turtles to escape from a capsized 44-gallon drum and head for nearby salt water, as happened on one occasion I observed in the Wik region, was regarded as a potential disaster to be headed off by a collective sprint to intercept them. In the same region only senior men were supposed to drink water from baler shells, at least in earlier times. Wells were to be closed in again with sand after use, otherwise one courted the possibility of lethal thunderstorms. Wells dug out near sacred sites by unauthorised visitors, even those who had an ordinary right of passage through the same country, were considered to be the causes of illness or threatening electrical storms, and certainly of anger among those to whom the wells belonged. At one off-shore place of importance north of Archer River, it was permitted to spear fish, but only if the man held a baler shell on his head and stood on one leg at the same time. At a certain lagoon, where people caught long-necked turtles, the normal words for turtles could not be used in speech and they had to be referred to by a term based on the word for baler shell, an oblique reference to the carapace of the unmentionable turtle.

In Wik classical traditions, as in so many others, there are numerous other restrictions on who can consume which species at which maturation stages. There are restrictions on the gender, age and health status of persons permitted to eat certain foods or go to certain places or to dig certain ground. There are restrictions on fishing at a certain place or extracting water from a certain well after dark, and certain camping areas or whole estates may be 'closed' due to recent deaths. In the 1970s these closures were normally for a year. One could bathe in most streams, lagoons and lakes but the use of soap in any natural water body was, and I believe still is, strictly prohibited. To move about the bush with people who had been socialised in it was, for this visiting anthropologist, to be in a constant state of apprehension about making mistakes, going to the wrong places, and doing prohibited things. At that time, no one, Aboriginal or otherwise, was simply free to roam the Wik lands unsupervised or out of communication with relevant landowners. Once radio communications to outstations arrived, advance notice of visits, using the radio schedule, became at least for a time *de rigueur*, assuming the older role of smoke-fires lit by approaching visitors.

These examples of specific restrictions on rights, some of them rather baroque to an outsider's view, could be readily added to in vast quantities from the same region and from many others. The point here is that an 'economic right', like even the most unquestioned tenure right, is never a completely untrammelled right. This applies also to Westerners. Lawyer Hal Wootten wrote of an owner's capacity to enjoy their Australian freehold title: 'There are innumerable activities that are forbidden unconditionally or conditionally, or can be carried out only with some form of permission. Is the "owner" free to dispose of, or refuse to part with, the land as he or she chooses? By no means in all circumstances, either during his or her life or after death by will.'[55]

For example, to forage as of right is also to forage 'properly'. Such rights carry responsibilities with them. To forage 'properly' is to carry out only what one has the right to do, something which arises from one's standing in relationship to the country and its owners. Foraging 'properly' is also partly a matter of how it is done, where it is done, at what time it is done, who is doing it, and with whom. It is arguable, therefore, that when modern rural or urban Aboriginal people define 'proper' foraging as requiring a conservation ethic they are doing nothing very new at the level of basic principles, even if conservation in the modern global sense was not a classical Aboriginal value. The conservation of supplies of particular species at particular locations was certainly important if for no other reason than the avoidance of shortages, in the pre-conservationist era, and there is a range of evidence on the question of how much this occurred as a matter of deliberate action and how much was embedded in a religious framework of restrictions. This is not, however, to suggest that classical Aboriginal thought was traditionally conservationist in the modern global sense. Simple-minded assertions that pre-colonial Aboriginal people always 'lived in harmony with nature' and had an altruistic approach to all creatures great and small have long since been debunked, almost for as long as they have continued to pour out unabated from uninformed sources.

What certainly is a classical Aboriginal value is an emphasis on 'looking after', 'caring for' and 'growing up' the country which continues to inform the attitudes of many. To refer to one's country as an object of emotional attachment, as 'poor-bugger', as something one 'worries for', is similarly a classical value. Such continuing values have been the basis of different forms of the exercise of care and protection over time. Those who assert an obligation to care for the country they claim thereby assert a right, the right to act as primary custodians. That they now do so in new outward forms is hardly surprising.

I think it can be argued that there is a common basic hierarchy of restrictions on using the resources of Aboriginal country. Those resources which were most desired, which were immobile and thus a permanent feature of an estate, and especially those which were non-renewable, attracted the greatest restrictions.

In the Wik region, certain natural resources were more or less freely available to be taken and used by those who were traversing or living legitimately on the countries of others. These would include the basic necessities of life such as firewood, shade, water from unrestricted sites, the indispensable and multi-functional paperbark, most fish and game animals and many vegetable food sources, such as fruit and lilies. But the taking of certain items was subject to a more exclusive approach than the taking of others, as was the burning of certain sections of country.[56] In the Wik region there was in general less restriction on clearing up a forest area with fire so as to make it more habitable prior to camping, than there was on the firing of grass plains rich in game such as small mammals and reptiles. The latter were once organised and collective events which could involve neighbours invited to partake of plenty, whereas any small camping group, at the appropriate season, would normally burn off nearby vegetation as it moved about. One qualification to this is that restricted sites, and estates closed due to a death, could be subject to prohibitions on burning except by those in particular authority.

In the Wik region a more exclusive attitude was held towards certain immobile resources of a precious or thinly distributed kind, such as the more important ground tubers, pandanus trees whose fronds were used by women for string-making, stands of hibiscus used for spear-handles, stands of large bamboo, and mangrove oysters. There are no narcotics or similar drugs naturally occurring in the region but if there had been, one would expect the attitude to them to also have been very restrictive, as it was in the Lake Eyre basin.[57] A similar attitude was held towards the ochre sources.[58] There are no stone quarries within the study region for which I have good information, and indeed there is no stone at all on the Wik coast, but in other regions it is notable that non-renewable and immobile valued resources generally tend to stand high on the list of things to which access is restricted. These, such as knife and axe blanks, along with certain kinds of artefacts or forms of adornment (including shell) and much-desired drugs such as pituri, also tended to be among the major trade items. Spear handles, especially bamboo ones, are a major trade item between coastal and inland Australia; although renewable, they do not usually occur in anything other than small isolated stands.[59] Site restrictions are thus sometimes dependent, at least in part, on the character of the resources of the site.

One aspect of the extracting of non-renewable resources that is probably relevant here, and which is true also of yam digging and well digging, is that of the breaking of the ground. Breaking the surface of the ground is, in the Wik region at least, always potentially more dangerous and hedged with restrictions than other forms of exploitation. Marking the country in a durable form also seems to me to be something highly restricted in classical Aboriginal practice. Given the length of Aboriginal occupation of the Australian continent, the quantity of parietal art is not at all vast and the proportion of it that has been attributed specifically to non-religious activities is minute. Given the very restrictive attitude towards permanent engraving, painting and stone-arranging, it is to be expected that those with less than core rights or less than solid religious authority would have been under very severe taboos preventing the leaving of durable traces on the country.

Those resources and sites subject to the greatest restrictions of access are those most subject to concentrations of authority within groups, and thus those most likely to attract descriptions which portray them as subject to the personal rights or wishes of one or more senior custodians. This is the case even though the underlying title of the country concerned remains communal. The few ethnographic records of Aboriginal Australia which suggest explicitly that country could be privately owned by individuals might perhaps be explained by this analysis.

COEXISTENT RIGHTS: THE CASE OF PASTORALISM

Both Aboriginal and European tenure systems separately embrace the sharing of rights and interests over the same parcel of land or waters, and its products, by more than one entity.[60] In this section I make a brief excursion to look at the conditions under which the legal rights of pastoral lessees and the customary rights of Aboriginal people in the country of their pastoral leases have tended to coexist as a matter of fact.

Where Aboriginal people were not physically removed from their homelands by colonising interests, they were generally better able to preserve their traditional connection to their lands than other groups who were early centralised on mission stations or in towns far away. The geographically decentralised pattern of pastoral development, combined with the need to muster large areas of land on the stations by horseback each year, and long periods spent as shepherds guarding flocks of sheep against wild dogs, meant that opportunities for station-based Aboriginal people to learn and remain in touch with the cultural traditions of even remote parts of their countries were comparatively plentiful. For many groups this close contact with their countries was more or less abruptly cut off by the requirement that Aboriginal stock workers be paid the same as others, a situation which came into reality at different times in different places and which finally was enforced in the Northern Territory as of 1 December 1968.[61] While this was a progressive decision in terms of equal rights, for many people it was also the catalyst for their movement to wholesale dependency on welfare, their centralisation in townships where they came to live among people with whom they had traditional conflicts, their suddenly increased physical alienation from at least parts of their countries, and their movement to greater proximity to alcohol outlets. Over much of remote Australia this shift took place in the decade 1965–1975. For many families the shift to equal wages, unaccompanied by counter-measures, can only be described as a social engineering disaster. Although there have been many small communities established on excisions from pastoral leases in recent decades in the Northern Territory, for example, their economic base largely remains that of welfare payments.

Pastoral work offered Aboriginal people opportunities for maintaining economic relationships with their homelands, something that was often a matter of necessity as well as of choice. Station-based people, part-time during work seasons and often full-time during lay-off periods such as the summer or wet season, continued to hunt and gather wild food, to drink from waterholes and soakages, and to extract natural resources for medicinal and technological purposes. Given the monotony and scarcity of the food and other resources provided to them by many pastoralists, these supplementary and replacement sources of the necessities of life effectively constituted a subsidy for the pastoralists' activities. It is well remembered among older people that the north Australian wet season lay-off period, when Aboriginal employees conducted initiations and other ceremonies and travelled from area to area visiting their relations, as in fact large numbers still do, was at that time one in which the people relied mainly on bush tucker and did not receive regular rations from their seasonal employers. That is, the viability of the granted leases was in some measure enhanced by, if not dependent on, the maintenance of Aboriginal foraging. And foraging 'properly' in Aboriginal customary law is something that ultimately rests on the system of rights and interests in land that 'native title', as a legal concept, attempts to reflect. The maintenance of traditional rights in coexistence with pastoral occupation often enjoyed several generations of continuity.

One could not say this quite so confidently if there were no evidence of territorial stability among station-based Aboriginal people, particularly during the earlier phase of pastoral expansion. But the evidence for such stability is widespread, and in many remote regions it has largely been maintained, especially up to the completion of the spread of equal wages in the late 1960s. For example, a map of the Northern Territory showing the physical location of primary affiliates of particular Aboriginal languages as of 1972 was published by E.P. Milliken in 1976. A comparison of this map with information on the location of traditional countries associated with those same languages shows comprehensively the significant degree to which station-based people in that part of Australia kept to bases within or near to their own traditional areas long after pastoral occupation occurred. This is not to suggest they were completely immobilised. Visits to relatives alone would require people to travel some distance from their own homeland areas, but as the classical Aboriginal marriage preference system, certainly in the monsoon belt, aimed for geographically close marriages, the distances would not have been great until recently. Lyn Riddett has pointed out that, in the Victoria River District from 1900 to the 1940s, Aboriginal people moved in and out of the pastoral industry when it suited them and moved from station to station more or less as it suited them. This type of mobility, especially in the early period of colonisation, was dependent on the ability of people to live off the land, at least while in transit but also for longer periods when not working.[62] But much more detailed evidence along the same lines, for specific stations, has been repeatedly given before Aboriginal land claim tribunals in the Northern Territory and Queensland over the last two decades.

This stability of associations between Aboriginal groups and pastoral stations in or close to their traditional countries dates from the period usually known as 'letting-in'. Ever since Elkin's useful (if rather dated) synthesis of 1951, the following basic phases have been recognised in the history of relationships between local Aborigines and incoming colonists, especially pastoralists:

1 There was an initial period during which Aboriginal people were curious about the newcomers but did not often attempt to drive them off their land in an organised way. Both sides usually sought some means of coexistence. Conflict over the use of waterholes, spearing of stock, or relations with women, for example, eventually occurred in many cases and violence could erupt. In Queensland the Protector of Aborigines, who was widely experienced in the field, reported to Parliament in 1901 that

> Another contentious matter which must be approached with great care is the right of the aboriginals to hunt and fish on the watercourses. It is their right, and it is their only means of existence when in their natural state. ... To deprive them of this right means wiping them out or driving them into the smaller townships ...[63]

2 Another alternative, and in fact one largely reached in pastoral areas, was for the original inhabitants and newcomers to reach some arrangement by which resources were shared. The pastoralists themselves were a resource. For example, the mutual dependency of small farmers and Aboriginal people seems to have been quite extreme in the Daly River area prior to World War II, and particular farmers and farms became subject to competitive claims by Aboriginal people who sought to control access to them.[64] It is not stretching things to say that,

in this kind of situation, among the Aboriginal rights being asserted were those over people as resource providers.

3 For a time, sometimes for a decade or more, 'wild' or 'bush' Aborigines kept away from, or were kept away from, the pastoral homesteads, and sporadic violence out on the runs continued, while a proportion of Aborigines were employed on the stations, thus giving rise to a major distinction between those still mainly dependent on the bush for survival and those more heavily dependent on station rations and payment in kind. Many 'bush' Aborigines would maintain a furtive and touchy relationship with their relatives in the station 'black's camp' at this time, for example, visiting by night to obtain meat.[65] Thus there was, on many pastoral leases, a period of uneasy coexistence not only between Aborigines and non-Aborigines, but between sets of Aborigines, and also between the two economic modes, pastoralism and foraging, the mutual dependency of which was sometimes most notable.

4 When the pastoralists considered the 'bush blacks' sufficiently settled down or untroublesome to be allowed to reside near the homestead and take part in the station economy, they would 'let them in'.[66] This was not only in order to end hostilities, but also because the pastoralists had an economic incentive: they often needed the labour, even if only seasonally.[67]

5 A period of mutual adaptation and some equilibrium then usually followed, often for some generations. This phase has been called by some scholars one of 'accommodation'.[68] The tendency of Aboriginal people to try to remain close to their traditional areas continued to be supported by the decentralisation of pastoral activities. The resulting access to the bush and bush resources continued to support the maintenance of Aboriginal knowledge of country and of foraging skills. This was a period in which traditional continuities and gradual changes were intermingled.[69] The economy of stations was not purely pastoral, but a mixed economy of pastoralism and foraging. For example, the Koolpinyah station diaries (Northern Territory) give the 'distinct impression of two economies and cultures meeting at the point of labour and commodity exchange...'.[70]

I do not pursue Elkin's paradigm or its relatives any further in this context.

The pastoralists, of all the colonists, offered the form of colonisation most compatible with the maintenance of traditional Aboriginal connections to land. Intensive farming of small plots, town life and even seasonal maritime work could be less conducive to this kind of continuity. Diving and other work in the lugger trades was seasonal and for the first decades allowed many to return to their bush homes during the off season, but many also were taken far from home by sea, and a significant number did not return, given the rigours of the life. On the other hand, in a region where Aboriginal countries were and are very small, as in the Bloomfield rainforest region of Cape York Peninsula, the coming of small-scale tin-miners could be incorporated into local Aboriginal practice and actually helped the survival of close traditional associations with the lands on which the mines, scattered as they were rather than centralised, were located.[71] Pastoralism was more like the hunting life than agriculture or town occupations, as it involved tracking and capturing animals across large areas of bush, and it provided opportunities for meeting the obligations of remote site custodianship. Ann McGrath writes of the Top End pastoral stations: 'While travelling around the station at various tasks, Aborigines maximised any opportunity to "look after" specific sites for which they had individual or group responsibility.'[72] Pastoral work also involved semi-nomadic seasonal shifts both at mustering times and lay-offs; it was frequently participation in an economy of kind rather than cash, and it offered access to a wide range of bush resources, the latter being at least a part-time necessity.

Furthermore, there was often no direct philosophical assault on Aboriginal cultural traditions under pastoralism, as there was under the Christian missions with their common, though not universal, enforcement of bans on ceremonies and the use of Aboriginal languages, and their widespread practice of forcible separation of children from parents using locked dormitories. The pastoralists by and large were not there to change Aborigines ideologically, or to get them to abandon their bush knowledge and skills. Local geographical knowledge was a field in which pastoralists could not, at least initially, compete with the original inhabitants. Knowledge of the land's waters and other resources, of its vegetation associations and physiography, and of the mythological and spiritual landscape, were constitutive or substantive aspects of local systems of law and custom to do with rights in land and waters.

Far from being 'extinguished' by the coming of the first lessees, such knowledge was offered an additional role, and its continuity became an asset to lessees just as much as a prize bull could be. They had no interest in destroying it. The persistent coexistence of customary rights and leasehold in many areas was not, in this sense, an accident. Pastoralists who recognised and accepted the rights of their Aboriginal co-residents to make use of natural resources on the countries of their leases, and to pursue their religious interests in those countries, in a sense were exercising a customary or de facto recognition of the persistence of a pre-existing (sub)set of indigenous rights, whether or not their leases contained reservations in favour of those rights.

The usefulness of distinctions such as the one I have proposed be made between core and contingent rights, and between the sets of people who have either contingent rights only or both core and contingent rights, should not blind us to their complexities and difficulties. Like several of the other kinds of rights discussed above, this pair probably suffers from the oversimplifying effects of dualism, or the tendency to want to break things down into contrasting pairs. Yet in so many cases it seems that such a distinction, or one very like it, is a part of Aboriginal customary systems of land tenure and land use.

There will be times and places where such a distinction may be somewhat weakly established as a matter of customary practice. In some regions, the Western Desert in particular, this may be a situation of long standing. In some other regions, those where older traditions have received the greatest impact from non-Aboriginal society, the core/contingent distinction may have been eroded or it may be the focus of disputation as to its validity as a principle. On the other hand, in

New South Wales it is reported that, in spite of a state land council system based on current residence rather than traditional connections, many Aboriginal people continue to privilege the most ancient or 'way back' connections in disputes about control of land or heritage issues.[73] But the New South Wales legislation imposes legal structures in which there is a failure to distinguish 'traditional owners' from 'historical people', and thus technically amalgamates those who hold only contingent rights with those who hold both core and contingent rights. Nicolas Peterson said, of residence-based models of land rights, that 'it needs to be recognised that [they are] an interference in the traditional system since [they are] likely to result in advantaging those with weaker interests by equating them with the strongest if litigation takes place'.[74] Some people may seek to use existing contingent rights as a springboard for the attainment of core rights, at least in terms of bureaucratic recognition.

In spite of the complexities that may arise, the core/contingent distinction is one that ought at least to be taken into consideration in the making and processing of native title claims. There is much ethnographic evidence to suggest it is a common feature of Aboriginal land relationships, but of course its applicability to any case is a matter for local testing and demonstration. To ignore it, where it applies, would be to court a native title determination which offered support to those who hold marginal interests in the country but who have ambitions to attain a dominant status in controlling its resources. It is also to court negative reactions from those who fear that their privileged core relationship to their country may be downgraded or displaced by the homogenising of all kinds of rights-holders in a determination, or in a prescribed body corporate, which sets up a single recognised set of 'native title holders' without internal distinctions.

2 | Local organisation before the land claims era[1]

T HERE IS NOT enough space here to offer a comprehensive history of ideas about Aboriginal local organisation and land tenure, but gaining some grasp of that history is relevant to understanding the anthropological evidence that is put forward in native title cases. This is partly because significant early records of Aboriginal societies and their normative practices were made by people who framed the publication of their results in terms of the theoretical apparatus of their time. Some used technical terms of the day, many of which still survive, often with different meanings. Readers unfamiliar with anthropological terms of art, especially in the field of kinship, should read Chapter 7 before proceeding.

We cannot assume that a technical term in common use in 1890 has the same meaning attributed to it by present-day scholars, for example. More importantly, it is always sobering and informative to learn to what degree the empirical observations and insights of the past were moulded, in their public presentation, by the intellectual schemes and paradigms brought to them by those earlier practitioners. Les Hiatt has provided a valuable historical analysis of some major topics in Australian social anthropology of the colonial era and up to recent times in his *Arguments About Aborigines*, including a review of the evolution of ideas about local organisation.[2] Here I focus on fewer sources in greater detail, but refer the reader to Hiatt's book for some wider context.

Slicing history into epochs is always rather artificial, but it can make the patterns of change easier to grasp, especially for people new to a subject. In the case of the theory of Aboriginal land tenure and local organisation, there have been perhaps four most influential bodies of thinking and writing among anthropologists.

Among the colonial-era writers, A.W. Howitt and Lorimer Fison were pre-eminent influences, especially Howitt. It was an era when social and cultural evolution and history were central interests for many anthropologists. The period of modern professional anthropology began, in the Australian case, in 1926 with the appointment of A.R. Radcliffe-Brown as Australia's first Professor of

Anthropology, and his writings on local organisation held considerable sway until the Hiatt-Stanner debate of the 1960s. The 1930s–1960s was the era when the structural-functionalist paradigm was dominant in much of the world's anthropology, Australia included. A third phase can be distinguished with the commencement of land claims research on a large scale in the Northern Territory from 1976. From that time the number of players in the field of applied anthropology in Australia increased dramatically, but the 1970s was also a period of greatly increased activity in land-based studies of a purely academic anthropological kind, given the interest in ecology and ethnoscience in those years, and it is harder to identify a limited number of influential individuals for this third phase. A fourth phase, the native title era (1993–), began while land claims in the Northern Territory and Queensland were still being researched and heard under different legislation. Some scholars who had begun their interest in Aboriginal land relations before the land rights era thence became engaged in preparing reports on behalf of organisations acting for claimants, although most senior scholars did not, leaving much of the field to those who were newly trained. Many of the latter came to be employees of indigenous organisations, carrying out their research 'in-house', as it were, and thus limiting the extent to which they might be perceived as independent experts, regardless of their actual practice.

I do not attempt here an historical overview of the ideas which have been evolving in this field since the 1970s. In many ways it is too soon to have a well-resolved understanding of the pattern of historical developments in anthropology, especially when one has been an active participant in them. Later chapters, however, do refer to developments of the last thirty years in the writing on Aboriginal land tenure, but on a topical rather than a chronological basis.

HOWITT AND FISON

Perhaps the earliest terms used by Alfred William Howitt for local groups were 'sub-tribe', 'subdivision' and 'small family' in his discussion of the Diyari of the Lake Eyre region published in 1878.[3] He was later to refine his thinking on the subject quite considerably.

In 1880 Howitt, in a joint work with Lorimer Fison, wrote that in Gippsland, 'an aggregate of families, all being intimately related by common descent through the father', formed what he called a 'division'. Two or more divisions combined to form what he called a 'clan'. Clans were named, divisions were not. Three of the five clan names were based on roots meaning 'east', 'west' and 'the sea/south', one was untranslated, and another was based on a term meaning 'manly'. Clans included all those individuals acknowledging common descent, their members inhabiting a certain area, including the country of their several divisions, and claiming certain distinctive qualities. The clans had geographical 'positions' or 'countries', and together these clans made up a tribe. Their countries made up a tribal territory.[4]

In 1883 Howitt and Fison said that an Australian 'tribe (or community)', in its 'local and physical aspect', had 'subdivisions' which they termed 'clans' or 'local groups'. They said that recruitment to these local groups was by 'perpetual succession through the males'.[5] In another paper of the same year, Howitt said that the tribe was 'divided geographically, either into what may be termed hordes with uterine [matrilineal] descent, or into clans with agnatic [patrilineal] descent'.[6] The Kurnai of Gippsland only had 'clans' and no 'hordes', because Howitt reserved the latter term for 'local divisions of tribes having uterine descent'.[7] The suggestion that Howitt use the term 'horde' to refer to a local group of a tribe with uterine descent, even though no matrilineal 'hordes' were described, came from Fison.[8]

A reader may be forgiven for understanding this 'horde' therefore to be itself recruited matrilineally, but it seems that it is intended to refer to a local group in a tribe which has (predominantly) matrilineal social organisation (that is, with mainly or wholly non-local classes and totems determined through the mother); this local group, however, like that of a tribe with patrilineal institutions, is itself also perpetuated through the male line. Elsewhere, for example, Howitt said that

> the Kurnai tribe is divided into five clans, each of which has succession from father to son in the same portion of the tribal territory. I use the word 'clan' advisedly, because, this tribe has agnatic descent. When I use the word 'horde' I refer to a local division of a tribe having uterine descent as to its *social* organisation.[9]

As far as I am aware, no ethnographer has ever produced any convincing evidence that any territorial transmission system in Australia was or is matrilineal by rule (see further Chapter 7). Indeed, this is clearly implied by Howitt and Fison's own statement that 'descent through the mother ... *has to do with the social organisation only: it does not touch the local*'.[10]

Howitt considered the Kurnai to be a socially advanced group because, in his opinion, they had moved from a predominance of matrilineal institutions to having no matrilineal institutions, and to having patrilineal descent of rights in country. This was a 'progressive social change'.[11] The idea of a struggle between matriliny and patriliny was conceived of by Howitt as correspondingly a struggle between the social organisation (largely uterine in transmission) and the local organisation (largely, perhaps wholly, agnatic in Howitt's experience). Where the local organisation gained strength it could take to itself 'all the powers which the social organization formerly possessed'.[12] The 'aggressiveness of the local organisation' was an unconscious social process. Local organisation was 'hostile to social [organisation]' and its tendency was 'to bring about descent through males, to arrange society on its own basis, and finally to make itself paramount'.[13]

But the change in local organisation to which he referred does not seem to refer to the way rights in land were transmitted, as he claimed that both less advanced and more advanced tribes had the same form of local organisation in this respect. Instead the change he referred to seems largely to amount to a shift of dominance, in the aggregate, between the various matri- and patri-based kinds of institutions used by a society.

In their 1885 paper, Howitt and Fison revised their terminology. Instead of the term 'local clan', and presumably also in place of the restricted (and impossible to apply?) definition of 'horde' cited above, all local or geographical divisions of the 'community' or 'tribe' would now be known as 'hordes'. A horde is a group which 'occupies certain definite hunting-grounds'. A child belongs to '*the horde in which it was born*'.[14] All members of the horde share in common a 'hunting right' over a certain area. But '[t]he succession of the son to the father's horde can scarcely be called inheritance from the father. It is mere continuance in the locality where he was born.' 'The daughter may go away when she marries, but the son remains in the father's horde.'[15]

On the basis of these statements one might conclude that Howitt (and Fison) considered that locality of birth and subsequent presence in one's father's camp was the critical basis of rights in country, not descent from the father as such. Yet Howitt describes a Gippsland man (Gliun-kong) who 'having been born at Lake Tyers, it [the Wurnungatti geographical division] is his country by birth, as Raymond Island [the Binnajerra geographical division] is by inheritance from his father'.[16] This suggests that descent could confer landed identity and rights independently of birthplace.

The Krauatungalung and other clans of Gippsland were subdivided into local 'divisions' which were further divided into 'subdivisions' such as 'the *Bunjil-baul*, or men of the island, who lived on Raymond Island in Lake King', and who were a subdivision 'mostly' of the Tatungalung clan and 'partly' of the Brabralung clan.[17] It would seem that these 'subdivisions' of Howitt's 1904 version are the same as the 'families inhabiting a certain locality' that 'formed that aggregate which [Howitt] …termed the division' in his 1880 version.[18]

What Howitt called a 'clan' is in all major respects the same kind of grouping which Meggitt and Hiatt called a 'community' (see below).[19] His 'divisions' correspond to what most present-day Australian anthropologists would call a 'clan' or a 'patrifilial group'.

Howitt and Fison wrote, as did Howitt repeatedly elsewhere (see below), as if only sons received such rights from fathers, even though they implied that a female joined the horde at birth just as males did. It is implied, but not discussed explicitly, that they considered a woman's horde membership to be that of the people with whom she lived at any particular time. But, as is overwhelmingly demonstrable from other sources, under classical Aboriginal rules, women carried with them their ancestry-based identities, most often as members of their father's land-holding group, no matter where they went to live either before or after marriage.

Only a few years after the 1885 change of terminology just discussed, however, Howitt reverted to his old terminological practices. In 1888 he wrote: 'Horde is used to designate one of the local divisions of a tribe which counts descent through the female line. I only use the word clan for the local divisions of a tribe which has descent in the male line.'[20]

In 1891 he wrote similarly, but with less clarity: 'I use the term "horde" when there is maternal descent, and "clan" when descent is in the male line', and he proceeded to refer to the adjoining 'hordes' of the Wiradjuri (NSW) in contrast with the (similarly adjoining) 'local clan[s]' of the Kurnai (Victoria).[21] In the same year in another paper he stated that the 'class divisions' (moieties, sections, etc.) of tribes were not, 'excepting in very exceptional cases, aggregated into localities. They then become "local clans" with descent counted through the male line'.[22] In his major work of 1904, he made his usage clear once more:

> Horde, the primary geographical division of a tribe having female descent, for instance, the Ngadi-ngani.
> Clan, the primary geographical division of a tribe with descent in the male line, for instance, the Krauatungalung.[23]

Describing the Ngadi-ngani of Lake Eyre, Howitt refered to the 'definite tract of hunting and food ground' of each local group, and added:

> The sons inherit, or perhaps to speak more correctly occupy, as a matter of birthright, the country which their fathers hunted over. Such is the local organisation of a typical two-class tribe with descent in the female line.[24]

Once again it is clear that such a 'horde' was not asserted to be matrilineal.

Howitt (with or without Fison) defined what he meant by the word 'tribe' more than once. In most cases these definitions included words to the effect that the tribe is a community occupying a common tract of country and sharing a common language or dialectal variants of a common language.[25] The presence in the tribe's area of people speaking other languages he regarded as an exception brought about by marriage – not knowing, or not taking into account, the fact that such inter-language marriages were quite common in much of Australia. These inter-language marriages alone are fatal to any 'tribe' definition that seeks to combine unity of language with some neat kind of unity of residential range. In any case, common language was usually integral to Howitt's (and Fison's) definitions of 'tribe'.

Howitt (at times with Fison) made frequent reference to Aboriginal 'communities'. In their first work together they said that 'the word *tribe* [is] used as synonymous with *community*'.[26] They would not, they said, use the term 'tribe' to refer to any division within a community.[27] Later, Howitt was to do so (see below). In 1883 they said that 'the Australian tribe (or community) presents itself under two aspects... [a] social aspect ... [and a] local and physical aspect'.[28] Here again was a simple equation of a 'community' with a territorial language group. This kind of tribe was in part defined essentially as the entity which bore, contained or maintained both the system of local organisation *and* the system of social organisation to which its members subscribed. The fact that such systems were frequently shared in detail with several or many neighbouring 'tribes' does not seem to have discouraged such authors from locating them principally as features of tribes rather than as features of larger regional populations or social fields. I would much prefer the latter. This is not only because systems of social and local organisation typically occur regionally and 'supra-tribally', but also because some language groups may be subdivided on the basis that some of their subgroups may have one variant of social organisation and some may have another.

In an 1883 paper Howitt referred to the Wolgal, Ngarego and coast Murring tribes of the area between the upper Murray, the Monaro and the coast at the Shoalhaven River as together constituting a group which is 'indicated by the community of initiation ceremonies'.[29] In a subsequent paper he added to this set the Theddora and the Wiraidjuri (Wiradjuri), commenting:

> These five tribes, or perhaps tribal groups, represent a social aggregate, namely a community bound together, in spite of diversity of class system, by ceremonies of initiation, which, although they vary slightly in different localities, are yet substantially the same, and are common to all. Again, each of these five tribes, if regarded separately, is found to be not only connected in the way I have mentioned with the other four, but also with other neighbouring tribes in a similar manner, so that "the community", as indicated by the initiation ceremonies, spreads over even a wider extent of country than that which these five tribes occupy.[30]

As Howitt then pointed out in a footnote, 'the community of initiation-ceremonies and the practice of [tribal] intermarriage did not prevent the tribes from making raids into each other's country in the olden time'. Two of these tribes were 'constantly and desperately at war' and the Wiraidjuri even made raids on the coast.[31] After the ceremonies were over, the extracted tooth of the novice was passed from headman to headman until it had made 'the complete circuit of the community, which was present at the initiation'. 'The circuit in which the tooth is carried marks the extent of the epigamic [intermarrying] community.'[32]

Here we have several contradictions or changes. First, the tribe is no longer coextensive with the community as defined elsewhere by Howitt. Second, members of the same community as defined on the basis of joint initiations and intermarriage may have different forms of social organisation depending on their particular tribe, whereas elsewhere Howitt said that social organisation is a feature of the tribe itself and the tribe itself is the community, thus implying that different forms of social organisation must belong to or imply the existence of different communities. Third, where the community is a tribe it has a uniquely defined, invariant territory, but where the community is a set of people who jointly initiate youths with varying sets of their neighbours depending on occasion, the geographical correlate of a person's community of initiation varies with the event and is not a constant. A Northern Territory parallel here would be that while the Warlpiri lands can be defined with some constancy, Warlpiri people may be found participating in initiation ceremonies along with people from the lower Roper River, the Victoria River, the East Kimberley, and as far south-west as Kiwirrkura in Western Australia, depending on the event. Another problem for Howitt's analysis is that initiation was or is only one part of the regional ceremonial lives of Aboriginal people. There is no reason to expect that any one local or tribal group's ceremonial networks should be isomorphic with another's and reflect a single community.

In their 1885 paper Howitt and Fison reflected some of their accumulated preceding definitions when they wrote that

> The [initiation] ceremonies are held by the assembled community periodically; the community being the aggregate of hordes, or of tribes between which there is epigamy [intermarriage].[33]

Howitt speculated that such ceremonial assemblies, and similar festivals such as the bunya nut harvest in south-east Queensland, represented the probable initial condition of Aboriginal society as an 'Undivided Commune'. Howitt also used the term 'Commune' to refer to the hypothetical social whole that may be conceived of as distinct from any of its various divisions into tribes, hordes, nations, classes and sub-classes. Social and territorial 'divisions' within this hypothetical Commune were thus, for Howitt, not just structural features of contemporary society but were also likely to have been historical events in Aboriginal social and cultural evolution.[34]

RADCLIFFE-BROWN

A.R. Radcliffe-Brown (1880–1955), an Englishman, was one of the more important figures in the history of modern anthropology. He was founding professor of Anthropology at Cape Town 1921–26, Sydney 1926–31, and Oxford 1937–46. During his time in Australia he established courses and stimulated much post-graduate research in Aboriginal Australia and in Papua New Guinea. He emphasised careful and extended fieldwork and laid special emphasis on social and local organisation. Kinship studies were central. He was one of the main figures in the development of what is known as the structural-functionalist theoretical paradigm in anthropology, a paradigm which is no longer dominant.

His views on Aboriginal local organisation, as he expressed them in his writings, seem to fall into two phases.

The early Radcliffe-Brown

Radcliffe-Brown carried out fieldwork in north-west Australia near Port Hedland in 1911, assisted by Daisy Bates.[35] In 1913 he published a map of Kariera tribal country and showed on it the approximate locations of nineteen '*local groups*' each with its own defined territory'.[36] He guessed that the tribe had 20–25 such local groups.[37]

> Membership of the local group is determined by descent in the male line; that is to say, a child belongs to the local group of its father and inherits hunting rights over the territory of that group.[38]

Ownership of the land and its products was collective, not individual. A man could not leave his local group and become naturalised or adopted into another; local group membership was for life. Members of one local group could not hunt or gather anything from the country of another group without permission; trespass was punishable by death.[39] However, visits to other countries were frequent and there was a 'perpetual shifting to and fro both within *the country of the group* and *from one group to another*' by '*families*'.[40]

Here we see the slippage from '*group*' as a land-holding patrilineal descent group to a '*group*' as something one can visit, namely a residence group not a descent group. 'A single individual, or a family, or several families, might pay a visit to a *neighbouring group*.'[41] Why not '*family*', especially as he says 'the unit of social life in the Kariera was the family, consisting of a man and his wife or wives and their children'?[42] Or he could have referred to visiting neighbouring '*camps*', as he also says that a native camp is composed of two parts, the married people's camp (which includes unmarried women and widows) and the bachelor's camp (which contains the unmarried men, including widowers).[43] But this does not sound like 'the family' or the 'local group'.

Radcliffe-Brown tells us that 'On the occasion of the performance of a ceremony, members of different local groups might be found camped together often for weeks at a time'.[44] Each local group is exogamous (out-marrying).[45] It seems odd that he did not see the implication of this exogamy – namely that every pair of spouses in every 'family' and 'camp' already consisted of members of 'different local groups'. He says that local group members had to marry outside their own local group but post-marital residence was in the husband's country. Women lived with their husbands' groups but retained 'a sort of right' over the country of their birth. A man had a 'sort of secondary right' over his mother's country and was welcome both there and in his wife's country.[46]

'[I]n *the camp of a local group* would be found only men and unmarried women and children who belonged to the group by birth...'[47] Here we see the essential seeds of Radcliffe-Brown's later more fully expressed confusion between a band (that which has a *camp*) and a clan (that which has an *estate*).

Colonisation, he said, referring to 1911, meant that 'the country now belongs to the white man' and Aboriginal people had to live where they could, but 'a man's' attachment to his own country had not been destroyed.[48] This makes it clear that the clans and their estates, which, Radcliffe-Brown himself was able to record from informants and put on a map, had survived an abrupt change to the pattern of physical occupation of the land.

In 1914 Radcliffe-Brown published a paper called 'The Definition of Totemism' in which Kariera local groups were most frequently described as 'clans'. There were, Radcliffe-Brown said, two kinds of divisions of tribes into clans, clans with male descent and clans with female descent. He gives as examples Yualai (unlocalised matriclans) and Kariera (localised patriclans). Among the Kariera, he says, 'each clan is localised, or in other words, the local groups of this tribe are clans'. A clan is exogamous, and is made up of 'a number of persons who regard themselves as closely related to one another, and who therefore owe each other certain specific duties'.[49]

Radcliffe-Brown said that we have to clearly distinguish between:
- the place of a clan in the wider social structure;
- the way its members are supposed to behave towards each other according to custom, i.e. its moral and juridical elements, e.g., the rule of clan exogamy; and
- religious beliefs and customs associated with it.

This is an early and crucial example of the evolution of structural-functionalism. The advance it represented in its own time was its clarification of muddied waters. Previously there had been insufficient clarity, among anthropologists, about the need to separate out structures from functions among social institutions.

The later Radcliffe-Brown

In 1918 and 1923 Radcliffe-Brown published his 'Notes on the Social Organization of Australian Tribes', a paper not to be confused with his 1930–31 series of papers called 'The Social Organization of Australian Tribes', which was a revised and expanded version of it. Here he presented the results of field work with people on the Lower Murray River, the Murray–Darling system, and north-central New South Wales. This time he was at pains to clarify his terminology and set down definitions of nine key expressions. I will refer to only some of them.

'*Tribe*' he defined as a 'collection of persons who *speak* what the natives themselves regard as one language'.[50] Here we see the same confusion of category with action. It is clear from what he writes that his 'tribe' is not made up of all who speak a language, but only of all who are identified with or own a language.[51]

'*Horde*' was a term Radcliffe-Brown appears to introduce in this paper, as if it had not already been in use by others: 'I shall use the word "horde" (from Tatar *úrdú*, a camp)…'.[52] Howitt had already been using it in print for decades at this time. The *Macquarie Dictionary* gives its etymology as 'Pol[ish] *horda*, from Turkic *ordu* camp', but is misleading in its definition of the word, as it gives the Aboriginal 'section' as an equivalent.[53] The only scholar who used 'section' to refer to a local group, as far as I am aware, was T.G.H. Strehlow who wrote of Aranda clan estates as '*njinanga* [*nyenhenge*] sections'.[54] The *Macquarie* also captures the literature's ambivalence over whether a horde was a camp or a clan: '3. any nomadic group … 5. an exogamous kinship grouping within an Australian tribe.'[55]

Of 'the horde' Radcliffe-Brown said that
- it consists of persons who regularly live together in one camp;
- it is the 'primary land-owning group, each horde owning and occupying a certain area of country';
- each horde is independent and autonomous and manages it own affairs by means of a camp-council often directed by one head-man;
- recruitment to the horde is strictly patrilineal, that is, a child always belongs to the horde of the father, *but* 'a woman, on marriage, *joins and lives with* the horde of the husband';[56]
- it acts as a unit in its relations with hordes of the same or of other tribes.

'*Family*' Radcliffe-Brown defined as a social group consisting of a man, his wife/wives, and their dependent children. At times, however, he seemed to also use the term 'family' to refer to certain kinds of camp compositions.

'*Clan*' he defined essentially as a unilineal descent group that is marked off in some way, for example by having a name, or by having certain totems. Radcliffe-

Brown must have realised the overlap between this definition and that of horde. He said there were two kinds of clan, matrilineal and patrilineal. '[I]n some tribes the horde is a clan' (in the patrilineal sense), 'and such hordes may be called *local clans* or *clan-hordes*'; they are often totemic. Matrilineal totemic clans are '*non-localized*'.[57]

In 1930–31 Radcliffe-Brown published 'The Social Organization of Australian Tribes'. Here he again presented some broad Australia-wide generalisations, but this time, as far as local organisation is concerned, he moved even further away from ethnographic reality. According to this work, *tribes* are sets of hordes whose members speak the same language and enjoy a 'unity of custom', even though hordes lying on tribal boundaries may belong to more than one language group, and language group areas are thus often 'indeterminate'.[58]

Much of his definition of the horde remained the same. It was 'the important local group' and 'the *primary* land-owning or land-holding group'. But it was also 'a small group owning and occupying a definite territory or hunting ground'. Note the possible conflation here of a 'territory' as something owned, with a 'hunting ground' as something physically occupied – unless one thinks of a hunting ground as a tenure unit not coextensive with anyone's pattern of hunting. Radcliffe-Brown stated that its membership was determined by the descent of 'children' – not just male children – from the father. But, he said, 'male members enter the horde by birth and remain in it till death'. In many regions the horde was exogamous by rule and in any case the majority of marriages were outside the horde. 'The woman, at marriage, leaves her horde and joins that of her husband.'[59]

This contradicts later statements in the same paper where Radcliffe-Brown distinguished clearly between the 'father's horde' and the 'mother's horde'. For example: 'In Australia the conception of kinship is very definitely bilateral. It is true that everywhere the important social group, the horde, is patrilineal. But the individual is very closely bound to his mother's horde.'[60] If the mother became a member of the father's horde upon marriage to him, then how is there a difference between the mother's and father's horde? To return to the early part of the work: 'The horde, therefore, ... consists of (1) male members of all ages whose fathers and fathers' fathers belonged to the horde, (2) unmarried girls who are the sisters or daughters or son's daughters of the male members, (3) married women, all of whom, in some regions, and most of whom, in others, belonged originally to other hordes, and have become attached to the horde by marriage.'[61]

Surely, on this model, one's own horde (as a male, or unmarried female) was also that of one's mother, so how could relationships with *father's and mother's hordes* be an example of 'bilateral kinship'? Later in the paper, in what looks like an attempt to clarify all this, Radcliffe-Brown wrote again of the Kariera, saying that in that tribe '*connected with each horde* there is a *clan*'.[62] The male members of the clan stay in the connected horde all their lives. The female members of the clan leave, not their clan, but the connected horde on marriage and join the connected horde of their husband. Then comes a footnote in which he appears to be grappling with his own contradictions and almost gets out of them:

> This distinction between the horde and the associated local clan is, I think, a very important one... A horde changes its composition by the passing of women out of it and into it by marriage. At any given moment it consists of a body of people living together as a group of families. The clan has all its male members in one horde, but all its older female members are in other hordes. It changes its composition only by the birth and death of its members.[63]

But Radcliffe-Brown then immediately contradicts this by saying that it is the horde, not mentioning the clan, that has totems, possesses totemic centres, has a territory and is 'the patrilineal local group'.[64] This would imply that a woman changes her totems on joining her husband's local residential group, but this is not what Radcliffe-Brown intended and is not true. When writing about the 'Talaindji type' (Thalanji, Western Australia) of social organisation, Radcliffe-Brown again appeared to pull himself up when he said: 'Each horde, or rather the patrilineal clan connected with it, is a separate independent totemic group.'[65] He returned to the Kariera again and said that 'the individuals *born in one horde* constitute a patrilineal local clan ... Each local clan is also, in a certain sense, a totemic clan, having a number of totems. In the territory of each horde [why not clan?] are found a number of totemic centres ...'.[66]

It seems that Radcliffe-Brown slips into using the terms 'horde' and 'patrilineal hordes'[67] whenever he starts writing about 'territory', and he closely associates the 'horde' with land possession and the 'clan' with kinship. This is apparent from the comment at the end of Part I of the work: 'Individuals are united together into groups on the basis of sex and age, of community of language and customs (tribe), of possession and occupation of a territory (horde), and on the basis of kinship and marriage (family, clan, section, moiety).'[68]

That phrase '*born in one horde*' recurs in Radcliffe-Brown's writing about various types of Australian social organisation. For example, when writing about the 'Mara type' of the Gulf of Carpentaria he says 'It seems likely that all persons born in one horde form a single totemic clan'.[69] 'For a large number of Australian tribes it can certainly be said that the persons born in one horde form a patrilineal clan ...'[70] Thus the horde precedes the clan in his construction of the process of the latter's social reproduction. One gets one's clan membership, not primarily from descent *per se*, but from making one's first appearance in a certain kind of family camp in charge of a 'hunting territory', *and* having a certain ancestry.

Much of what is problematic about Radcliffe-Brown's horde/clan writings also applies to what he says about 'the family'. Radcliffe-Brown was trying to correct earlier descriptions of Aboriginal marriage, such as those of Spencer and Gillen, in which the economic aspect of the relationship was neglected and marriage was represented wholly or mainly as a form of sexual union.[71]

In 1935 Radcliffe-Brown published further on the local organisation question in an important paper called 'Patrilineal and matrilineal succession'. But again he reproduced the old confusion, even though he introduced the, then, novel idea that the Aboriginal land-owning groups he was writing about were 'corporations' that had 'estates'.[72] This idea, or parts of it, has had some long acceptance. In this later paper, however, the 'clan' has disappeared from the terminology and the 'horde' is the only name for the land-owning group.

Radcliffe-Brown made his last public pronouncements on Aboriginal local organisation in 1954 and 1956.

In 1954 Radcliffe-Brown took issue with Elkin's view that there was insufficient evidence to conclude that patrilineal local groups had existed in south-east Queensland and north-central New South Wales. On the contrary, Radcliffe-Brown's own fieldwork in both regions had confirmed that their local groups had been patrilineal. He continued, however, to speak of them both as unilineal descent groups and as travelling and camping groups which, for example, visited other clans for ceremonies, thus maintaining his clan/horde confusion but not mentioning the horde.[73]

His last word was in 1956. There, he said an Aboriginal clan was what others might call a unilineal descent group, one which was corporate in the sense that its adult males engaged in collective action. As a clan they had collective ownership and control of a territory, including its material and spritual resources. The horde, on the other hand, was a collection of 'parental families', and a 'quasi-domestic' group, who hunted together. All married men in a horde were members of one particular clan. This clan unity of men grounded the unity of the horde and its connection to a territory. A woman belonged to her father's clan and her husband's horde. The patrilineal local clan had a 'dependent associated horde'.[74] As we shall see later, this neat picture was contradicted by some good field data.

Radcliffe-Brown on wider relations

Later in the book I deal with ideas about 'nations', 'culture blocs' and so on (Chapter 4), but this discussion is included here for its demonstration of the fact that Radcliffe-Brown was not confined only to 'tribal' and smaller levels of resolution in his thinking about Aboriginal social and local organisation. He also went to some lengths to discuss what he called 'factors tending towards an expansion of social solidarity, and other factors tending in the opposite direction towards a contraction of social solidarity'.[75] He advanced the argument that some Aboriginal systems showed wider social integration through kinship and ceremonial links than others, and some showed greater emphasis on 'the solidarity of the narrow circle of the horde' than others.[76] Minus the word 'horde', most specialists in the field would still agree with him.

His discussion of this topic, framed very much in terms of the role of the horde and the role of the web of kinship connections between members of different hordes, occupied eleven pages of his main treatise on Aboriginal social and local organisation, but is rarely discussed in the literature.[77]

CONTRA RADCLIFFE-BROWN

Although widely credited with having struck the sledgehammer blow to Radcliffe-Brown's Australia-wide model of local organisation, L.R. Hiatt was not the first scholar to differ with Radcliffe-Brown's views on the matter, as writings by W.E.H. Stanner, Donald Thomson, Phyllis Kaberry, A.P. Elkin and Ronald and Catherine Berndt attest.[78] Nevertheless Hiatt's classic paper of 1962 formed a watershed in the development of ideas about the subject by bringing together widespread evidence from different regions, and by encapsulating many of the relevant observations of earlier scholars whose findings were incompatible, or only partly compatible, with Radcliffe-Brown's views on Aboriginal local organisation.

Hiatt's critique

Hiatt's 1962 paper produced evidence from five regions of Australia where local organisation had been studied since 1930. He did not propose an alternative universal model as a replacement of Radcliffe-Brown's. Some of the more telling evidence was as follows:

Central Australia: The Arrernte had patrilineal clans who owned territories, but members of them roamed over each others' countries.[79] Meggitt had found among the Warlpiri that people lived in communities of up to several hundred members consisting of six to twelve patrilineal descent groups. Such descent groups did not necessarily, or even commonly, constitute residential and food-seeking on-the-ground groups.[80]

Western Desert: Berndt used a somewhat Radcliffe-Brownian definition of the land-occupying group in this case, but stated that it had no territorial claims as such.[81]

The Kimberleys: Piddington, for example, found that small parties from hordes would go on hunting expeditions lasting months, 'over the territory of any other horde', without asking the permission of the owners, who would not object'.[82]

Arnhem Land: Stanner had found in the Daly River area that the hordes or residence groups were 'aggregates of contiguous local totemic clans' and that people passed between their own and neighbouring countries with great freedom and confidence.[83] Hart found at Melville and Bathurst Islands that the Tiwi had residence groups of very fluid composition and each horde contained members of different clans (matrilineal totemic clans associated with a particular locality). McCarthy and McArthur in 1948 had studied a bush-dwelling group in the Arnhem Land Reserve and found its male members came from at least two patrilineal land-owning groups.[84] Warner had earlier found in North East Arnhem Land that while land was owned by patrilineal descent groups or clans, friendly clans always lived together when seasons were plentiful and entered each other's lands without invitation. People could spend more of their lives on territory of other clans than on their own.[85]

At Groote Eylandt, Worsley found the same – 'there were no tribal rules against entering or exploiting the territory of another clan'.[86] (I am leaving out many other examples here.) Hiatt himself found in north-central Arnhem Land, very soon after the first settling of people at Maningrida, that the land-owning unit was a small patrilineal descent group (or several of them amalgamated) (average 9.3 persons, range 1–29). Gidjingali people, before settling, lived in four loose common residence groups that were named. At times such communities combined into bigger residence groups. Members of land-owning units moved freely over each other's territories and residence groups were not recruited only, or even mainly, on the basis of patrilineal descent.[87]

Cape York Peninsula: McConnel's findings in Cape York Peninsula had more or less reproduced the Radcliffe-Brown model, but they were not borne out by follow-up studies. Sharp's ethnography among the Yir-Yoront and others represented better ethnography than McConnel's further north. Clans gave a 'standing permission' for members of other land-owning units to use their country, a freedom only withdrawn for *persona non grata*. Sharp thought his discovery was of an 'aberrant form'.[88]

Hiatt said that we need to distinguish 'ritual relationships from economic relationships'.[89] A spiritual link does not automatically imply a material one.[90] This idea was followed up in some detail by Grahame Barker.[91]

Stanner's reply to Hiatt

For good reasons, W.E.H. Stanner in his reply to Hiatt's paper attempted to defend Radcliffe-Brown's continual association of the residential group or 'horde' with the landowning group or 'clan'.[92] He admitted Radcliffe-Brown's confused statements, but felt it was important not to dissociate the two completely, saying that the estate, the land owned by a *clan*, and the range, the land used by a *band*, both formed parts of an ecological 'life-space' or domain. However, he failed to rescue much of Radcliffe-Brown's confusion. He tended to use some of Radcliffe-Brown's more accurate statements, for example, from earlier papers, to refute allegations made against Radcliffe-Brown's later statements. This did not work, naturally. Radcliffe-Brown had contradicted himself.

What Stanner did in his 1965 paper was to establish more clearly the terminology for such things, and his *clan/band*, *estate/range* dichotomies have endured.

He also, in that paper, argued for much better ethnography of Aboriginal land use.[93] This challenge was not, in the main, taken up until the ecologically-oriented field studies of the 1970s, especially in Cape York Peninsula but also elsewhere.

Another positive contribution of Stanner here was to emphasise the role of tendencies for at least some members of land-owning local descent groups, especially senior males, towards a pattern of repeated residence on their own country.[94] Claims of continued residence can sometimes become converted into claims of ownership in time. But Stanner still thought of tribes (as language groups) as congeries of bands,[95] as Tindale always did,[96] but this is not sustainable on the evidence.

Hiatt's counter-argument and the enduring consensus

Hiatt replied cogently and clearly to Stanner in 'The Lost Horde'.[97] Hiatt successfully refuted most of the charges made against him by Stanner. He showed that Stanner's arguments had certain deep internal logical and philosophical flaws.

He showed that Stanner had misrepresented or under-represented Radcliffe-Brown. He showed again how the empirical evidence he had put together countered Radcliffe-Brown's generalisations about the horde. He refuted Stanner's suggestion that Hiatt had put forward a new generalisation about Aboriginal local organisation (that is, that all groups wandered about in an area regardless of local clan estate attachments). In fact Hiatt did not think all groups conformed to a single general type.

Why did the great man (Radcliffe-Brown) fall into this trap? I think there are several reasons. He adopted an underlying colonial view that, as physical occupation of the country had been disrupted by Europeans, and this meant Aborigines no longer owned the land in law, ownership and physical occupation had to be understood as essentially coextensive. He lacked adequate ethnographic material to address the question. It was the latter that Hiatt supplied, and, since then, others (notably Peterson and Long[98]). He was a victim of the double bind of the systematiser of what had formerly been a rather messy picture: in order to see the wood for the trees, there is a temptation to suppress known facts that do not fit into the scheme.

Radcliffe-Brown's sexism was also a problem for his analysis. His ethnography appears fundamentally male-oriented. For example he defines the Kariera local group as 'a "clan" with male descent, all the male members of the clan being "father's father", "son's son", "father", "son" or "brother" to each other'.[99]

There is no mention of the female members of the clan.[100] In the Kariera ethnography he refers to 'the women of the clan' who take part in increase ceremonies 'as well as the men',[101] in spite of the fact that the totemic centre, or *talu*, at which these ceremonies were performed was initially described by Radcliffe-Brown as a site that belongs to the *men* of the local group in whose territory it is found.[102]

When he is engaged in ethnographic description, as opposed to theorising or providing definitions of words, Radcliffe-Brown almost always uses the term 'horde' in the sense of 'land-owning group',[103] and not 'clan'. I think that for him, 'horde' had an ethnographic immediacy and concreteness that attracted his cast of mind as someone who was philosophically a British empiricist. But it is not clear that he ever saw a bush camp composed on classical lines.

Nicolas Peterson and the band perspective

In many ways, the success of Hiatt's arguments against Radcliffe-Brown's model relied mainly on published summaries of local situations as found by anthropological fieldworkers. One advantage of this method was that some questions could most conclusively be addressed at the fine ethnographic level of specific field observations, rather than using generalisations based on them.

The concrete and reliable evidence as to classical band composition in Australia published subsequently by Peterson and Long reinforced Hiatt's argument considerably.[104] Although published in the Australian land rights era, I refer to it here as it really put the last nails in the coffin of the Radcliffe-Brown model. In the cases of fourteen of the bush bands on whom census data was available, Peterson and Long were able to present information about the estates or clans of the individuals present in them. Contrary to Radcliffe-Brown's model, there are many more clans (and thus estates) represented in these bands than just the clan of the patrilineal core members, or that clan plus those of incoming spouses. In fact the average number of clans with members in a single band, on this sample, is more than six (Figure 1).[105]

Band	No. of people	No. of estates/clans
AL14	23	10
AL15	30	5
AL19	21	3
CY1	16	8
CY2	22	9
CY3	14	7
CY4	15	4
CY5	19	8
CY6	17	5
CY7	8	5
CY8	16	7
CY9	10	5
CY10	13	6
CY11	11	4
Average	**16.78**	**6.14**

Figure 1: Arnhem Land and Cape York Peninsula bands and estates or clans represented in them (based on Peterson and Long 1986: 74–99)

I have presented this brief history of ideas partly because some of these older ideas and models have survived into the present era, often after much refinement, and it is sometimes important to know where one stands in the history of their development. Especially in the more settled parts of Australia where there has been much social and cultural change since colonisation, older ethnographic evidence frequently cannot be checked with living informants, nor is it useful to pluck it from the older sources in a way that takes it merely at face value or out of context. Understanding where source authors stood in relation to competing anthropological paradigms of their day, and what their own standing and reliability as scholars might have been, can affect the usefulness of early information as evidence, especially in a context of litigation.

The history of anthropological studies of Aboriginal land tenure and social organisation has generally been one of increasing refinement of models on the basis of an increasing quantity and quality of empirical data. The models of today will no doubt give way to others in the future, but it is worthy of comment that each phase of scholarly history in this case, regardless of demonstrable errors and intellectual dead-ends, has left a stratum of insights and factual recording that remain of value.

3 | Aboriginal country groups[1]

INDIGENOUS COUNTRY GROUPS AND THE COMMUNITY OF NATIVE TITLE HOLDERS

Proving NATIVE TITLE involves, among other things, a process of cultural translation. An indigenous person or group, usually on behalf of other persons and groups as well as themselves, makes application to have their customary rights and interests in an area of land and waters, as held by the group, recognised in the form of a determination in accordance with the *Native Title Act*. Most determination applications are on behalf of a set of people delimited along the lines of a collective identity such as a language group or a set of smaller identity groups such as descent-based or other groups with particular interests in different parts of the area concerned, or all of it together.

In the case of *Ward*, for example, the trial judge, Justice Lee, found that native title existed in the determination area, and it was held by the Miriuwung and Gajerrong people (the first applicants), and in respect of that part of the determination area known as Boorroonong (Lacrosse Island) native title was held by the Balangarra people (the third applicants). The second applicants sought to establish a determination of native title for three 'estate groups' (Dumbral, Nyawanyawam and Binjen) of the Miriuwung 'community', but instead the judge found that the native title that existed in the determination area was a communal title held collectively by members of the Miriuwung and Gajerrong 'community'. These are significant indigenous groupings. Other significant groupings whose members were found to possibly have native title in part of the determination area were Malngin and Gija. Like Miriuwung and Gajerrong, these are names of languages. However, no independent determination of the Malngin and Gija interests was made under the *Native Title Act* and they did not lodge their own application.[2]

Under the *Native Title Act* the Federal Court has jurisdiction to hear and determine applications relating to native title.[3] However, a hearing is not an investigation into all kinds of customary rights in the area covered by an application. In most cases it will involve an investigation of the rights and interests of members of a 'native title claim group' on whose behalf an application for a determination of native title has been made to the court. The customary rights of those who do not belong to the claim group, including those of their spouses (other than those drawn from the claim group), neighbours and nearby holders of religious connections which extend into the application area, for example, will not necessarily be captured or recognised by the legal process. On the other hand, respondent parties may bring forward evidence that people other than the claimants have native title over the claimed area, and they may then become a represented and joined applicant group.

It is usually the case that anthropologists are engaged to investigate the claims of claimant groups and report on them, rather than being engaged to investigate who holds any and all kinds of customary rights in an application area. Typically this is after the claims have been lodged. Indeed, application areas have frequently been defined by local conceptions of traditional territories or wider cultural 'nation' blocs, as understood by a local solicitor on instructions from clients. It can sometimes be the case that one anthropologist is hired to work with and seemingly on behalf of one group, while another group with a separate and neighbouring or overlapping application may work with a different anthropologist.

This can mean that no one anthropologist is in a position to provide expert opinion to the claimants, their representatives, or to the Federal Court, as to the character of all and any customary interests in an application area, or as to the basis on which applications over a common area are in conflict. After all, to understand a conflict well is to know quite a lot about both sides of the argument. Anthropologists may at times be placed in the position of knowing only one side, in a context where they are expected to comment on conflicting claims being made. This alignment of experts with particular group aims, no matter how 'objective' the researcher manages to be, is hardly in line with the spirit of the Federal Court's practice directions for experts, which require that an expert's first duty be to the court.[4]

The anthropologists frequently have little to do with the initial applications for determinations. That such a crucial document should be lodged prior to any serious research being carried out on the area concerned seems to me to be not only entirely counterproductive but in fact quite astonishing, given the risks of unnecessary conflict and expense that this practice has led to repeatedly.

It is not untypical for there to be a patchwork of applications in any one region, applications which abut or overlap, which may be in overt conflict, and which may be made on different bases. For example, one group may assert its interests based on descent from certain forebears known to have lived on and been identified with a country, while another group may assert interests in the same area on the basis that it holds the sacred Law for sites on the land and has an untrammelled right of use of the country. A small local group or set of such groups may make an application for an area contained within a wider language group territory which is also being claimed by other people of the same language affiliation as themselves, and many of whom are relatives. The first and second applicants in *Ward* were not alone in this situation. Some claims in the same area may be based on a traditional territory associated with a named identity (a 'tribe', geographic grouping and so on) while others may be based on a past history of land use and travel regarded as legitimate under customary rules. In this last example the two kinds of determination areas are founded on contrasting principles, even though the different claimants may share a common system of laws and customs and a common history of land use in the region. However, the Federal Court can make only one approved determination of native title in relation to a particular area and if two or more claims share a common area the applications are to be dealt with in the same proceeding.[5]

In *Ward* the trial judge upheld just one basis for the possession of native title rights and interests in the area concerned, and thus only one 'level of resolution', in making a determination. Justice Lee opted principally for a higher-order entity, a combination of two language groups and their territories. Understandably, some who viewed their 'lower-level' interests in certain estates to be paramount considered them to have been submerged or in some other way unacceptably bypassed in the determination, hence the second applicants' unsuccessful appeal. In this case, Greg McIntyre was counsel for the third applicants, the Balanggarra peoples and the Kimberley Land Council (the fifth respondent, representing Aboriginal people other than those claiming on behalf of the Miriuwung and Gajerrong people) and Kim Doohan was the anthropologist who gave evidence for those parties. McIntyre and Doohan have argued:

> Many … examples of apparent conflicting or inconsistent use of labels were given during the hearing by Aboriginal witnesses. Similarly, the naming or identity of the land claimed was also limited to one or both of those labels [Miriuwung or Gajerrong]. … The danger that this adherence to identity labels posed was that it would become a basis for denying full membership to title holders within the claim area who identified themselves by a label other than Miriuwung or Gajerrong.[6]
>
> The challenge of the decision is now to devise a process for ascertaining, when that becomes necessary, who is within the native title holding group. That will be based on a collection of indicative factors, none of which may be in itself definitive…[7]

Then followed a list of ten 'indicia of membership' of the native title holding group: descent from forebears connected to the area, self-identification with it, recognition by others, birthplace, conception, adoption, regency, religious responsibilities and participation, and marriage to a person connected to the area.

Among those who can justify traditional connections to any one area there can be much political life. There are many cases when this activity influences, even drives, the particular boundaries set for the membership of the claimant group in a way that excludes others with recognised rights. Yet such politics is often internal to a wider regional 'community' of people, most of whom are usually related somehow, and most of whom may be able to legally establish various pathways of traditional connection to at least some part of the common region.

A very real fear of being ignored or bypassed may add encouragement to atomistic approaches to having native title determinations processed. It is not the only factor leading to atomism in this context. Others may include a history of social fragmentation among descendants of the original occupiers, and the encouragement of separate representation by some members of the legal profession acting out of self-interest. If determinations give rise to an appearance of a body of internally undifferentiated rights and interests held in a common area, and the design of prescribed bodies corporate (PBCs) also fails to protect the existing interests of various subsets of the community of native title holders, the result may be a legal 'flat earth'. Although it is said that the differentiation of rights-holders is an internal matter for the title holders to sort out among themselves, I do see value in some external finding on the matter. A flat earth approach seems to me to be a natural platform for renewed conflict and potential litigation, in the event that some classes of native title holder remain unsatisfied with merely having the same class of rights as any other. This is not to suggest that some groups of native title holders will not in future opt for a 'one member one vote' level-playing-field, corporate style of doing business. What I do suggest is that such a style cannot be imposed. Where PBCs are very small, they may be tailored just to the interests of a smallish, relatively coherent set of people and thus the issue of internally differentiating rights among native title holders may or may not be so critical. On the other hand, there are many arguments against small PBCs and many arguments in favour of a regional approach to PBCs.[8]

Even where one has a clear preference for a regional PBC, should it be based on an indigenous cultural or political bloc of some kind, in order to provide internal consistency of customary laws and a degree of social integration, or should it be arbitrary in shape so as to avoid conflicts over boundary questions? If keeping the political temperature down is a prime consideration, I would incline towards encouraging large PBC areas based on some kind of history of cultural and political integration among the indigenous people who come from there; but I would suggest that traditional named entities be avoided when identifying any new organisations. Such names and the 'groups' they conjure frequently become the focus of conflict. More neutral entities such as names of river valleys, plateaux or deserts attract less competition and emotional feeling.

If the clock could be turned back I would be strongly urging potential claimants and those responsible for the bureaucratic generation of native title applications to lodge none until each manageable region had been researched sufficiently for the picture of the different bases of claims to emerge more or less clearly. How a legal strategy can be mounted in the absence of some substantial field work and library study, when the applications themselves are for the recognition of historical and contemporary cultural practices, many of which are complex, foreign and puzzling to the uneducated, remains a mystery. (This point does not apply, however, to applications in response to 'future acts', which are often lodged on short notice.)[9]

Then I would suggest that a single anthropological team carry the investigation for each region through to the end, if necessary into the litigation phase. This would help avoid the current spectacle of wasteful duplication of expensive archival searches, for example, and decrease the work pressures on the small number of anthropologists available and sufficiently qualified to do the work.

A determination would thus be for an unambiguously defined region, one delineated using boundaries such as highways, railway lines, drainage systems or mountain ranges and so on. Such a region would be deliberately designed so as to avoid any implication that it was a territory of traditional cultural significance, even if it contained several such territories that fell together under a reasonably united regional system of laws and customs. It would be a unit of investigation, not of bounded rights, since a number of those with interests in it would also have similar interests outside it, and a number of those with primary connections outside it will often have individuated or even collectively institutionalised rights and responsibilities within it. In regions where there is an 'owner–manager' dichotomy for countries, those in the 'manager' role are sometimes said to be in a secondary role, sometimes in a role level with that of the 'owners', and, on occasion, even in a role superior to that of the 'owners'. These relative powers lie in the domain of responsibility and action, especially ritual action, rather than of essential identity with the country concerned.

Levels of resolution

A former shorthand title for a draft of this chapter was 'Levels of resolution'. One reason for abandoning it was that it might suggest that Aboriginal country-related groupings generally fit together in a pyramidal structure, in the form of a nested hierarchy, such that each higher-order grouping is more or less neatly made up of two or more segments of a smaller or lower order. The higher up the pyramid you go, the fewer the number of groups and the bigger their populations are.

This actually does apply to certain kinds of Aboriginal country groupings, as reported, but by no means to all of them. For example, in a part of south-east Cape York Peninsula Christopher Anderson found the following arrangement after very detailed long-term research:

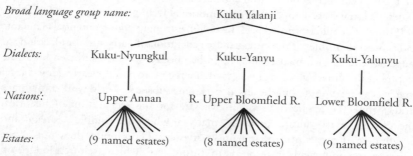

Figure 2: Nested groupings, south-east Cape York Peninsula (based on Anderson 1984:91)

The 'nations' as they are called in local English, or *jawunkarra* in Kuku Yalanji, are clusters of estates sharing common drainage.[10] Estate groups have names formed by the addition of –*warra* to estate names. In the earlier literature on the area it tended to be these small –*warra* groups which predominated and were called 'tribes' by writers. In the 1930s it was the riverine dialect group which tended to attract the attention of anthropologists and to be labelled 'tribes'. Anderson used the term Kuku Yalanji for people belonging to all three nations for convenience and because it was in use by people in the region. 'As one goes through time with the sources, the labels used by observers get more inclusive and the units larger.'[11]

The neatness of this schema cannot be replicated in the Wik region of western Cape York Peninsula, where linguistic varieties do not map uniquely onto drainage subsystems in this way, nor are local environmentally based estate clusters aligned with single linguistic varieties in each case, as they are here. The Bloomfield arrangement is much closer to that reported for an area of northern New South Wales by Malcolm Calley.[12]

Nevertheless, in any region, there is always a variety of groupings of people in relation to country and some of these are smaller in scope, others larger. In that sense, all regions exhibit country-related groupings of different degrees of resolution, even if these degrees are not always arranged in a single structure that has different levels.

Words and things: labels, groups and territories

In an industrial society there is a great need for precision and consistency in the description of land tenure units and the boundaries of governmental entities such as shires, postcode areas or cities. This need applies not only to boundaries but also to how labels are applied, such as 'Lot 22, Fenchurch Street' or 'Wallagandra Shire'. A lesser degree of exactness and common agreement is required for districts such as the Monaro, the Wimmera, or the Kimberley. Even these rather loose appellations may become subject to the measuring and straitening of the law when bureaucratic or industrial implications arise, as in the recent history of the name of one of Australia's most famous wine growing districts, the Coonawarra, which now has a legal definition.

Under classical Aboriginal cultural conditions, there were no centralised and theoretically neutral official records of a similar kind. This is not to say that non-verbal and durable media such as rock pictures played no role in the transmission of knowledge about countries, but such media were not normally focused on boundary matters nor were they concerned with recording names. Authority and consensus on such matters was verbal, localised, and subject to the influence of the history of face-to-face relations between individuals. This situation persists for many.

While Aboriginal terminologies for countries and country-related groups have been shown to be systematic, and they often enjoy a high degree of agreement between people as to what they refer to, they may also be subject to some inconsistent use and even, at times, considerable debate. It is not always easy to differentiate between the analysis-defying complexity of a naming scheme which a scholar has only partly understood and a naming scheme which itself contains inconsistencies or gaps. There are surprisingly few comprehensive and linguistically sophisticated accounts of group and territorial naming schemes in the ethnographic literature for Australia. Here I am referring to deeply local accounts such as Nancy Williams's chapter 'Names and meanings' in her 1986 book on land tenure in north-east Arnhem Land. Perhaps the report with the widest range of ethnographic detail and depth of treatment is that of anthropologist linguist Bernhard Schebeck for the same region.[13]

Schebeck suggested various criteria for the assignment of names for groupings in that region, presenting the following scheme:

I	nicknames	1. warnames of the *Murrnginy* ('Murngin') type
		2. bynames (environmental typifiers)
II	ceremonial names	1. warnames of the *Melthanggimirr* type
		2. religious names
		3. phratry-like names
III	local names	1. territorial names
		2. locality names
		3. regional names
IV	linguistic names	1. general classification
		2. special classification[14]

Yet Schebeck said:

Personally I feel still incapable of giving a rigorous system. It rather looks to me as if several tendencies were constantly at work, giving this picture which is somehow confusing – because of the concurrent use of several criteria – and never fully accomplished – because not using all criteria together in a parallel way in all cases. It is only when one type of distinction is formulated into a native theory that anthropologists have been tempted to work out a clear schema. I have tried to show that even then the schema is much less clear and consistent than is often assumed. The richness of distinctions does not seem to allow us to postulate a completely formalized system such as those to which the natives are so much inclined. We seem to touch here on two basic human tendencies, namely stematisation and formalisation, that is rigid simplification and generalisation on the one side, and a permanent development of new distinctions and richness of expression, i.e. unsystematic and individual 'reality' on the other side. It is here where I must stop and where the anthropologist must take over the discussion.[15]

Old group or territory names may change meaning and applicability over time. Where this has happened in an accelerated way due to colonisation, the combined evidence from early and late cultural histories may be confusing. Not all variability in a group name's scope of reference over time may be attributable to a relative absence of system, or to population movements, however. For example, in North

East Arnhem Land the leaders of a group may give one of its names to another group, 'often in exchange for a comparable name'.[16]

Over time, names applied to a group by outsiders may become adopted by members of the group itself, as has been the history of names such as Luritja, Antakirinya (both eastern Western Desert) and Lamalama (Cape York Peninsula), and regional group names such as Yiithuwarra (east of Lamalama). But if a record is made part-way through such a transition the evidence from different informants may understandably be inconsistent. In such circumstances, older and younger people, or nearer and farther people, may simultaneously hold different views of the appropriateness of particular terms. Luritja, for example, has gradually moved from being a pejorative outsider-term for a kind of people to being internalised at settlements such as Amunturrngu (Mount Liebig) as a dominant self-name for a linguistic variety and its people, a people whose identity is in part an emergent one arising from histories of settlement life on the frontier with the state.[17]

Social and cultural transformations such as the Luritja case remind us that all ascriptions of names to groups, or countries to people, are part of historical events and processes. Some seem to have great staying power, others less. But past documentary evidence about such things, drawn from a century or more of time, cannot simply be pooled as if all evidence about a single topic from any era can or must be perfectly integrated. Naturally I make these remarks from a scientific point of view. Within Aboriginal tradition in any one instance it can be expected that those in authority will regard territories, group names and rules for recruiting people to country groups as having been the same 'from the beginning', not secular creations of recent human societies but spiritually grounded Law handed down from the original Dreaming era.

A typical debate between native title claimant group members often proceeds in terms of such objectifications. People may disagree as to 'where the real boundary between the territories of tribes A and B lies', or 'what the real and true name is for the group, X or Y'. Native title claimant groups occasionally disagree over group names derived not from differing oral sources but from differing non-Aboriginal records. In a number of cases the debate can be sourced to two slightly different spellings of the same word, the spellings themselves having now achieved the status of objectifications that stand for much else in the way of local political tensions. It is not enough simply to respond that such debates are about nothing important. Group labels are always signs which can attract powerful political emotions and offer means for maintaining distinctions between groupings. (Consider the likely political reactions to a movement to rename Australia as Aboriginalia.) It is tempting for professionals engaged in native title case work to also adopt this language of objects, in which a name implies a group. But from an anthropological perspective the entities here are not objects in the sense that a creek or a bettong is an object. An indigenous country group, as a social entity, is not something one can see. Even a territory is something other than a set of rocks, streams and vegetation. It is a culturally reproduced landscape, a mental map more than just a part of 'nature', the latter notion being in any case a concept foreign to classical Aboriginal traditions.

That is not to say dismissively that such debates about boundaries and names are 'only about words', because they are also about identity and rights. But the anthropologist cannot afford to merge the word and the world in the same way. The anthropologist needs to be able to separate out terms from groups or territories. The latter may or may not be definable entities on grounds other than that they fall under a single common name. In fact the terminological apparatus used by a claimant group to refer to people and places needs to be understood as part of a set of linguistic practices, and not treated only as evidence for subjective knowledge. This is one way of avoiding confusing terms from one set (e.g. dialect names) with terms from another (e.g. environmental typifiers or totemic groupings). What someone says to you, and what you write down as your understanding of what they *mean*, can often be different. Even where you have got it right, the potential message includes not just what is meant, but also the outward form in which it is conveyed. It may be relevant, for example, that a group name is offered which contains a sound sequence or lexical item found in a neighbouring language and not that of the speaker, yet is being applied to the speaker's own group. In general, I urge anthropological practitioners in the native title field to pay close attention to the ethnography of the means of communication as well as to what one thinks is being communicated.[18]

The greatest challenge in dealing with group and territory names seems to arise when there are many early written records. For example, one often finds a scatter of rarely recorded and sometimes variably defined terms for territorial groups in a particular area, perhaps alongside a range of much more frequently and securely used terms. The rarely recorded terms may come from written sources that are a century or so old, and the terms are no longer known, or are remembered only by the elderly few. There may be little evidence as to whether or not such a term was relatively precise or highly loose in usage, an enduring element in a naming system or an ephemeral one used for an occasion or a period, or a term closely relevant to land tenure as against one that merely described unwelcome kinds of behaviour on the part of distant neighbours.

Especially under conditions where the use of labels X, Y and Z found in the literature may well have been loose, ephemeral or merely descriptive of the behaviour of certain neighbours, it is not advisable in my view for scholars to rely on such terms for the ordinary purposes of social and territorial description. Where, for the sake of argument, a manuscript by Daisy Bates records once or twice a group label written as 'Katakurawonga', but the word is not an entrenched group name, it belonged to a fluctuating set of ephemeral names, it occurs in no other record, or it is now unknown even if the language is still spoken, and so on, there is no basis for saying things such as, 'The Katakurawonga group seems to have disappeared'. One can become sure that a label is no longer in use, but unless it can perhaps be argued that the label is a critically essential element of group identity, rather than one of several ways of referring to it, label extinction cannot be assumed to imply group extinction. From time to time one comes across allegedly 'extinct' groups of this kind whose contemporary memberships indeed continue to reproduce themselves but who no longer bear one or more of their older names. Members of claimant groups in native title cases may, however, take the view that without acknowledging and bearing a certain collective name, or even just the right version of it, one cannot belong, and therefore cannot enjoy native title rights and interests in the area concerned. This would be a question of what constitutes the normative rules of the relevant society and therefore a question of fact to be decided on the evidence.

Identity and action: similarity versus connection

The tendency of native title applications, as mentioned earlier, has been to frame them in terms of culturally significant groups which endure through time and are not physically observable on the ground populations or area residents *per se*. It is interesting in this regard that many Aboriginal people over the years, when explaining their territories to me, have often couched their accounts in terms of physical presence and action. That is, when asked where an ancestor's country lay, a not infrequent answer has been put to me in terms of 'how far that old man would go', or of how he and others would 'meet up with' members of neighbouring land-holding groups at a certain site, and where primary rights in a site were shared with another group he might be said to 'come into there too'. This is the language of action, but it is clear on other grounds that these are not historical accounts or memories of events so much as the substitution of the idiom of practice for the idiom of claims. The descriptions are, to borrow a phrase, those of 'lawful occupation' rather than of travel.

Similarly, mass events such as feasts, ceremonial gatherings or battles are often described in the anthropological literature as the coming together of named groups such as 'tribes' or 'clans'. Again, this can be the common idiom in which descriptions of such events are phrased by Aboriginal people recounting events of the past. But on closer inspection it is sometimes possible to specify in more detail who was present at such an event. The whole memberships of named groups were in fact highly unlikely to be present at these events unless the groups were very small ones, consisting of only a handful of individuals. But even if only five per cent of a 'tribe' were present at an event, the tribe's name may still have been used as the most appropriate shorthand for specifying who was there, especially if the event lends itself culturally to being interpreted as a meeting of representatives of 'tribes' rather than as a private encounter between individuals. This is not merely the result of not wishing to use the names of individuals, as Aboriginal languages are astonishingly rich in resources for specifying individuals without having to resort to naming them. What the collective idiom does is to phrase the actions of individuals in terms of their implications for relations between kin (occasionally non-kin) within a particular geopolitical framework, and thus in terms of their implications for that fabric itself.

In my view the idea of a private encounter between ungrouped individuals is not easily assimilated to classical Aboriginal views of how such events have meaning, although I concede that this varies regionally, the Western Desert being the extreme and exceptional case where a kind of individualism may be said to prevail. By contrast, for example, stories about past ritual cremations in the coastal Wik region abound with the specification of who was there but mainly do so in terms of group names which are based on the ecological niches of estates owned by clan members, only some of whom were present at the event. I do not have as much data on inland cremations but in the inland case best known to me the groups lined up in combat at a pericoastal cremation were described by reference to named language groups, some from the inland and some from the coast – a model which in fact does not match the way coastal people themselves think of the relationship between country, named language and political group. But my informant was an inlander.

There is, of course, a feedback relationship between identity and action. Social and territorial identities do not perpetuate themselves but are maintained, and transformed over time, or lost, by human action or lack of it. Thus, while one's identity as a member of a land-holding group may not depend on one's continued personal physical contact with the land concerned, it is arguable that some level of continued contact with the same land needs to be maintained over the generations by at least some members of the group if group descendants are to keep hold of the same land over a period of, say, a century. Whether one visits the land or not, the maintenance of connection is primarily achieved through its assertion and social recognition. The maintenance of connection is never a function of presence itself, but of what that presence may mean to the relevant people within a certain system of attitudes characteristic of a region. Knowledge of country is difficult, not impossible, to maintain without a local presence on it, but this knowledge thus becomes increasingly generalised, or focused on sites and songs that form part of ongoing rituals, for example.

It should be borne in mind that 'diaspora' people have maintained various forms of their original landed identities over several generations while living *in absentia* in missions and other settlements, even where group members have been unable to physically visit their homelands for decades. Parallels from the early contact period in the bush are harder to find. David Turner, however, has put forward such a case for a group which migrated from North East Arnhem Land to become associated with a part of Woodah Island near Groote Eylandt:

> By the time of prolonged White contact, the Durili [local group] had already migrated to Groote but say today that they do not 'own' [ie. have spiritual or mythic links to] territory there. Members of this group insisted that they were really 'Balamumu' [from North East Arnhem Land] and Änindiljaugwa [the Groote Eylandt language] was not their native language.[19]

But customary rights in country are not just a matter of identity. They are also a matter of continuing responsibility, at least for adults.

Any particular spot on the ground may have identified with it a range of identity-groups of differing degrees of scope. It may be part of a small sub-estate (see below), and also part of an estate, part of a local environmentally defined estate cluster area, part of a dialect group area, part of a wider language group area, part of a culturally well-defined region encompassing several linguistic territories, one of a string of sites linked by a continent-crossing sacred legend, and so on. For each of these entities one may be able to describe a reasonably well-bounded group of persons and at least some such persons may be engaged in meeting responsibilities towards the site or may have certain rights and interests in the site. Those taking responsibility and asserting rights belong to active social networks as well as to more or less bounded identity groups. Networks may be open-ended and groups relatively closed. Both, regardless of this, are sets, and both sets have structure.

It is the groups, however, which attract formal names in Aboriginal languages, not the networks. As has often been observed, it is enduring entities such as descent-based land holding groups, or subsets of them such as environmental clusters, or language groups, which may have formal names, while camps, current members of households and other residential aggregates in a strict sense do not. (A modern settlement community identity is normally tagged by the name of the township, plus 'mob'.) The strongest and deepest and most long-lived customary rights in countries tend to be those attendant upon membership of an identity group rather than those of members of an action group, except where a certain kind of action group directly gives rise to a long-term identification group, as in certain kinds of ritual participation in some areas. As usual one has to bear in mind that there is a range of relevant phenomena, with the Western Desert lying at one extreme or perhaps even as something of an outlier to the general picture. In the Western Desert the maintenance of claims over sites, while collectively shared, depended to a greater extent than elsewhere on significant life events and active participation, as against life-long category memberships that elsewhere were usually more stable, at least in most of north coastal Australia.

Overall there has been more successful maintenance of Aboriginal identity, both broadly ethnic identity as well as localised place-of-origin identities, than there has been of Aboriginal cultural distinctiveness in the sense of classical cultural practice. We tend to use phrases like 'our culture' in rather different ways. In one usage, 'our culture' refers to the speaker's day-to-day speech, economic life, cooking preferences, methods of handling conflict and so on, which the speaker shares with others. In another usage, 'our culture' may refer to forms of speech, economic life, cooking preferences, methods of handling conflict and so on which characterised our identity group's members in the past, and which we know about, but which have not been practised for generations.

When Captain Cook visited Australia in 1770 he found a people among whom there was a consistent coincidence of physical type with cultural and economic type. He did not find, for example, any Caucasians living an Aboriginal lifestyle, nor any Aboriginal people living, say, a Danish lifestyle. The arrival of permanent British settlers added a new element to race and culture: namely ethnicity. For a while there was largely now a coincidence of all three: an Aboriginal person (of indigenous ethnicity) looked a certain way (was of a certain 'race') and had a certain distinctive way of life (Aboriginal culture). Since then, however, the potential for these three aspects to move apart and achieve independence from each other has become gradually realised for many people. It is now possible to be ethnically Aboriginal but, in terms of appearance, no different from a Dane, and in terms of day-to-day lifestyle some Aboriginal people differ in no significant way from their non-Aboriginal fellows, but may still be visibly different from average Caucasians. Most fall somewhere between the two extremes. The extent to which the maintenance of day-to-day cultural difference is critical to proof of native title is an area of divided opinion.

ESTATES AND ESTATE SETS

Individuals, sites and countries

While there are a few scattered references in the earlier ethnographic literature suggesting that land could be owned by individuals, as such, in Aboriginal Australia, the anthropological consensus for a long time has been that most of these instances are likely to be misleading.[20] Bronislaw Malinowski reviewed the available relevant Australia-wide literature and came to this conclusion for the whole continent.[21] Gerald Wheeler earlier reviewed a similar range of sources, concluding that 'there are a few indications that the ownership [of land] might even be vested in single persons within a family other than the head', but 'it seems ... that the rights of families or of individuals, as also those of the local groups, were, in general, subject to tribal overrights'.[22]

The latter comment has some resonance with the approach I suggest be used in framing native title determination applications. Individuals certainly have specific links to places and may have special rights in them, and these may well be recognised by a court as individuated native title rights. Having a culturally significant link to a birthplace, initiation site or a parent's grave site, for example, may confer certain clear rights and responsibilities on a person.

Writing of 'the Yir Yoront' of Cape York Peninsula, Lauriston Sharp said that individuals could hold powers of economic exclusion from one or more tracts of land, and the 'actual rights of ownership are thus vested in the individual members of the clan', but these places had to be within their own clan's country, country to which 'the clan holds the clan title'.

> [I]t would appear that the clan, as a corporation, holds a primary title to all the countries within its domain ... yet the actual rights of ownership of any particular clan country at any given time are vested, not collectively in all clan members, nor in any person or persons who could properly be considered representative of all clan members, but in particular individual members within the clan membership.[23]

Note that Sharp's definition of ownership was 'the moral right of a person or persons to a relatively exclusive use and control of an economic good, which thus becomes property'.[24] Inheritance, conception and gifting between patrikin seemed to be the main pathways to individual rights in this area, but gifts and inheritances had to be within the clan.[25] While succession to countries without owners was by individuals, there was a strong practice under which the former clan's 'totemic complex' associating their country with certain ancestors, names, totems, rites and legends was passed on intact.[26] Sharp's detailed ethnographic backing for this unusual description may assist in the understanding of fragmentary accounts from places like New South Wales and other regions where 'gifts' of economic resource sites to individuals by individuals, and 'inheritance' by an individual upon the death of an individual, were sometimes reported.

In most cases a place controlled by an individual is normally also subject to collective rights and interests of a more corporate or at least aggregated kind held by a recognised group. If such a group has been reduced to one member, the latter does not have individuated rights so much as the individual enjoyment of the collective rights of the group. Where a culturally significant collectivity's rights in such a site are those of a group to which the individual born or initiated (etc.) there does *not* belong, then a determination application framed only in terms of group identities such as language groups or estate groups will fail to encapsulate such individuated rights held by non-members.

Domestic space, rights of way

There is a fairly rich ethnographic literature on the organisation of traditional Aboriginal camps of the colonial era. It shows that the larger camps, at least, were commonly organised into sub-camps or sets of hearth groups arranged in a kind of microcosm reflecting the directions in which lay the countries of the relevant sub-camp members, or rather their bosses.[27] Thus a normal right to be present together at a place may not be enacted with complete disregard to the insider/outsider distinction as far as deep rights in country are concerned. To lump all camp members together as having a common right to camp at a certain place would not reflect customary law in such a situation, given that visitors may be told where to camp, asked to leave, and so on, by those with strong ties to the site.

Perhaps more relevant here is the observation that hearth areas were areas of particular rights for those camped at them, a practice which has led Bruce Rigsby to distinguish 'domestic space' from 'public space'.[28] Thus non-local people would have rights in a domestic space which were in contrast with their relative lack of deep rights over the earth beneath it. This has some parallels with a tenant's rights in a rented property. In any case, the houses and yards of non-local people are normally treated with a similar respect to those with stronger local claims in Aboriginal communities today; it usually requires a very serious breakdown of relationships between locals and non-locals before a local person might seriously suggest that a non-local vacate their dwelling, drawing on the high card of traditional land rights.

Sub-estate country

In a region where parcels of land and waters are named and form primary elements in a tenure system, elements of the classic 'estate' kind, it is sometimes reported that there is some subdivision of the estate. In North East Arnhem Land, for example, 'ideally the estate of a land-owning group is the sum of smaller parcels, each of which it is the primary responsibility of a mature man, the head of a family, to look after', even though all estate group members would regard the most sacred site of the estate as being most important to all of them.[29] In the same region most patrifilial estate groups or clans 'distinguish at least two sub-groups within their own ranks, usually named ... "top" and ... "bottom". This distinction can be more or less clear and sometimes it seems the last step before a real scission takes place...'[30] If over long periods of time such groups and their estates have become subdivided and later perhaps reunited, it is not surprising to find examples where anthropologists have been undecided between referring to them as two estates or as one. Caught in mid-process they may be clearly neither. In the Wik region there is some evidence of the historical waxing and waning of such 'subdivisions' between 1928 and the 1990s, but there they are not so much subdivisions of single large entities as sets of closely linked estates which at times may amalgamate, perhaps due to loss of population and the later emergence of a powerful clan leader able to unite them.

Estates

While W.E.H. Stanner made the term 'estate' a matter of standard usage in the anthropology of Aboriginal relations to country, in his classic paper of 1965, he was not the first to use it. In 1952 A.R. Radcliffe-Brown wrote of the Kariera people of north-west Western Australia:

> It is convenient to speak of such a group as the Kariera horde as a 'corporation' having an 'estate'. ... By an estate is here meant a collection of rights (whether over persons or things) with the implied duties... The corporate estate of a Kariera horde includes in the first place its rights over its territory. ... Now a member of the horde has certain rights over other members and over the territory of the horde.[31]

Stanner's usage was somewhat distinct:

> The estate was the traditionally recognized locus ('country', 'home', 'ground', 'dreaming place') of some kind of patrilineal descent-group forming the core or nucleus of the territorial group. It seems usually to have been a more or less continuous stretch. The range was the tract or orbit over which the group, including its nucleus and adherents, ordinarily hunted and foraged to maintain life.[32]

The group which had a range was a band, commonly described as the land-utilising or camp group. Thus, in the simplest terms, a clan had an estate and a band had a range, the two geographic areas together being what Stanner dubbed a 'domain', which was an 'ecological life-space'.[33]

This scheme has been subject to considerable debate and revision since 1965, although I do not recount that history here. In particular, the evidence for the dominance of patrifilial descent groups or similar formations was not as widespread as Stanner had considered it, and even groups which formerly had such structures have in many or most cases now modified them in a range of ways.[34] Furthermore, the extent to which bands were, in bush times, constituted of a strong core or nucleus of people from a single estate and hence of a single descent or totemic group focusing its residential pattern on that estate, for example, is greater even in Stanner's formulation than the empirical evidence will support.

A number of those who earlier wrote about these things considered there to be a close resemblance between what Stanner called clans and bands, such that most members of a camp group, or at least a clear core of them, would be living on their own clan estate most of the time except when visiting neighbours.

For example, Norman Tindale published photographs taken at Groote Eylandt in 1921–22, among which were two captioned 'Men of Bartalumbu' and 'Men of Talakurupa' respectively. These were among six 'local groups or sub-tribes' on the island.[35] In 1948 Frederick Rose obtained identifications of most of the men from those who remembered them.[36] The 'Men of Bartalumbu' included seven men from four different totemic clan countries, and the 'Men of Talakurupa' included ten men from three different totemic countries. Rose says:

> …in both cases although the majority of aborigines come from one country … there is a considerable proportion of the aborigines who come from other clan countries and are in different moieties. It seems clear from this that even in 1921/22 when the aborigines had been exposed to very little white influence there were considerable comings and goings between the various clan countries and that the aborigines did not confine themselves to their own country.[37]

That this was not a unique observation is suggested by the table overleaf (Figure 3), which is drawn from other observations of bush camps in three regions of north Australia by Peterson and Long.

Stanner's basic notion of the estate as a primary unit of tenure has endured. It is typically characterised as a set of sites and surrounding landscapes considered to belong to a single, relatively small, country. The degree to which this set of sites is conceived of primarily in terms of key sacred sites over which religious authority was exercised especially by senior members of the estate groups, as opposed to an approach in which the whole estate as a 'block', including its non-sacred sites, is at the forefront of its conception, is a matter of regional variation. So also is the extent to which estates may overlap and intertwine. Such variations to a significant extent are in line with the aridity of the region, estates being less neatly bounded and more inclined to intertwine along Dreaming track segments, and to rest elementally on the sites of Dreaming track or songline segments, in semi-desert areas.

The estate may or may not be named. It may consist of a cluster of sites forming a single continuous tract, or it may consist of a number of sites and tracts separated by sites and tracts belonging to other estates. With the major exception of the Western Desert, where the estate construct is of debatable usefulness at least in several sub-regions, estates appear virtually everywhere. If one defines an estate by

BAND	PEOPLE	CLANS	LANGUAGES
Arnhem Land: Groote Eylandt			
AL 9	25	5	—[38]
AL10	23	6	–
Arnhem Land: North-East			
AL14	23	10	–
AL15	30	5	–
AL19	21	3	–
Cape York Peninsula[39]			
CY 1	16	8	2
CY 2	22	10	2
CY 3	14	7	2
CY 4	15	4	—[40]
CY 5	19	8	–
CY 6	17	5	–
CY 7	8	5	3
CY 8	16	8	2
CY 9	10	5	–
CY10	13	6	–
CY11	11	4	2
Averages:[41]	17.68	5.94	2.16

Figure 3: Arnhem Land and Cape York Peninsula bands, band sizes, and number of primary language affiliations represented in bands (based on Peterson and Long 1986:80–99)

reference to an individual, egocentrically, rather than sociocentrically, it ceases to be a collectively and uniformly held objectification but it remains an objectification nonetheless. It is in this sense that 'estate' remains a useful term for the Western Desert, as a property of an individual.

Estate sets: non-contiguous

Estate sets include geographically separated estates which share a form of common identity, and also contiguous clusters of estates. The groups associated with the estates in these sets may thus be presented to the ethnographer as higher-order categories or linked sets of groupings both of territories and people. There are many different forms of such sets. They lie in scale somewhere between the minimal territory and personnel of an estate (or sub-estate) and the often larger collectivities of people and country associated with, for example, different languages or other broad regional groupings. As we shall see below, language group areas are not always particularly broad geographically nor do their people always have even reconstructible numbers as high as the hundreds.

In at least one well-documented case of strings of non-contiguous estates joined by ties of legend and ritual the resulting 'groups' are not well-bounded and there may be rather different views among senior people as to which estates are included in a particular string that is named or otherwise identified some way, for example by reference to a common Dreaming figure or song type.[42] Some such strings have been called 'phratries' or 'phratry-like' entities, although this term is not now in common use.[43] These kinds of arrangement have perhaps been best reported from North East Arnhem Land and the Mitchell River area of Cape York Peninsula.[44]

Other forms of discontinuous unity include the patchwork mapping of four semimoieties onto estates in the wider Roper River region, a system which facilitates estate succession by members from the same semimoiety as the estate of a group that has died out.[45] They also include non-contiguous estates of a common moiety linked by ritualised trade connections as in the case of the Wurnan of the Kimberleys.[46] In some cases there are reports of estates of the same moiety occurring more or less together in blocs, as in Spencer and Gillen's account of Kingili and Wurlurru moieties in the Tennant Creek district, and Blundell's account of estates of the Wodoi and Djungun moieties 'forming two contiguous curving areas of country' in the Kimberley region.[47] The Spencer and Gillen account is not supported by more detailed and later research.[48] In general, moiety countries do not seem to occur in blocs like this. On the contrary, in some parts of north Australia they exhibit a tendency towards regular alternation, but perhaps only a tendency. For example, in eastern Cape York Peninsula patrimoiety identities of sandbeach estates running from north to south between the Olive and Stewart Rivers alternate in the following pattern: ABBAABABABAABABAABAABBABAABAAB.[49] Of these 30 estates, contiguous same-moiety estate pairs (AA, BB) occur only eight times. Whether or not this is well below a prediction based on an assumption of randomness I do not know, but it certainly meant that, when moiety exogamy and geographic closeness of marriage partners were the dominant trend, as they were in the past, marrying a person whose estate was contiguous with one's own was certainly facilitated.

In parts of western Cape York Peninsula between the Embley and Edward Rivers there are at least two systems of linked estates. In the southern Wik region two or more estates may be identified as belonging to a single 'company' or single patrifilially recruited group under its totemic emblems, yet subgroups are identified which possess non-contiguous tracts that may in fact be ascribed different linguistic identities and that have no identifiable common ancestor. That is, custodians of different parts of what might be called by an analyst a single estate (or set of sub-estates) assert ownership of differently named and linguistically distinct speech varieties.[50]

To the north, around the mouth of the Embley River, there is a case where three groups with adjacent estates have a high proportion of overlapping totems, all three being Gecko, Crow, Darkness, White Cockatoo and 'Wattle Tree'.[51] Two of the three are said also to share Arrowroot, Saltwater Crocodile, Oyster, Porpoise, Cyclone, Bonefish, Frill-necked Lizard and a small Mullet species. And yet the three estates and groups are distinct and each traditionally owns a distinct speech variety, respectively Alngith, Linngithigh and Mamangathi. Of these, Alngith and Linngithigh are close dialects, but they belong to a separate technically-defined language from that of Mamangathi.[52]

The estate group sets in either kind of case cannot be described as subgroups of single language groups, although this may be true of their component segments or sub-clans severally. That is, a clan of this Embley River type or a sub-clan of the southern Wik 'company' type may belong to a culturally recognised local unity that is linguistically diverse and at the same time may belong to a distinct grouping of neighbouring estate groups whose members enjoy a single common linguistic identity. I have no doubt that both kinds of collective identity could be brought into play in different contexts and for different purposes, depending on the fluctuating fortunes of alliances. Along the coast, however, unity of named linguistic variety was not normally a basis for concerted political action.[53]

Western Arnhem Land's estate groups (*kunmokurrkurr*, *mowurrwurr* etc.) exhibit a pattern whereby two or more may share a common name and a certain culturally recognised level of unity under such a title, but their estates may be quite long distances apart and each may have a distinct linguistic identity. For example, of six Mirarr estate groups, one each is identified with the Kunwinjku, Urningangk, Amurdak and Erre languages and two with Gaagudju.[54] Both linguistic identity and *kunmokurrkurr* identity are transmitted in largely the same way, by patrifiliation. The transmission of linguistic identity, here as in some other areas, is 'predominantly ... patrilineal' but less so than that of clan membership.[55] In one part of the region, land is held by small language groups rather than by clans.[56] People may be named with the same *kunmokurrkurr* name but, in terms of anthropological analysis, belong to distinct clans, or perhaps distinct sub-clans, or to one clan. At times people refer to a set of clans of the same name as a single *kunmokurrkurr* that has different countries, or as several *kunmokurrkurr* of the same name.[57]

Clearly *kunmokurrkurr* are not subgroups of language groups in any simple or obvious sense in this context, but they have some obvious similarities and are frequently conjoined in the construction of landed identities: to specify which particular Mirarr *kunmokurrkurr* a person belongs to, the linguistic identity of their estate is commonly combined with their clan name, hence Mirarr Erre, Mirarr Gaagudju and so on. The fact that such linguistic identities may outlive clan identities as a primary means of identifying people with country perhaps suggests a strong pre-existing connection between the two.

On the other hand, in the south-western extremity of this region especially, while clan identities may be remembered, they are no longer very specifically tied to particular sets of sites and in some areas may even be no longer linked to place at all, except in the sense that those belonging to them principally identify with a 'tribal' language group territory such as that of Jawoyn.[58] Francesca Merlan describes Jawoyn *mowurrwurr* as 'lower level units ... participating in one or another higher-level identity'.[59] This does not explicitly propose a structural model of subgroups within a language group, but rather the 'participation' of lower-level groups in higher-level ones.

In present day bureaucratic and legal contexts it may be that Gaagudju *kunmokurrkurr* can now be regarded as subgroups of Gaagudju, Jawoyn *mowurrwurr* as subgroups of Jawoyn and so on, given that it is at the language-named tribe level that legal incorporation and official decision-making about land are now concentrated for these people.[60] The expression 'language-named tribe' comes from Bruce Rigsby. It is a useful term because not all such groups represent the descendants of people of just one language group only. For example, in Cape York Peninsula 'the contemporary Lamalama tribe includes the descendants of at least 35 clans associated with six separate languages, and the contemporary Kuku Thaypan tribe includes the descendants of an unknown, but lesser number of clans associated with four languages'.[61]

Whether or not a web of shared but non-contiguous patrifilial identities such as Mirarr would have manifested more social and political unity than could be found among the members of one of the linguistic identities of the Mirarr clans in the early colonial era remains unclear,[62] but on the grounds that amity suffers from distance I would think it unlikely.

I would apply the same remark to the *yikurrumu* names associated with *kunmokurrkurr* in the region. According to Berndt and Berndt these were 'stylized exclamation[s] … used also in ritual invocations' but they were not aligned with the linguistic affiliation of a *kunmokurrkurr* and several different *kunmokurrkurr* of different areas and different linguistic identities could share a common *yikurrumu* 'name'.[63] For example, 'Magaliraga' (*kunmokurrkurr*: Danek, Djalama, Mandjurlngunj, Yakitjakit), 'Neiilibidj' (*kunmokurrkurr*: Dorlmanngarr, Mirarr), and 'Nabambidmag' (*kunmokurrkurr*: Barrbinj, Maninggali).[64]

Distant estate groups without a great deal in common other than shared totemic identities, but no common name, may also assert their unity at times. In the absence of any single inclusive formal title for themselves or of ritual or other action-based links, and especially in the absence of regular social ties of some kind or another, these may form rather weak kinds of sets politically, although such links may definitely come into play during occasional interactions between more distant groups, for example at meetings and ceremonies.[65]

As non-contiguous estates linked in these and various other ways are not necessarily identified with one particular linguistic identity, they are not necessarily conceived of as subgroupings within a language group. They may be, but that is a matter for local empirical demonstration.

Estate sets: contiguous

Estates which form contiguous sets, and their primary custodians, may be grouped together on a variety of grounds. I deal with those which share linguistic identity in another section below.

Contiguous estates may be linked by a local totemic cult, for example, as in the cases of Shark on the lower Kirke River and Dog on the lower Knox River in the Wik region of Cape York Peninsula.[66] They do not, however, share a common linguistic identity in those particular cases. The five Shark cult clans early in the twentieth century were affiliated to three differently named language varieties, and the four Dog clans to four, that is, one each.

Contiguous estates may also be linked by a common environmental identity, one that is often formally named, such as 'forest people', 'mangrove people', 'lancewood ridge people' and so on. The same terminological system may also subgroup estates of the same area under the name of a single important feature such as a prominent hill or large swamp, the name of which has an extended scope of reference in this context. There seems to be no kin-class unity of such sub-groupings – for example, where there are moieties, the component groups may come from either or both moieties. For the north-central Arnhem Land region Hiatt calls them 'loosely-knit communities' and Bagshaw calls them 'regional designations'.[67] I prefer the unwieldy but more specific 'environmental identities'.

In fact, in general, the membership of a kin superclass such as a particular subsection couple, a section, a semimoiety or a moiety (see Chapter 7) is distributed across the memberships of a number of disparate and separated country-based groupings in any region, and there is little reliable evidence of local clustering of kin superclasses in terms of estate groups.

In the Daly River area Dek Dilk, Dak Kenyim, and Dak Milngin were environmental identity names that encompassed two distinct and un-named estates each,[68] but Dek Deliken, like several others, referred to just one estate. Such names in the region were based on either a major feature (Dilk is a particular hill, Karriyel a particular water body), a typifying kind of geomorphology (*milngin* is 'stone country') or a species typical of a particular vegetation association (*delik* is a plant species). The first pair of estates (Dek Dilk) were both Malak Malak by language identity, the second Madngele, and the third Kamu. Wak Karriyel, however, covered four estates, three of them Malak Malak and the fourth Kamu. Thus I concluded that 'those entities designated by single country names [that is, environmental identity names] are not structurally sub-units of linguistic groups'.[69]

Environmental identity names in the Wik region, known as 'nicknames' in English, may cover two or a few estates, often just the one.[70] They have high political content and were often used in situations of conflict. The estates in such a cluster include this typifying kind of country or species. In many cases the estates and their custodians are un-named as such, although of course there are ways of specifying them in speech, for example by reference to a principal totem, a leading person, or a focal site. Perhaps for this reason, it is often the environmental estate clusters which find their way into the literature, especially the older records, as the smallest kind of formal country grouping of persons that is noted. This over-concern with what is named as against what is un-named has been a limiting factor for the value of such older records, as well as the less thorough recent ones. The literature on a vast area of eastern Queensland contains multitudinous group names which end in the suffixes *–barra* or *–warra*, for example. One cannot assume that these necessarily refer to the most significant groupings of people with traditional connections to the land concerned, or even to groupings of the same type. Unfortunately for the latter-day researcher of old documents, the grammar of such names may also be extended to different kinds of collectivities, for example both to small estate groups and to those of a much wider and more sub-regional environmental or areal type such as 'sandbeach people' or 'river people'; or names that remain unetymologised such as Yiithuwarra (eastern Cape York Peninsula). In the latter case, four distinct languages were encompassed by the set of estates falling under this single name, which covered people whose estates lay between Bathurst Head and about Red Point. A further complication may be that such names of a geopolitically broad character may be found in use only among neighbours, as in the example just given. The names outsiders and neighbours use for a grouping such as this may have no equivalent used internally by those referred to, even if their unity is recognised by all.

LINGUISTIC IDENTITIES AND TERRITORIES[71]

In perhaps the majority of cases, but with some serious exceptions including North East Arnhem Land and the coastal Wik region, sets of estates and their custodians which share a common linguistic identity will be found to be contiguously distributed. Such sets may or may not be accompanied by an active ideology of linguistic group unity. From time to time one reads the speculation that linguistic groupings were, or were not, politically significant territorial groupings at the time of colonisation in Australia. A review of the evidence makes me conclude that in some regions such groupings were of political significance, and in other regions they were of less significance or virtually none. Both Lauriston Sharp and myself, in different parts of Cape York Peninsula, concluded after detailed research that for coastal people, at least, common named linguistic group identities were not of major political importance within the societies concerned. While Sharp wrote of 'the Yir Yoront tribal territory',[72] he also said,

> The term Yir Yoront is purely a label for a linguistic class or category of people who in no sense constitute a corporate or organized entity. ... Indeed, one cannot even speak of Yoront country or of Yoront customs, but only of Yoront speech – Yir Yoront – and of people who speak it. ...[73]

> ... a majority of them also understand or 'hear' a second language, and many, a third. The 'network ... of understandings' thus exists which might serve, regardless of language differences, as a basis for a society or for a community of interests. Yet it is impossible to locate a fixed population associated with a single bounded territory which might constitute a social or cultural community. ... everywhere there is flux or overlap of people with their mutually understood but different behaviours. ...

> What we cannot ignore in this area is the named patrilineal totemic clan. The clan is the only corporate entity found among the Yir Yoront and their neighbours, and it is the clan which is the only landholding unit.[74]

Further north, in the region of Cape Keerweer, I found that coastal people likewise did not regard commonality of language as a major structuring element in their political relationships. A relevant factor here was that in the Wik region a number of languages, in both the named-variety and technically-defined senses, were found to be discontinuously distributed in terms of the locations of the estates identified with them.[75]

Language groups and native title applications[76]

Many native title claims have been lodged in the names of language groups, or in the names of families or other collectivities whose members also identify as being of a particular indigenous language in their applications. One occasionally hears criticism of this on the grounds that the anthropological literature on Aboriginal land relationships has tended to emphasise the small estate-holding group as the primary or even the exclusive locus of rights and interests in country. Indeed one finds sometimes the statement that such a group is '*the* land-owning group'. Similarly one at times sees an early author seeking to find '*the* warmaking group' in a particular society. The danger of such a simplistic approach is usually increased dramatically by a failure to recognise that a neat category such as '*the* land-owning group' may be something brought to the field by the researcher rather than an indigenous cultural institution. The fact is that members of several different kinds of grouping may engage in warfare, may be ascribed rights and interests in sites and country, and may be said to intermarry, for example. Both Sharp and Meggitt defined Aboriginal land 'ownership' essentially (and only) in terms of economic exploitation rights, a position few would hold to now.[77] That only one kind of grouping is given the privilege of being the locus of features that can be translated as some kind of proprietary relationship to country in this way seems contrary to the complexity of the facts.

Language groups or 'dialectal tribes' are usually described as collectivities of smaller groups, and linguistic territories (such as 'Yidinji country', 'Guugu Yimithirr country') as consisting of those estates whose owners share the same linguistic affiliation. In the Cairns Rainforest region, groups of people who own the same language may be named by adding a variety-specific 'having' suffix to the name of the language: hence Yidinji people have the Yidiny language, Gungganyji have Gunggay, Madjanyji have Majay, Jirrbalngan (or Jirrbalji) have Jirbal, Warrgamaygan have Warrgamay, Girramaygan have Girramay, Biyaygiri have Biyay, and Jirubagala have Jiru.[78]

As R.M.W. Dixon has pointed out, one must be aware that what is considered a 'different language' by members of a particular society, and which may have its own name, may range from being an isolate, like Basque, to being just one of several closely related varieties which share a largely common grammar, vocabulary and sound system, as in the case of Danish, Swedish and Norwegian as standard languages. These last three are different 'languages$_1$' – especially in terms of geopolitics – but constitute a single 'language$_2$' in terms of a technical linguistic definition. What constitutes a single technically-defined variety (or language$_2$) varies somewhat among linguists. Some will base the definition mainly on the problematic device of 'mutual intelligibility',[79] others on whether or not it is most efficient to write a single description of the grammar or more than one, others on statistical cut-off points such as 'sharing more than 70% basic lexicon', and sometimes these different ways of subgrouping varieties are each useful in different analytical contexts.

Given the extent to which non-linguists are now writing about linguistic topics in native title legal contexts, it is perhaps not going too far to mention also that technical genetic and typological subgroupings of Aboriginal linguistic varieties by comparative linguists are not 'language groups' in the sense that the phrase is normally used in Australianist contexts. ('Genetic' here is meant as a reference to 'origin' not 'genes'.) One exception to this comment on usage, at least, comes from Jeffrey Heath:

> There are no clearcut 'tribal' entities in the portion of the Northern Territory of Australia where I have done fieldwork (the coast along the south-western part of the Gulf of Carpentaria). Frequently, however, we can say that a particular language was the principal medium of communication within a number of affiliated clans who resided together during a portion of each year … These confederations of clans had no institutionalised corporate identities in ritual, politics, or the exchange of women. Thus 'language group' is a linguistic rather than a social grouping, and in some cases (e.g. where a clan or other unit was strongly bilingual) it is even difficult to demarcate the boundaries among language groups.[80]

Thus Heath ascribes languages of the region to clans on the basis of some kind of regular behavioural pattern, not on the basis of a native ideology of clan possessory rights in linguistic varieties.

Technical linguistic subgroupings in the Aboriginal context most often form a nested hierarchy intended to reflect hypothesised historical relationships, a common terminology being one in which the widest kind of genetic grouping, in this case the Australian phylum, is subdivided into phylic families, then into groups of the same phylic family, subgroups of the same group, languages of the same subgroup, and dialects of the same language. This kind of model has, however, become a matter for some debate among linguists.[81] As far as I know, no native title claims have been lodged in the name of any such scientific linguistic groupings *per se*. One reason for this, apart from the obvious (that is that it is a scientific categorisation, not an acknowledged cultural feature of the claimants), is that the relationship between genetic linguistic closeness and inter-group cultural closeness and political integration is seldom exact and the two can at times be heavily out of kilter. For example, stone tool distribution may reflect social networks that only sometimes seem close to genetic linguistic subgroupings.[82] Or the current sound systems of a set of languages may be relatively homogeneous, reflecting regular interaction or at least a chain of connection via others, while the same languages may be deeply split along genetic lines. For example, Warrungu (far north Queensland) has largely the same sound system as its northern neighbours of the Atherton Tableland but is a close dialect of the same (technically defined) language as Gugu-Badhun, its southern neighbour, with which it has some phonological differences that are immediately apparent.[83] In a reverse sense, people can have very similar language varieties but belong to different political spectra. For example, two estates identified with the Wik-Mungkan linguistic variety in Cape York Peninsula are coastal 'outliers' separate from the majority of estates of the same language affiliation, which lie inland. Political, ritual and marital connections were largely with their immediate and middle-distant coastal neighbours, who had different languages, not with inlanders of the same language.[84] Perhaps similarly, Terry Crowley argues that the New England Tablelands languages belong genetically with the coastal languages to the east and prehistorically may have come from the coast, while a range of evidence indicates that their social networks were oriented in historic times more towards the western slopes people, whose languages were genetically more distant.[85]

'Patrilects'

There is a quite common assumption that the Aboriginal local estate group was not a linguistic group of any kind, and its estate was not a linguistic territory, in classical times. In some native title cases it has been argued that estate groups were land-owning groups (or, in some more extreme versions, merely groups of religious responsibility), but linguistic groups were just groups of shared identity or ethnicity.

There is good evidence that this is false, at least in a number of regions. In those regions the smallest and most elemental linguistic-territorial entity, in the minds of the people themselves, is traditionally that of the membership of the estate group. The linguistic varieties identified with estate groups have been called 'patrilects'.[86] I adopt this term, though it might skew attention more to patrifilial groups rather than to estate groups as such. The distinctiveness of their dialects is usually attributed to the innate characteristics of the estate group's principal founding Dreaming figure, or may be identified by the name of such a figure. The dialect varieties of such small groups are commonly subgrouped by the people themselves into one or more higher-order linguistic categories, although these do not always have names. Case material on patrilects varies in detail but comes from a huge area from about the Ord River in Western Australia east to the Barkly, Roper, North East Arnhem Land and Cape York Peninsula regions. Territorial linguistic sub-units below the level of the (usually) named broad linguistic identity have been reported for northern Warumungu, north-eastern Warlpiri, Warlmanpa, Mudburra, Jingilu, Wampaya, Gurindji, Ngarinyman, Ngaliwurru, Gija and possibly Nungali;[87] Wardaman;[88] Ngalakan;[89] north-central Arnhem Land (Ndjébbana);[90] north-east Arnhem Land;[91] and several parts of Cape York Peninsula: Princess Charlotte Bay,[92] Barrow Point–Flinders Islands,[93] and the Wik region.[94]

Critics of the emphasis on language groups in certain native title cases have included at least two anthropologists. Perhaps the main thrust of their critiques lie in asserting that land tenure in classical Aboriginal systems was not located within language groups *per se*, but in local estate groups or similar. There are two main issues here. One is whether or not supra-local groupings were merely about shared identities and practices and did not impinge directly on the distribution of rights in land and waters, or conversely had a role in the allocation of rights, in classical Aboriginal societies. The other is whether or not the emergent post-classical 'tribal' entities based on language group identity and territory represent departures from the classical past that are so dramatic as to represent a fatal break with the continuity of traditional connection to country.

Language group size

Although in some areas, as detailed above, it is reliably reported that the estate-owning groups regarded themselves as constituting linguistic (sub-)units, in a large number of cases they are described as constituting the elementary particles of a larger sociolinguistic entity, a 'tribe' or similarly identified entity. In a wide range of different areas it is also reported that each estate group had its own distinctive dialect even if it shared a dialect name with a number of others. Those estate groups whose members shared the same linguistic variety name are often said to have typically numbered or averaged about 500 people at the time of early European contact.[95] A close inspection of a wide range of data on the question has led me to the view that in different regions the average number of estate groups per named linguistic variety may range from a low of about two to a high of about 70 in north Australia, and probably much higher in parts of southern Australia.[96] In other words, to assume that all such linguistic identities and groupings and territories were very much of the same order and had similar socio-cultural under-pinnings is probably a big mistake.

For example, between the Embley and Archer Rivers in Cape York Peninsula an estimated 31–35 estates were affiliated to at least thirteen named linguistic varieties in an area only about 100 x 75 kilometres in extent. This gives an average of a little over two estates per named linguistic variety, with a range from one to possibly ten at the outside. If we reduce the picture by subgrouping these varieties into technically defined single languages, of which there were at least six, this still only yields between five and six estates per language (in the technical sense). At an assumed average in the range of 15–25 people per estate group, a figure that certainly seems to have empirical support in this region, a reconstructed population for the Embley–Archer Rivers area of 465–875 seems realistic. Thus thirteen named linguistic varieties would have had an estimated average of 35–60 people each, in terms of primary linguistic identifications, and even the six technically defined languages would have had an average in the range of only 78–146 people who had primary identity with varieties subgrouped together in this way.[97]

At the opposite extreme, in western New South Wales, the reconstructed populations for language-named identity groupings such as Kamilaraay (6,000–7,000 people), Wangaaybuwan (some thousands), Wiradjuri (3,000) and Baagandji (3,000), on the assumption that localised countries of something like the estate type were present, imply a huge number of such countries per language.[98] Some 7,000 people divided into an average of 25 persons per localised tenure group yields a figure of 280; but it is unlikely that empirical evidence will now be discovered that would confirm or negate this kind of estimate. It may be possible for the south-west of Western Australia, where an estimated minimum of 7,500 people[99] spoke dialects of a single language[100] which had a number of differently named varieties. The descendants of the people of the region are now commonly categorised overall as Noongar (Nyungar, Noongah, etc.) as also may be their language.[101]

The difficulty of simple generalisations

The view that language groups have emerged as political units only in response to land rights opportunities is sometimes put in anthropological evidence in a native title case. It is not too difficult to refute this in specific cases, but one has to be specific. There are cases where people who were brought up without learning a traditional label for their identity, and who believe they must have this tribal or other classical name in order to pursue recognition of their native titles, have researched the record and reinstated their language or tribe name, for example one drawn from Tindale's map.[102] The suggestion that these attempts are inherently illegitimate in some way, an opinion sometimes conveyed by innuendo rather than in a transparent and scientific fashion, begs the question, or rather two of them. First, have members of the group maintained a connection to the area under traditional law and custom, with or without a label? If so, the label question pales somewhat. (Recall that the search for a name for a language may be futile, in the sense that not all languages had names.) Second, it would be surprising if legal opportunities did not stimulate a renewed interest in the past when the law requires continuity with the past as proof of native title – the taking up of an opportunity is only opportunism under certain conditions, and separating the two is a notoriously subjective area of judgement.

My basic point here is that broad generalisations about the role of languages in the framing of political life and land-related rights and values are not easy to make. For example, in contrast with parts of western coastal Cape York Peninsula discussed above, where language group identity played at best only a very modest role in inter-group and territorial politics, there are opposite reports, such as that of Meggitt for the Warlpiri (Walbiri):

'There are two kinds of blackfellows,' they say, 'we who are the Walbiri and those unfortunate people who are not. Our laws are the true laws; other blackfellows have inferior laws which they continually break. ...'

The Walbiri maintain their identity wherever they settle. When one takes a wife from another tribe, the children are Walbiri, no matter if the couple live in the wife's tribal territory or even in the same camp as her near kinsmen. ... The people cannot believe that a person fortunate enough to be born a Walbiri would ever allow his 'citizenship' to lapse, and I have never encountered a Walbiri who has done so.[103]

Even in the Yir Yoront case mentioned earlier Sharp found that there was a tendency against the alienation of estates to successors who came from a language group different from that of the deceased former owners.[104] The tendency for linguistic territories to be relatively stable in this kind of way has also been reported for the western Roper River: 'This situation strongly suggests that 'Mangarayi country' [baṉam ṉa-Mangarayi-wu], conceptually associated with the Mangarayi language, has in fact been much more stable an entity, at least over the past several generations since contact, than has the personnel.'[105] General territorial stability for sets of related languages has been demonstrated now for a number of different regions, the most dramatic thus far being that of the Iwaidjan language family of the Croker Island–Cobourg Peninsula area of the Northern Territory as reported by Nicholas Evans, whose highly detailed work led him to conclude that the patterns of relatedness of the geographically rather restricted Iwaidjan family of languages reflected 'the accumulated effects of gradual changes, *in situ*, over many thousands of years'.[106]

Sociolinguistic territories or language group memberships are not based in any immediate sense on the ability to speak a language. People identify with a language most commonly on the basis of parental filiation – it is an identity passed down through the generations – or ultimately on some other criterion such as place of conception or birth, as in the Western Desert. Most often one acquires the linguistic identity of one's estate. Estates at the peripheries of linguistic territories may carry two or even three linguistic identities, and their owners will normally identify with each language variety so named. One may belong to a language group and not be able to speak the language. A typical example from among very many is that reported by Merlan for the western Roper River area: 'Today, native language competence, as well as inclination to use the native languages, are declining rapidly among younger people, but the sociolinguistic identity of the country as "Mangarayi" persists'.[107] In at least one native title case an anthropologist has argued that loss of language results in loss of language group membership, an assertion that flies in the face of overwhelming evidence. Conversely one may speak five or six languages but claim only one of them as one's own 'real, proper' language. Because one has at least two parents and four grandparents, for example, people may claim varying levels of identification with several languages and their associated groups.

Can rights-holders be definitively listed?

The unattainability of definitive lists of rights-holders is not just a result of the breaking down of traditional discipline, although it can be greatly exacerbated by it. It is abundantly clear that some rural and urban claimants exhibit a lot more mutual denial, overlapping claims and overt conflict over who has what rights than would have been possible among their ancestors. The erosion of ritual and gerontocratic authority, the general suppression of execution as a way of dealing with the bucking of senior men's authority, and the imposition of Australian law in regard to assault, may to a degree have opened Pandora's box. One cannot assume that eruptions of conflict over who holds what rights are merely the result of loss of knowledge of the country, or of each other, among the claimants. Declining fear of the consequences of counter-claiming may at times be more significant.

But objectified and definitive lists of rights-holding groups may also be impossible even among the most classically-oriented people of remote Australia. Fred Myers has long worked with Western Desert Pintupi people, whose adherence to traditional religious Law is legendary. By collecting claims from many people Myers found that he was unable to 'delineate sets of people everyone agreed were identified with a place. The isolation of finite groups proved impossible ...' People might say 'that's my country' without necessarily having custodianship of the ritual associations of the place. Claims of identification with a place remained 'ambiguous and open-ended'.[108] Land-owning groups overlapped in membership and were bilateral in composition (hence they were not, for example, patrilineal). People could be recruited to a country directly; that is, they could belong to a country group without descent from one of its members. Membership involved individual choice.[109] Because of this multiplicity of claims, land-holding groups essentially took the form of bilateral, descending kindreds.[110]

Pintupi people could thus give conflicting accounts of who was identified with a particular country. They were not in the habit of presenting 'balanced, sociocentric accounts of "ownership", listing [as in a legal context] for the benefit of outsiders all owners and the ordering among them'. The 'abstract serving of "justice" is not the immediate issue; *there is no third party to judge the claims'*.[111] Pintupi were primarily concerned that everyone be satisfied with the results of negotiated claims, and sought to avoid the danger of open denial and rejection of claims. The latter offered the potential of violence.[112] On the other hand, making trouble was also used as a means of influencing people, although it tended to be rooted more in self-regard than in a desire for power.[113] No one was prepared to be told by others what to do.[114]

> Identification refers to the whole set of relationships a person can claim or assert between himself or herself and a place. ... Identification is an ongoing process, subject to claim and counterclaim, dependent on validation and acceptance or invalidation and nonacceptance. ... [S]uch a political process ... enables claims of identification to be transformed into rights over related aspects of a country. Such rights only exist when they are accepted by others. ... This graded range of claims, though not well-marked by linguistic forms, is an important property of a state of affairs open to much negotiation.

> Landownership in the Western Desert is thus an elusive matter. Only belatedly did I come to see the mystery as part of the system itself: Ownership is not a given, but an accomplishment.[115]

There are elements of Myers' account which raise further questions. It is not really laid out clearly why he opted to summarise certain kinds of relationships to country as 'ownership', given the European cultural baggage that comes with that term. Certainly there are examples in Myers' work of people expressing their relationship to places by means of possessive pronouns, as in '*That's my country*', and at that elemental level 'ownership' as a folk term is appropriate. Of more relevance here, however, is the argument that ownership depended on negotiated claims and counterclaims, and land-owning groups were egocentric kindreds, not sociocentric objectifications.

If the rights conferred by land ownership 'only exist when they are accepted by others', as Myers says, it seems unlikely that many claims would amount to 'ownership', or could do so for long periods, if the bar of social acceptance were set very high and many claims were disputed. Social acceptance is a concept that is very difficult to make precise. It is not just a matter of numbers. One's many equals and juniors may agree with what one says, but what if just one far more senior person contradicts it? The people with whom one lives day to day may also accept it, perhaps out of respect, fear or a desire for peace, but what if the members of neighbouring communities do not? And how does one interpret situations of public consensus about a claim, when it is preceded or followed by private dissension? As 'ownership', or the absence of it? Given Myers' emphasis on the event-specific nature of consensus or 'determinations', and the fact that Pintupi do not necessarily feel bound by collective 'decisions', perhaps 'acceptance' is a difficult concept to apply in such a case.

Even if wide social acceptance of an individual's land claims is achieved, that may not be the end of the story. Myers tells us that Pintupi determinations were available to renegotiation. 'Closure, in the form of a final or definitive account, is unusual. Just as with land ownership, so also can promises of [wife] bestowal be changed as current relations alter.'[116] In stark contrast with this world of indeterminacies, minimal structuration and contested claims, was the *Tjukurrpa* or Dreaming. This lay outside of people, an objectification to which people had to conform. It was the Law.[117] Society itself was a precarious achievement under the economic circumstances of the past. The Dreaming transcended the immediate and provided a stable, theoretically timeless and unchanging basis for social life. Initiation, marriage and how to deal with death, for example, were matters for customary law instituted by the Dreaming.[118] The Dreaming narratives, and Dreaming sites themselves, formed a kind of durable, bony foundation of relative consistency and permanence. One might ask, though, from whose vantage point this consistency and permanency existed, in the event that conflicting versions of Dreaming narratives or site locations were to be put forward by different individuals. In this *Tjukurrpa* domain, at least, objectification may be a target or ideal not always achieved.

Such Western Desert people are at the least firm extremity of the phenomenon of elusive 'groups' of holders of rights in country, and should not be taken to be archetypal of Aboriginal Australia. One could put forward descriptions of far less elusive systems from other parts of the country. But the native title legal and administrative system, if it is to be pragmatic rather than ideological in cast, has to be capable of living with the fact that it is not normally possible for an anthropologist to make simple and dogmatic statements about which rights in which areas are held by exactly which people, and expect that witness evidence will match the description. This cast-iron approach suffers from the legendary failings of cast-iron – it fractures easily.

I have suggested, partly for reasons of sheer Aboriginal cultural complexity, that no single level of territorial grouping in Aboriginal Australia is overwhelmingly the natural candidate for translation into the legal concept of the community of native title holders. This has implications not only for how native title determination applications are framed, but also for how they are researched and, in the event of litigation, what kinds of evidence are appropriate to the process of proof. In the end, also, this complexity represents a serious challenge to the bureaucratic incorporation process that accompanies recognition of native titles.

4 | Atomism versus collectivism[1]

A TENSION BETWEEN ATOMISM and collectivism appears at more than one point in the processes by which Aboriginal and Torres Strait Islander people seek to achieve legal recognition of their title to traditional land and sea areas.

Where small landed groups belong to larger congeries, and also may overlap considerably in memberships and geographical scope, subgroups may pursue their interests rather atomically unless convinced that their interests are better served by some form of coalition. This will usually be true before a land claim is begun, and its pattern may be fairly well entrenched. The ultimate form of atomism is the individual pursuit of control. Some attempts at control by individuals may be masked by their public description as the actions and beliefs of a group. Some small informal groupings in an indigenous context are basically the pluralisation, some of it fairly fictive but nevertheless highly customary, of the persona of a single focal individual, without whose existence the group itself would not exist.[2] Most, however, have a more widely distributed basis. Ultimately, as I suggest below, this basis is typically regional rather than local, although locally manifested.

Once the native title claim process begins, the devising of a list of named applicants or the determination of the membership of a claimant group will often throw the atomist/collectivist tension into some relief. Anthropologists may be engaged on a land claim or native title claim after some meetings have already been held and a claimant group has more or less been identified, perhaps by in-house anthropologists of an indigenous organisation, perhaps by others. I would advise anthropologists new to this situation not to take this kind of preliminary grouping for granted, but to carry out their own careful investigation of whose interests are at stake and whether they have been included or excluded on appropriate grounds.

As a general rule, for reasons that are ancient in origin, desert Aboriginal people are on the high end of the collectivist scale in their public approach to actions such as land claims, in spite of their relative individualism in assigning interests in places, and coastal people tend more strongly towards the atomic or sub-group approach (and less towards individualism). This partly accounts for the differences in how claimant groups have been defined in different regions over the last twenty years.

Anthropologists themselves, mainly for reasons of personality and political persuasion, may also be ranged along the atomist/collectivist scale. Rod Hagen has referred to people at the two ends of this sliding scale as 'lumpers and splitters'.[3] Such differences among Australianists seem to me to be rather slight at the present time, but were more pronounced in the 1970s and 1980s. Among anthropologists of that era working in the Northern Territory, the regionally uneven influences of feminism and socialism, combined with the very distinct political origins of the Central and Northern Land Councils, made it possible to hazard a rough generalisation that the anthropological interpretations then coming out of the CLC were typically more collectivist than those coming out of the NLC. That this also matched the hinterland/coast dichotomy of Aboriginal practice seems mainly – perhaps not entirely – fortuitous. The point I wish to make here is that anthropologists, like anyone else, bring to their work not only a set of skills but also certain attitudes. A rugged individualist of maverick persuasion will not see things in quite the same light as someone committed more to a communalist perspective. This distinction comes out in the way conflict between claimants is perceived, for example: whether conflict is something to be left aside for the benefit of a claim or an inherent part of the claimants' system for dealing with land interests that needs to be faithfully represented. The same distinction may come out in the anthropologist's attitude to acting for one group or two groups who have differences over the nature of the claim, or to acting for a small subgroup of a larger group whose other members may nevertheless have certain interests in the area claimed.

This leads to yet another manifestation of the tension between atomism and collectivism. As Mary Edmunds has pointed out, while most statutory land claims in the Northern Territory under its *Land Rights Act* have been free of overt or significant disputation between claimant groups, many native title cases have showed the opposite tendency.[4] Although one reason for this difference is probably that land-based Aboriginal political mechanisms outside remote Australia are understandably in a more ragged state as a result of shattering histories, I suggest there may be another reason, one already alluded to by Mary Edmunds.

In the Northern Territory the *Land Rights Act* claims have mostly been brought before the Aboriginal Land Commissioner by the major land councils. It is understandable that such organisations, with their historically modest funding for land claims work, would normally be unwilling to commence financing the processing of a claim until the claimants had sorted out a reasonably settled position on who constituted the appropriate claimant group in each case.

Where disputation has occurred openly in Northern Territory cases (for example, *Finniss River*, *Lake Amadeus*), this occurred after a unified claim had already been lodged and the legal process begun. Under the native title legislation and its early implementation, money for developing and commencing claims was supplied directly to claimant groups as well as to a number of regional organisations, although the latter are now the sole conduit for official funding of native title claims. Has it been true here, then, as in the coast/hinterland case, that affluence facilitates atomism? If there were enough money, would each nuclear family or even each person making a native title claim be entitled to, and achieve, separate representation and study?

MEETINGS AND FIELDWORK: STARTING RESEARCH ON A CLAIM

There are some critical moments at the very start of the process by which a native title case is researched by an anthropologist. There have been two main techniques for beginning the fieldwork part of the process. I have tried both. They are at opposite ends of the atomist/collectivist spectrum. They can have an impact on the final shape of the claimant group.

One way is for the researcher to travel extensively in the area, engage quietly in conversation with a wide range of individuals with interests in the case, and thus work out who might be authoritative people with whom to concentrate the early phase of the research. A handful of knowledgable people may then accompany the researcher to the claimed land where they map its cultural significance and customary tenure interests, later to be checked against a wider selection of people. A similarly handpicked set of people may commit themselves to the demanding grind of providing genealogical and biographical information for the emerging set of relevant families. The trust and personal relating that helps make this a rewarding experience for all concerned are also helped along by this small-group approach. There is, further, a technical reason for this focused approach: if researchers do not already know the local people and culture fairly well, they cannot make significant advances of knowledge in the time available if they scatter their fire and carry out shallow survey work with many people but in-depth work with no people.

The other way to start off is to attend a series of mass claimant (and possible claimant) meetings organised by a relevant indigenous body, and go on a tour of the claimed land with several vehicle-loads of people. This is very helpful for the getting-to-know-you phase, although the claimants mostly end up knowing who the anthropologist is while the latter can be overwhelmed by having to remember too many names and faces in a short time. The main advantage of this phase is that it encourages group dynamics to become well oiled and to focus on the claim and on the question of who should be making it. Its main disadvantage is that the ability of some powerful people to perform well in a public and ritualised context is not usually matched by that of some others who may also have claim interests that the general population regards as legitimate, but who are less publicly adept.

I would conclude that both methods should ideally be used. Apart from the fact that both public and private contexts provide important but distinct types of knowledge for the researcher, and enable him or her to serve the client better than by using one means alone, there is another reason why both need to be used. That is, that the researcher needs to maintain a high degree of independence and avoid coming under the undue influence of a few people who may or may not have the interests of others at heart.

In the end, a line is typically drawn around the claimant group, unless an 'exemplars of system' approach is taken instead. The anthropological reportage for a native title claim is there to establish, among other things, whether or not a certain kind of normative system of country relationships existed in the pre-sovereignty past and has persisted into the present. On this basis the reportage may concentrate on presenting selected claimants or subgroups in detail, so as to show 'how the system works'. In the case of applications for compensation for extinguished native title, the question is centrally one of who held native title rights and interests just before the time when the native title was lost, and whether there remain identifiable people who may be eligible for compensation for that loss, rather than one of providing a definitive list of compensation group members. In both cases, exemplars of the system may be presented, leaving the precise determination of the boundaries of the group to the internal processes of the regional society at any one period. The Native Title Act allows for the Federal Court to either name the persons entitled to compensation or, alternatively, to set out a method for determining who they might be.[5] In many cases, however, researchers have defined claimant groups by naming individuals. Nonetheless, anthropologists usually make it their business to understand the complexities of how the relevant regional society is constituted. Unlike legal representatives, they do not seek or take 'instructions' about how it is to be subdivided.

SLICING THE PIE

In each part of Australia there are many kinds of Aboriginal group that can be defined in relation to interests in, and associations with, land. Many of these have labels, but many also do not. Whether labelled or unlabelled, no one of these geographically definable sociopolitical Aboriginal entities is ever simply synony-mous with '*the* territories of Aboriginal people', because the same population can normally be divided into a number of different landed entities, such as small unilineal land-holding units, local sets of totemically or ritually linked units, language groups, named sets of distinct languages, groups holding environ-mentally similar country, people coming from the same direction ('westerners', for example), people who hail from the same residential community, members of the same legally incorporated body, and so on.

Identifying these different kinds of geographically definable entities in a particular area yields a number of overlapping 'territories' for the same population, and the question then arises as to whether or not one of these candidates is to be selected to be the relevant locus of communal interests in land for a land claim, or not. Even if, for pragmatic reasons, one of the alternative ways of slicing the same pie is to be chosen as the starting point or primary structural envelope within which a claim will be made out, one has to be clear about what the result-ing description or map, or both, is intended to do in order to motivate such a choice.

The scale of the context determines how widely the net of interest-holders should be cast in any particular case.[6] Specific connections to and rights in land or sea areas, as compared with relatively context-free and outright possessory relationships, typified by authoritative statements such as 'That's my country', are far more contextually determined. But I would raise this question: are the interests of members of a wide regional group simply political interests based on their living in the same region and being citizens of the same polity, or may they be a form of proprietary relationship as well? Arguably they can be both, depending on the case. I say this partly on the basis of analysis of details of such relationships, but also on the basis of the confirmatory tendency of some people, at least, to feel free to say of their home region, not just their home estate or Dreaming track segment, 'That's my country'.

THE REGIONAL BASIS OF LOCAL ENTITLEMENTS[7]

The authoritative assertion of customary–legal interests in land and sea, while it may place a presumptive emphasis on small-scale relationships to land and sea, includes the expression of a wider responsibility for decisions affecting small areas physically but large numbers of landowners socially, culturally, or politically. The wider set of people in such a case is recruited not merely on the basis of residential proximity but above all on the basis of their shared status as customary-law landholders in the same region. While they do not, in a simple sense, 'claim each other's land', they have a collective interest over the whole region that arises from rights and interests rooted in particular homeland areas. This can form the native title basis of a regional agreement where the impetus for such an agreement arises from a major development that physically occupies only a small part of the region. While developers in the past typically preferred making deals with the smallest local indigenous group available, local customary landowners are increasingly wary of effectively committing others, without consultation, to the consequences of such deals, and developers are more committed to working through regional indigenous bureaucracies.

To give an example from a classical north Australian system, each person may have a range of differentiated rights and interests in as many as five or six distinct estates (e.g. father's, mother's, father's mother's, mother's mother's, spouse's, a vacant estate where they have a long history of residence, and so on). It is thus possible under certain circumstances for a person to say of a substantial part of their region, or even of that region as a whole, that their relationship to it is one of belonging as well as of personal historical origin. Typically their region will be criss-crossed by such lines of interconnection between individuals and particular land/sea areas. As a member of the wider regional group of origin, it is one's neighbours among whom successors are most likely to be found if one's own estate should become vacant on the extinction of one's clan, in regions where such analytic terms are useful.

For this reason, as well as others more to do with access and use rights, a small-scale land-holding group in such a system cannot simply or always be said to have a clearly and completely exclusive relationship with their land. It is not necessarily 'against the rest of the world' that they hold it, in a simple sense. On this basis, and according to context, regional group members may be entitled, under indigenous customary law, to play some part in decision-making about land use in large sub-areas of their region's lands or even those lands as a totality, even though their individual primary clan estate or Dreaming track interests are confined to only part of it. (It is not irrelevant, for example, that Dreaming story and songlines may travel on a continental scale in Australia, thus perhaps expressing symbolically the role of these wider jural networks.)

The more eminent of these people will tend to be put forward as claimants, even if others of their subgroup are not, especially in arid Australia. This raises problems for a wholly group-centred pathway to defining customary interests in the land. This role for eminent individuals is part of the ethnographic reality that cannot merely be laid aside because people may have a preference for communalist interpretations of indigenous proprietary relationships to land. The *Native Title Act* does say that native title rights and interests are the 'communal, group or individual rights and interests' in land and waters.[8] However, customary proprietary relationships, whether couched in terms of small groups or individual interests, have a communal foundation.

The argument that large-scale decision-making, such as that involved in a regional response to a major development proposal, had no place in Aboriginal life before colonisation and therefore cannot be part of Aboriginal tradition can be refuted on two grounds. First, Aboriginal tradition is grounded in, but not bound by, the conditions and practices of the pre-colonial past, a point I would now regard as beyond dispute, not only among anthropologists but often in Australian legal practice as well, in spite of the requirement for proof of native title that the relevant pre-sovereignty traditions be substantially maintained. Second, large-scale gatherings were typical of ceremonial events in early times, as is attested by many reports dating from earliest contact. Old people have many times recounted memories of bush events involving the attendance of members of many subgroups recruited from their region as a whole. And then there is the general point that, in indigenous custom in this country, where one comes from is 'everybody's business', at least regionally.

Where a native title claim is a large one, particularly if it is strongly opposed, it is unlikely, in my view, that the Aboriginal people concerned will seek to represent their interests in a totally atomic way rather than a firmly collective one that presents both the atoms and an account of how they are connected into a larger, customary–legal whole. This 'whole' is typically a fabric that fades into the distance, not a neatly finite unit.

REGIONS AND 'NATIONS'

After an era in which anthropologists long focused their attention on one or more localised populations such as tribes and villages, anthropological theory has in recent decades given greater emphasis to relationships between the local and the national, and the local and the global. An earlier concern with regional levels of sociocultural integration in Aboriginal Australia has long apparently faded, in spite of Nicolas Peterson's noting with surprise and disappointment, as long ago as 1986, how little attention had been given to the subject.[9]

A stimulus to re-engage with regional studies among Australianist anthropologists may be provided by the engagement of indigenous peoples with Australian law at various regional levels. This is particularly so in the context of native title law and its implementation. Given the role of regional populations in indigenous land use agreements, the creation of native title prescribed bodies corporate with regional responsibilities, and the regional base of constituencies such as those served by native title representative bodies, anthropological reconsideration of the topic may have some practical implications. This is in spite of the fact that indigenous land use agreements and the prescribed bodies corporate which are involved in them typically relate to land and waters that form only a sub-part of a region's titles.

Traditional Aboriginal localism, whereby political power and decision-making are highly decentralised among small populations and also characterised quite often by high levels of contestation and conflict, is not readily compatible with the idea that large-scale regional corporations are integral to the implementation of the native title regime.

In their book *Native Title Corporations: a Legal and Anthropological Analysis*, Christos Mantziaris and David Martin discussed the collision of indigenous localism with pressures for 'wider imperatives for efficiency, cost effectiveness and accountability'.[10] The reluctance of local groups to cede autonomy and power over their interests to wider-based structures could partly be overcome by various kinds of federated structures whereby umbrella organisations acted for legally distinct small groups, but this did not remove the essential problem of tensions between the local and the regional. Mantziaris and Martin said 'it is arguable that the origin of native title rights in regional *systems* of traditional law and custom should be recognised in the design of native title institutions so far as is practicable, rather than just the locally based rights and interests that derive from the regional system'.[11]

One problem with this suggestion, which I should admit is partly based on some work of my own, is that regional systems of land tenure are seldom in a neat isomorphic relationship with the shape and content of regional polities. Furthermore, we use 'system' in a variety of senses.[12] One has to distinguish *system as active network* from *system as a body of principles and sanctioned practices*. In the latter sense, land tenure systems are typically far more widespread than in the former – that is, people with the same way of assigning rights in country may not necessarily interact closely with each other because of distance. Conversely, people may interact, including ceremonially, with others whose land relationship systems differ significantly from their own, as when Western Desert and Arrerntic people (such as the Western Arrernte of the Hermannsburg area), or Warlpiri and Warumungu, combine in rituals.

Unfortunately there is no ready manual for looking up the nature and geographic distribution of systems of indigenous customary law relating to rights in country across the whole of Australia. There are now many reliable local studies, especially in land claim case materials, and some regional studies, but it takes a long period of research and experience to find one's way among the hundreds of sources in order to form even a partial picture of Australia as a set of regional systems of indigenous land and marine tenure.

Perhaps more noticeably we do not have any up-to-date Australia-wide studies of indigenous cultural and social regions that are broadly based. The extent to which such regional systems have played a part in the reproduction of local land tenure arrangements is also not well established in the literature. While many of the mysteries of Aboriginal local and linguistic organisation have been unravelled over the decades, especially by anthropologists, there are several cases of relevant large-scale phenomena that still remain mysteries, at least to many of us.

One is the various levels of cultural and social regions themselves. How such coherence was or has been maintained over time, in the absence of any centralised powers, is not explained merely by appealing to notions such as 'the force of custom' – especially when we know that custom can change, and contradictory customs can abut.

THE ANTHROPOLOGY OF ABORIGINAL REGIONS

Between the local and the continental lie many differently defined 'regional Aboriginal Australias'. These remain rather patchily and often poorly documented, in spite of a number of achievements in mapping indigenous cultural and social regions, many of them carried out between about 1880 and the 1930s. (A review of the history of some anthropological ideas about Australian Aboriginal regional 'communities' is given in the next section.)

Even where regional studies have been made, the content of the relevant regions has often been conceived primarily as isomorphic with the envelopes of their constituent groups and territories, usually groups or territories identified and often named by their members and neighbours. There is often some difficulty in clarifying the extent to which these regional entities are defined by the enjoyment of common cultural traits, as compared with regional populations characterised by relatively bounded patterns of interaction. Even where common cultural traits are clearly the main basis for describing a particular indigenous region, it is often unclear whether the region is mainly the product of the outsider's analysis or also a construction of indigenous people's own consciousness of kind.

It is also quite often unclear whether these larger, supra-local aggregates of the literature are intended to be 'typological', to use Peterson's term,[13] or are meant to refer to on-the-ground populations. Typological aggregates are sets of people defined by some kind of common identity, such as having a particular linguistic or 'tribal' affiliation or supra-tribal regional identity as a 'nation', or by sharing common social institutions and other cultural traits such as kinship systems or forms of initiation ceremony. Such people are usually distributed among populations which do not exactly match, and may in some cases only weakly match, the geographic distribution of their typological identities.

I refer here to 'sets' advisedly, since there are relevant population aggregates which are co-located and there are others whose members belong to *networks* which overlap and may be differently constituted on the basis of different contexts. Thus a set of trading partners or ritual celebrants may be distributed as a string of individuals or small groups across a wide landscape, interspersed among other similar or different strings or 'chains of connection'.[14] Individuals may belong to one such set for one purpose, and to another set for another purpose. In this chapter, however, my focus is on regional sets, whether typological or demographic.

It can be argued that any distinction between the local and the regional is bound to be an inadequate and counterproductive dualism. The most obvious ground for this criticism is that applying the distinction in practice is always likely to be arbitrary, as small populations – defined on whatever grounds – combine in a bewildering range of ways and at many different 'levels of resolution' into smaller and bigger entities, depending on context. The distinction is most useful as a relative one – the scope of some entity or other can be described as more local, or more regional, than that of another, without too much fear of contradiction, except for the odd close call.

Ethnographic writing in Australia often begins with a wide-ranging account of a regional context, but the main work itself is usually restricted to a particular group of people or a particular place. Among the better known ethnographies that come readily to mind are those such as Howitt on 'the Kurnai', Spencer and Gillen on 'the Arunta', Sharp on 'the Yir Yoront', Meggitt on 'the Walbiri', Hiatt on 'the Gidjingali', Myers on 'the Pintupi', Warner, the Berndts, Williams, Shapiro, Morphy and Keen on 'the Yolngu' (or 'Murngin', 'Wulamba', 'Miwuyt'), the Berndts on 'the Kukabrak' (or 'Yaraldi', 'Narrinyeri', 'Ngarrindjeri') and so on. While these culturally salient entities are of varying scales and composition, they have much in common conceptually. That is, a collectivity culturally significant to Aborigines becomes the main reference point for descriptions of patterns of thought and action.

In an earlier phase, Australianists often used the term 'nations' to refer to 'congeries of tribes' or regional 'communities', defined on a number of different bases. These 'nations' were typically described as consisting of a number of different 'tribes', that is, sets of people named after their various languages. The most common basis for identifying 'nations', in the literature of the late nineteenth and early twentieth centuries, was either their social structural organisation or their ritual life, plus additional elements such as shared customs and beliefs. But the literature also identified explicitly *interactive* entities such as trade networks, sets of people with common or overlapping speech repertoires, sets of people who intermarry, and people who aggregated for the purpose of warfare. There was a tendency to fail to distinguish patterns of interaction from patterns of shared and unshared geopolitical identities. Roth referred to larger aggregates in western Queensland, probably reflecting local English usage, as 'messmates':

[T]he Boulia District, the limits of which have already been defined …, comprises in all a score or so of tribes, each having head centre or chief encampment. Speaking generally these same tribes are able to render themselves pretty mutually intelligible, and possess in common various trade-routes, markets and hunting grounds, customs, manners, and beliefs; in other words they might, as a whole, be well described as "messmates," though in the aboriginal language there appears to be no one word which would express them collectively. Still deeper bonds of comradeship connect them in that all these tribes, with certain individual limitations to be subsequently discussed, are intermarriageable, and furthermore, in cases of warfare with outsiders, would join in making common cause against the enemy.[15]

Roth's experience of an identifiable large-scale aggregate whose members had no name for themselves can be repeated many times over around the continent. There is evidence, however, that while members of such aggregates may have had no term for themselves as a whole, in a number of cases their neighbours certainly did.

NINETEENTH- AND EARLY TWENTIETH-CENTURY REGIONAL STUDIES

This was an era when anthropologists took rather more of an interest in cultural and social regions than they have since. Theories of diffusionism and culture circles were enjoying their heydays.

In 1892 John Fraser twice published a map of New South Wales indicating fourteen regions which were territories associated with 'native tribes'.[16] This is largely a map of regional blocs rather than a map of language group territories, but in some areas it is a mixture of the two. For example, he distinguishes 'Kamal arai proper' from 'Wal arai', but these would usually be combined at the regional level, as they were by R.H. Mathews. In 1898 Mathews published a somewhat similar map to Fraser's, but in this case it was a much more consistent attempt to indicate major sociocultural blocs only, and within the state borders there were at least parts of nine such blocs.[17] Mathews based this map on variations between types of initiation ceremonies, stating that the boundaries indicated 'the several districts within which each type of ceremony is in force'.[18]

Mathews modified this map on its western, southern and northern edges in other publications.[19] In 1900 he published a more complex map of South Australia showing at least parts of eight 'nations', one of which was shown as subdivided into ten 'tribes'.[20] This map also showed the important circumcision and subincision lines, a mapping tradition maintained by Davidson in 1928 and continued into the 1970s by Norman Tindale and Ronald Berndt.[21]

One of Mathews's most ambitious efforts in this regard was his 'Map Showing Boundaries of the Several Nations of Australia'.[22] This shows 28 'communities or nations' based on the sharing of 'divisional names', which are the names of moieties, sections, and subsections, to use the modern terminology.[23] His 'nations' bore the following names, which seem mainly or wholly to have been selected by Mathews himself:

1 Bangarang

2 Booandik

3 Barkunjee

4 Yowerawarrika

5 Parnkalla

6 Kookatha

6a Tardarick

7 Wiradjuri

8 Kamilaroi

9 Darkinung

10 Thangatty

11 Dippil

12 Kooinmerburra

13 Kogai

14 Mycoolon

15 Goothanto

16 Warkemon

17 Koonjan

18 Joongoonjie

19 Arrinda

20 Yeeda

21 Wombya

22 Ulperra

23 Inchalachee

24 Adjadurah

25 Narrinyeri

26 Kurnai

27 Thurrawall

The use of social organisation as a basis for defining a 'nation' was common both to Mathews and to Howitt, although both also used initiation rituals as a basis. On this latter score, they alternated between using commonality of the *form* of initiation practice, and active participation in shared networks of initiation performances, as a basis for asserting that various sets of groups formed a 'nation'. It is clear, however, that sharing a type or form of initiation practice is a matter of shared customary laws and practices rather than a shared world of social interaction *per se*. In that sense, the two should not be conflated. One should not forget, either, that forms of initiation were not unrelated to forms of social organisation, but the earlier ethnographers did not tease out the implications of this fact in any detail. For example, moiety divisions tend to play an important role in initiations.

Actually it seems to be particular *combinations* of social structural and other cultural features which allow one to identify some of the more obviously coherent and distinctive regional systems. Certain extensive areas of south-eastern Australia, for example, were characterised by a widely reported classical complex in which were to be found matrilineal moieties, sections, matrilineal unlocalised social totems, single linguistic groups numbering several thousand (not just a few hundred) people, a *bora* (sacred ceremony) type of initiation system, emphasis on site-bound increase rites, a prominent religious and social role for medicine men of high degree who were believed able to fly, a belief in an 'All-Father' figure located in the heavens, fragmentary evidence of a primary recruitment to country through birth or possibly conception and, probably, a system of individualised lifetime site or tract tenure resting on an underlying communal estate title system. In the latter case it appears from some accounts that life interests in particular places were acquired through gifting or bequeathing, in some cases ratified 'through the *bora*', but not necessarily (in some places not at all?) on a principle of descent. This kind of complex was probably not confined to eastern Australia but at least several aspects of it, such as the combination of matrilineal social totemic clans, extremely large linguistic unities and some firm individuation of site or land entitlements, appeared in a different form in the south-west of Western Australia.

Howitt offered a rather curious definition of a 'nation' as a 'larger aggregate' where the word for 'man' was the same in all the relevant languages.[24] On the other hand he, like many others, also said that he was sometimes unsure as to whether a particular named group was a 'tribe' or a 'sub-tribe'. Presumably he would also at times have been unsure as to whether or not a middle-sized aggregate was a 'nation' or just part of a 'nation'. This emphasises the inadequacy of a simple dichotomy in each case.

In the 1970s there was some revitalisation of interest in the Aboriginal regions question. Nicolas Peterson's work especially emphasised ecology as well as culture and society. Peterson's emphasis in his 1976 paper was on populations occupying regional areas, especially drainage divisions, rather than on 'typological' aggregates such as peoples who shared common systems of social organisation, or common linguistic heritages. As he put it: 'The question is whether there are boundaries with natural significance and historical consequences, around regional clusterings of bands such that interaction among the clusters is greater than beyond, producing culture-areas.'[25]

Bands are land-utilising aggregates rather than typological units such as clans, language-owning groups or members of particular cult lodges, for example. However, in his maps showing correlations between drainage systems and Aboriginal groupings Peterson emphasised matches between linguistic territories and drainage when it came to the more localised maps. In general he did not attempt to align his suggested Australian culture areas with genetic linguistic subgroups. The proposals were very useful, although I think that further research will need to proceed from more localised studies outwards to the definition of larger areas such as most of those proposed by Peterson.

It is important to keep the interactive populations and cultural traits that suggest patterns of interactions such as common economic strategies and patterns of exploitation of resources, archaeological trade evidence and superficial phonetic features of languages, or 'art' styles, for example, distinct from culturally significant ethnic or structural entities. The latter include language-owning groups, riverine identity groups, or sets of groups who share common kinship systems, prescriptive marriage rules and other aspects of social organisation such as sections, sub-sections, matrilineal social totemic clans, and patrifilial totemic estate groups.

Ian Keen has been working on a large project looking at selected representative regions of Aboriginal Australia, and with a focus on economics and social networking. One of his central tasks is to examine regional networks of connection along a continuum from the more localised to the more regionalised to the continental.[26] Like many of us now, and indeed since Lauriston Sharp's time some decades ago, Keen avoids the illusion of a 'cookie-cutter' approach to Aboriginal society in which there are or were discrete, cell-like societies.[27] Keen, rightly I believe, recognises the whole of mainland Australia, at least, as a single ancient regional system. Within it, he has expressed strong doubts about endorsing notions of 'regional system' that suggest firm closure anywhere short of the ocean beaches. 'Local' and 'regional' are, as he argues, relative terms.[28]

And yet Keen is open to the empirical possibility that there are points of cleavage and discontinuity, what he aptly calls 'fissures and lesions', in the social, cultural, economic, marital and other communicative and culturally constructed fabrics of Aboriginal Australia.[29] Examples of this can be put forward, I think, with some solid empirical grounding. The great continuous chain of connections across the vast Western Desert runs into something of a crevasse at certain well-known points around the edge of its extent. One of the more dramatic of these is the eastern area in the region of Hermannsburg and the George Gill Range. Here the historical, linguistic, ceremonial, mythic and biogenetic evidence come together to reflect not just a discontinuity but a historically comparatively recent abutment of two varieties of Aboriginal culture and two originally distinct populations. In McConvell's view, this abutment is only some centuries, not thousands of years, old.[30]

THE REJECTION OF 'NATIONS'

Norman Tindale campaigned vigorously against the concept of Aboriginal 'nations'.[31] He was happy to write about 'intertribal relationships',[32] and made considerable use of the notion of the Western Desert (or 'Great Western Desert') as a regional sociocultural population area. Lauriston Sharp was also unconvinced by the utility of the 'nation' construct in the region where he conducted his in-depth research with Aboriginal people.[33]

Ronald and Catherine Berndt, for all of their many differences with Tindale, also rejected the term 'nation', along with 'confederacy'.[34] Of aggregates such as 'the Aranda', the Berndts said that they were 'linked tribes, or a cultural bloc, rather than ... one large tribal group'. The term 'nation' was not a happy choice of language as it 'suggests a degree of political unity'. The Berndts gave examples of the Western and [sic] Great Victoria Deserts, the 'Narrinyeri' confederacy of the lower Murray River, and the so-called Brinken groups of the Daly River area, as examples of linked tribes or cultural blocs.[35] The Berndts also referred, for example, to regional 'constellations'. These were comprised of 'dialectal units'.[36] From their various references it seems plain that the Berndts were referring to identity groups, or sets of linked identity groups, not interactive population sets per se, when writing of constellations. It is important to remember, however, that the larger the identity-based aggregate or constellation, the greater the likelihood that its members will also belong to a population whose members' interactions with others, including marriage ties, fall mostly within that constellation.

In more recent times the 'nation' term, if not the ethnological concept, has again arisen in Aboriginal affairs, mainly playing a role in political discourse. Thus the 'Larrakia Nation' of the Darwin area, for example, has attained sufficient currency to be the title of a formal organisation. Coordinated action at this level of several hundred people is not easy, however, and there are competing groups using the Larrakia title or rejecting that title in favour of another. For many individuals in such circumstances there is a tension between the greater political certainty of smaller groups bound by concrete ties of kinship and mutual familiarity, and the benefits of greater influence and visibility offered by collective action on a greater scale.

ABORIGINAL 'COMMUNITIES'

The term 'community' is used in several different ways in writings on Aboriginal people. One refers to what Barry Smith has called the 'geographic community',[37] which is basically the population of people at a particular Aboriginal settlement such as the many former missions or government stations, regardless of how socially integrated such a collectivity may be or how few of its residents may subscribe to a notion of the common good. This is a very common sense of the term 'community' as used in Aboriginal affairs. Newcomers to such places sometimes have to be disabused of the warm and cooperative images conjured up by the idea of a 'small community'. Nevertheless, those who have lived all their lives in such places can experience acute homesickness even when theirs is a community racked by serious problems of conflict, substance misuse and ill health. Attachment does not require harmony.

Such a community is at once a place, a population of residents (in some cases frequently shifting about, in other cases very sedentary), a collection of subsets of ethnic, territorial and other groups, a focal concentration point in a regional system of overlapping egocentric social networks, a local cultural milieu, a mini-economy, a rallying badge of identity in competitive and combative contexts such as football and fighting, a political unit both formal and informal, and a unit of local governance.[38]

Another sense of 'community' refers to an Aboriginal social field within the wider context in which it is embedded, such as the Aboriginal community of Sydney, or the Aboriginal community of Australia. While some members of such a community live together in a single house or street, most do not.

Like the geographic community, what I shall refer to as the interspersed community is normally a population that is not in any neat way coterminous with any formal culturally-based territorial, linguistic or religious grouping of the kind that typically attracts a name. 'Clans', 'tribes', 'language groups', 'patrifilial groups' and so on are categories of person, not residential aggregates. It is notable that most if not all native title determination applications have thus far been made exclusively, or in the first place, on behalf of non-residential categories of person, even where a local resident population is somehow covered or referred to in the finer detail or in a subsequent determination.

It is thus plain that the 'community of native title holders', however legally defined, is not going to be the same as, or even necessarily closely aligned with, populations living within determination areas or even at a nearby township. This is not to say that a residential community's members cannot form a significant class of legal native title holders, especially under the rubric of those who enjoy contingent rights.[39]

And while it may be true that for large determination areas, at the time of sovereignty, there was a far greater identity of holders of core rights with those frequenting the area physically, the evidence is overwhelming that core rights-holders were typically durable classes of persons whose members at any one time could be interspersed with others across a wide area in a number of separate camps. This is why a sovereignty-era 'tribe' or 'clan' was no more a residential aggregate than one of today, at the level of principles, even though identity groupings and interactive networks may have enjoyed a closer match. And it is also why such a 'tribe' or 'clan' or similar category of persons, if it is to be recognised as holding native title, is always likely to remain an interspersed community rather than a geographic community.

If, 200 years ago, people used their own country only for part of each year or in certain cases only for a part of their lives, both of which undoubtedly would have happened in my view, and people also regularly lived, foraged, cooked and extracted raw materials on country for which they denied having any claims of a proprietary kind, then to recognise 'use' of country as a native title right is to perhaps speak of two rather different kinds of use. A man who is digging for water is 'using' the country. The same man may sing about the same well during a ceremony 400 kilometres away in some other region where he is visiting for ceremonies. Is this not also 'using' the well, even if *in absentia*?

The singing of a religious song verse about a well *in absentia* might sound to some like a flimsy, abstract or ethereal stretching of the meaning of the humble word 'use'. On the contrary, starting the singing of the verse under ceremonial conditions may well be deeply integral to maintaining one's customary proprietary rights over the site, while getting a drink from it might be open to any bona fide traveller through the area. It is not the right to sing that is a native title right, but it may underpin, or provide evidence for, the right to exert authority over use of the land.

The 'community' of Meggitt's Walbiri (Warlpiri)

As we have seen above, there are several senses in which anthropologists have used the term 'community' in their writings. One particular technical use of the term is confined not only to anthropological writings, but mainly to the work of two scholars, Mervyn Meggitt and L.R. Hiatt. It is the former that I wish to focus on here.

Mervyn Meggitt thought of land 'ownership' in the Aboriginal context as being defined in essence by the exclusive right to reside on and make economic use of the land.[40] This was something distinct from the question of religious authority over sites or Dreaming tracks or local estates. According to Meggitt, it was not the individual residential food-gathering camp which was the locus of economic land rights among the Warlpiri of Central Australia; instead it was the 'community'. There were 'no individual or family possessive rights over tracts of land or waterholes', he says.[41]

Michael Niblett's 1992 thesis includes a valuable critique of Meggitt's assertion that land 'title' was held essentially by 'communities' in the Warlpiri case. The core of this critique asserts that Meggitt did not explicate adequately the land interests of communities *vis-à-vis* the ritual property interests of patrifilial groups and their *kurdungurlu* or ritual managers. A similar critique had already been advanced by Nicolas Peterson. Peterson pointed out that while Meggitt had said that the 'community' 'had custody of totemic sites within its territory'[42] there was no single community ritual, communities had no formal power structure, and ritual roles were primarily determined by real rather than classificatory kinship. The vital participation in such roles of affinal relatives of the patrifilial kin identified with particular sites in a community area often involved members of 'other communities', thus vitiating the notion that members of a single community had any kind of exclusive custody of its members' sites.[43]

Derek Elias's recent detailed study of the Tanami Desert offers much new information about developments in Warlpiri land relations and a commentary on Meggitt's 'community'. Meggitt's view, Elias said, was influenced by learning about the 'communities' *in absentia* from people settled at Hooker Creek. Had he had the advantage of extensive field mapping, as Elias has done, he would have formed a rather different view. The 'community' level of subgrouping was only one of several and was only used under particular circumstances during Elias's field work. There were no well-defined estates or indeed any well-defined other clusters of places forming sub-territories of Warlpiri country, although major places and Dreamings, for example, were used as reference points for referring to areas of land. Songline handover points at the edges of 'community' zones were not as fixed as Meggitt had imagined, and although they could be very important especially at transitions between different languages or systems of assigning rights in country, they were contested. They could also be understood as forging links between people by unifying different kinds of interests in common places, and in that sense they actually erased boundaries.[44]

Cultural practices and structures are thrown into particular forms of prominence where they are called upon in the pursuit of concrete objectives, and in some ways this is at the heart of the differences Niblett and Elias have noted between Meggitt's descriptions and those of more recent ethnographers working in the same region. In Meggitt's fieldwork period, Warlpiri were not concertedly pursuing concrete land uses across a broad spectrum of country, but were fairly localised or demographically concentrated; much of their vast region was for the time being unpopulated, and Meggitt's assessments of the nature of land-holding relationships were highly retrospective or 'reconstructionist'. A different picture may have emerged if Meggitt had been among the Warlpiri either while they were economically dependent on the land alone, or were pursuing current forms of legal tenure, decentralisation and resource allocations based on royalties and government transfer funds. His fieldwork coincided with a window between two distinct eras of concrete political action focused on land as a material resource base.

What did Meggitt mean by 'the community'? Although he described it as 'an active group and not merely a social category',[45] his own account suggests strongly that this entity is something of an abstraction in its 'social category' sense.[46] If its membership ever resided together in time and space it was seasonally restricted, in Meggitt's description.[47]

In my own view, on the internal evidence and in a strict all-members-present sense, it would have been at the best unlikely that a Meggitt 'community' would ever be assembled as one on the ground. For example, on the one hand we are told that during autumn and part of winter the community would congregate in one or two large groups. Yet these were coalescences of smaller food-gathering groups which he describes as 'too labile, too dependent on the changing seasons, the alternation of quarrels and reconciliations, the demands of non-agnatic relatives, and so on' to have been 'simple patrilineal and patrilocal hordes'.[48] It is hard to imagine the composition of a camp of 300–400 people remaining constant for three or four months of the year.

The Meggitt 'communities' were very unlike those of Howitt and Fison, even though both were at heart abstractions. The Meggitt 'communities' were subdivisions of a tribe, not tribes.[49] The 'community' names were also used to refer to countries.[50] Meggitt's Warlpiri countries were Waneiga, Walmalla, Yalpari and Ngalia. Later work in the same region by Michael Jackson resulted in a map which shows Warnayaka (Waneiga), Pirlinyana , Manyangarnpa and Ngarliya (Ngalia), not a close match, perhaps due to the passage of time, perhaps not.[51] It may also be oversimplifying to define the four Meggitt 'communities' simply as being 'Warlpiri' by linguistic identity. Some 'Warlpiri' sub-groups have mixed linguistic affiliations, sometimes to mutually unintelligible languages. They identify, for example, as Ngarti-Warlpiri and Warlpiri-Kukatja in the north-west, and as Warlpiri-Warlmanpa, Warlpiri-Anmatyerre and Kaytetye-Warlpiri in the east.[52]

Nevertheless, linguistic differences between such subdivisions were among the most obvious markers of cultural distinctions between them.[53] They were not definable by any statistically significant frequency of in-marriage versus out-marriage, although they were slightly endogamous (in-marrying) on the figures.[54] They were not sets of people bounded by mutual participation in joint initiation ceremonies.[55] Although a community's members were to be found living in different combinations at different times, in Meggitt's reconstruction of their bush life, as a whole they were a set whose members knew each other and had dealings face-to-face with each other at various times and places. This abstract set from which action groups were drawn was 'in many respects the maximal political entity' – again, one should read this, I think, primarily as a reference to a constituency rather than to an assembly.

Meggitt referred to community members as 'countrymen', as displaying 'in-group ethnocentrism', and indicated that they enjoyed solidarity in that they found scapegoats in other communities and protected fellow community members from attack.[56] Inter-community visits, unless by invitation, could produce feelings of embarrassment, shame or fear if travellers encountered tabooed persons unexpectedly, the environment being structured into regions of greater or lesser personal mobility. 'The whole concept bears a certain resemblance to the Lewinian notion of the life-space.'[57] This particular passage was the inspiration for Stanner's use of the term 'ecological life-space' as a gloss for his notion of 'domain', but Stanner used it in a much narrower sense as the intersection of a clan's estate with its members' range – a puzzling construct in that a clan, *per se*, did not have a range.

In spite of such action-based criteria as those just mentioned, these Warlpiri 'communities' were also collective identities which survived the 'displacement' and migrations of their members, at least for a time, and were thus not land-occupying groups in a simply immediate sense.[58] Meggitt considered that in time, new residential arrangements at modern settlements would facilitate the adoption of a new definition of the community. Both 'community' and conception-based attachments to country were thus subject to a kind of historical impact that 'lodge-dreaming affiliation' was not, and Meggitt considered that changes in the latter would probably occur much more slowly.[59]

Still, the limits to 'community' countries were not defined merely by habitual physical presence. Meggitt tells us that their boundaries were 'fixed, validated and remembered through the agency of religious myths'.[60] Such stories specified the places at which songs, rituals and designs should change hands, so that it would be possible to 'produce from such data a detailed map of the borders of the four countries'.[61] Furthermore, part of the community's title to its country and its resources lay in its members' collective memberships of ritual lodges, which were the sets of people identified with and responsible for certain sacred sites of particular Dreamings in segments of the community country, for 'lodge and community affiliation are commonly related'.[62] Sacred boards owned by patrilodges are associated with the Dreamings of the lodges and are 'maps' of the Dreaming countries and Dreaming tracks of a community country, 'so that the boards form part of a community's title deeds to its territory'.[63] In these features, the Warlpiri 'community' countries closely resemble religious units or estates, not ranges. Overall, Meggitt's descriptions may be broadly divided between the 'community' as a stable jural construction that outlives individuals, and which also functions as a political constituency, and the 'community' as an active entity composed of living individuals sharing a time and space.

In line with this ambiguity in his usage, there is evidence in Meggitt's work that the 'communities', or rather their names, were applied in two distinct ways in Warlpiri discourse: a strict or narrow way and a looser everyday way, the latter being an extension of the former and used in a rather weaker or perhaps less formalistic sense. The two senses severally reflected a 'fundamental difference' in what they referred to, not a blurred merging of multiple concepts into a single indeterminate one:

> Community affiliation depended primarily on birth (or, more strictly, conception) and subsequent residence in the territory occupied by the community and totemically associated with it. There were no ceremonies that facilitated the conversion of non-members into members. The fact of residence itself gave only economic, and not ritual, rights to immigrants. ...

Whereas in everyday life people apparently treated a long-term resident from another community (especially a wife) as a countryman, their actions at the death of the outsider revealed the *fundamental difference* in the latter's status. Classificatory kin of the appropriate categories might mourn and carry out the duties connected with the disposal of the corpse that close kin and countrymen normally undertook; but the avenging of the death still remained the prerogative of the deceased's *own matriline and natal community*.[64]

It is clear from Meggitt's work that men stayed in closer proximity to other men from the same 'natal community' than women did to women of their own 'natal community' because of patterns of postmarital residence.[65] Assuming Meggitt's major informants were men,[66] this may have coloured his account by creating in the evidence a stressing of the – perhaps retrospectively idealised – alignment of spiritual connections with residence. In any case, we have here a clear distinction between community of residence and community of birth that is maintained until death. The community identity of birth depended on descent and was portable. Co-residence with members of such a community yielded economic 'privileges' (see Chapter 1), not ritual authority rights or rights of intrinsic spiritual and cultural identification with the country of members of the 'natal community'.

One must consider it axiomatic that, of the two, it is the latter, not foraging rights, that would normally give rise to the assertion that a particular area is a person's own true or proper country. In this feature, the membership of a Meggitt natal community is just like 'patrilineal' group membership. Indeed, as he makes clear, the former is based upon the latter. Patrilineal group membership is the primary entry-point to the natal community, as it normally is also to primary language affiliation, although this is not to discount conception and matrifiliation as factors.[67]

Not only is patrilineal group membership one's entry-point to the Meggitt natal community, it is also one's entry-point to the political authority system of that kind of community. In Meggitt's own description:

> Although the members of the community conceded some of their fellows the right to co-ordinate certain activities, the ascription of authority to particular men on particular occasions depended largely on considerations of kinship status and, by extension, of descent-line and moiety affiliation.[68]

Given that the Meggitt 'communities' themselves, on the evidence, look rather more like aggregates of estate groups than large bands in their core and formal definition, and if we think of the 'community' countries as being like macro-estates, then it is justifiable to say that the Meggitt 'communities' are in principle presented to us very like a Radcliffe-Brown 'horde' and a Howitt or Tindale 'tribe' – namely, an amalgam (if not a 'confusion') of a formal cultural category with a supposed face-to-face population. Frances and Howard Morphy made a similar observation: '[Meggitt's] community title is really the debate between clan and band as right-holding groups projected onto a higher plane. Just as the band consists of members of a number of clans, so the "community" consists of members of numbers of communities since communities are not endogamous units...'[69] I think it very likely that this kind of amalgam was itself part of Aboriginal ideological discourse, and that ethnographers have been misled by it accordingly. Given that there is a feedback relationship between continued political presence and the maintenance or attainment of religious interests in country, I am not suggesting that the two can be regarded as analytically isolated from each other.[70] Nor should they be analytically confused. The amalgam probably lies in the way things were represented, rather than in how they observably were.

Groups of the (Meggitt) 'community' and (Tindale) 'tribe' size, namely those often in the hundreds, may lend themselves to such analytical blurrings between abstract categories and behavioural ones much more than smaller entities such as 'clans' and 'bands' do. Up to a certain limit, the larger the abstract set of people who belong formally to contiguous or adjacent countries, the more likely they are also to belong to an interactive set, a set of people who actually know and are 'used to' each other. It is thus more likely in such circumstances that such 'community'-level entities will be both religious and political in their foundations, in classical terms.

Meggitt tells us that a man's political status depended ultimately on which community he belonged to. His ritual status referred to which particular lodge of which community he belonged to. 'Lodge, and hence patriline, membership may be an index of community affiliation and, indirectly, of political status.'[71] There is a stronger version of the latter remark elsewhere in Meggitt's work:

> In short, patrilineal descent is the main determinant of lodge membership, which by inference also involves community affiliation. A boy is initiated into the lodge of his patriline, and this is almost always connected with a dreaming located somewhere in his own community country.[72]

Warlpiri patrilines had 30–35 members at a given time. Warlpiri 'communities' had up to 300 or 400 people.[73]

The 'community' of Hiatt's Gidjingali

A close inspection of Hiatt's data on his 'communities' of north-central Arnhem Land indicates that, in at least one sense, which I take to be the primary sense, these 'communities' were environmentally-based categories whose constituent members were land-holding units which themselves were composed of patrilineal subgroups, which he called patriclans. In this respect Hiatt's communities were not said to own land and in this there is a crucial difference between Hiatt's and Meggitt's 'communities'. Hiatt has recently written:

> With regard to land use and residential associations, my findings were similar to Meggitt's. Concerning ownership, however, I had no hesitation in ascribing primary proprietorial rights to patriclans. The estates that made up a community's domain

each belonged either to a single named patrilineal descent group, or to several such groups that had amalgamated to form a single land-owning unit.[74]

On the other hand, he asserted that 'communities' were the primary land-utilising group.[75] This is not to say that clan estates had no special economic status for their clan owners. Men tended to build fish-traps in their own estates, sharing the proceeds with the general camp. Between ceremonies small groups of kin and affines 'often left the main community for a while and lived by themselves on their own estates' – presumably those of the implied core of patrilineal kin. Hiatt drew attention to two other cases, of an axe quarry in Victoria and stands of *pituri* (a narcotic) in south-west Queensland, where resource exploitation was controlled by small local groups and the precious items were not freely available to the regional 'community'-scale population.[76] The same applies to Howitt's observation of special 'division'-level 'property' rights in the swans' eggs of Raymond Island in Gippsland.[77] To these I can add the coastal Wik distinction between open camping sites and 'secret waters' within any clan estate. Knowledge of the latter's where-abouts is said to have been formerly very strictly controlled and restricted to a small core of male clan elders. This appears to have been related to the estate's role as a fallback refuge during conflict.[78]

Hiatt presented a table showing the four 'community' identities of the nineteen land-owning units which made up the Gidjingali language group at the time of his research.[79] There was no suggestion by Hiatt that the relationship between the 'communities' and the land-owning units which belonged to them was anything but a relatively stable one. Hiatt did not suggest that a person's 'community' identity changed weekly or seasonally with shifts of camp residence. However, the evidence is somewhat perplexing.

Hiatt's introductory definition of the Gidjingali 'community' as 'a group of people who customarily moved about together' was followed by the statement that it normally consisted of men who belonged to one of a number of patrilineally constituted land-owning units which were the constituent elements of a community, plus the wives and unmarried children of such men.[80] He presented a table showing that such a community may include wives from outside itself and women of such a community may marry into another community. On his sample of two communities (Anbara and Nagara), more marriages occurred between communities than within them. Upon marriage women generally went to live with their husbands in the husband's father's area.[81] It flows from this that a majority of married women would at any time be living on the country of a community into which they had not been born. The question here is whether or not women relinquished their birth-community identity (and the patrilineal group membership on which it was founded) upon marriage to and residence with a man of a different community. The evidence (see below) seems to be to the contrary, and may also be implied in Hiatt's later use of the phrase 'natal community', familiar to us from the work of Meggitt.[82]

Hiatt at one point presented a list of owners of dwellings in a single clearing, showing that the seven senior men living at the five dwellings belonged to five different land-owning units which fell into three different 'communities'.[83] If these 'communities' were simply residential aggregates rather than forms of enduring identity this description would not be possible. The individual men in this case carried their 'community' identity with them wherever they camped, it would seem. The same applies to the six bachelor households at Maningrida, four of which included men of two different 'communities'.[84] The same would appear to apply also to those 'communities' which spent one or more months of the year living in the area of a different 'community' prior to settling at Maningrida. The Anbarra community for a month or so each year, around August, were guests of the Marawurraba community. In October–November five or six communities camped at a large swamp which belonged to members of only three communities.[85] It would follow that the 'communities' as described by Hiatt could not have been residential aggregates, nor even a set from which such aggregates (camps) exclusively or normally drew their personnel.

On his stated criteria, Hiatt's 'communities' were either residential aggregates such as one could see on the ground, or a population from which such visible aggregates would be drawn on occasion. The criteria are discussed, after all, under the heading: 'Residential Associations'.[86] But his listing of communities and their component patrilineal groups might convey the impression that communities were entirely made up of a limited set of small patrilineal groups whose estates clustered together in the same area.[87]

The 'communities' were subdivisions of a language group in the case of the Gidjingali language group, but in the case of four other language groups of the same area the language group as a whole 'formed the basis of a single community'.[88] The phrase: *the basis of*, may be a clue here to there having been a somewhat loose relationship between a local person's description of a residential aggregate as 'Anbara', 'Nagara', etc, ('community' names) and the actual community affiliations of the persons who lived in such an aggregate. A problem here is that some of the constituent patrilineal groups making up 'Gidjingali' land-owning units named languages other than Gidjingali as their primary tongue. There is thus no neat categorial alignment between 'community' and single-language affiliation in this case.

Furthermore, people did not switch primary language affiliation upon residentially joining a 'community' other than their own. Hiatt presents statistics showing very substantial proportions of inter-community and inter-language marriages.[89] Thus, even if we consider only married couples, the members of a single community (according to Hiatt) would be typically have been found living with members of a range of different 'communities'. It is therefore unlikely that such 'communities' were residential associations *per se*.

In his construction of the north-central Arnhem Land 'community', Hiatt may be said to have described a kind of grouping that in some ways resembled Radcliffe-Brown's 'horde', but at a larger scale of social grouping, rather as Meggitt had done for the Warlpiri. In doing so, Hiatt may have been swayed by the local idiom in which such 'community' names may be used on occasion to refer obliquely to a particular camp or contiguous set of camps dominated by members of such a 'community'.[90] Geoffrey Bagshaw, who has worked as an anthropologist in the same area for many years, confirms unequivocally that a Blyth River woman does not lose her own patrifilially-derived 'community' identity upon marriage and residence in her husband's country. Bagshaw calls these Hiatt 'community' names 'regional designations'. They translate as, for example, 'river mouth', 'grass plain',[91] 'mangrove fruit', 'tree blossom' and so on. These environmental terms refer to the typifying environments of the combined estates of their constituent patrifilial groups.[92] They are not sets of combined band ranges.

In Cape York Peninsula, among Wik people, it is also my experience that an environmentally- or location-based category of the same type can be used in both ways.[93] This is not ambiguity. It is a case of a primary and 'hard' usage that gives rise to an extended and 'looser' usage, on occasion. The root sense of the category remains the shared local environs in which particular subsets of owned estates are located. It does not primarily refer to the range of a band or coalescence of bands, or in essence to the estate of a single clan, even if some such 'nicknames' cover only a single estate and its group. Nor do those who belong to such a category normally constitute the set of all persons actually present in a camp or cluster of camps. Recruitment to these Wik categories, as in the case of the Hiatt 'communities' and Howitt's Kurnai 'clans', is ultimately by patrifiliation to a constituent or member subgroup which is a theoretically perpetual group identified with, and which is in a custodial relationship with, certain places and their sacra.

Gumbert's 'community' as a model for legal recognition

In 1984 Marc Gumbert, a lawyer with anthropological training, suggested that the emphasis of the Northern Territory land rights legislation was misplaced because it was based on small patrilineal corporate groups such as clans and lodges which were ideological rather than economic units. They were sociocentric rather than geocentric. The 'community' was the appropriate land-owning body, he argued, and he defined this entity as: '[t]his collection of people who, from time to time, exercise economic rights over the land or who have a variety of ritual rights and responsibilities over it...'[94]

Although paying heed to non-economic relations to land, Gumbert's primary emphasis, partly hinted at in the ordering of this phrasing, was on a model 'which commences with the land itself (the economic base)' and which thereby generates a grouping which is not 'sociocentric' but 'geocentric'.[95] While agreeing that a geocentric emphasis is better than a sociocentric one when carrying out an investigation of customary rights and interests in a tract of land, the privileging of economic rights in defining who should hold key decision-making powers over Aboriginal land seems to me to be flawed, not just ethnographically, but also in practical terms.

What Gumbert's approach failed to deal with was that ultimate control of land use in Aboriginal tradition is not, at its root, a matter of economic rights but of jural authority, something that is based on personal and group identity as well as achieved standing, and on mutual recognition of that identity and standing between members of different groups. It is from these bases that economic use rights ultimately flow. People with the same ordinary economic use rights, such as the right to forage, to get water and timber, or perhaps even to be compensated for the disturbance caused by forced relocation in the case of railway construction, are usually rather clearly divided between those who can also assert a primary right to make decisions about where buildings and roads are constructed, for example, and those who cannot. Gumbert's model seemed to combine the two into an internally undifferentiated community of legal landholders: '…if there is to be any use of such terms as "ownership" of land, then they should be used only where there is actual convergence of both ideological [e.g. patrilineal totemic clan] and economic rights.'[96]

Gumbert also said that 'there is no possible responsibility for the land below the level of the community'.[97] This ignores the contextual nature of responsibility for country and sites in Aboriginal practice, in that some matters may well be defined as simply the responsibility of a small set of people, while other kinds of events or proposals require wider sets of people to be involved in decisions.[98] In certain cases the wider sets may require people from a number of 'communities' or 'tribes' to take part in decisions that have regional repercussions.

One of the major problems with Gumbert's proposal, however, is that his 'communities' are not well-bounded and thus difficult to define: estate groups may have members distributed across more than one such community in terms of where they exercise their ordinary economic rights of foraging, and people change their geographic community of residence from time to time. Above all, members of groups responsible under Aboriginal Law for the lands concerned would be likely to object strongly to his proposal. Authority over decision-making for land use was not clearly distinguished, in Gumbert's model, from the possession of economic use rights such as foraging rights. Foraging may not change the physical or social environment itself in a dramatic way, at least in the short term, but modern decisions over land use are often concerned with excavating deep holes, mass clearing of vegetation, and the introduction of outsider workforces. To conflate all these with berry-picking and skink-roasting under the heading of 'economic rights' is to ignore the distinction between important business involving economic and social change, on the one hand, and business as usual on the other.

Povinelli's challenge to the culture/economy divide

The other anthropological book which goes to some length to criticise the *Northern Territory Land Rights Act* and suggest an alternative approach is *Labor's Lot* by Elizabeth Povinelli.[99] This book was in part 'an effort to challenge the theoretical divide between Aboriginal culture and economy'.[100] She also challenged the subordination of foraging to social and cultural expressions of land attachment, as it exists in the Act.[101] Her book is about the people of Belyuen, a community on the Cox Peninsula near Darwin. The people have detailed knowledge of the surrounding countryside, use it regularly for economic and religious purposes, have many biographical and spiritual links to it, and take much care of it. Most, however, at the same time maintain a primary form of identification with their ancestral homelands to the south around Anson Bay, from which they or their recent ancestors migrated to settle at Belyuen; many continue to visit and derive economic benefits from that homeland area. With the rarest of exceptions they are not prepared to say, in vernacular English terms, that they are 'traditional owners' of the Cox Peninsula area, unless they are among the handful of Larrakia people who are based at Belyuen. The Belyuen people have repeatedly acknowledged that the Cox Peninsula country is Larrakia country.[102]

Povinelli highlights the difficulties of such long-term residents in trying to have their interests afforded appropriate weight under the *Land Rights Act* regime, especially in a case where the majority of residents are of immigrant stock and the majority of those with ancient ancestral affiliations to the area live outside it. While highly sympathetic to these difficulties, I do not regard her analysis as one which could justifiably lead to a collapsing of the categories of ancestral affiliation and long-term resident.

THE ASSIGNING OF TITLES

A tension between atomism and collectivism not only affects the way a claim is researched and argued, but also the way it is put into legal concrete after the process is all over. Claims are usually made to areas of land and/or sea according to cadastral or administrative boundaries, although some follow geographic features dividing the claimed from the unclaimed. Typically the claim areas subsume parts of several different areas of land associated with distinctly definable indigenous groups or subgroups. The history of such claims has been that, while several groups may be recognised as successful claimants, courts and tribunals have not sought to partition the available land into sections for each of the groups severally when recognising or granting titles. While each group may claim only a portion of the block available, all may be found equally successful in law as claimants to the block as a whole, that is, to the block as a unit in the Australian land tenure system. This does not mean they all have equal customary interests in all parts of the land, far from it. The sorting out of administration of the block, once title is recognised, is left to the successful claimants and those others who may also establish such a relationship to the same land, in conjunction with their regional land council or similar body. Apart from the practical difficulties of arriving at enduringly agreed 'boundaries' within such a block – a situation that has almost never occurred, with the exception of the much-disputed internal partitioning of the old Hermannsburg Mission area – there can be no neat assumption of a closure of interests between 'neighbours' in such cases.

This may not always be the case. It is true that all these legal processes shift the emphasis of indigenous land relationships away from classical Aboriginal and Islander practice and towards codification or, at least, the recording of certain states of custom and consensus in a permanent medium. But one has to allow for the possibility that the relative indeterminacy of indigenous people's land relation-ships, as compared with the tenure systems of nation states – an indeterminacy that has long formed part of their traditions – may not always be something that indigenous people want to maintain in its fullness. The forcing of a vigorous oral tradition towards a document-based set of rights in land is sometimes perceived as unjust. It would also be unjust to deny people the right to move away from an inherently conflict-prone system towards the greater certainty and stability they might hope to achieve from engagement with the Western legal system. Whether this is a false hope, or a hope at all, remains to be demonstrated.

5 | Underlying and proximate customary titles[1]

WHILE ABORIGINAL LAND use patterns may have been fragile in the face of colonisation, and severe limits were consequently placed on Aboriginal people's capacity to physically enact local traditional entitlements on many lands, the basis and key content of traditional title to such lands is not fragile but has generally been maintained with considerable robustness. In this chapter I suggest that this robustness arises in a critical sense from the pre-existing and widely continuing dual structure of traditional land tenure, which may be understood as consisting of an underlying title held within the relevant regional jural and cultural system, which underpins proximate entitlements enjoyed by small groups of individuals.

The Australian *Native Title Act,* at section 223.(1), defines native title as the 'communal, group or individual rights and interests' in relation to the land or waters that are '*possessed under the traditional laws* acknowledged, and *traditional customs* observed, by Aboriginal peoples or Torres Strait Islanders'.[2] That is, the rights and interests derive from and are rooted in a wider set of living principles. These are also defined as rights and interests in the land and waters where the Aboriginal peoples or Torres Strait Islanders '*by those laws and customs*' must 'have a *connection* with' the land or waters. That is, it is not sufficient to establish just any connection, either by continuing physical occupation or in more cerebral ways. The connection must be derived from and rooted in the system of law and custom relating to country and country-related groups of people.

In the *Mabo (2)* decision, Chief Justice Brennan said:

> ...[W]here an indigenous people (including a clan or group), as a community, are in possession or are entitled to possession of land under a proprietary native title, their possession may be protected or their entitlement to possession may be enforced by a representative action brought on behalf of the people or by a sub-group or individual who sues to protect or enforce rights or interests which are dependent on the communal native title. *Those rights and interests are, so to speak, carved out of the communal native title.* A sub-group or individual asserting a native title dependent on a communal native title has a sufficient interest to sue to enforce or protect the

communal title. A communal native title enures for the benefit of the community as a whole and for the sub-groups and individuals within it who have particular rights and interests in the community's lands.[3]

Since the passing of the *Native Title Act* it is now the Act, not *Mabo (2),* that is the source of law on native title. The Act envisions two distinct but related kinds of whole-part dependency relationships. (I use 'whole-part' here in the logical sense, with no implication that a cultural entity has an ascertainable 'whole' in the sense of a putative 'complete' account by an anthropologist.) One is between particular rights and interests and the wider system of customary practices in which they are embedded. The other is between the rights and interests held in land or waters by subgroups or individuals, and the communal native title out of which they are 'carved'.

In this chapter I argue that these requirements themselves are in essence an accurate reflection of the relationship between wider Australian Aboriginal systems of land tenure and the granting of local entitlements under those systems. While there has been some debate as to how much of the detailed content of native title has to be proven in legal cases, there has been little debate about the Act's reflection of the proposition that 'Native title has its origin in and is given its content by the traditional laws acknowledged by and the traditional customs observed by the indigenous inhabitants of a territory'.[4]

ABORIGINAL LAW AND LAWS

Gaynor Macdonald has produced a good deal of evidence to show that the Bogan River Wiradjuri, acting as the Peak Hill native title claimants (New South Wales), have a sense of their own culture, rules and custom as a distinctive system.[5] An emphasis on this is not an artefact of the native title context. The short title of her PhD thesis, completed in 1986, was 'The Koori Way'. Constructs of the same type are well documented, not only for remote regions where classical traditions persist strongly, but also for people of rural and urban backgrounds not unlike those of the Peak Hill people, where those traditions have been subject to considerable historical transformation.

Jerry Schwab's PhD thesis on Aboriginal people of the Adelaide region was called 'The "Blackfella Way"', a reference to a particular complex of values, social rules, beliefs and style that carries customary–legal force in the area of obligations towards others and may be referred to as 'our Law'.[6] In far north Queensland the terms '*Murri Law*' and '*Bama Law*' (Aboriginal Law) embrace the same basic concept, and this Law governs, among other things, who has rights to land.[7] These concepts are arguably direct post-classical descendants of more classically framed and expressed notions that are usually translated into English as 'Aboriginal Law'.

Kenneth Maddock has published a brief review of such concepts, using as his examples the term *julubidi* in the Mardu region of Western Australia and the term *djugaruru* among the Warlpiri of north-central Northern Territory.[8] These terms typically refer to a body of designs for conduct, and range widely from religious acts such as 'going through the rules' (being initiated), to marriage rules, kinship etiquettes, the butchering of game, the making of fire and even forms of animal behaviour, for example.[9] Land law falls under the same rubric.

This should not be taken to suggest that indigenous terms for Aboriginal Law are vague or nebulous. Where well documented they are polysemous, that is, they have several related but distinct senses of different scopes, context indicating which one is in use. For example, the relevant term in Kayardild (Gulf of Carpentaria) is *birrjilka*, defined by Nicholas Evans as '1. Time, occasion; 2. Way, manner, pace; 3. "Law", way, custom; 4. Morals, way of living; 5. Something (event)'.[10] In the case of Arrernte (Aranda, Central Australia) John Henderson and Veronica Dobson define *atywerrenge ('tjurunga')* as '1. sacred objects; 2. sacred; 3. traditional law; 4. precious to someone, much-loved'.[11]

It is always integral and common to these concepts that the Law is something derived from ancestral people or Dreamings and is passed down the generations in a continuous line. In the Flinders Island language of Cape York Peninsula the term translated as 'Aboriginal Law' is *epiy-abiya*, literally 'from father and from father's father'.[12] Although transformations between ancient and modern practices are recognised by people such as the Wiradjuri of 'settled' Australia, their customary land law still has this same essential feature of being something that derives much of its authority and sanctity by being conceived as a body of principles transmitted down the generations from elders to younger people. In the case of a Wiradjuri subgroup such as the Bogan River people (or 'Peak Hill mob') their own customary land law is embedded in a wider regional system of similar cultural institutions.[13]

It is useful to try to be precise about the way local entitlements to land can be said to be derived from a wider set of customary laws and cultural principles held by members of the social field or network concerned.

'Laws and customs' derived from a set of wider living principles

This notion can be understood in two ways, both of which are relevant here.

First, a particular land-related law or custom[14] may be shown to be part of, and embedded in, a wider set of such laws and customs that in some sense cohere among themselves, and are also held in common by a particular group of people. It is in each of these distinct senses that the system may be said to be a whole system underpinning a communal title, rather than merely an accidental set of principles or practices found across a population. This is important to interpreting the terms 'possessed under' and 'confer' in sections 223(1) and 225 of the *Native Title Act*.[15]

Second, a particular law or custom, or a local group's system of laws and customs to which the particular law or custom belongs, may in turn be shown to be part of and embedded in a geographically and socially wider set of similar such laws, customs or systems. In normal Aboriginal terms, the proprietary relationship, or occupation as of right, is usually the state from which specific rights, interests and responsibilities flow. If members of surrounding groups are asked if a certain person has the right to fish or hunt somewhere, or, more critically, if they have a right to assert control over the area, they would be expected to first want to know what country, and thus whose country, is being talked about. The proprietary relationship is not built up from fragments of rights and interests. It is usually the other way around.

The need to show how laws and customs are derived from a *normative system* has direct implications for the nature of evidence in native title and similar cases.[16]

In the first place, where one is trying to show that a particular customary rule or practice is part of a locally coherent system possessed by a group, and the system has been acknowledged by the group and its antecedents in a substantially uninterrupted and consistent form since pre-covereignty, it may be useful to show that several such laws and customs are and were related to each other in principle. For example, the right to assert that one is Wiradjuri, and from a particular Wiradjuri subgroup identified with a particular river system, may be recognised only if one meets certain criteria, such as a licit form of descent from a Wiradjuri forebear of the appropriate subgroup, combined with active involvement in the group's affairs upon reaching adulthood. That one meets such criteria may be established on the principle that elders of the relevant community know and accept one's genealogical position in a certain family, and know and accept one's degree of involvement in the affairs of the community.[17] This may be the basis on which speaking possessively of the land is considered proper or improper, or the basis on which one may be delegated to take public responsibility for looking after the cultural heritage of the group and its land, for example in transactions with the National Parks and Wildlife Service.

This principled basis, however, may be shown not to be restricted simply to matters of landed identity. It may also be the basis on which sexual relationships are considered legitimate or illegitimate in the group, or it may be a prerequisite for certain kinds of political office. In such a way, one could show that a specific strand of rights and interests is constituted by a law that is part of a system of like laws. They constitute a system because their licitness and enactability rests on, and in that sense is derived from, and rooted in, common principles that drive much of the group's customary–legal behaviour across different domains (property, marriage, public office). Whether or not people have such rules as a matter of regular contemporary practice, or largely as unrealised ideals, or only as memories of the past, or something in between, can be relevant to the fortunes of their case. So also can be the question of whether or not such rules have remained substantially the same since pre-sovereignty.

It is a basic principle of ethnography that where there is a superficial patterning in speech or behaviour, this may well be evidence of a deeper system at work. It is important to pay attention, for example, to the specific language of land relationships when trying to understand those relationships. Let us say that by careful observation there seem to be three roughly equivalent ways of speaking of the most fundamental level of connection to land, in a particular group from New South Wales. First, people use possessive constructions (*my* country, *their* place,

Granny's home) or are in a sense said to be possessed by places (we *belong to* Dubbo really). Second, people use ablative constructions (she's *from* Wagga but lives in X, he's *really from* Trida, my people are *originally from* Murrin Bridge). Third, people use juxtaposition (they're all *Bourke mob*, the *Wanaaring fellas*). This type of discourse would suggest a land relationship system in which the salient and highly compatible principles were: *possession, origin,* and *identification.* This system of principles of connection to land, at this underlying level, seems not so different from those of more recently colonised parts of the country in the interior and far north. The deeper the principle, the less likely it is to be confined to smaller regions.

But there is another side to such systems, namely the way assertions deriving from them are policed. In a modest sense such statements are policed as to their idiomatic naturalness, their grammar, and the definition of what contexts are appropriate for saying them at all. These are sociolinguistic rules, and they are integral to culture. One could properly describe them as 'customs'. But such statements are policed in a stronger sense as well. If the same people have regular ways of controlling false or exaggerated statements put in this type of language, by shaming people, by socially ostracising them, and so on, then they clearly have a system for distinguishing licit from illicit claims of connection to country. That is, sanctions apply. This itself is a critical part of the system of laws by which they are connected to land. Such a socially broad-based policing system belongs to the wider social domain, not just the level of local entitlements to small parcels of land.

To return to the earlier discussion: there is thus a second sense in which a particular law or custom may be shown to be part of a system. That is the regional sense. It is normally the case that one local group's laws and regular practices, including those which underpin its entitlement to publicly identify with a particular traditional country, are only part of a web of similar laws and practices in the wider region. For this reason it can be useful, in legal proceedings for establishing native title, to call witnesses from surrounding groups, who are recognised senior members of them, who can testify (as non-claimants) as to the propriety of the claimants' evidence and claims. This is not to suggest that there is a fixed 'council of elders' for each of a set of regions, but there is sometimes remarkable agreement on the subject of who the authoritative elders are within any particular context.

This 'witnessing' can be most useful on two fronts. First, 'neighbours' can assert who are the right people to identify with the area in which the claimed land falls, and can usually give a name for them or at least name the main kin groups concerned. They may also give a general statement of how far such a claimant group's interests extend geographically. Such people may also state why they themselves are not claimants, and may say that for them to be claimants would be in contravention of Aboriginal Law. Secondly, they may also give very useful evidence as to the lawfulness, under Aboriginal custom, of the claimants' evidence. Their role is not so much to corroborate or assert the veracity of the statements of autonomous others, but to enact their rightful role as keepers of the regional system which holds in its ultimate gift the local entitlements that are under discussion. This is one of the reasons why such elders are often referred to, in Aboriginal English, as 'the Law men' or 'Law women'. They have supra-local, regional roles in relation to local land and other matters. This social role itself reflects the local/regional duality of rights and interests in land.

UNDERLYING TITLES AND PROXIMATE ENTITLEMENTS

The indigenous customary laws and cultural practices of mainland Australia that give rise to traditional land tenure, are arguably dual systems that recognise both an *underlying title* and a *proximate title* in land. In the first draft of this chapter I referred to these as radical and beneficial titles respectively. Lawyers who commented on that draft tended to suggest these terms be replaced, in order to avoid confusion with their function as key terms in Australian and other English-based land law. 'Underlying' is particularly apt in the sense that Aboriginal people will sometimes refer to the Dreaming as 'underground culture', as they did in the Elliott (Northern Territory) region in my experience.[18] I use the term 'proximate' in the senses '1. next, nearest; 2. closely adjacent, very near; ... 4. next in a chain of relation'.[19]

The living holders of specific traditional land interests, often now called the 'traditional owners' in a vernacular sense across much of Australia, hold title to those lands in the proximate sense, while underlying titles are maintained by the wider regional cultural and customary–legal system of the social networks of which they are members. The distinction I make here is akin to, but clearly not the same as, the distinction in Australian law between radical title and beneficial ownership.

A more closely related distinction has occasionally arisen in the literature for Aboriginal tenure systems. Marie Reay referred to '*residual rights*' held in the estate of an extinct clan by others of the same semimoiety in the Borroloola region of the Northern Territory.[20] In that region such rights are central in facilitating succession to estates vacated by other groups. This analysis has gained further support from subsequent work in the same region by David Trigger.[21] Nancy Williams, writing of North East Arnhem Land, distinguished '*radical title*' to a clan estate from 'a specific and subsidiary right in [small parcels of] land' vested in a group other than the owning clan by a procedure of formalised 'granting'. No 'absolute right in perpetuity is entailed; the continuance of the grant is subject to renegotiation at any time'.[22] Ian Keen described the same process in the same region as the granting of rights of 'ownership' of small areas within a clan estate, 'while the "*root title*" remains with the clan of the encapsulating estate'.[23]

These usages refer to constructs that are different from the underlying/ proximate distinction I wish to explore here, although they perhaps indicate that a common principle of layering of entitlements may operate at a number of levels within Aboriginal land tenure systems. The cleavage I discuss here is one I regard as foundational, however.

Underlying title in the case of Aboriginal customary law consists of the cultural and jural constitution of a particular area of land, including

- its geographical limits and/or focal points as a unit of tenure or a district;
- its internal structure (e.g., drainage subsystem, ecological zone, etc.);
- its association with markers of a particular cultural identity (e.g. a particular language, a subsection couple, a focal residential centre (campsite, old mission, etc.), certain totemic entities, site-specific myths, songline verses, sacred objects, etc.),
- its characteristics as a form of property (e.g. not being available for treatment as an alienable commodity, the communal basis of its tenure); and
- the acceptable norms by which claims as of right may be made over it by Aboriginal people (e.g., a certain kind of descent from former landholders, conception, modes of ceremonial incorporation, long residence combined with other preconditions, etc.).

These and other components of the underlying title may be established in evidence for the purpose of legal proceedings such as a native title determination application, whether or not the land concerned has, for the time being, living claimants with unambiguous primary entitlement to it. Since this kind of situation must have occurred countless times pre-sovereignty it would appear to be an onerous situation if the law were to demand that all areas under claim must have living proximate holders of rights and interests. Uncompleted succession to a vacated proximate title or a proximate title in dispute between rival groups are both contexts which make it plain that underlying title may be distinguished from any current state of active claimancy. Where rival groups have radically different understandings of the content of the underlying title, in the sense laid out above, they will probably have more of a legal problem in establishing their claims than if they merely disagree over who should hold it. In my experience, while rival groups (and even non-rival groups) often have differences about the cultural content of a particular land area, they do tend to agree on much or most of it and tend to coincide strongly on what should count as jural principles in the recognition of customary proximate rights in land. Ian Keen repeatedly cites evidence of variation between different versions of myths, song interpretations and other land-related cultural forms in North East Arnhem Land, but at the same time emphasises the fact that Yolngu have a form of social organisation and religion in which there are many universal categories and symbols and predominantly agreed ways of dealing with land tenure.[24]

Proximate entitlement entails the right to publicly claim the particular country concerned and to exercise the rights, and fulfil the custodial obligations, that flow from such standing. While proximate entitlements of particular human beings may come and go, the underlying relationships between foundational Dreamings and certain landscapes are theoretically eternal. Particularly in remote Australia, the entitlements of people to places are usually regarded as at their strongest when those people enjoy a relationship of identity with one or more Dreamings of that place. This is an identity of spirit, a consubstantiality, rather than a matter merely of belief, but it is still in one sense a pendant relationship: the Dreaming pre-exists and persists, while its human incarnations are temporary.

In some ways this pattern resembles the doctrine of tenure in English law, under which the Crown holds radical title to all the land over which the Crown has established sovereignty, and all property interests of those other than the Crown are 'held of' the Crown. 'Tenure' derives from Old French *tenir* which in turn is cognate with Latin *tenere* 'to hold'.[25] In feudal-based legal terms, 'tenure' does not refer to the holding of the land but to the relationship between Paramount Lord and tenant.[26] Land in Australian law is thus 'held of' the Crown, not held absolutely, unless by the Crown. While such 'held' interests come and go and are transformed from time to time, the radical title may go on undisturbed. This fiction of ultimate ownership by an individual office is nonetheless legally real, just as the superorganic constructions of the Dreaming or Aboriginal Law have reality in Aboriginal culture and society.

Similarly, underlying Aboriginal titles are always present if the system of traditional land relationships persists, whether it does so in a conservative, classical form or in some post-classical, transformed way that has evolved more recently but which is still rooted in the classical. Underlying titles are usually enjoyed in the proximate sense by extant groups, but for various reasons they may not be instantiated in this form at all times, or even at all. Extinction of landed groups and out-migration may leave country untenanted for a time. (I do not refer here to physical absence from the land, but the absence of active claims as of right over the land, whether made *in absentia* or not.) The area may then be described by some Aboriginal people as 'orphan country', that is, country lacking living or competent custodians who claim it as their principal estate, even though individuals or groups from surrounding areas may be active in looking after it as regents.[27]

The survival of an underlying title over a parcel of land is not vitiated by the temporary disappearance of local proximate title-holders. In terms of the *Native Title Act* the reverse may not be true. That is, for the local, proximate native title to endure as such, it must ultimately do so on the grounds that the society in whose culture it lies embedded maintains the relevant system of 'the traditional laws acknowledged, and the traditional customs observed'.[28] This does not mean, however, that regencies of active custodianship over vacant estates must be in place in order for the underlying title to remain alive within the regional land tenure system. People will sometimes say of a vacant estate: 'Nobody is looking after it at the present time'. The estate nevertheless retains a 'good' title in the sense that its cultural and jural definition as something to be claimed endures, and a successor claiming it 'properly' must do so under Aboriginal customary laws.

The wider regional social and cultural system in which Aboriginal-defined parcels of tenurable land subsist is not in general manifested as a formal adjudicatory body consisting of permanent offices. In Aboriginal practice it is typically objectified as 'the Law', which in this particular context refers to the sacred pattern integrating land areas with totems, Dreaming tracks, languages and other defining features of one's geopolitical landscape, a pattern that was laid down 'forever' at the foundation of the world. People do not make the Law. While senior practitioners of this Law may be, and often are, called upon to play a key role in influencing the outcome of debated cases of succession to vacant estates, or boundary disputes, for example, they do not usually arrogate to themselves a role of formally 'representing' the regional tenure system in which they have become eminent. However, by playing such roles they emphasise the relatively unitary regional character of the system of underlying titles.

The regional Law, rather than a group of elders or 'tribal council', is what has proximate land entitlements in its gift. That is, the wider system maintains the underlying titles while at the same time it maintains the principles and lawful procedures by which proximate entitlements are allocated to or achieved by living people. This is, of course, hypostasising. I am treating a cultural system as if it were an actor, a controlling being, just as the English doctrine of tenure was founded on the fiction that all the land belonged to the Sovereign.[29]

This is indeed how Aboriginal tradition treats it also: the Dreaming Law, Blackfella Way, Koori Way, Murri/Bama Law, are what Ian Keen has called 'a control practice or institution, that is, an organised set of long-term and short-term, specific and diffuse actions, coordinated roles, and a body of norms. ... The overall control effects are not achieved by any one action, although individual actions are indispensible'.[30] The Law may be an intersubjective construction, but it is not simply an analytic construct of anthropological study. For those who live by it, it is regarded as a permanent reality beyond individual human agency.

Gerontocratic authority, as Myers says of the Pintupi, is legitimised as the carrying on, following up and passing on of the Law and looking after the young, and thus as the responsibility to mediate a taken-for-granted cosmic order.[31]

> In Pintupi representation, what we might call 'public goals' and legitimate injunctions of personal autonomy at the collective level existed, as it were, prior to society itself. Far from being able to rightfully coerce their juniors in personal matters, the norms, rules, and constraints older men could be said to represent and speak for to juniors were not the product of their wills; from the Dreaming, they were imperative for all.[32]

Definitions of 'all', in such a context, are something of a minefield. I agree with Ian Keen that neatly bounded collective social universes in Aboriginal Australia do not exist, and that network-based models of sociality are for many purposes much more appropriate.[33] (But this is not to say that Aboriginal collectivities, however lacking in neatness of boundaries or agreement on their status, are not to be captured by anthropological analysis but displaced only by attention to networks.) It is also clear from the evidence that transitions between different Aboriginal Law systems, and, in particular, areas of distinct and abutting land tenure arrangements, are sometimes graduated, sometimes rather abrupt, but tend to be managed through the bicultural skills of those living along the edges of such differing systems.[34] There are occasions when such differences are great, especially where people with only a recent history of non-Aboriginal contact assert their own Law in contradistinction to that of the weakened and disarrayed populations they have encountered on their exodus from the hinterland.[35] This type of disjunction raises serious questions for applicants in native title cases, especially if a claim is contested by groups who do not recognise, or only partly recognise, each other's systems of customary land law.

Even where two adjacent regional populations hold to the same essential principles of land tenure, and agree on the character and content of underlying titles in the zone known to both of them, cases may still arise when their senior practitioners disagree over the allocation of proximate tenure to a particular area or estate. This occurred, for example, in the case of some Stormbird Dreaming sites on Muckaty Station in the Northern Territory. Senior men from the Tennant Creek region controlled this songline from just north of Muckaty and south for a long distance. Senior men from the Elliott region to their north controlled it south from about Mataranka for a similarly long distance to just north of Muckaty. In the early 1990s senior members of the two regional ceremonial regions disagreed firmly over the allocation of members of one particular patrifilial group to the holding of Stormbird sites on Muckaty itself. These men had traditional interests in both regions. The Tennant Creek and Elliott men were both 'claiming' them at the same time.[36]

Such cases are less problematic for claimants, in my view, because it is not difficult to establish the content and coherence of the underlying title, and there is an expectation that even members of different regional systems can come to accommodations over such disagreements, over time, and in some kind of customary-lawful manner.

This principle of the chartering of the local by the regional is perhaps figured, among other things, in the very many founding myths of the different regions of Australia. In these myths, what typically occurs is that a heroic ancestral figure or pair of figures travels across the landscape, allotting land areas to particular groups.[37] Quite often a superordinate mythic figure is explicitly not only the founder of cultural diacritica such as language but also of the Law, as in the case of Ngurunderi on the Lower Murray River.[38] Like other 'mythic instigators' of this level, Ngurunderi originated from outside the region of his greatest fame. Perhaps this pattern of external origins reflects the distinction of the underlying Law from its instantiations, since the ideology that normally applies to holders of established proximate entitlements to land is that they have been there since the start of everything, and immigration is denied. By contrast, for founding major Dreamings, a story of an initial immigration or passage through the known region is extremely common.

Local landed groups are not *sui generis*, but are perceived as being, from their foundation, members of a multiplicity of like entities which belong to a coherent regional cultural system. W.E.H. Stanner wrote, in relation to this theme:

> When everything significant in the world was thus parcelled out among enduring groups, the society became made up of perennial corporations of a religious character. ... The religion was not the mirage of the society, and the society was not the consequence of the religion. Each pervaded the other within a larger process.[39]

The wider Aboriginal land tenure system and society holds underlying titles in, as it were, a communal wellspring from which individuals and groups may establish local entitlements by way of birth, conception, ancestry, succession, ritual incorporation and so on. And the communal nature of the title is not vitiated by the fact that a local land-owning group may, at times, be reduced to a single individual, or, in cases of succession, when the replenishment of an extinct estate-holding group begins with the conception or succession of a single person. The title retains its communal character even in its proximate embodiment, a point explicitly recognised in the Queensland Aboriginal Land Act which defines a 'group of Aboriginal people' in part as: 'if there is only one surviving member of a group of Aboriginal people – that person'.[40] One would expect the same principle to apply in certain native title contexts.

The main bodies of evidence for the general proposition that Aboriginal land tenure may be understood as consisting of two main levels, the underlying and the proximate, seem to me to be the following:

- the status of estates of recently extinct proximate title-holders, prior to completed succession;
- the status of estates subject to disputed proximate title;
- the distinction between public and private lands or sites;
- the role of regional elders in validating proximate entitlements;
- the possibility of the divestment of proximate entitlements by regional elders, voluntarily by out-migration, and retrospectively through genealogical forgetting;
- the relative stability of geographic units of land affiliation, in the face of group extinctions and fissions;
- the linguistic evidence that classical conceptions of landholding emphasise custodianship, belonging and landed origin rather than absolute ownership.

I will deal with each of these in more detail in the following sections.

Continuity of underlying title during processes of succession

When a local land-holding group dies out, as indeed happens from time to time in Aboriginal Australia,[41] their erstwhile proximate title may be without living holders for some time, perhaps even a generation or more. Customary devices for succession to it, and for the recognition of both individual and collective 'regents' who look after the local title in the event of delayed succession, are well documented.[42] Where succession to a vacant estate remains unresolved, there is no hint that the land has ceased to be an estate, with all the economic, spiritual and other cultural content to which a title-holder would be entitled. It is not 'no-man's land', or exposed to the unilateral assumption of occupation-as-of-right by some far-distant group that has no existing connections to the area, simply because it has been 'orphaned'.

There is in fact very little reliable evidence of 'conquest' or the forcible unilateral takeover of land by Aboriginal groups although a number of cases are on the record.[43] It is certain that it is sufficiently abhorrent to Aboriginal people for the very suggestion to have been met by many blanket denials, duly reported in many ethnographies. Also uncommon, and perhaps contingent on dramatic events of depopulation such as epidemics (or colonial conquest in the last two centuries), is the filling of territorial vacuums by uninvited migrants. Both forms of change in proximate tenure would normally, one expects, be succeeded in time by the restoration of a sense of lawful standing for the incoming groups as landholders, or as residents with lesser rights than landholders, or their rejection.

The status of estates subject to disputed proximate title

If native title is just the ability of living people to legally establish their entitlement to possession and use of land or waters, then an unresolved conflict between rival groups over a parcel of land might suggest that no native title could there be found. But conflicting parties in such cases will normally agree that there is a 'thing' to be fought over which includes the land physically but which is also something more abstract than the land and, from an anthropological point of view, is culturally constructed.

Just as a deceased person's freehold title may be 'good' legally, in spite of being fought over by the recently bereaved, so also may a native title be both 'good' and subject to mutually exclusive claims. This is a prime reason why I argue that mediations and adjudications over Aboriginal traditional land ownership generally should not seek to compile invidious 'complete' lists of individuals as landholders, but should instead recognise the processes, categories and principles that generate the relevant proximate entitlements within the regional system and from the underlying title.

The distinction between public and private lands or sites

Observations from widely different parts of the Australian continent indicate that, in the absence of local resources or remarkable features, areas on the periphery of local estates or Dreaming track areas are typically either shared by adjoining landed groups, or perhaps regarded as the property of all the locally linked groups, and at these zones the abutting estates lack specific boundaries. This is true both of Arnhem Land and Central Australia.

In Central Australia anthropologist Olive Pink gave the results of field observations made during travel with senior Arrernte people across country by camel. She specifically addressed the question of clan estate boundaries and so-called 'no-man's land'. While the totemic sites of a clan's estate were strictly respected by non-owners as if they had been pastoral 'boundary posts', typically poor and waterless country at the outer edges of estates was also typically lacking in associated sacred songs and paint designs and was held in common as 'tribal land' rather than as the 'private' land of particular clans.[44]

This rather unusual record is suggestive of a plane of tenure at the supra-local level that emerges in, but is not confined to, a specific context (boundary phenomena).[45] My view is that it may reflect a cognate principle to that of the dual system of title to which I am referring here, or an instance of it.

A related phenomenon may be the basis of what Gerald Wheeler described, based on his Australia-wide literature survey, as 'tribal overrights'.[46] His sources indicated that while small areas were subject to ownership by small groups, all members of the 'tribe' to which such groups belonged had a general right of access to each other's estates, and thus the 'rights of families or of individuals, as also those of the local group, were, in general, subject to tribal overrights'. Trespass was a serious offence but generally consisted of members of one tribe entering the territory of another, although it was important to bear in mind the loose way the term 'tribe' was so often used.

In western Cape York Peninsula it has been recorded that certain 'main places' (*aak mu'em* in Wik-Ngathan)[47] were available more or less freely for use by members of visiting groups with countries elsewhere in the same immediate region, but such people were not able to camp of their own free will at other more private places in the same estates, including the 'secret waters' referred to earlier.[48] Within *aak mu'em* the visitors might, for example, have regular shade areas allotted to them, and I was able to map some such places.[49] Someone once defined *aak mu'em* for me as 'just like a pub', that is, a public or shared space. Although these are statements about use rights, not tenure *per se*, they represent aspects of the formalisation of usufructuary rights within estates which may be held by those who do not claim the estates as their own. These statements also exemplify the widespread ethic of reciprocity that permeates the use of estates. This ethic and the intervisitation involved make it 'normal' that people know a great deal about each other's countries. This knowledge is important in enabling them to maintain a regional, rather than estate-bound, common system of constituting the cultural and ecological content of estates and of how they should be used, spoken for, and otherwise dealt with lawfully.

The role of regional elders in validating proximate entitlements

In a number of land claims heard in the Northern Territory and Queensland jurisdictions, elders from groups with country surrounding that of the claimants have appeared and given evidence. Not only do they typically vouch for the claimants' claims, they often also deny that they themselves are entitled to make any claim in the case. Especially within a claimant group, elders may also vouch for the standing, as traditional landholders, of those 'diaspora people' who have been physically alienated from the country to which they are entitled through descent and affiliation. In one Northern Territory case, a group of male elders drawn from the relevant wider region gave evidence which did not support a group's claims, but the group was nevertheless legally successful.[50]

It is too limited a view to understand this practice simply as external corroboration or credentialling. These elders are from *within* the regional system of authority in dealings with land, and their roles are integral to the maintenance of the 'system of law and custom' in which underlying title persists, if it persists at all. Their denials of local entitlements in the countries of others are denials of proximate title. They are not denials that the speakers are guardians of the wider, underlying system of title, and I argue that this is one of their key roles. As members of the wider kin network they can legitimately influence the public acceptability of claims of proximate entitlement.

Regional elders assemble from time to time to deal with conflicting land claims, usually with a view to helping settle them. I do not regard this as merely a recent development, although depopulation during the colonial era combined with cultural change and emerging new opportunities for establishing legal title have no doubt accelerated the need for such assemblies in recent decades. While it became fashionable for a while to deny that 'councils of elders' existed in classical Aboriginal traditions, the evidence for some kind of widespread system of assemblies of this kind cannot be ignored.[51] Even in the absence of explicit accounts in the older literature detailing land tenure dealings engaged in by such assemblies, the role of the senior jural public in religious matters is a commonplace theme in the ethnographies, and land tenure is at the heart of the religious system. It is inconceivable that assemblies of elders would meet to discuss religious matters, including sacrilege, without also addressing disputed land claims, questions of succession, and similar perennial and serious land tenure issues whose resolution is so typically framed in terms of religion. Even T.G.H. Strehlow, who was much inclined to stress the autonomy of Arrernte estate groups ('njinanga sections'), once described a land tenure succession dispute in Central Australia and then commented: 'The conflicting arguments were irreconcilable; neither of them was supported by sufficient legal authority to win general acceptance.'[52] This cannot possibly have been an intra-estate group matter, and here Strehlow explicitly acknowledges the role of the region's senior men, in this case, as those whose understanding of customary law had to be met by the opposing aspirants to succession.

Proximate title may be 'revived', when an estate-holding group has become extinct, so long as the underlying customary title continues and there are people in some kind of authority (or at least there is an acquiescent wider social network) able to eventually reassign it to proximate title-holders or accept their assumption of it.

In some regions tangible signs of the title to an estate include sacred objects. At times they may be held in the custodianship of a region's ceremonial elders pending the revival of living memberships for estate-holding groups that have become extinct. For example, a child may be conceived in the relevant area and thus become the founder of a new-old group holding the local title involved. Eventually the child may become the recognised holder of sacred objects relating to their estate. The same may apply to paint designs, songs and other sacra, which together may sometimes be called 'title deeds'.[53] The child itself cannot make claims over such sacra. They are bestowed on the child by decision of their elders and often with elaborate devices of divination.[54]

In the Roper River region, as in a number of others, young or even adult people may be 'put into country' (not their country of birth) during ceremonies conducted by senior ceremonial practitioners, and at such times sacred objects related to the country may be made for them.[55] In this way vacated estates may have their proximate custodianships restored, not by personal choice or whim, but by a collective, and collectively enacted, decision made by some subset of the region's senior Law people. Material symbols of this bestowal relationship mediate the new arrangements. These are perhaps concrete examples of the underlying/proximate distinction at work in daily practice.

The phenomenon of inter-group competition for individuals is another relevant example. As we saw earlier in the case of two Stormbird men from the Tennant Creek region, where two somewhat different broad regional land tenure systems and language types abut, they were 'claimed' by the collective ceremonial interests on each side of a regional ceremonial divide. In the same area, and involving the same two regional networks, some years ago a man from one group was killed by a man from the other. The compensation exacted, or perhaps offered and accepted, was that the father of the killer 'gave' him as a replacement son to the father of the man he had killed, who then incorporated him into his own land-holding group. The person thus bestowed retained a certain ambiguous landed identity nonetheless. His ancestral origin was not entirely erased by his re-identification through a form of fostering.[56]

The possibility of the divestment of proximate entitlements

I have a small but persuasive body of case material which indicates that, from time to time, the primary local entitlements of a group may be reduced or forfeited, not merely by the usual well-documented processes of reproductive failure or long-term out-migration, but by a communal decision authorised by elders of the region. If these cases are widely representative, which is unclear, in the final analysis no local entitlements are mechanistically and inalienably acquired, no matter how stable might be the rules under which they may be received and, in turn, passed on. Strictly speaking, all proximate title interests are ultimately maintained by consent, and lack absolute inevitability. This is not to say that people's proximate title interests chop and change rapidly – far from it in general – but merely to characterise the outer limits of the system.

One of the reasons why the divestment of or withdrawal from proximate rights and interests is possible is that individuals all have multiple legitimate pathways to rights in several different local countries, often because they have remembered ancestors from several different countries. That is, the 'withdrawal' of local tenure rights from a small group by wider consensus does not leave them landless, but usually shifts their primary focus elsewhere. Indeed the arguments used in these cases, and in the much more frequent cases of disputed local tenure, tend to be of the sort: 'They are not so connected here, this is only their mother's mother's country – they're really more from over there, where their father's father's country is.' These are cases of shifting emphasis, but occasionally a group's or individual's local proximate entitlements can be withdrawn completely. W.E.H. Stanner said that totemic disinheritance was 'not really possible', but went on to cite cases where the children of men who married wrongly were said to 'lose' their paternal totems, and he knew personally of one case where a man had abandoned his totem and publicly declared his intention never to return to his clan country. 'There are rules, both religious and secular, governing acquisition [of totems], so that a person's totem could be said to be a matter of right, but public ascription and agreement (disputes do arise) both seem necessary conditions.'[57]

Linked to these rather rare cases of withdrawn or reduced rights, is the practice of reducing a person's publicly acknowledged estate links after their death, a practice ritually made plain in the Victoria River District, according to Deborah Bird Rose.[58] This often means that they may basically transmit one particular set of local estate interests to their descendants, even though, while they were alive, they activated strong interests in two or more estates (e.g. father's, mother's, father's mother's). Without some such means of retrospective pruning of links, the system would have to face the spectre of individuals claiming and attempting to service interests in as many as sixteen different estates from their various great-great-grandparents. Rose's point is that in one region, at least, such pruning can be public and communally formalised. This is a form of retrospective divestment, at least for the purposes of focusing which rights will be passed on to successors.

Until the advent of written genealogies, most Aboriginal people have been able to ascribe multiple estate interests only to people of their parents' and perhaps grandparents' generations, if that. If the country interests of a great-grandparent is known, they will be in a single country, even though in their lifetime that person might have held three or four estate interests. It is also sometimes the case that an individual who exercises interests in a number of countries to which they are connected by ancestry or some other legitimate pathway will decide to relinquish one or more of those interests whilst still alive. If they are a senior person they might do so almost unilaterally, but where ceremonial obligations are involved this would be more difficult.

These occasional instances of reduction or effective removal of proximate title interests from individuals or small groups, including cases of self-divestment, again reinforce the notion of a distinction between underlying and proximate titles. They should not be understood as cases of the alienability of land. It remains impossible, under Aboriginal systems, to treat land held under customary law as a commodity or chattel that can be wholly alienated by sale or exchange. In the cases known to me, people may succeed to local proximate title by some lawful pathway, or may be divested of it by some customary process, and in that sense the people, rather than the land, might be regarded as potentially alienable.

The relative stability of geographic units of land tenure

The classical Aboriginal approach to the geographical definition of units of land tenure is highly conservative, especially in the better watered parts of the country. That is, there is a documented tendency for these units to be maintained in essentially the same shape, or at least focused on the same key sites, over long periods. The role of drainage in stably demarcating such units is probably one aspect of their capacity to endure.[59] On the evidence, though, I am not convinced that a comparable model of 'units of land tenure' can be applied to much, possibly any, of the Western Desert, except on its outer fringes such as immediately west of Hermannsburg.[60]

In western Cape York Peninsula, in a detailed, field-mapping-based study of traditional land interests, including disputed succession, I found that, in spite of the somewhat ragged facts of local claimancy in a number of cases, '[t]he shape and content of the territories remain relatively constant and unambiguous, and provide a matrix for ecological and political stability'.[61]

In the Princess Charlotte Bay region of south-eastern Cape York Peninsula detailed mapping combined with linguistic research has shown that the local clan estates, the smallest territorial units of the area, have very ancient names, most of them probably centuries old. This conclusion arises from the fact that, on a very large sample, they frequently have different but historically cognate names in several of the languages of the region. These differences among cognate terms indicate their continuing use in those languages over the centuries during which they have been diverging from a common original stock. A significant number of the clan names are based on particular names of focal sites or areas within the estates.[62] The clan names, if not their memberships, appear to have been highly stable.

Erich Kolig found that in the Kimberley region of Western Australia there was always the possibility of a land-holding clan becoming defunct, but the estates of such clans tended to be maintained as distinct:

> As soon as a clan had effectively ceased to perform its life-maintaining duty of tending the land it was in charge of, others had to fill the gap – and they did not hesitate. This development did not result in a clan's actually expanding its land holding. Those of the clan who were most closely affiliated with the new locality took over. However, within a few generations the ties between the two splinter groups and the recognition of a common origin would disappear since actual genealogical memory is traditionally very shallow.[63]

This accords with my own findings for the Cape Keerweer region of Cape York Peninsula, where evidence from clan totems, totemic personal names and language affiliations suggests very strongly that certain pairs of clans with geographically separated estates were formerly, in each case, a single clan with a single estate, although this origin is forgotten.[64]

In writing of North East Arnhem Land, Ian Keen was at some pains to correct the existing ethnographic impression that the area had 'rather clearly defined groups with determinate estates', and said that Yolngu people 'contested the definition of country, as well as rights over it. The definition of country was not "objective" but relative to a person's perspective, interest, and loyalties.'[65] He also said that the rich coastal countries tended to have spatial definitions on which people agreed more than they did in relation to inland areas, and the moiety and group identities of these coastal areas were less subject to dispute.[66] He confirmed that the 'identity and location of focal sites are fairly consistent through the literature on the region, although "clan" identity is not'.[67] As the literature in this case dates back to the late 1920s, this indicates that at least the geographic cores of the countries and their more important Dreaming identities have been relatively stable in the record for more than seventy years.[68]

In the pastoral district of the upper Roper River region of the Northern Territory, Francesca Merlan found a pattern of continuity of territorial boundaries, this time at the level of land units affiliated with particular language groups:

> This situation strongly suggests that 'Mangarayi country', conceptually associated with the Mangarayi language, has in fact been much more stable an entity, at least over the past several generations since contact, than has the personnel. ... The boundaries of Mangarayi country are permeable, so that new personnel may be recruited to it.[69]

Peterson's theoretical model of long-term changes in relationships between estates and ranges allowed for the expansion and contraction of estate sizes, but he nevertheless regarded a particular size relationship between estates and band ranges as 'modal'.[70] While it has been suggested that demographic decline in a land-holding group might result in a diminution of the size of its landed estate,[71] documentation of such cases has not been substantial. Nor has that of the amalgamation of estates into other estates.

Amalgamation does occur regularly in one sense, in that heavily impacted regional groups whose sub-group estates become vacated extensively and suddenly may assign conjoint succession to all of the vacated estates by those surviving in a few of them, as in the case of the Malak Malak of Daly River, the Yiithuwarra of eastern Cape York, and the Larrakia of the Darwin region.[72] But in these cases, even where an old vacant estate is still remembered, it is not combined with an estate of a surviving sub-group, but swept into the pool of the surviving regional or language group's overall territory.

The point here is that the system of localised land units is maintained by the custodians of a regional system, and the locations and focal areas of the units tend to be stable over time. That is, the wider system is far more stable than the identities of those who are recruited to fill the slots in the system from time to time. This is further evidence of the robustness of the underlying system of titles, rooted in and policed by the relevant wider social network, as compared with local entitlements held proximately by small groups or individuals.

The linguistic evidence

The linguistic evidence suggests on balance that classical conceptions of land-holding emphasise exactly that: 'holding', custodianship, belonging and landed origin rather than the kind of private ownership associated with chattels. Possession, in the ordinary sense, is nevertheless clearly implied.

In Aboriginal languages, possessive constructions are often used to describe the relationship between a person or group and their land, hence expressions that may be translated, for example, as 'my/your/his country' (using, for example, dative or genitive pronouns), or 'Topsy's country' (name + dative, name + genitive or similar).

There is also a frequent expression, which can be translated as 'own country', where the same word meaning 'own' is typically used also for one's relatives (for example, one's own family). There are similarities here with English, as in 'looking after your own', 'best wishes to you and yours', and the dialectal 'our Onslow'. In some languages there is a close connection, even homonymy, between expressions for 'own country' or 'owner of country' and 'own relatives'. For example:

Pitjantjatjara (Western Desert): *ngura walytja* 1. (one's) own place; 2. owner of a place, person who belongs there; from *ngura* camp, home, place, site, country, and *walytja* 1. a relative, someone you care for and who cares for you; 2. owner, someone who takes care of something; 3. doing something oneself.[73]

Eastern and Central Arrernte (Central Australia): *apmereke-artweye* an owner of land inherited patrilineally; someone who belongs to a country; from *apmere* country + *-ke* 'for' and *artweye* 1. owner; 2. one who belongs to a Dreaming, ceremony or song; 3. relations, ancestors; 4. a particular relation.[74]

Relatives are people one possesses (one 'has' a mother, nephew, etc.) but not as property or chattels. Relatives 'belong' to each other, although not as property. Something of this reciprocal claiming is also evident in the case of land – Aboriginal people often say they 'belong to' their country as much as it belongs to them.

These are all indications of a broad kind of proprietary relationship to land, and it is not often contested nowadays that certain traditional Aboriginal land relationships may be described loosely but correctly as forms of 'ownership' or examples of a system of 'tenure'.[75]

In many languages regular locutions may refer to the person/country relationship without using possessives, as in the case of:

Kayardild (Wellesley Group, Gulf of Carpentaria): *dulkuru dangkaa* (literally 'country person'), idiom: 'boss of country', 'owner or custodian of territory or sacred site'; (plural: *dulkuru-dulkuru* (country + reduplication)).[76]

Pitjantjatjara (Western Desert): *ngurara* 'resident, local, person that lives in a place'; *nguraritja* 'someone that belongs to a place, traditional owner' (from *ngurara* + *-(i)tja* 'of, from').[77]

Many Aboriginal languages have other regular locutions that consist of a place or country name plus some affix or similar device that indicates a group of people jurally related to that country:

Flinders Island language (Cape York Peninsula): *Yalgawarra* (members of clan holding *Yalga* estate); *Aba Yalgaya* (people from *Yalga* estate); *Walmbarrwarra* (members of clans holding the many constituent estates of the *Walmbarr* region; the *Walmbarr* 'nation').[78]

The relevant verbs in Aboriginal languages are most often those meaning to 'hold', 'look after', 'be in charge of', 'come from', 'belong to' and so on. Few, if any, Aboriginal languages have a verb that corresponds to English 'have' or 'own'. For example:

Nunggubuyu (eastern Arnhem Land): *warnaga-* 1. to hold, grasp; 2. to be in charge of (people, country, ritual). This is the closest Nunggubuyu verb to English 'have'. *lhal-warnaga* to hold or be in charge of country.[79]

Wik-Ngathan (Cape York Peninsula): *kooepe-* 1. wait for; 2. look after, hence [also] possess as country, totem; *poenche-* 1. descend into; 2. belong to (country).[80]

In 1978 I wrote, in relation to the people of the Cape Keerweer region (Cape York Peninsula):[81]

> 'Owning' land in this sense is spoken of [in Wik-Ngathan] using the verb /*kooepan*ha/ which means 'to look after, wait for, wait upon, guard'. The other verb of possession is /*pi'an*ha/ which describes holding of any kind, including possession of a wife, but does not apply in this situation. Thus land tenure is more a type of established custodianship rather than inalienable or alienable possession. The possessive pronouns used in this context are more frequently oblique than genitive [ie. the forms used are more often benefactive rather than truly possessive in meaning] (e.g. /*aak thananta* rather than /*aak thananga*/, 'their country'). Established custodianship of this kind, which is the target or archetype of person–land relationships, must be distinguished from 'minding the country' for someone else.[82]

More recently, in about 1993, a senior Cape Keerweer man steeped in classical traditions but also a committed and practising Christian, spoke to me with some sadness, mixed with anger, about a dispute then raging between local groups over the tenure of a particular estate. He then said: 'Brother, we don't *own* the land. We are the *stewards* of the land. *God* owns the land'.[83]

A somewhat similar syncretic view was reported in 1996 as coming from Jean George of Napranum (Weipa, Cape York Peninsula), while visiting Canberra to witness the High Court proceedings in the Wik case: 'Before they came to mine the place it was our land and it's still our land… We're not fighting for their land, we are talking about our land. The land was given to us by God.'[84] Ian Keen reported local Christian Revival leaders in Arnhem Land asserting, in the late 1970s and early 1980s, that 'God gave the various people of the world their lands, and God entrusted the ancestors with countries of Yolngu groups'.[85] The question arises, then, as to how independently such landholders, or those with only a classical Dreaming-based cosmology, may act.

HOW AUTONOMOUS CAN LOCAL LAND-OWNING GROUPS OR INDIVIDUALS BE?

I consider the answer to this question to be: Not at all in absolute terms or in principle, as far as assertions of tenure are concerned. In operational or day-to-day terms there is less autonomy for those who come from the harshest deserts than there is for those come from the better-favoured environments, given desert-dwellers' legendary mutual dependency in a marginal environment.

In relation to the Pintupi of the Western Desert, Fred Myers wrote:

> Identification [with country] is an ongoing process, subject to claim and counterclaim, dependent on validation and acceptance or invalidation and nonacceptance. ... Such rights exist only when they are accepted by others.[86]
>
> The primary basis on which identification [with country] is established is conception. Through such an incarnation, an individual is considered to be identified substantially with a place, as a mutual transformation of the same creative activity of The Dreaming. Yet however rooted it may be in the cosmological facts, identification becomes meaningful only when validated socially. It must be actualized and accepted by others through a process of negotiation.[87]

Most other Aboriginal systems, even those of the northern neighbours of the Pintupi, the semi-desert Warlpiri and Warlmanpa, exhibit lesser degrees of operational negotiability for land affiliations. In the latter region, the land claim book for a Northern Territory land claim over Muckaty Station reads:

> It would be tempting to regard the patrifiliates of Muckaty-area Dreamings such as Milwayi, Ngapa, Wirntiku or Yapayapa as in some sense the 'basic' landowners under Aboriginal tradition in the region. This would be neat and uncomplicated, and would resemble the European type of land tenure in which individuals or corporations hold exclusive title to discrete parcels of land. The actual system of relations with land in the region is far more subtle and complex than this.
>
> No Aboriginal country is an island. It exists only as an element in a system of interrelations between landscapes and the kin associated with them. Indeed, without such relationships, the countries themselves have no particular reason for existence. They are essentially relational in function. Just as the words that belong to the class of 'verbs' or 'nouns' in a language are defined as such only because of syntactic relations between subjects, objects and indirect objects, so the nature of 'countries' in this region is constituted by the relationships between people, Dreamings, ceremonies and places. These relationships are not enforcible paper contracts but states of mutual assent between people that are subject to continual, if gradual, renegotiation. These states of assent are not merely symbolised in religious imagery but are frequently attained and maintained through the very process of creating such imagery in the organisation, diplomacy and decision-making that make ceremonial events possible.
>
> The heart of the Aboriginal land tenure system in the Muckaty region thus lies not within the cell-like structures of the countries but in the local clustering of shared rights and interests in country, both agnatic and uterine, that provide the cultural, religious and political context for these apparent 'units'. They are not so much units, or self-existent territorial entities, as the bones of the system which, when articulated, make up the body of the system. Just as there is no system without its constitutive building-blocks, so there are no Aboriginal territorial building blocks without the wider set of relations between regional kin and landscapes in which they play their part. A brick is a brick because of the way walls are made.
>
> The customary use and exploitation of land, and decision-making about land in the new bureaucratic environment which is now so insistent, are also never by

intention or even common usage carried on by members of highly local country groups exclusively. Again, knowledge of the land is never in principle that of members of the local country groups exclusively. This pattern is general. The local countries provide an elemental structure over which the real determination of authority over land is actually played out.[88]

In retrospect, and with regard to the last sentence above, I would now say that 'real authority' over the definition of local land ownership will often be a matter of negotiation, in the sense that there is typically a dialectical interplay between the drive for local autonomy and a respect for 'the Law' of the wider society. Local autonomy may have more ideological emphasis than can be sustained in real life. T.G.H. Strehlow spent a lot of time emphasising the autonomy of Arrernte clans in relation to their estates (*nyenhenge* sections) in Central Australia.[89] On the other hand, he published richly detailed accounts of joint, large-scale involvement of members of many different clans in dealing with cases of sacrilege, including punitive action.[90] He also said that religious authority extended into the secular realm.[91]

Wider 'jural publics', moreover, are recruited differentially to adjudge particular events or contests and are thus context-dependent 'aggregate structures'.[92] What is not so labile is the Dreaming content of country, the geographic definition of sites and cores of estates, the linguistic identity of country, and the rules for recruitment to local estate-holding groups, which these wider publics and their senior practitioners know and apply to cases of disputed proximate title.

Small local groups often act with great autonomy in relation to land *use*, and such cases might be thought to alter the cast of my general argument. I will cite one example:

> In the early 1990s a small group of traditional land holders in the Western Desert region cut a private deal with a small mining operator to allow him to dig up chrysoprase on a Dreaming track. Strong disapproval among others in the region soon developed as many were highly critical that a few people had 'gone it alone' and had also agreed to the mining of a sacred site, thus literally 'breaking the Law'. There was also much criticism that the men concerned had failed to negotiate through the regional land council and had done the deal 'through the back door'. It became a case of a small group versus the rest of a large regional population. Talk of spearing and ensorcelling the offenders abounded but nothing apparently eventuated. In due course the regional land council held a meeting close to the mine site. At this meeting the decision to allow the mine was endorsed. The offenders were, in 1996, still held in a degree of opprobrium, however, and the verse of the song referring to the site has been deleted.[93]

This was not, of course, a case about land ownership but one about site use and site destruction. Nevertheless it seems that, even where a region's senior people disapprove, local forces may prevail in the contest between localism and regionalism. We cannot know how the region would react to a repeat offence in this case, so we also cannot know how long local forces could continue to prevail in the teeth of widespread opposition. It seems that the wider consensus in the region is that mining proposals should be dealt with through, and with, the legal and other support of, their land council. Here is one of many instances of a desire to engage with modern bureaucratic institutions in order to present the buffer of a regional will to pressures originating from outside, and local self-interest originating inside.

In regions heavily impacted by colonial and post-colonial developments, it is sometimes the case that some people maintain proximate entitlements to small areas such as classical estates as well as an identification with more widely-cast landed entities such as language groups; but at the same time others from the same region may maintain only the wider form of identification with land. Such a situation may lead to conflict. In the *Birthday Mountain* land claim in Cape York Peninsula this particular distinction came to a head when the claim was lodged solely on behalf of a small descent group within whose estate the claimed land fell in its entirety. This claimed land was part of the southern Kaanju language group area. Other southern Kaanju people lodged a subsequent claim over the same land. Just after the conclusion of the hearings the two sets of claimants came to a signed settlement to the effect that they agreed the southern Kaanju as a whole had traditional affiliation to the claimed land, the small descent group were the owners of the land under Aboriginal tradition, and the latter were therefore the appropriate people to act as trustees and grantees of the land under the *Aboriginal Land Act (Queensland) 1991*. This was reflected in the Tribunal's compromise recommendations, namely that (apart from a cemetery reserve) the land be granted in fee simple to the southern Kaanju, and that members of the small descent group be appointed as the grantees of the land as trustees for the benefit of the southern Kaanju as a whole.[94]

Here was a case in which an assertion of autonomy by a group holding proximate title failed, not completely, but partially, and as a result of the assertion of interests by those speaking for a wider group that included them. Spokespersons for both sets formally agreed that each had a specific form of right and interest in the land. Although the legal intermediary process was novel, and may have thrown interested parties into some disarray, it seems that some ancient principles concerned with the dual nature of customary title did emerge.

In writing a chapter such as this, one is always wary of engaging in 'codification' of tradition, or what Francesca Merlan has called 'the regimentation of customary practice'.[95] My intention has been not to encourage that practice but to try to stimulate debate and new insights into the fraught process of legal recognition of customary practice. Any legislation aimed at granting or recognising indigenous land and marine tenure, once enacted, immediately creates problems for those who wish to understand such entitlements in all their complexities, indeterminacies and contradictions, but who at the same time are assisting in their presentation and explanation to a tribunal or judge. The reductive impulse is usually something to resist as far as possible, but it is still an art form: one can schematise well, or badly.

Simple oppositions, such as the one I have considered here between underlying and proximate titles, easily sweep the complexities of real life under a rug. On the other hand, without the occasional broad generalisation it is difficult to advance discussion of a subject by anything other than slowly gained inches. We may take courage from the fact that failed hypotheses are often fecund ones.

6 | The system question[1]

INTRODUCTION

In THEIR reasons for judgement in 2002 in the *Yorta Yorta* appeal, three justices of the High Court of Australia expounded their decision on one of the more difficult issues in the native title regime. This was the question of whether current native title claimants may be found to be acknowledging traditional laws and acknowledging traditional customs even if those laws and customs have changed or diminished substantially, or there have been breaks in the transmission of those traditions, since the time when British sovereignty was established over the area in question.

They said in part:

> [I]t is important to bear steadily in mind that the rights and interests which are said now to be possessed must nonetheless be rights and interests possessed under the traditional laws acknowledged and the traditional customs observed by the peoples in question. ... For the reasons given earlier, 'traditional' in this context must be understood to refer to the body of law and customs acknowledged and observed by the ancestors of the claimants at the time of sovereignty.
>
> For exactly the same reasons, acknowledgment and observance of those laws and customs must have continued substantially uninterrupted since sovereignty. Were that not so, the laws and customs acknowledged and observed *now* could not properly be described as the *traditional* laws and customs of the peoples concerned. That would be so because they would not have been transmitted from generation to generation of the society for which they constituted a normative system giving rise to rights and interests in land ...
>
> In the proposition that acknowledgment and observance must have continued substantially uninterrupted, the qualification 'substantially' is not unimportant. It is a qualification that must be made in order to recognise that proof of continuous acknowledgment and observance, over the many years that have elapsed since sovereignty, of traditions that are oral traditions is very difficult... [B]ecause what

135

must be identified is possession of rights and interests under traditional laws and customs, it is necessary to demonstrate that the normative system out of which the claimed rights and interests arise is the normative system of the society which came under a new sovereign order when the British Crown asserted sovereignty, not a normative system rooted in some other, different, society. To that end it must be shown that the society, under whose laws and customs the native title rights and interests are said to be possessed, has continued to exist throughout that period as a body united by its acknowledgment and observance of the laws and customs.[2]

At the time of writing, the decision in *Yorta Yorta* represents the state of the law on the question. It sets the bar rather higher than had previously been considered appropriate by many practitioners in the native title field. Some would say that it has moved the law closer to the 'frozen in time' approach under which 'traditional' is considered to refer to how things were pre-sovereignty, but with the qualification that contemporary systems of customary rights in land and waters need only be 'substantially' the same as their pre-colonial predecessors. Many Aboriginal people and supporters of a generous view of native title have tended to find this view of *Yorta Yorta* extremely disheartening, concluding that claims made in 'settled' Australia rather than remote outback areas will now be doomed by a standard of proof that it will be impossible to achieve. Others take heart from the Court's statement that '[a]ccount may have to be taken of developments at least of a kind contemplated by that traditional law and custom. Indeed, in this matter, both the claimants and respondents accepted that there could be "significant adaptations". … [D]emonstrating some change to, or adaptation of, traditional law or custom or some interruption of enjoyment or exercise of native title rights or interests in the period between the Crown asserting sovereignty and the present will not necessarily be fatal to a native title claim'.[3]

The Crown acquired sovereignty over most of the Australian continent in a series of acts beginning in 1788 (eastern Australia) and ending in 1879 (some Torres Strait islands), although most of the continent came under British sovereignty in 1788 and the three subsequent largely western legal expansions of 1825, 1829 and 1831.[4] For all indigenous Australians there have been significant social and cultural changes in the relevant period. Whether or not these changes may prove fatal to their claims for recognition of native title in any one case is a matter for empirical argument, but there is inevitably a certain subjective element in deciding what constitutes substantial continuity of a normative system of rules and practices of a society over time. The subjectivity issue was confronted in the first *Yorta Yorta* appeal. There the Federal Court majority rejected the appellants' assertion that the test of whether a law or custom is traditional is a subjective test, saying instead that it was 'principally an objective test. The primary issue is whether the law or custom has in substance been handed down from generation to generation; that is, whether it can be shown to have its roots in the tradition of the relevant community.'[5] One could argue, however, that 'in substance' and, in relation to the High Court decision in the same matter, 'substantially', are words that may have different meanings to different people. There is no detailed criterial test for such a thing, and it is hard to see how such a test could be devised that would enjoy broad support.

In comparing present-day customary Aboriginal country relationships with those that can be reconstructed for the time of sovereignty one normally finds that changes have occurred, ranging from modest to substantial to thoroughgoing. If the classical country relationships were systematic and quite rigid in form, regularly enforced and held more or less unchanged over eons, then even substantial transformation, let alone utter rupture and reconstitution, might be considered out of character in terms of Aboriginal tradition. If, on the other hand, those classical arrangements for recognising rights in country were generally less systematic, or very fluid and flexible, then, one presumes, substantial and perhaps rapid transformation into something very different would not of itself necessarily result in currently observed arrangements being no longer regarded as 'traditional'. But anthropologists have put forward contrasting views on how systematic, and how fluid, Aboriginal traditional country relationships were or are. This chapter engages with those contrasting views.

THE SYSTEM QUESTION

Until fairly recently, one of the main tasks of anthropology as a discipline was to provide systematic and reliable accounts of how different societies resolve the problem of maintaining a reasonable amount of social order, one in which the passions of self-interest, sexual desire and aggression, for example, are channelled and delimited rather than allowed too destructive a liberty. Kinship, social organisation, the distribution of property, succession to office, the regulatory role of religion and sorcery, were therefore typical of the major concerns of anthropology in its classic period.

In studying societies that lacked written laws or separate judicial and policing institutions, and especially acephalous societies such as those of Aboriginal Australians, a great deal of attention was paid by scholars to the rules and collective organisational practices which stood between the populace and anarchy. It is significant that two of the three main founding figures in the emergence of modern anthropology in the mid-nineteenth century, Lewis Henry Morgan and Sir Henry Maine, were lawyers who took an interest in what was systematic and rule-driven in relationships between people, group identities, offices and property, among a wide range of societies.

Particularly since the 1960s, the anthropological project has broadened dramatically and one can no longer say that the discipline is particularly concerned with understanding the maintenance of the social order. This period coincides with the final ending of the isolation of most small-scale societies from the reach of the nation-state and its capacity to impose order externally. Even where social organisation continues to be of anthropological interest, that interest has for some time been one that can pay as much attention to the processes by which social institutions are evaded, reconstituted and imagined as it does to the way they are structured, how they are maintained sometimes over vast periods of time, and what they do for their members – as anthropologists will confirm, structuralism and functionalism have long since become devil worship. The very use of the notion of 'systems' sometimes looks as if it also might follow them down the same drain.

There has been a positive and general shift in Australianist anthropology away from structuralist emphases on relatively rigid social and cultural forms, and on cellular and segmentary analyses of those forms as if they were objects in space-time, towards greater recognition of their negotiability and fluidity as meanings. I have been in the habit of calling this the Seventies Corrective, but in fact, as Nancy Williams has pointed out, such a shift, at least in so-called 'hunter-gatherer studies', has been apparent since at least 1966.[6]

In this chapter I argue that in some of the literature on Aboriginal society, and especially as it relates to land and marine tenure, this pendulum has swung so far that, for some writers, 'fluidity' has acquired the status of an almost obligatory descriptor in spite of the ethnography of the case, and there is sometimes a kindred and, in my view, unjustifiable tendency to ignore or play down that which is systematic in Aboriginal cultural and social life, as a matter of principle or perspective rather than on empirically justified grounds.

In the context of native title claims, the issue cannot be ignored. The High Court in its majority decision *Mabo v. Queensland (No. 2)* referred to native title as resting not only on 'traditional laws and customs' but also on a '*system* of rules' or 'the overall native *system*'.[7] There is as yet no detailed and explicit legislative or common law yardstick against which evidence must be tested in order to support findings that the laws or rules enunciated by native title claimants or explored in anthropological evidence constitute such a system. Nor is there, to my knowledge, any consensus in this field as to what might count as a *system* and what might not. The High Court in *Yorta Yorta* has cautioned as follows:

> Indeed, reference to a normative 'system' of traditional laws and customs may itself be distracting if undue attention is given to the word 'system', particularly if it were to be understood as confined in its application to systems of law that have all the characteristics of a developed European body of written laws. Nonetheless, the fundamental premise from which the decision in *Mabo[No.2]* proceeded is that the laws and customs of the indigenous peoples of this country constituted bodies of normative rules which could give rise to, and had in fact given rise to, rights and interests in relation to land or waters. ... Of course, those rights and interests may not, and often will not, correspond with rights and interests in land familiar to the Anglo-Australian property lawyer. The rights and interests under traditional laws and customs will often reflect a different conception of 'property' or 'belonging'. But none of those considerations denies the normative quality of the laws and customs of the indigenous societies. It is only if the rich complexity of indigenous societies is denied that reference to traditional laws and customs as a normative system jars the ear of the listener.[8]

There are perhaps three main aspects to the system question in this context. First, are the relevant claimant group members' various relevant rules and practices themselves severally regular, or regulated, to a degree which would attract definition of them as normative and systematic, even though at times they may be breached or imperfectly applied? (Here I intend 'practices' to cover both the articulation of rules and observed action, and the often untidy mesh between them.) Second, do the group members' rules and practices, in combination, form a normative system of rules and customary practices rather than merely constituting an incoherent assemblage of opinions and activities, or merely a set of 'observable patterns of behaviour',[9] or perhaps a set of internally coherent yet mutually incompatible rules and practices engaged in by different individuals? Third, does the group's normative system, if it has one, show an acceptable degree of continuity with that of its predecessors back to the time when British sovereignty was established over the area in question?

Answers to such questions in specific cases will depend not only on the specific evidence but also on how such words are interpreted by the courts. The more basic senses of 'system' provided by the *Macquarie Dictionary* are of interest here:

> **1.** An assemblage or combination of things or parts forming a complex or unitary whole: *a mountain system, a railway system.* **2.** Any assemblage or set of correlated members: *a system of currency, a system of shorthand characters.* **3.** An ordered and comprehensive assemblage of facts, principles, doctrines or the like in a particular field of knowledge or thought: *a system of philosophy.* **4.** A coordinated body of methods, or a complex scheme or plan of procedure: *a system of marking, numbering or measuring.* **5.** Due method, or orderly manner of arrangement or procedure: *have system in one's work.*

Some recurrent elements of these various definitions suggest that a system might be described more elementally as an assemblage of things which are somehow correlated or coordinated among themselves, and in which there is an ordered complexity of some degree.

In his judgement in the *Croker Island* native title case, Justice Olney, in a section called 'The System of Native Title', observed there that the applicants' 'system of native title' had 'four components': the estate, the estate group, incidents of title held in an estate, and a mechanism of succession to it. Clearly these four components are integral to a single system and they all have the estate in common as a focus. In that sense they are coordinate. While the representation of the system as having only four components may make it appear simple rather than complex, Olney went on briefly to summarise a number of its other features, the relative complexity of which is suggested by local rules of descent, filiation and adoption in relation to estate group membership, the maintenance of a distinction between core and contingent rights and interests, the way boundaries are handled, and so on.[10] There will be other cases where tenure arrangements will not be so complex, and the question may arise as to whether or not their relative simplicity denies them the status of 'system'. I suppose a quick answer to that is to say that these may simply be 'simpler systems' rather than 'non-systems', depending on the evidence.

THE FLUIDITY PROBLEM: THE WESTERN DESERT VERSUS THE REST?

A parallel question to the one about complexity is that of how much fluidity in a set of customary tenure arrangements is sufficient to deny it the status of a 'system of laws'. Whose definitions of 'laws' or 'fluidity' will be privileged in these debates, for example? There is something of a debate in the anthropological literature on Aboriginal societies which is of increasing importance to this issue. The sections that follow, given their focus on the theoretical orientations of differing anthropological opinions, might be considered optional for non-anthropological readers. On the other hand, it is difficult for a lawyer or administrator to assess differing expert opinions without being able to put them into the context of the debates within the discipline itself.

In some of the more recent anthropological literature, fluidity is at times examined and 'problematised' in the absence of equal treatment being given to that with which fluidity is usually in constant dialectic, and without which it is a vacuous category, namely, stability. Increasingly one comes across evidence of an underlying assumption that the only alternative to fluidity is rigidity. A small number of exceptions to somebody's rules about how to do something apparently can mean that the cultural phenomenon being described is 'fluid' – full stop. A certain detectable glee in these small ethnographic defeats of overweening patriarchal restraint and regulation ironically suggests that things might not be quite so fluid out there after all.

The most classically fluid type of Aboriginal society, that of the Western Desert, and especially the Pintupi as described by Myers,[11] has for some scholars become the preferred source for generalisations about Aborigines anywhere, and in some instances one can see the Pintupi now exerting an exaggerated colouring influence on how other kinds of groups themselves are to be understood and discussed. There is a similar and related tendency to project Western Desert approaches to kinship and genealogy onto other groups. This applies especially to the view that the degree to which Western Desert people downplay both physical parenthood and the actual/classificatory distinction is typical of the whole continent. I would instead regard their genealogical thinking as being at one extreme end of the spectrum, a long way from the degree of emphasis on elaborated and socially very significant distinctions between various kinds of physical and social parenthood which have been reported for groups in better-favoured parts of Australia, where people also maintain the actual/classificatory distinction between grandparents, for example, with what seems to be a great deal more robustness than do Western Desert people. A psychologically interesting question here is what would motivate certain anthropologists to prefer to think that all Aborigines are like the Pintupi in just these particular respects – the fluid social groupings, a land tenure system that focuses more on individual connections than any other does, the absence of a strong descent principle, and the least emphasis on the physical aspects of human reproduction when it comes to reckoning kin. This obsession with fluidity, which began as a positive corrective to older static and cellular models, can now some-times amount to distortion, in my view.

In a careful comparison between Western Desert and northern semi-desert local organisation at McLaren Creek (Northern Territory), Ian Keen, while he avoided projecting the Pintupi onto different groups, argued that differences between Western Desert and McLaren Creek do not amount to a simple contrast between 'the presence or absence of patrilineal descent groups or corporate clans'. Instead,

> [t]he difference lies primarily in the relative weight accorded to, or the ranking of, various grounds for articulating identity and claiming to hold country, the ways in which these relate to one another, and the relevance given to naming systems such as subsections and moieties.[12]

Keen reported for McLaren Creek that people made land claims

> on a variety of grounds including filiation, initiation, conception, birth, a parent's death, long-term residence and consociation, and knowledge. These are the same kinds of claims as those made by people of the Western Desert, but ... McLaren Creek people rank them in a particular way.[13]

McLaren Creek station is not far south of Tennant Creek and straddles the Stuart Highway. The McLaren Creek claimants came from several groups which were affiliated (in various combinations) with the languages Warlpiri, Warlmanpa, Warumungu, Kaytej and Alyawarre. Of these, Warlpiri and Warlmanpa affiliates were linguistically and culturally those who most resembled Western Desert people. It appears that for McLaren Creek people it was patrifiliation that outranked these other bases of claim.[14] It is useful to distinguish ranking by cultural importance or ideological prescription from ranking in terms of frequency of action. The two seem at times conflated in Keen's account. It appears that patrifiliation was taken as a norm or default means of recruitment to country-holding groups, as six of the bases of claim that are typical in the Western Desert were 'especially important' at McLaren Creek '[w]here people claimed country to which patrifilial connections had been interrupted'.[15] That is, the salience of forms of connection other than those based on descent or filiation was generally higher where succession to an estate was in progress or in suspension. And while countries or estates generally had agreed core sites and mythic identities and were formally named, the ownership of such countries was contested. Not only that, but at least some people divided and reconstituted countries, and the common identity of particular individuals with others, defined in terms of connection to focal places, 'was hotly debated'.[16]

My problem with descriptions like this is that they leave unclear just how much of the land tenure situation can be characterised as subject to, for example, non-filial forms of recruitment to land-holding groups, events of succession to the country of groups which have no direct descendants, and hot debate over the placement of individuals within the scheme. Within the regional purview, and perhaps looking at the several ethnographic accounts available from a series of neighbouring land claims, was it the case that succession cases were frequent, occasional, or exceptional? Were there hot debates about a few dozen persons, or a few hundred, out of a few thousand? Are the McLaren Creek cases of recruitment by conception, initiation, father's initiation and father's birthplace restricted to the singular case of each that is cited by Keen?[17] How many of the 516 claimants[18] in this case fell into the category of those recruited to the groups principally (though not solely) by filiation or descent, and how many fell into the remaining categories? I am not arguing for a statistical anthropology but for some indication of where the great weight of the case material falls, if it falls at all.

There is a reason for wanting to know. If, for the sake of argument, around 90 per cent of McLaren Creek claimants were there on at least the basis of the single top-ranked criterion and the other ten per cent were distributed among half a dozen other criteria, this tells us something very important about the ranking involved. If, by contrast, the basis of Western Desert people's land claims are far more evenly distributed across a similar set of criteria, then the difference between McLaren Creek and the Western Desert is not merely one of ideological ranking and enacted preference but also one of relative homogeneity or unity of system.

Again, if there is a predominance of patrifilial group-based claims at McLaren Creek, and a rather binding consistency between estate Dreaming subsection couples and those of their principal patrifiliates, and such totemic groups persist at all substantially down through at least several generations within substantially the same family trees, then the McLaren Creek system is clearly far more corporate in character than that of the Western Desert where individual bases of claim are common and enduring genealogical groups of a corporate character have not been reliably recorded. This is a systemic difference, not a difference of emphasis on common principles. The archival resources probably exist that could answer the question of how stable McLaren Creek land-holding groups have been from at least about the 1830s to the present, as T.G.H. Strehlow and W.E.H. Stanner worked in the region in the 1930s and Stanner, at least, recorded genealogies.

Fred Myers wrote:

> My contacts with Warlpiri were considerably different [from those with Pintupi]; as informants, they were inclined to treat kinship, social organization, and language in more systemic terms.
>
> Evidence of the difference between Warlpiri and Pintupi people in regard to 'systematizing' does not depend on my impressions alone.
>
> …we might classify the Pintupi as phenomenological rather than structuralist in their approach to cultural forms.
>
> The greater definitiveness with which Warlpiri [land and ritual] groupings are made implies that some rights may be asserted by them without fear of abridging or rejecting relatedness among people. It is as if these distinctions were not matters of personal will and rejection, but rather were already achieved understandings to which one assents: objectifications.[19]

There is a further contrast between Western Desert people and their north-east neighbours, among whom are the Warlpiri who were numbered among Keen's McLaren Creek informants. The McLaren Creek system, especially if non-descent criteria are as rarely invoked as in, say, ten per cent of cases, is one that seems strongly committed to attempting to maintain stability in relationships between countries and sets of people who stand in certain kinds of ancestor–descendant relationship to each other. The Western Desert systems do not, at least until recently and in restricted areas, show such a commitment. '[A]mong Western Desert people, social attention to temporal continuity in terms of mortuary, clan structure, or even the reproduction of alliances is insubstantial.'[20] This is a systemic difference that far exceeds mere contrasts between rankings of the same criteria.

The extent to which a tenure system was stable in the pre-colonial past cannot be taken for granted. The Western Desert is the region that seems to have been in the greatest demographic instability at the time of colonisation. This is often attributed to the ecological uncertainty the people faced there before the arrival of water bores and imported food. I am inclined to consider, however, the possibility that the recency of their presence in at least the eastern part of the Western Desert, a range of evidence for which has been assembled by Patrick McConvell, may account for some of their relative geographic instability among themselves, as it may for the fact that they seem to have been making incursive movements at least on the east and south-east and taking over certain parts of the country formerly associated with different languages, in the earliest colonial phases.

McConvell, using linguistic, archaeological and genetic evidence, estimated that the spread of the Western Desert language and its speakers east from the Hamersley Ranges began less than 3,000 years ago, and their intensive contact with people who have Arrerntic languages (for instance, in the Hermannsburg–Alice Springs area) was probably only achieved in the last 1,000 years.[21] There are multiple records of Western Desert expansion occurring on its eastern, southern and western fronts, at least, at the time of colonisation.

Annette Hamilton earlier considered the possibility that ecology was not the only factor at work here:

> The whole of the Western Desert cultural area was, at the time of the arrival of the Whites, in a state of transition, in which indigenous cultural institutions were undergoing transformations without having yet achieved any kind of balance. A static model of social organization could not possibly account for the structural features found under these circumstances. Where such transitions had already occurred and been stabilized, a static account appears much more successful (see the Walbiri, the Aranda). It remains a moot point whether such a stabilization would indeed have been possible, given the ecological constraints of the area. Strehlow repeatedly attributes the social organization of the Western Desert to its extreme aridity and lack of resources. This question cannot now be decided empirically, since that particular trajectory has now ended for good, to be replaced by another of equally doubtful outcome. We may however construct an ideal model to account for the features of the system of local organization in the Western Desert as they might once have been, and another to describe *the system as it was straining to become*.[22]

One can always say that all peoples are struggling with their systems of local organisation and social organisation, but even within Aboriginal Australia it seems that some groups literally have or had *more* in the way of system than others. Even in the demographically more stable parts of the continent, however, some writers have been reluctant to suggest that unified and integrated systems of local and social organisation have been achieved. In the early 1960s, W.E.H. Stanner wrote of the Murinbata people of the north-west Northern Territory that their

> society and/or culture cannot be set up as a "unified whole" … The 'principles' of social interaction do not appear to have a ground of unity which can be stated. … the totality of Murinbata life is one of multiple principles. Because the principles are conjugate they affect different regions of life which overlap and are in conflict. … If the principles have a unity among themselves I have not been able to find what it is, and doubt if it exists. Certain aspects of Murinbata tradition suggest a working toward a unified system or unified whole.[23]

Referring to the period from the early 1960s to the late 1980s, and especially in relation to studies of social organisation, Ian Keen wrote about the decline of 'systems thinking' among anthropologists, and their paradigm shift from 'a systems approach to a "structurationist" perspective in which social life is pictured as a looser weave across the warp of time'.[24] Not only is there no universal yardstick for distinguishing 'a system of customary laws' from 'a swag of unconnected customs', for example, but there remains the perennial problem of subjective preferences – could not the same social institutions be described by one anthropologist as a 'system' and by another as a 'looser weave' without their disputing the ethnographic base account?[25] I believe they could, depending on the anthropologist's intellectual and political temperament. In the context of land tenure matters, this recreates a classic problem for courts attempting to come to conclusions after listening to conflicting expert evidence from anthropologists, all of whom have been confronted with the same ethnographic and evidentiary materials.

SOMETHING OF THE TIMES

In the present intellectual climate in the social sciences it often seems that it is transgression rather than repetitious conformity that fascinates, as indeed it might. Atomic human agents, evanescent action and the dynamism of power and process are sometimes preferred to the stodge of intricate and formal classes of person, complex enduring structural groups and their associated paradigms of cohesion, articulation, subordination and oppositional coherence. Cohesion may be structural more than interactive, and sometimes it is both. (Even conflict can be a form of interactive cohesion, especially where those in conflict share large common grounds of culture and social organisation.) In such an atmosphere, to note that some people within a single region assign groups to segmentary hierarchies in somewhat contradictory ways might become the springboard for simply saying the people have no hierarchical social structures, just overlapping personal networks – but that can hardly be the end of the story.

Of more concern is the privileging of meta-discourse over ethnographic craft in defining what is glamorous in anthropology. While not present everywhere in the academy, this has certainly become rather widespread and meant that in the 1990s and early 2000s it was often not easy to find recent anthropology graduates who were employable as native title case researchers. Nor was the emphasis on postmodernist and cultural studies paradigms in social science teaching doing much to provide undergraduates with essential field and analytical skills for the much needed work on indigenous tenures. Michael Silverstein's 1980s definition of 'Yuppie anthropology' as 'Geertzian blurred genre, post-structural deconstru-phenomenocrititerpreteneutics' had apparently failed to stem the tide entirely.[26]

Loss of craft means a decline in the power of ethnography to act as a natural brake on the theoretical schema we bring to experiencing another people. It is easy for us now to identify the distorting effects of the assumptions and values of the ethnographers of a century ago, because so many of those assumptions and values have become outmoded and sound weird. Their death knell was often sounded by the arrival of new and better ethnographies, for which older paradigms had no adequate analysis. The problem in dealing with one's own distorting presuppositions is that it is so hard to achieve any distance from them, something made harder by working only within one's own social and cultural world. The corrective process of self-knowledge through contrast is as much an aspect of reflexivity as is the recognition of one's own presence during ethnographic field-work, although one might not think so after listening to the way the term 'reflexive' is often used by anthropologists. Acquiring the skill to reach this kind of distance from both others and oneself is hard, but not impossible.

Anthropologists of the 2000s are less in agreement than they formerly were on the question of whether, or how far, one should make efforts to hold one's presuppositions at bay. Since so few anthropologists now come to the discipline from a scientific background it is perhaps unsurprising that there seems to have been a serious decline in the extent to which empirical rigour is required of an academic ethnographer and anthropological writer in recent decades. In a time when there are now many very different ways of 'doing anthropology' this may be no great loss, except that students are not always taught more than one way. If that way fails to inculcate in students an attitude of humility towards knowing about the world, and a healthy respect for the persuasive role of systematically researched ethnography, then they may have great difficulty treating their presuppositions with the necessary scepticism. Those with a healthy scepticism about their presuppositions are likely to be far better received as expert witnesses in native title cases.

It is sometimes the most valued of our presuppositions that cause us the most difficulty in recognising them as problems. The replacement of positivist structural-functionalism by a view that anthropology is primarily about the earnest critiquing of unequal power relations will not guarantee that native title representative bodies will never sue us for negligence on the grounds that our basic description of the local land tenure system was so far from the empirical situation that it could not be confirmed by claimant evidence.

Defective views are not the exclusive property of the old-fashioned. Our capacity to perceive different societies with clarity gets hampered by the very fact that anthropologists, like anyone else, are daily tempted to see themselves in others, just as some of their forebears were tempted to see their own evolutionary ancestors or fancied and primitive inner opposites among the tribal peoples they studied. An expectation of constant change and novelty, liberation from Victorian mores and their victimless crimes, unfamiliarity with the experience of physical violence, the efflorescence of personal choice, an assumption of security, the advancing conquest of patriarchy, a shift from the public to the private in so much modern cultural life, the validation of narcissism through technology and affluence, and the very rise of the individual, can colour the way we understand other societies perhaps much more than we are able to bring to consciousness. On the other hand it seems perfectly reasonable to experience desire for a little chaos when one's own society is documenting, registering, superannuating, monitoring and regulating one's life with what appears to be an increasing relentlessness. Anthropologists' emphasis on the fluidity of others with whom they have worked may therefore, at times, be mixing memory with desire. On the other hand, a bias towards finding much order even where it is only partly present has arguably characterised some of the ethnographic writing on Aboriginal Australia. This bias too, in its time, has been progressive, as cultural relativists have sought to prove that Aboriginal society was complex and organised rather than primitive and chaotic.

DARWIN FRINGE-DWELLERS

The most extreme example of fluidist ethnography in Australia remains Basil Sansom's work among Darwin fringe-dwellers. To read his publications on these people is to be confronted with a world in which there are no enduring social groups, no corporate structures, no stable forms of property, and little or no continuity in relations between people and each other, or between people and specific areas of country.[27] For example:

> In constructing the reality they experience and know, Northern Aborigines treat groupings as the product of process and recognise an achieved grouping for what it is – a realization of the here and now. ...
>
> The Countrymen belong to a range or stamping ground ... The Countrymen call this range their country...
>
> Knowledge of country, and, hence, title to it comes only of experience. ...
>
> In Northern Australia, social identity is established with reference to the distribution of knowledge among persons and groups of persons. ... Folk modelling in this region has always to do with the comprehension of emergent social states and forms – with an emergent and changing pattern of land occupancy and use, with an emergent population made up of Countrymen who are currently but not permanently counted as such, with mobs or local groupings that are neither fixed in composition nor in membership nor location. ...
>
> In the first instance, Countrymen are constituted as an ego-centred set. ...
>
> [S]ocial continuity is processurally [*sic*] achieved by organizing "companies for business" into whole mobs and drawing on whole mobs to recruit their members to

form "companies for business". The "company for business" ... is a grouping recruited to a purpose and will disband as soon as its declared purpose is fulfilled. ...

With reference to such people, the sociology of the corporation, the study of hierarchies of office, the ethnography of propertied family lines must all be put aside. ...

In the Darwin hinterland, "continuity in the arrangement of persons in relation to one another" is uncharacteristic and the search for this order of continuity is pointless and unreal. ...

Continuity in Northern Australia is in the perdurance of cultural forms of and for action.[28]

What is not made clear in Sansom's work is the extent to which these same people whose urban fringe-camp daily lives were dominated by discontinuity and fluidity also identified with enduring totemic estate-holding descent groups, and with descent-based language groups associated with mostly stable areas of country, on other days and in other places. Some of Sansom's 'Wallaby Cross' people have been among those who have advanced land claims under the *Aboriginal Land Rights (Northern Territory) Act 1976 (Commonwealth)* and appear in the relevant ethnographies as members of more or less classical kinds of land-holding descent groups. Some of them were from families with whom W.E.H. Stanner had also worked in the early 1930s. A number of these people told Stanner about the identities and countries of their own grandparents born a century earlier. Later in this paper I show that, contrary to the impression one might gain from reading Sansom's work, customary title-holding groups in at least one part of the relevant Darwin hinterland region, namely Daly River, can be shown to have been predominantly stable totemically, geographically and genealogically since at least the 1830s. This is not to suggest that the area had not been through serious demographic loss and upheaval in the colonial era and afterwards, nor that succession claims were undisputed, nor that the linguistic identity of one or two extinct clans was in dispute, for example. But what is in fact most impressive is the extent to which they had held to certain basics among their ancient principles of landed and group identity throughout this traumatic era.[29]

The answer to this apparent contradiction seems to be that the Wallaby Cross mob's members led double lives. In the urban fringe-camp context they played down and actively suppressed their concurrent memberships of fourteen different descent-based stocks affiliated with fourteen different hinterland languages, and the mob's 'members could at any time reclaim original identities and so go separate ways'.[30] (In pre-colonial times there were also labile camps or residential aggregates of people with different languages, but it is unlikely they would commonly have been as heterogeneous in ethnicities as the Wallaby Cross mob.) But when representing themselves as the Wallaby Cross mob they 'generally submerge original ethnicities and present themselves as a grouping united in what they call "that Darwin style we got"'.[31] Sansom describes all members of the mob as 'escapers',[32] but fails to sketch for us the lives from which they were escaping and to which in many cases they continued to return.

So Sansom's sweeping statements about the nature of continuity, group composition and entitlement to country in 'Northern Australia', which I have quoted above, can only be justified as descriptions of one aspect of one particular kind of residential aggregate in one aspect of its members' lives. As generalisations about all Northern Australian Aboriginal groups over time and in relation to country, and even merely as generalisations about Wallaby Cross people as whole persons, the generalisations I have quoted above from Sansom's work are unjustifiable.

The Wallaby Cross milieu was certainly one riddled with indeterminacies and a large amount of disorder, despite the fact that, as Sansom so ably showed, its residents did live according to a code that could be subjected to the ethnographic process and described in a series of generalisations. It is partly because of such works as Sansom's that we can see the indeterminacies of social and cultural life with far clearer an eye than our order-obsessed scholarly ancestors. This has been a signal advance. The question I raise here is whether or not we may have gone too far and are becoming unable to place the determinacies and indeterminacies in accurate balance.

RULES VERSUS ACTION: THE CASE OF PRESCRIPTIVE MARRIAGE SYSTEMS

Aboriginal prescriptive marriage rules of classical type have long been famous for their precision and complexity, and also their regionalised variety. With our current attraction towards the recognition of indeterminacies and suspicions about the neatness with which a people's rules match what they do in practice, it is perhaps easy to treat such ideals as just another case of prescriptions which, as everybody knows, did and do get flouted or bypassed.

While it is historically the case that these elaborate prescriptive systems have collapsed partly or dramatically in many regions of Australia, this should not distract us from considering just how much of a match there was, during the earlier phases of colonisation, between marital theory and action. This kind of consideration is important if we are to place discussion of formations such as country-holding descent-based groups into a meaningful context, and to get a handle on what kind of yardstick is used to characterise practices as systematic or anarchic or otherwise.

A number of scholars have compared traditional marital prescriptions and prohibitions with substantial samples of actual marriages. To do so appears to have been a common or standard practice in the writing of ethnographies in the past, but has become very rare. Under a subheading, one rather typical of its era in being titled 'Maintaining the System', Kenneth Maddock wrote:

> There is evidently a strong sentiment in favour of the traditional regulation of marriage. Thus, in spite of the restrictiveness with which potential spouses are defined, infractions are unusual.[33]

Maddock went on to cite case material as follows, giving the percentages of marriages which were licit unions according to local rules:

Pitjantjatjara (Yengoyan)	95.5
Mardutjara (Tonkinson)	97.0
Warlpiri (Meggitt)	95.8
Kimberley (Kaberry)	85.5[34]
Groote Eylandt (Turner)	89.1[35]

To these one could add Hiatt's sample of marriages from the Blyth River region of Arnhem Land of which 94 per cent were 'proper' and six per cent 'improper',[36] and Shapiro's figure of 95 per cent for the extent to which men of the Elcho Island (Galiwin'ku) area had married women of the prescribed kin-class.[37]

The twelve specific cases given above yield an average of licit marriages of 90.5 per cent, and come from widely scattered parts of north and central Australia. Although six come from Kaberry's Kimberley fieldwork, they involve both desert and monsoon savannah peoples. In western Cape York's Mitchell River area, Lauriston Sharp found that 'The preferred marriage is with my own mother's brother's daughter, and the genealogies show that this ideal is realized in a large majority of cases'.[38] Sharp did not, however, provide figures. From the Milingimbi region of Arnhem Land where he worked in the 1920s, Lloyd Warner reported that

> [e]ach individual feels it is his right rather than his duty to keep his part of the system working; hence the proper functioning of the whole. A proper marriage is preferred because a Murngin man and woman usually feel that they have a right to each other, since their relationship has destined them to marriage. ... Nevertheless, wrong marriages occur. ...[39]

Ian Keen, who worked in the same region about fifty years later, also found that 'most marriages were between people who were in a correct [FZS/MBD] relationship'.[40]

However, the latter statement occurs in a passage under a subheading which, also true to its times, is called 'Indeterminacies and Variation'. It begins: 'Let me conclude this brief outline of *gurruṯu* [kinship] by stressing variation and indeterminacies; although *some* widespread common axioms *could be isolated*, there was *no uniform* Yolngu "marriage *system*".'[41]

Coming after a masterly presentation of what must seem to many or most readers like a vastly complicated and in fact highly uniform system of kinship and marriage, one taken so seriously by its practitioners that most marriages actually conform to a specific and extremely narrow ideal pair of relationships, the passage may seem anomalous. So, in the material that follows it, one could reasonably expect to find, perhaps, evidence to the effect that some Yolngu traditionally eschewed other Yolngus' ideal of cross-cousin marriage altogether, or, say, that Yolngu differed among themselves as to whether the cross-cousin a man married should ideally be the daughter of a mother's younger brother but not that of a mother's older brother. But it turns out that the 'widespread common axioms' which are not classed as subject to variations or indeterminacies are indeed just that: axiomatic aspects of how Yolngu reckon 'relations based on (although not restricted to) genealogical relationships grounded in beliefs about procreative processes'.[42] What could be more foundational to the coherence and relative stability of the fabric of such a social field than *gurruṯu*, given the bedrock role of kinship in classical Aboriginal life?

However, the evidence Keen provided for this foreshadowed 'indeterminacy and variation' seems to me mainly to entrench the view that exceptions, manipulations and variable degrees of knowledgability fail to dislodge the prevailing impression of orderliness conveyed by the more constant and universal adherence to rules and practices of the region's people. Here I leave aside the question of recent changes due to the impact of non-Aboriginal society. The indeterminacies Keen cites are as follows:

- A person would emphasise or deny a real or close relationship on the grounds that the person nurtured them or because of a grievance.
- People would manipulate categories and rules in their own interests, for example by saying that a union that was improper on kinship grounds was correct on subsection grounds, or that a wife's group and country were of that of the man's mother just because his mother's and wife's countries were on the same river.
- There was some choice as to which kin terms to apply to people, because anomalous marriages meant that people ignored the paternal factor and computed relationships through the mothers only. (Here as in some other cases one can take the evidence in two ways. One could read it as evidence of rule-breaking and thus of the indeterminate character of, say, patrimoiety exogamy. On the other hand, one could also read it as a powerful sustaining plank in the argument that patrimoiety affiliations and their relationship to the transmission of country interests are so vital to the stability of the social fabric that a firm and sacrificial method of dealing with intra-moiety (or other wrong) marriages has long been instituted that yet again removes or vastly reduces optation.)
- There were slight sub-regional variations in the use and semantics of some kin terms.
- There was perhaps variation between the coast, where there was formalised sister's daughter's daughter exchange, and the inland where apparently there was not.
- The Djinang people at the western extremity of the region appeared midway between the reciprocal marriage-exchange of their western neighbours and the asymmetrical exchange of Yolngu to the east.
- There were some variants in local meta-theories of marriage practice.[43]

It seems to me that it is these pieces of evidence, not the greater body of basic kinship-related categories, rules and practices, that should be characterised as '*some*' aspects of Yolngu society that '*could be isolated*' as evidence for the point that Yolngu marriage constituted a less than perfectly neat, homogeneous and adhered-to system.

Part of the problem here is that while the term 'marriage system' is something Keen prefers to place in quotation marks, giving it something of the status of a dead cat on the dinner table, he is quite happy elsewhere to refer to 'Yolngu marriage-practices'.[44] These are not a 'system' but a regional set of sub-regional variations on a theme, as we see in the list above. But there is a problem here that remains: namely, the 'Yolngu' category. As one gets close to the edges of the Yolngu region, variations between local usage and the usage of the north-east corner of Arnhem Land, both of marriage rules and kin terminologies, increase. However, to characterise this as evidence for the absence of a uniform Yolngu marriage system is a doubtful solution.

Having emphasised a single large-scale reification called the Yolngu, one then proceeds to find they are not an island but have neighbours with whom they interact, to whom they are both similar and different, and thus that 'Yolngu' 'marriage-practices' are not 'a unified system'. On closer inspection, however, these 'practices' are uniform at one level and variable at others. This is how it is right across the continent. But since so much of this variation is successfully subject to generalisations formed by the anthropologist, why can it not be called 'systematic variation'? As David Nash has pointed out, this phrase is ambiguous between 'variation that is regular' and 'variation (possibly irregular) of a system'. I mean it in the first sense here.[45]

The use of the term 'indeterminate' for these circumstances is problematic. The *Macquarie Dictionary* defines it in major part as '1. not determinate; not fixed in extent; indefinite; uncertain. 2. not clear; vague… 3. not established. 4. not settled or decided'.

If people subvert and manipulate kinship and marriage norms from time to time in ways that themselves are also subject to successful generalisations by the anthropologist, and these fudges or wrongs themselves have limits and also belong to a limited set of classes, and they are fudges or wrongs built precisely on the fact that some highly shared prescriptions are being flouted out of self-interest or conflict, then why cannot these exceptions and anomalies and fictions also be characterised as cases of 'systematic variation' rather than as 'indeterminacies'? One could say that what they show is that the regional marriage system has some exceptions and breaches that are of a generally predictable form – what is unpredictable, perhaps, is who will indulge in which exception or breach and when.

NORTH EAST ARNHEM LAND: PATRIFILIAL GROUPS

In North East Arnhem Land, Ian Keen found that earlier 'segmentary' descriptions, especially those preceding the work of Nancy Williams, were misleadingly neat. They emphasised units clustering into higher order levels of inclusiveness, and described the 'clan' as a basic unit of Yolngu society. I will return to the clan question below.

Keen used the image of 'strings' in 'networks' in preference to that of 'enclosing sets' in order to discuss the way groups are constituted in relation to each other in the region. He found that the identity and boundaries of groups were often ambiguous. People also disagreed about their internal structure, including who was leader. The groups did not sort into a taxonomic hierarchy of different levels of inclusiveness of the kind implied by 'clan' and 'phratry'.

> Connections among groups were not those of enclosing 'sets' but extendable strings of connectedness... . Yolngu groups were not like the corporations in Roman or English law or corporate groups of anthropological theory, but 'kinds' of people with ancestry and attributes that both linked them to, and differentiated them from, others.[46]

The kinds of groups which others might have described as 'patrilineal clans' were referred to by Keen principally as 'patrifilial groups'. Some may see 'filiation' as a weaker or 'lighter' basic recruitment mechanism than 'descent', for a group with collective interests which are supposed to exist over time, because filiation involves only one or two steps of genealogical reckoning and deals with 'the recent', as well as being focused on pairs of individuals rather than on lineages. (Warren Shapiro, however, rejected the view that filiation is to descent as individuation is to corporation.)[47]

But one can also see this in reverse: descent from a known ancestor can only go back so far, while classical Aboriginal serial filiation is often thought of by its practitioners as being continuous back to an ancient time out of mind, and as continuing to an indefinite future. Rather than 'serial filiation' it might more properly be called 'perpetual filiation' from an 'emic' (insider) perspective. Especially if historical evidence suggests considerable stability in the serial transmission of collective and property-related identities down the generations, such that living group members are seen as temporary embodiments of enduring spirits and their relationships to country, what impediment is there to referring to such groups by the structural, collective, diachronic and bodily metaphor of the corporation?

Strings of patrifilial landed groups such as Cloudy Water, Mangrove, Sunrise, Thunder and others were described to Keen as 'one group' called *Ma:tjarra* or *Bungunbungun*, a set whose members had 'one ceremony' and had the *Djang'kawu* as common ancestor.[48] But each country was connected to several such strings; a group had several string-oriented names, each of which linked it to a different string; and people often used their own group name to identify others of the same string of groups. So Keen does not identify the strings as 'phratries'.[49]

Yolngu themselves, in addition to using the proper names of groups, argued about whether or not the people referred to were 'same' or 'different' or 'one' or 'separate', not using specialised terms that were equivalents of technical terms like 'clan' or 'phratry'.[50] A *mala* is any kind of group. A *ba:purru* was a relationship between totemic ancestors, spirits of the dead and those yet to be born, and places and elements of ceremonies associated with the group, and implied a shared form of identity, through those connections, which came from one's father (*ba:pa*).[51]

Keen distinguished 'least inclusive' from 'more inclusive' kinds of groups, rather than 'clan' from 'phratry', for example, because at any one degree of inclusiveness the groups did not have uniform or common structures. For example, not all cases of these 'least inclusive, common *ba:purru* identit[ies]' had subgroups with their own names, but some did.[52]

People disagreed about the genealogical structure of a group in certain cases, but this principally referred to linkages between upper generations of deceased people and the proportion of disputed cases to the rest was not stated so it is not clear whether such cases were uncommon, common, or very common. For related reasons people disagreed with each other over whether, for example, there were three Crocodile groups with distinct countries, or one Crocodile group with common rights over three countries.[53]

People also differed as to the proper forms of ceremonies, but Keen nevertheless showed how these 'incommensurable traditions' lay embedded in a 'network of qualified agreement as to the constitution of "law" or "right practice" (*rom*)'.[54] Differing understandings of myths and rituals did not prevent frequent and elaborate cooperation in ceremonial events by members of conjoined social networks. Although '[g]roups were not the bounded entities or fictive property-owning persons of corporation theory', their members had 'shared, though ambiguous, negotiated and hence open languages and frameworks'.[55]

Patrifilial group countries had definitions that were 'not altogether agreed', although their boundaries were marked by natural features 'more or less unambiguously' in ecologically rich areas, even if members of groups with adjacent countries 'were likely to disagree about which mark was significant'.[56] The moiety and group identities of focal rich areas of Yolngu country were subject to much less ambiguity than those of less favoured areas; indeed there is great continuity in the record of the last seventy years of the mapping of patri-group names onto core areas of country in North East Arnhem Land generally. This fact is partially obscured because Keen removed almost all of these names from his published detailed ethnography. One also has to bear in mind that the majority of Yolngu estates, perhaps as many as 90 per cent of them, lie in this richer country, and the majority of Yolngu people, both as groups and as individuals, therefore come from the areas of least ambiguity and dispute as to the identities of tracts of country. These two issues directly affect the extent to which one can characterise the regional system as one marked by indeterminacy, as against noting there is a systematic relationship between *degree* of determinacy and type of ecological context.

NO CORPORATIONS VERSUS CORPORATIONS

How strictly corporate does something have to be before it can be called a corporation? This raises the age-old question of how long is a piece of string. In between the Mitsubishi Company and the local school working bee lies a rather large territory.

Like Howard Morphy,[57] I am not persuaded that the patrifilial land-holding groups of North East Arnhem Land should no longer be described as 'clans', nor do I see evidence that they should not be described, as has been done by Nancy Williams, as 'corporate groups'.[58] Were they property-holding groups of no consistently specifiable structure which failed to outlive their memberships, or enduring structural groups without any property, or groups with common voluntary identity but no particular social structure or property interests, then one could dismiss the claim that they are corporations. But Yolngu clans, both as targets and also as variably achieved states, do appear to have the elemental requirements of a corporation: an enduring group recruited on definable and predominantly consistent criteria, the members of which possess a recognised common identity, and whose members possess common jural status in relation to something valued, in this case country, sacra and so on.[59]

Morphy noted that was the 'fuzzy nature of Yolngu clans that has persuaded Keen to simply use the word group rather than clan, which he sees as being indelibly contaminated with the connotations of a determining bounded corporate entity clearly inappropriate in the Australian case'.[60] Morphy pointed out that clans had a significant place in Yolngu ideology and while they were 'emergent, contextualised, and transforming', and were not 'rigid, pre-existing components of social structure', nevertheless

> there was a continuous process whereby people were divided into groups, and links were established or asserted between these groups, a set of ancestral beings, and a number of areas of land; and this process was part of the structuration which resulted in the reproduction of the regional system and provided the framework for individual action.[61]

In a narrowly technical sense, Keen's rejection of the term 'clan' for the patrifilial groups of North East Arnhem Land is correct, assuming one treats 'clan' as an international anthropological term of art rather than explicitly using it in the broader of its ordinary English senses or in some localised specialist usage. That is, 'clan' in a technical sense is usually held to refer to a unilineal descent group whose members can, at least theoretically, trace descent from a single common ancestor (the 'apical' ancestor).[62] If people such as Yolngu don't have apical ancestors, they don't have clans.

I am not sure the choice is that simple. Certain singular Dreaming figures are sometimes regarded as having been founding clan ancestors in parts of Aboriginal Australia, including the Yolngu region.[63] Patri-group members' kinship organisation often reflects at least a powerful metaphor of common patri-descent even in the absence of a traceable apical ancestor. The earliest remembered ancestors are often a set of siblings, their very status as such being something that rests on having an implied common parent or two, but the emphasis is often on this siblinghood rather than on a single (implied) apical ancestor. There are now some parts of Australia where historically recorded ancestors have become pivotal figures in the reckoning of serial patrifiliation. This includes at least some Arrernte in Central Australia.[64] In North East Arnhem Land, in the Laynhapuy region, Komei Hosokawa found that

> it is often the case that several outstanding male individuals (charismatic leaders, warriors, or negotiators with Balanda [Europeans]), usually 3 or 4 generations up from the present, are regarded by the clan members as 'No. 1 person of the tribe'. E.g. Gumana in Dharlwangu clan, Wonggu in Djapu clan. It is important to notice that these recent ancestors are quite often the starting point of a new named lineage (sub-clan). Gumana is now a Dharlwangu surname and people tend to consider that Gumana Dharlwangu and non-Gumana Dharlwangu constitute separate *bäpurru* (clans, ceremonial groups). Both groups require representation in land rights talks such as [Northern Land Council]-organised meetings to deal with mining company's exploration proposal etc...[65]

Keen's argument that anthropological constructs such as the clan were alien tropes which should be replaced by local Yolngu tropes in anthropological descriptions, on the grounds that they distorted the representation of Yolngu institutions, was rejected by Nancy Williams. Williams asserted that Yolngu land-owning groups do have apical ancestors, they recruit by serial patrifiliation, they are corporate by virtue of their members' joint interest in land and waters, they hold a lineage ideology, and are patrilineal. Genealogical subgroups within a clan could be hierarchically ranked and persons could be ranked as individuals within a clan, although their hierarchical model was a template to which life did not always conform. It was not necessary to find that Yolngu clans belonged to a strictly segmentary system or had impermeable boundaries in order to call them clans. Nor, on the other hand, did their variability from the template imply fuzziness. Yolngu could be as precise or imprecise as context required.[66] She also sought to clarify her former use of the concepts of corporateness and of group:

> By corporateness I meant (and continue to believe this is an appropriately descriptive term for a particular social form that carries no excess connotative baggage and conforms to its generic usage among English-speakers) a set of people whose identity as a set arises from their common interest in an estate in land and/or water such that the set has a jural existence distinct from that of its individual members. ... [A] Yolngu title-holding group's relationship to land ... is corporate ... and their interaction is predicated on their joint interests.[67]

That is, Yolngu clans also matched Keesing's technical definition of a 'social group' as 'people grouped through social interaction and who are corporate in one or more respects'.[68]

Here I simply draw attention to the fact that it is not easy to say categorically that Aboriginal totemic, country-holding patri-groups are constructed in the absence of a notion of common ancestry, even where unconnected genealogical subgroups subscribe to a common Dreaming and homeland.

Perhaps partly because of this difficulty in focusing the picture, Australianists have long been in the habit of using the term 'clan' in a looser sense than that which the technical dictionaries suggest; and given the range of variation in the way Aboriginal filiative groups are constructed, the use of a reasonably flexible cover-term for them seems to me preferable to one that is narrow.

I struggled with the same issue in the Wik region of Cape York Peninsula: 'I have been using the term "clan" without defining it. It is a convenient cover term, rather than a name for a simply definable, locally universal social structure.'[69]

I then described the modal form of the Wik clan as one or more patrilines whose members claimed the same land as primary country, and who had the same patrilineal totems and the same totemic names. (There are actually some names that are not so shared between senior and junior segments of the same clan in some cases.) I then referred to cases of adoption, clan fission, and incomplete estate succession, concluding:

> In other words, 'clan' may be more neatly applicable in some cases than in others; not all clansmen are clansmen in relation to all the country claimed by any one of them, and not all territories have a 'clan' in possession of primary and unique rights over them. But it is fair to say that the clan as a patrilineal land-holding totemic unit with a unique country is *the target towards which the flux of reality is continually pushed*, and forms the model into which people attempt intellectually to compress the often somewhat ragged facts. It is the social and political facts which are ragged. The shape and content of the territories remain relatively constant and unambiguous, and provide a matrix for ecological and political stability.[70]

The ultimate Wik target in this domain was to belong to a descent-based group whose claims over a particular estate had been recognised by members of the wider society since time out of mind. Another way of putting this, however, is to say that the desired state was one in which the present jural public repeated what their predecessors had said about one's own clan predecessors. And one 'repeated' one's patrifilial forebears by having the same names, totems, ceremonial identity, language affiliation and estate as they did, and even on occasion people would claim the same personality traits, body build, skin colour and hair type as such forebears from the same estate, at times linking these traits with the main totemic being present in the estate, and emphasising the repetition of ancestral essence in one's living body and appearance.

To craft the analysis of such views about the importance of repetition within country-holding groups simply in terms of deconstructing the contemporaneous production of meanings concerned with an imagined past is, in my view, to leave out part of the story. That is, in the absence of any immediate evidence that might affect the verifiability of what people think about the past, such approaches seem to consider the past to be just an idea lodged in the present. This is too reductive and, perhaps, narcissistic.

In 2000 Keen replied to the various critiques summarised above. He said the patrifilial criterion for membership of the relevant Yolngu groups was not rigidly applied, and people did not hold uniform views on which groups were part of or separate from other groups. Serial patrifiliation alone did not define such a group, as groups could consist of genealogically unconnected lineages, and views on which people shared apical ancestors could be a matter of dispute. So-called clans were not equivalent components (homologous segments) within a segmentary system. They did not fall neatly into an objectified taxonomic hierarchy. Yolngu represented them metaphorically by organic and branching tropes, and their interconnections among themselves by string-like tropes, while the technical language anthropologists had applied to them imposed segmentary tropes that were foreign.

Only by stretching the use of the language could technical definitions of corporate groups be applied to the Yolngu case, although there were resemblances between the two. People from the same patrifilial group could have differentiated rights in different areas of country, so membership of a group did not grant a common (corporate) interest. Rights in countries were actionable by a variety of people genealogically connected with members of the group but who were not members of it. Sets of groups were often circumstantial in conception and could be extendible depending on context. They were aptly described as strings, webs or networks rather than, for example, 'phratries'. Keen was skeptical about the notion of an imperfectly realised target or ideal model of clanship, as had been suggested by several critiques. People shared principles and ways of doing things, but one could not expect either achieved uniformity or a common modal type for country groups in the region, as there was no overarching authority which could impose them.[71]

Keen made these points well, even though regional specialists and others may continue to debate them. But the project of replacing anthropological meta-language with region-specific language and translations of it remains troubling in my view. Social anthropology as a globally comparative discipline has traditionally rested in part on its capacity to discover patterns of similarity and difference between related human institutions and practices. That Aboriginal group structures are not constituted as others are does not mean that they are merely unique, or that they and others cannot be ranged together and discussed using some common meta-language; indeed we all do this at least to some extent in anthropological discourse.

Australia is not Africa, but on both continents there are kin groups recruited by, among other things, some form of parental filiation whose members traditionally hold particular rights in areas of land and waters. Here, as in other areas of customary law, one often sees a family resemblance between the more precise and tightly-crafted institutions of more complex societies and the looser, rather more anarchic manifestations of similar cultural creations in Aboriginal societies. It is difficult to identify these resemblances in shorthand terms if each ethnography is presented more or less *sui generis*, and only in localised conceptual terms. This is clearly not what Keen proposes, but rather a privileging of informants' conceptual apparatus over the preconceptions that may be imported when global terminology is employed. The refinement of anthropological terminology over the last century or so has resulted in some terms of importance being defined so narrowly that they can only be applied to a restricted number of peoples, leaving something of a vacuum in a number of cases.

These are not arguments merely about words, but about the adequacy of descriptions and analyses. They have implications for the way ethnographic accounts are treated as evidence in native title cases, since they raise again a central question confronted by Justice Blackburn in *Gove* in the early 1970s: to what extent do Aboriginal land interests in any case rest on a 'system' of 'rules' and 'laws' of a 'society' or 'community'? To what extent are these interests controlled ego-centrically rather than collectively? Are individual versions of them too idiosyncratic to constitute, even together, a communal normative system? These are questions that have to be answered on a case-by-case basis.

It may be that detailed histories of Yolngu patrifilial groups and countries using both recent and older records will shed more light on the degree to which their indeterminacies have affected their long-term composition and territorial locations. If structuration is in part a matter of repetition and variation over time, it is tempting to want to see some empirical quantification of both as contained in the record.

PRODUCTION, REPRODUCTION, REPETITION

It is a matter of concern that all kinds of 'production of meanings' are sometimes lumped together in anthropological discourse, especially in the postmodern era, by a common emphasis on *cultural production,* without much attention being paid to contrasts between the continuities and discontinuities that characterise multiple acts of production over time. That is, the fact of 'production' has at times been allowed to overshadow perceptions of differential patterning of productions. Reduced to 'production', all more or less patterned or unpatterned cultural phenomena can appear equally solid or flimsy. But they are not. What the 'cultural production' metaphor tends to elide is the distinction between production and *reproduction,* that is, repetition of form and substance versus single events or series of unlike events. It is by finding patterns of repetition that the ethnographer finds longer-term order and is able to describe the local processes of structuration in a series of generalisations that transcend the moment. As Anthony Giddens explained:

> The 'structure' of an organism exists 'independently' of its functioning in a certain specific sense: the parts of the body can be studied when the organism dies, that is, when it has stopped 'functioning'. But such is not the case with social systems, *which cease to be when they cease to function*: 'patterns' of social relationships only exist in so far as the latter are organised as systems, reproduced over the course of time.[72]

One sometimes sees, in anthropological writings, an Aboriginal view that the meanings of places are forever being contrasted with an anthropological perspective under which such meanings are always newly constituted. Indeed, knowledge, in the neural sense, is constantly flashing into renewal or it would evaporate. But to contrast this academic view with Aboriginal perceptions of permanence may suggest to some people that the Aboriginal perceptions belong to the realm of the imagined, while an anthropologist's emphasis on some combination of repetitive renewal, evanescence and innovation belongs to the realm of reason and, dare I say it, science. Thus there is now a folk version of all this which says that Aborigines encourage fictions of continuity and order, while anthropologists know Aborigines really indulge in constant fluidity and ambiguity. No doubt anthropologists would generally reject such a crude version of what is being asserted, but it seems to me to be available from certain approaches.

THE LONG VIEW

It is wildly unfashionable to draw attention to the fact that some kinds of social practices are adaptive and others are not. A society in which the economy produced a fairly dense and sedentary population, but which arranged its land tenure allocations on the basis of weekly contests at arms, would very likely be one that was seriously maladapted to creating a good environment in which to raise future generations. Even in the Western Desert of Australia, where the classical economy was one that wrestled with perennial unpredictability and terrible basic scarcities, and where rights and interests in country were more strongly individuated than elsewhere and subject to considerable short-term change by comparison with other parts of Aboriginal Australia, there is always a huge emphasis on country rights mediated by religious knowledge. In fact, as a basis of tenure interests, such knowledge perhaps reaches it greatest prominence in that region. The Dreamings (*Tjukurrpa*) and their sites and tracks seem to be the most stable elements of the system, one that was demographically porous as individuals came and went over long periods.

Even so, Western Desert ideology does not locate country interests in the individual *per se*, however understood. One of the key values associated with enduring institutions such as the *Tjukurrpa* is their very transcendence of momentary and egoist will. Whether internalised as the Law of the Dreaming, or merely respected or feared externally as a matter of determination by the polity collectively and in ways that are subject to negotiated 'consensus', though often based on both, Aboriginal country interests are typically conducted on the premise that full private ownership is not really possible.

'The wisdom of these organic provisions'

Ideally, the 'enduring institutions' of classical land tenure to which so many Aboriginal people remain committed, at least in principle, provide them with some ability to predict what will happen. They narrow the range of licit choices, they keep a lid on brute force, and assist society to be a relatively safe one in which to hope to bring up children. They do things for people. To make a smart and insightful analysis of these cultural phenomena, while ignoring what they might do for those people and their forebears and descendants as a population over long periods such as millennia, is certainly possible. Not all accounts of things have to look to what they might do or fail to do to assist people in the project of running their lives or those of their descendants. To make such functionality constantly the main plank in one's analysis is indeed to hark back to a functionalism that has gone. But to reject thinking about the functionality of a social practice on the basis that that itself would be an act of function*alism* is to eject the baby with the bath water. And yet one comes across just such reactions from time to time when trying to teach anthropology in recent years.

The definition of a social group or institution that outlives its current members is not exhausted merely by alleging – truthfully as may be – that it is an illusion, a case of hypostasis or reification, the objectification and projection of the momentary as the long-lived and thus yet another kind of imagined community. One could go further and say that a perpetuable customary corporation is just another case of persistent delusion as to the existence of the machine-in-the-ghost. But while we are now highly resistant to reifying the dynamic process of repetition or near-repetition of social acts into a crudely objectivist notion of 'enduring structure', I think there are many of us who are reluctant to thoroughly embrace individual-focused and subjectivist 'agency-driven' synchronist theories of sociality at the expense of trying to understand the social and cultural sum that is greater than its combined parts, and which has a history that outlives its mortal practitioners – as well as, perhaps mercifully, the anthropologists who study them.

Lewis Henry Morgan said, in *Laws of Descent of the Iroquois*, that a crucial test of 'the wisdom of these organic provisions' was whether or not the people who tried to live by them could enjoy reasonable security as a result: 'for, during the long period through which the league [of the Iroquois] subsisted, they never fell into anarchy, nor even approximated to a dissolution from internal disorders.'[73]

How Morgan knew this about the more distant past of the Iroquois was not revealed, and it may have been merely a speculation of Morgan's or a case of just reporting the beliefs of his informants – or both. The point, however, is that the Iroquois had law, not just kinship. This was even though their legal institutions were 'founded upon the family relationships; in fact, their celebrated league was but an elaboration of these relationships into a complex, and even stupendous system of civil polity'.[74] What is not well developed, in the Australianist literature, is a theory of how the various social institutions articulate with each other, or not, to form regional 'civil polities' that are more than the sum of so many domesticities.

How stable have Aboriginal country groups been?

In 1938 D.S. Davidson broached this issue in his paper, 'An Ethnic Map of Australia', under the heading: 'Stability of Tribal Territories'. He concluded from his survey that:

> The tribal distribution as shown apparently represents the status quo for an undeterminable but considerable period. There seem to have been no major

movements of population in late prehistoric times nor are there any obvious indications that such have taken place at any time in the past. Australian traditions not only do not emphasise migration legends for political or ethnic groups but for the most part are quite deficient in them.[75]

He added that stories about the movements of legendary ancestors were myths about the establishment of totemic centres and were not intended as, and could not be interpreted as, tribal migrations. He was sceptical about evidence suggesting that some tribal movements in the Lake Eyre region arose because some tribes forcefully ejected others from their lands: 'Our reasons for suspecting that warfare may not have been necessarily the cause for such a change are to be found in the Australians' complete lack of interest in land aggrandizement...'[76]

One cannot, however, rest too much on such an *a priori* argument. More convincing evidence can come from detailed records.

John Morton has made a study of genealogical and other information recorded for Western and Central Arrernte people of the Alice Springs region. Using the late-nineteenth-century work of Baldwin Spencer and Francis Gillen, that of Carl Strehlow and later work by his son, T.G.H. Strehlow, and more recent research of the land claims era, he has found that the Arrernte families of the present have generally been associated with the same Dreamings and same core sites and estates since at least around 1800 and in some cases the evidence goes back further.[77] One can, of course, say that this is just a conservative approach to serial patrifiliation, and therefore that to hypostasise the existence of 'patrilines' or 'patrilineal clans' in such a case might be taking things too far. Some might say that what we have here are conjoined but very short 'strings' of parent–offspring relations which extend backwards in time only in the sense that certain identities have been passed on repeatedly. But this repetition itself is done according to local ideology, under which such repetitions are considered truly ancient, and it is projected forwards as well, at least in the minds of the people concerned. The records show that this cultural construct of perpetual corporations has been strongly reflected in behaviour and history in this case.

Country-holding groups in Aboriginal Australia often have metaphors and idioms for these sets of filiative links that are not 'string-based' but rest on other kinds of images. In some areas the antecedent–descendant relationship is conceived as a circular and 'rolling' model of perpetual cycling of spirits.[78] In others it may be thought of more as a unidirectional 'stem', 'spine' or 'tree trunk.' Wik ancestors are, in Wik-Ngathan for example, *wuut mangk, thaameth mangk*, literally 'old-man back/stem', 'old-woman back/stem'. The head of a clan, and the oldest of a sibling set, is the 'root person' or *pam yuk*, literally 'tree man'. In the Perth region of Western Australia, subsets of matriclans or 'great families' were described as being of *Matta Gyn* or of 'one leg'.[79]

In such metaphors, family trees are just that: while they stretch back to an ill-defined past, or to a remote past defined by a world beginning, and forward to an open future, and rest on parent–child relations, they are not conceived of essentially as unidirectional sets of single-chain links but as multiple outgrowths from a set of common sources. What is noticeable in such native models is their emphasis on perpetual repetition, combined with a plastic structural image drawn from a life-form, usually anatomical, and involving at any one generation sets of kin, the latter being unified mostly on the basis of commonalities of ancestry. Self-perpetuation, usually under some strongly constraining recruitment rules, is axiomatic for some such sets, which are often symbolised by totems and may be the locus of primary language affiliations, hold common property interests, are often formally named, and so on. There are other kin-sets based to varying degrees on filiation but which lack these features – for example, personal kindreds, and residential groups composed entirely of kin.

It is the theoretically 'perpetual' nature of land-holding groups, at least in ideological terms, that has been an integral characteristic of their definition as corporate entities by many scholars. That is, a corporation is something that, by intention, may or should outlive any individual member of the group. To attempt to reduce a people's conception of their corporations, no matter how they put them together, to merely a contemporaneous strategy for 'getting a slice of the action', for example, would be to suggest the absence of a prime consideration for the actors who put such strategies into place – the need to suborn potential eruptions of sheer new power to old and distributive ways of regulating society, ways which established rights in country ultimately on an extra-personal and lawful basis.

But are the Hermannsburg-Alice Springs data just an isolated case? What evidence is there that the stability and predictability that might flow from all this structuration is actually achieved in a widespread way?

Luise Hercus's genealogical data for the eastern Simpson Desert go back to the late eighteenth century and indicate similar land-relationship continuities on a smaller scale, although the earliest data were not obtained from documentary sources but from living informants born as long ago as c.1888 and who were still alive in the 1960s. The named individuals in the genealogy of Mick McLean Irinyili, for example, include one at the great-grandparental level (his father's father's father), and there are four other great-grandparents whose linguistic affiliations were remembered but not their names.[80] These people would have been born approximately in the period 1770–1830, assuming an average intergenerational gap as low as twenty years for women and as high as 40 for men.

Hercus's detailed knowledge of the comparative linguistic picture in the adjacent regions from Lake Eyre to Adelaide via the Flinders Ranges has led her to the conclusion that the language varieties of that large zone have been evolving more or less *in situ*, and in diffusional and other relationships with each other, over an extremely long period. The period involved here would have to be reckoned in terms of millennia, not just centuries. One exception to this general picture of enormous stability in the language/country relationship in the region appears to be Kukata, a fringe Western Desert language, whose people were actively pushing east and south at the time of colonisation.[81]

In far north Queensland there is also relevant case material. We know that the Guugu Yimithirr language recorded by James Cook and Joseph Banks at Endeavour River in 1770 is, as far as has been ascertainable by linguists John

Haviland and Gavan Breen, very largely the same language as that spoken in the same location in 1970, and the language is still in use there at the time of writing.[82] The comparison was restricted to lexicon and phonology as the Cook and Banks material did not include sentences or text. Barry Alpher has calculated that the 200-year vocabulary retention rate for Guugu Yimithirr has been 87 per cent, but even this is lower than it would have been if stable items such as pronouns had been included in the Cook and Banks list.[83] The South Australian language Parnkalla evinced no significant change in vocabulary between 1844 and 1960.[84] Linguists Black, Alpher and Nash have argued in considerable detail that the rate of lexical replacement in Australian languages is not particularly rapid at all, that borrowing between adjacent languages proceeds at a modest rate, and the evidence suggests that a minimum lexical retention rate of roughly 80 per cent per millennium is not inapplicable.[85] These conclusions add to the wider picture of long-term linguistic stability in Australia up to recent times. R.M.W. Dixon argues that Australia has been largely in a state of linguistic equilibrium for a very long time, by world standards.[86]

This is not to infer from the geographic stability of languages that population movement and stability simply matches that of languages, since in Australia the memberships of language groups can change slowly over time and one might describe such language-group categories as being somewhat porous, in the sense that people may slowly pass into and out of them.[87] The same may be said of lower-level country-holding groups such as estate groups. In the native title context, continuity of licit connection to a country is not vitiated because a country-holding group exhibits some dynamism in its membership, especially given the fact that this dynamism is largely restricted to shifts experienced by individuals and small genealogical branches and is not the equivalent of whole-group migration.

There are many examples of migration made evident in the distribution of languages in other parts of the world, migrations that occurred before the dramatic impacts of the colonial era. Indigenous languages of the Americas which belong to the same families are frequently distributed in a patchwork way, sometimes across very large distances. For example, the Algic family has an Algonquian subgroup in eastern North America, while its two other units, Wiyot and Yurok, are isolates spoken along the northern coast of California – they are a continent apart. The Athapaskan family contains over thirty closely-related languages spoken in three areas: western Canada and interior Alaska, Arizona and New Mexico, and the Pacific Coast.[88] Navajo, of the south-west USA, is related to widely-separated languages in the Pacific west coast, as well as some in Alaska and western Canada. Prehistoric migration is given by scholars as the usual explanation for these mosaic patterns.[89]

Other cases can be cited from other parts of the Americas. Families such as Mayan in Mesoamerica and Arawakan, Tupian and Cariban in South America have their members scattered over vast distances, interspersed among languages of different families. Such discontinuous language families are graphically visible in a number of Lyle Campbell's maps.[90] Migrations may be long remembered in oral histories of some native American groups, for example the Gitksan of British Columbia.[91]

In Australia there are extremely few examples of geographically separated languages that are members of the same language family, and thus very little evidence of Aboriginal migrations in recent millennia, apart from those coming after colonisation. Yolngu Matha, the language of North East Arnhem Land, is cut off from other members of the Pama-Nyungan family by a set of languages of different stocks. This has been the conventional way of putting it since Hale's work of the early 1960s, although R.M.W. Dixon has questioned the Pama-Nyungan genetic grouping. Nevertheless, Dixon does say that there are only two exceptions to the statement that all members of genetic linguistic subgroups in Australia are geographically contiguous – presumably referring to the Yolngu and Barkly cases.[92] Certain languages of the Barkly Tableland are related to, but geographically separated from, certain other languages near the coast to their north-west.[93] This evidence suggests either that some people of the same language family migrated, or people of some different language family penetrated a pre-existing area of relative linguistic homogeneity, thus creating outliers. But in these cases the separation events are extremely ancient. In a third case, a language found at the mouth of the Murray River in recent times may be considered originally to have been on the Upper Murray in far earlier times. Interestingly, the people in the latter case have oral histories in which their forebears are said to have migrated downriver.[94] With these three exceptions and that of the Western Desert (see above) there is no compelling evidence of significant Aboriginal migrations in recent millennia. The mosaic geographic patterning of language varieties which are associated with sets of non-contiguous clan estates in the Wik region of Cape York Peninsula is only a partial exception to this, as the languages concerned are all of the same subgroup and the 'migrations' that would explain the pattern are highly localised cases of personal or small kin-group succession at the estate level, not movements of whole language groups across the wider landscape.[95]

While such phenomena as living languages are constantly reproduced, albeit with gradual change, rather than being fixed entities 'out there' in time and space, their geographic stability in Australia seems to contrast massively with known historic cases of migration and official deportation, of language extinction and replacement, and other dramatic forms of discontinuity, most of which are identified with the conquest period and its aftermath.

In the Princess Charlotte Bay area of Cape York Peninsula the evidence for ancient continuities in the naming of both estate-holding groups and also in a significant number of sites seems quite clear, although much detail remains to be published. Bruce Rigsby and I have overlapping data on over 150 named geographic groups, most of them estate groups, for this area, and hope to publish an analysis of them at a later date. This is an area of great linguistic diversity where the people had a classical tradition of high linguistic exogamy and multilingualism, and their languages had a range of rather distinctive sound systems. While the languages are related, there have been many sound-changes in their history of divergence from a common stock over the centuries. To exemplify this material briefly, note that members of one Barrow Point estate group were known as:

Ama Ambiilmungu (in Barrow Point language)
Aba Almpilmiya (in Flinders Island language)
Mba Almbiylmakaram (in Lamalama Variety 1)
Mba Mbilmu (in Lamalama Variety 2)
Bama Gambiilmugu (in Guugu Yimithirr)

The first element in each rendering is the term 'person', which descends in each case from the ancient proto-form **pama* after which the Cape York Peninsula language family Paman is known. The second element consists of the estate name plus a grammatical suffix indicating that the person is from that country (*-mungu, -miya, -makaram, -mu, -mugu* respectively). The proto-form of the estate name in this case may be reconstructed as **Kalmpiil*. How stable was the relationship between such estate names and the country onto which the names were mappable in the 1970s and 1980s is not subject to strict proof, but it seems abundantly clear that many of the estate names themselves descend in a continuous line from past forms spoken several centuries or more ago.

The stability of the Wik

On the opposite side of Cape York Peninsula the highly parochial, insular, boundary-focused members of Wik coastal groups long ago developed a complex system of patri-group-totem-place-dialect associations, the high conservatism of which came in part from their maintenance of complex batteries of gender-specific (human and dog) clan member names and other practices that made it extremely difficult for clan/estate 'fluidity' to occur on anything but a very modest and gradual scale. So long as such complex brakes on change are constantly reproduced, they are reproduced on a pattern of continuity that stands in stark contrast to the relatively discontinuous patterning of Western Desert people's heavily biographical approach to the assignment of person/ place/ Dreaming identities based on birth district, conception site, place of initiation, site of parent's death, and so on. This is not to say that shallowness of historical and genealogical connections to a claimed area represents no problem for Western Desert claimants. Such depth has been reported as an internal criterion for evaluating strength of traditional connections to places among people from the Ayers Rock region. In such a cumulative system of achieving recognised rights, however, it is only one criterion of many.[96]

Having said that, I have also in the past taken the view that Sharp's image of lower Mitchell River society (Cape York Peninsula) as one consisting essentially of 'an ego-centred *set* of societies' is an apt description of an aspect of classical Wik society as well, albeit one that has to be reconciled with the fact that ego-centred networks do relate in various ways to regional and localised groups including corporate groups, and are in no sense independent of them.[97] But the view I expressed in 1978 was essentially synchronic, not diachronic, and was worked out from my position at the Cape Keerweer heartland of the Wik region, instead of after having worked with other Wik subgroups and seen something of their different perspectives, as I have since done.

By contrasting the synchronic and diachronic here I do not mean to suggest either is free of time, merely that the synchronic is an event or set of states belonging to a short time, relative to the question or project at hand, and the diachronic is one belonging to a suitably longer time, again relative to the question or project at hand. One cannot take one's own ego-centred network picture, formed after a couple of years, as a substitute for a more experienced and travelled ethnographer's picture of the polity and society concerned. To do so is to repeat the mistake of ahistorical synchronism but to do so in spatial terms. It is to look at the *here* without sufficient recognition of the *there*, just as we have often looked only at the *now* instead of also looking at the *then*.

What impresses about the hundreds of different ego-centred networks in the Wik case is their high coherence and mutual conformity at the level of principles, ways and means, as well as in many details of the symbolisms through which relationships are transacted. Individual Wik assertions about personal autonomy ('I am me, I am different, Nobody is boss for me' etc.), vigorous and repeated as they might be, must be understood against this background of collectively-shared rules for belonging, of shared understandings of means of construction of various kinds of groups, and a high degree of intersubjective agreement about how these principles map sets of persons onto the landscape at any one moment, and in a corporatist tradition. (There is considerable variation in the construction of the individual across Aboriginal Australia, contrary to the rather unitary impression one might gain from reading Hoyt Edge's paper on the subject.)[98]

All of this occurs in the presence of some rather frequent conflict between members of labile residential aggregates. The musical metaphor that seems most apt here is jazz, central elements of which may sound like disorder to some listeners coming to it from the outside. Insiders hear the musical sub-orders of syncopation, improvisation and deliberate variations from harmony consisting of dissonances cast against the main melodic line. What is notable about much 'disorder', in my field experience, is its intentionality.

I regard this kind of coherence in the midst of uncohesiveness, this mutual commitment to *system*, as the factor most likely to account for long-term stability in the relationship between Aboriginal groups and country. As a result of research into Moravian and Presbyterian church records and the pre-World War II manuscripts of Ursula McConnel and Donald Thomson, during the preparation of the Wik native title case, I am able to see the temporal picture of Wik social organisation in a rather different light from the view available in 1978. What is readily apparent from tracing the histories of a wide range of Wik clans and estates over a period as long as approximately 180 years is their great genealogical, totemic and geographical stability, the persistence of their structural commonalities, and the rule-governed character of changes they may have undergone as to content. That the Wik have not been exceptional in this regard is illustrated by the following example from 1,200 kilometres to their west.

How continuous was serial patrifiliation on the lower Daly River?

It has been possible to trace a number of clan/estate histories for the middle Daly River in the Northern Territory. There is good empirical support for the view that this area was overwhelmingly characterised by continuity of landed identity between generations, rather than by discontinuity, over a period of some 150 years. The principal device of this continuity has been serial patrifiliation.

In the *Malak Malak* claim book for Daly River I wrote:

> Genealogies elicited from claimants indicate that traditional rights of land ownership are inherited from the father. This is *not* to say that there is an ideology of *patrilineal descent* as such. That is, long lists of ancestors in ego's patriline are not assiduously remembered and handed on, there is no identification of a single founding lineage creator for each land-owning group, nor are forgotten ancestors in ego's patriline automatically assigned the same estate as ego. When older claimants were asked about the estates of their fathers' fathers, they said they were the same as their own only if they knew this about the grandfather in question, and preferably if they had actually seen him. The same applies to linguistic group affiliations and dreamings.[99]

There is, however, also an argument for describing the system as one in which serial patrifiliation yielded, or perhaps reflected, the long-term existence of a set of groups which may be said to be *patrilineal*. After reading a draft of the *Malak Malak* claim book, W.E.H. Stanner wrote to me giving his reactions to it, and one of the passages with which he disagreed was the one just quoted. He said in part:

> The whole question of estates, places of residence, patrilineality and patrifiliation still seems to me to need clarification. I incline to think that Scheffler has not really made his point, or that you are wise in following him.[100] My opinion is that there *is* a strong tradition of patrilineality: this is the *why* of patrifiliation. But there is insufficient time to go farther. Nor am I sure that Mr. Eames [Counsel for the Malak Malak claimants at that time] can safely draw the points into his presentation of the case. I trust you will not cite me as in agreement.[101]

The main reason why I have re-thought this issue, so that I am now more in agreement with Stanner's views, is because the historical evidence presented below suggests that the patrifiliation principle in this region, over time, resulted by and large in a set of continua which were structurally important to the society, and which were greater in temporal span than any one generation could attest to through personal knowledge. The 'patrilines' had in this sense a life of their own, something that is not captured by an analytic focus only on one-step filiations to fathers reported by their offspring.

A comparison of Stanner's 1932 field data with my own of 1979, combined with some intermediate data gleaned from the Register of Wards of 1957, revealed that the countries, patrifilial totems and languages of those living in 1979 were predominantly the same as those of their distant patrifilial forebears who were described by Stanner's informants in 1932. A number of totems and language affiliations were also recorded for members of the same groups by a patrol officer in 1957 and these intermediate data fill a chronological gap between the two main sets of records.[102]

I found only two cases where the patrifiliation mechanism did not apply wherever it could. In one case the estate of a man called Lukana did not pass to his children for some reason. In another case one man, Nugget Majar, together with his descendants, pursued as their primary estate interest an area different from his father's Madngele country, the latter being on the middle Daly. The area he pursued was on the Reynolds River to the north. His siblings remained primarily affiliated to their father's estate at Daly River and he also retained an interest in it. He was found to be a traditional owner of the Malak Malak/Madngele claim area by Justice Toohey in 1982.[103]

In the middle Daly record to 1979 the relevant patrifilial strings were up to six generations deep and stretched back, on a very conservative estimate, as far as the 1840s, more likely to the 1830s or earlier. In constructing guesses about birth dates of nineteenth-century people here, I have used 25 years as a conventional estimate for a generation, but in the case of father–child average age gaps it has to be regarded as a minimum. Many times in the data one finds the first child was born when its father was about 25, but later children were still being born when the man was in his fifties, for example. Overall it may be that 30 or 35 is a more useful rule of thumb and the birth dates of the earliest recorded estate group forefathers could thus be closer to the 1810s than the 1840s and 1850s. Frederick Rose found at Groote Eylandt in 1941, where polygyny was high (men having up to six wives), that for wives aged approximately between 14 and 39 'the *average age* of the husband was almost constant at about 42 years and it did not vary with the age of the female'. The average age difference between a man and his wife was 17.75 years, the maximum being 41 years.[104]

By contrast, at Angas Downs in Central Australia, where polygyny was very rare (only one case, a man with two wives), Rose found the average age difference between husbands and wives to be only 6.8 years.[105] At Daly River polygyny had been the rule, although it had fallen into disfavour with the Malak Malak by 1932, but the age gap between women and men on first marriage was still considerable, women getting married soon after puberty, men getting married only after reaching the third stage of initiation and often much later.[106]

In many cases even my most senior informants were only children or were very young adults in 1932, and Stanner's informants were by and large senior people from the same families who were deceased by 1979. I did not convey Stanner's information on these topics, nor that of the 1957 Register of Wards, to my informants. In that sense the record was greater than the knowledge of any living Malak Malak person, either in 1932 or 1979, and the continuities it revealed were in that sense 'innocent'. It is theoretically possible that Stanner's informants systematically guessed at the affiliations of the grandparents they had not known personally, but I regard this as unlikely, given that in so many cases no affiliations were recorded beneath their names.

Briefly, patrifilial totems and estate affiliations at Daly River were more stable than language affiliations, although the latter were also very conservative in patrifilial transmission. Among the extinct totemic clans were one or two whose remembered linguistic affiliations were in dispute, a situation that presumably would not have been likely had they survived. Preferred estate names had sometimes changed over time, involving a shift of focus from one main site to another, but these sites generally can be shown to belong to the same continuing estate. This is likely in my opinion to have been a product of biography in some ways – key individuals and their entourages becoming identified with different base camps at different times. It suggests a nexus between use of country and the way it is constructed in terms of named units of tenure.

It is in this case complicated by the fact that some estates overlapped at major resource sites or shared a similar environment and thus in several instances two or three estates could be known by the same name, namely that of a major place or that of a species used as an ecological typifier. This kind of 'ambiguity' of group names may have been not so much a case of 'blurring' but a kind of polysemy, one that was both a reflection of alliances between neighbours and, quite possibly, a device which lent itself to smooth processes of estate amalgamation, fission and succession.

To take one case as an example, the family tree for Malak Malak Land Claim Group 3, as remembered in 1979, and as is so often the case, only went back as far as the grandparents of the oldest living members, to their father's father. Stanner, however, had worked with the father of these oldest members, who was able to name and assign country, totemic and linguistic affiliations to his own ancestors to the grandparental generation also. As he was born in 1895, the birth dates of his grandparents could have been in about the 1840s, but probably earlier for males because of both their expectable later marrying ages than females and their capacity for a higher reproductive age. In this case the estate of Dek Dilk and its clan's principal totem of Red Kangaroo were thus recorded for all patrifiliative generations from the early or mid-nineteenth century to 1979. There are a number of other similar cases.

But language affiliations were a little more unstable: the 1979 members identified their language as Malak Malak. Stanner's informant's language is surprisingly recorded as Marranunggu, but his own father's (and mother's) language as Madngele. In 1957 he was recorded as Malak Malak but this has long been used not only as a name of a particular language but also as a kind of 'nation' name for members of both the Malak Malak and Madngele language groups, so the evidence there is inconclusive.

For those thirteen patrifilial groups still extant at the time of my own research on the Malak Malak, Madngele and (part of the) Kamu areas, the following figures can be derived:

Estate same in 1932 and 1979: 10 out of 13; 3 uncertain
Totem same in 1932 and 1979: 8 out of 13;[107] 4 uncertain, 1 same 1957/79
Language same in 1932 and 1979: 9 same;[108] 2 shifts, 2 unclear

While I do not suggest that such findings should be turned into a universal 'objective test' of both systemic and substantive continuities from the time of sovereignty to recent times, anthropologists working with claimant groups may find it useful to address similar patterns in the data, where it is available.

To establish that native title exists today, claimants will need to show, among other things, not only that they have rights in country according to their own system of laws and customs, but also that those laws and customs have their origin in the normative system of a society which existed in the area before sovereignty. At any point the relevant society comprises people who are united in their common observance of a relevant body of laws and customs.

In the ethnographic writings of the colonial era and later, one can detect a certain relationship between sympathy for Aborigines as human beings and the degree to which writers took an interest in and informed themselves about the systems of social and local organisation of the people about whom they wrote. Detractors of Aborigines not uncommonly accused them of leading a Hobbesian kind of life, of being not only nomadic and lacking property but also capricious in decision-making, lacking law and religion, and thus deeply unsystematic as a people. Their ethnographic defenders often said very much the opposite, but the ethnographers tended to do so in the context of providing evidence as to how local Aboriginal society was organised, rather than as political defence *per se*. This is not to suggest that defenders of Aborigines in that era rejected terms such as 'primitive', 'stone-age' or 'savagery' in describing Aboriginal societies, and many used these descriptions at the same time as they explored intricate local rules relating to descent of kin classes and totems.

A.W. Howitt, for example, said in 1888 that the Kurnai people of Gippsland had 'an "unwritten law" of extraordinary force'[109] and then proceeded to demonstrate this in a series of publications covering kinship, marriage, inheritance of property, camping rules, social and local organisation and many other aspects of what would now be called their system of customary law. But he also felt constrained to defend the Kurnai against 'the usual charges which are made against the Australian aborigines generally... The counts of indictment may be said to be – Superstition, untruthfulness, selfishness, ingratitude, immorality, cruelty, and finally, disregard of human life'.[110] And, he might have added, disorganisation, although this is hardly of the same order as these moral states.

In the jargon of earlier days, the more organised a society was, the more 'advanced' it was, and the more it had to be taken seriously by colonial powers. If a society failed to exhibit a certain ill-defined quantum of organisation – and especially if it failed to exhibit sedentism and horticulture – its lands might be regarded as *terra nullius*. Curiously, this idea resonates again in the context of proof of native title, and at both historical ends of the process: the indigenous society at the time of sovereignty has to be shown to have a system of a certain order, and the claimants themselves do also.

So once again a certain mutually reinforcing relationship between support for indigenous interests and a stress on systems thinking in anthropology becomes possible, albeit in a different way. In making a defence of 'systems thinking' at this time, I do not wish to underestimate the evils of a temptation to exaggerate system at the expense of ethnographic honesty. But there is also a counter-temptation: an anthropologist who was politically hostile to native title claims, at least those in areas where classical cultures had been most affected by colonisation, might equally be tempted to exaggerate the disorderliness and fluidity of evidence as to the persistence of customary tenure law among the claimant groups.

It is, however, a third temptation which has mainly been the subject of this chapter. This is the seductive progressivism of certain recent developments in social theory, under which ethnographic evidence of fluidity and non-lethal forms of anarchy enjoys a rather more glamorous standing than evidence of regularity, regulation, stability and more or less continual repetition. Given all these temptations, and while none of us ever escape from our conscious and unconscious theoretical leanings, in a forensic context such as native title research and writing it is increasingly important for us to somehow separate ethnography from interpretation where we can.

One approach to writing anthropology is to make a series of general or theoretical points, perhaps addressing some current issues or, in a forensic context, legal requirements, and in each case to draw on one's ethnographic knowledge in order to provide evidence or illustration of the general point. I think this approach lends itself to the three temptations discussed above. A rather opposed approach is to systematically and non-selectively lay out the ethnographic and other evidence that properly falls within the domain of the piece of writing, and then separately to raise the relevant theoretical points or legal requirements of proof, using the ethnographic and other evidence as a source against which to test various competing interpretations. This is a not uncommon procedure in the writing of grammars of little known or previously unrecorded languages.[111] It is of itself no guard against selective attention during the processes of fieldwork and literature research. It is also no guard against poorly framed instructions provided by clients to experts hired to research native title claims. Instructions which fail to identify the legal requirements of proof, and which thus put the onus on an anthropologist's (possibly inaccurate) understanding of those requirements, are an example of such inadequate instructions.

There is an anthropological aphorism that 'you can't separate ethnography from theory'. In some contexts this is true, but in other contexts a broad separation of this kind is common sense and common practice. One can easily point to vast bodies of evidence that demonstrate, for example, that while anthropologists may agree as to what terms and behavioural prescriptions are used among which kin in a certain society, at different times their theoretical interpretations of 'how the kinship system works' in that case can vary considerably.

It is at this level that I suggest practitioners consider the advantages of distinguishing evidence from argument, especially in the context of proceedings that may end up being litigated in the Federal Court of Australia. The guidelines for expert witnesses in that jurisdiction require experts to disclose, among other things, the 'facts, matters and assumptions upon which their [opinion] report proceeds'.[112] To that extent, Australian law requires a separation of ethnography from interpretation in some of our work. Before engaging in reflex actions to this imposition based on our usual critical view of the positivism that pervades legal culture, anthropologists could consider the advantages of such separation for the enduring value of our work and for its credibility when communicated to others.

7 | Kinship, filiation and Aboriginal land tenure[1]

NATIVE TITLE CLAIMANTS, while not required to have any particular form of social organisation, need to be able to show that they are a part of an organised society which derives at least substantial elements of its organisation and its relevant rules from those which obtained in the same area pre-sovereignty. While claims may be made on individuated bases and on many other bases other than those mediated by relations between kin, they still need to rest on a shared normative system. A defining element of distinctively Aboriginal societies is the centrality of kinship as an organising principle. In this chapter I focus on Aboriginal systems of genealogical relationships in relation to the transmission and recognition of customary rights and interests in land and waters. There is no suggestion here, however, that such transmission is always and wholly mediated by genealogical relationships.

THE KINSHIP POLITY

Those sets of Aboriginal people who hold the same or neighbouring countries under traditional forms of connection are normally kin, or relations, and address and refer to each other as such. This is certainly true where classical cultural traditions persist strongly, but it is also true of many groups, perhaps most, that have undergone cultural transformations as a result of their colonial and post-colonial histories.

Nevertheless, as a result of these transformations, and especially because of population displacements, some descendants of former landholders from a single area do not now necessarily know or regularly interact with certain others. That is, while two subsets of native title claimants may assert that they belong to a single land-based grouping such as a clan or tribe, at the time they made their application(s) they did not necessarily belong to the same social group of regularly interacting kin. This is a good illustration of the rather complicated way we use words like 'group'. It is sometimes useful to make a three-way distinction between a social group (set of interacting people who may not all ever assemble as a whole but each of whom is linked to the others by interactions), a social category (set of people who have some common social identity or recognised cultural feature but who may not interact), and a gathering (a set of people physically co-present for an event or task who may or may not belong to a single social group or category).

When engaging in the process of making a native title determination application, people may discover relatives of whom they were previously unaware. This may happen through attending land claim meetings, through receiving anthropological advice, or through access to documentary sources. In this way, lapsed identity-connections and inactive kinship links may be re-established, although the process may be long and slow. A common basis for questioning the credentials of those asserting connection to such groups, particularly people who have recently discovered or activated their shared ancestry with members of those groups, is that of motivation. They are often referred to as 'coming out of the woodwork' in order to gain some material advantage. Such comments may or may not be a sign of intra-community politics.

Most meaningful human relationships in classical Aboriginal practice involved dealings between kin. Prior to colonisation, judging from the early colonial literature, non-kin or complete strangers were not frequently encountered in daily life. Personal mobility was largely restricted to that region in which one could count on being able to trace some kind of kin relationship to any person one was likely to meet. Reserve and even great hostility, depending on the context, would normally mark encounters between people who were non-kin. The classical Aboriginal conventions for visiting between distantly related or unrelated people were highly elaborated, formal, and typically drawn out.[2] Unless such conventions were observed, an uninvited stranger was potentially subject to physical attack, possibly homicide, on sight. Under modern conditions this has been heavily modified, but aspects of the past endure and it may not be at all easy for native title co-claimants who do not have a known kinship connection, let alone an active one, to collaborate in pursuing their entitlements.

This is not to suggest that all Aboriginal kinship is based on a traceable genealogical relationship to others. Where such concrete links are recognised by the people themselves, the relationships are usually referred to by anthropologists as being 'actual', and they tend to be the relationships of greatest weight for those who have them. This is not to say that anthropologists regard such relationships as objectively 'actual' in, for example, a biological sense. It just means that the people whose relationships are under study regard such relationships to be 'real', 'full', based on 'blood' links, on 'being married' and so on, rather than on extrapolation from other relationships. To say that kinship is not about biology at all but only about cultural constructions is to oversimplify, and perhaps to miss the point. Many would argue that kinship is at essence the cultural construction of relationships arising in the first place from the nature of human reproduction.[3] The position taken here is that the anthropological study of kinship is, among other things, the study of relationships built on beliefs held about reproduction and nurturance in particular cultures, not the study of the biology and genetics of human reproduction. Where anthropologists study kinship in a context where DNA testing, for example, is an issue, there is a particular link between kinship and biology.

Most of an Aboriginal person's kin cannot be traced literally via connections of believed consanguinity or marriage and are referred to by anthropologists as 'classificatory' relations. In Aboriginal English one's classificatory kin may be referred to as 'tribal-way', 'outside' or 'long-way' relations, and one's actual kin as 'real', 'full', 'full blood', 'proper' or 'own', for example. These uses of 'full' are to be distinguished from the anthropologist's distinction between *full siblings*, who have the same mother and same father, and *half siblings* who have only one parent in common. Full siblings, in Aboriginal English, are often spoken of as having 'one father, one mother'. People with the same father and different mothers may be referred to as 'from two mothers', and people in the reverse situation as being of 'one mother, two fathers'. In some regions, the Western Desert especially, where one has been reared by more than one mother or father all may be recognised as one's real parents, so that 'I had three mothers' is quite a normal statement.

In Aboriginal languages, actual kin may be distinguished by locutions such as the Wangkangurru terms *arla* ('true') or *wathili* ('own'), e.g. *anthunha ama wathili* 'my own mother' (not a mother's sister or more distant kind of mother)[4]. In Eastern and Central Arrernte such a distinction may be made in this way:

Meye atyinhe ayenge-arle atnerte interleke re meye atyinhe anthurre.
My real mother is the mother whose stomach I was in.

Meye atyinhe, meye atyinhe-kenhe yaye re meye atyinhe antime.
My mother and my mother's sisters are all my mothers too.[5]

The actual/classificatory distinction is not the same as the distinction between primary and extended senses (denotata) of kin terms. For example, in Aboriginal languages the term used for one's own birth-mother is used in an extended sense also to refer to one's mother's actual sisters. This relation to one's mother's sisters is an important close relationship and is 'actual', even though the terminology *classifies* mothers' sisters as mothers and anthropologists will tend to refer to one's actual mother's sisters as one's 'classificatory mothers'.

At a further remove from the heartland of actual parentage is, for example, one's relationship to one's actual mother's mother's sisters' daughters, who are also usually classed as one's 'mothers' and with whom one shares considerable ancestry. Even more distant relations, and ultimately perhaps those strangers who have been integrated into a person's social field, may also be one's 'mothers', typically on the basis that one's own mother would have called such women 'sister' or on some similar basis for starting the kinship calculus. But as one moves further and further away from the actual mother, first to the mother's actual sisters, then to the mother's female actual parallel cousins, and so on through more attenuated blood connections to no known actual connections with one's many other 'mothers', it is clear that *genealogical distance* plays a major role in Aboriginal kinship and society. Its fine calibration far exceeds that of any simple actual/classificatory distinction. Especially in the past, and still for many today, genealogical distance has been closely correlated with geopolitical distance. That is, the more distantly related one is to others, the greater the likely distance between one's own traditional country and theirs.

Working out what kinship relation holds between oneself and a newly encountered person may take some time, unless the relationship is found to be fairly close. The solution to the calculation problem usually focuses on a meaningful relationship each person holds to a common third party.[6] One thereafter may call the new person 'sister' or 'grandfather' etc., 'from' or 'through' that significant third party, for example: 'I call him "uncle" through old Packsaddle, my father's father, who called him nephew'. One may trace such a connection in more than one way, through more than one third party, and thus end up able to define the mutual kin connection in more than one potentially acceptable way. For example: 'I should call him "uncle" through my grandfather, but I call him brother-in-law through my ex-wife, because I got married to his sister Delphina'. The usage adopted may depend on complex circumstances and it may be altered over time to take account of shifts in the fortunes of relationships: 'Since me and Delphina split up and we didn't have any kids I went back to calling him "uncle" again'. Disjunctions often occur, especially in cases where unrelated or very distantly related people interact as kin. For example, of two men who call each other brother, one may call a third party 'mother' while the other calls the same woman 'sister', tracing (or 'tracking') their kin connections via distinct pathways to the same person. There is no particular pressure, in my experience, to regularise these triangular cases of apparent disharmony.

In a general sense one treats classificatory kin according to an etiquette similar to the one used with actual kin, although with important exceptions, especially when following those graduated etiquettes which are based on degrees of genealogical distance. While much early anthropological literature on Aboriginal people concentrated on formal matters such as kin term systems and so-called 'marriage classes', there is also quite detailed information on the behaviours, rules, privileges and obligations expected of people of particular genders and seniority levels who stand in certain specified kin relationships.[7] Prescribed kin behaviours can vary widely according to the degree of distance involved, even where the people concerned stand in the same basic relationship of brother–sister, or two cousins, or father–daughter, or whatever. For example, pairs of the same kintypes who must be very restrained and basically avoid each other when closely related, such as certain kinds of cross-cousins, may have to joke together if middlingly related, and may be relatively free of both prohibitions and obligations if they are only distantly related.

The actual/classificatory distinction is only blurred under certain circumstances. For example, when elderly people are 'remembering' the relationships between people in the upper generations of a genealogy, they may reclassify two cousins who had the same grandparents as actual siblings, perhaps on the overt grounds that they addressed and referred to each other as such and had a close relationship. If relationships between their descendants were to be riven by conflict, however, they may be recalled as distant cousins or 'only cousins tribal-way'. Similarly, a man who was someone's stepfather may, after a period, be 'remembered' as that person's actual father and the memory of the latter expunged. In these retrospective cases the past may be brought into alignment with the demands of the present through structural amnesia. This is far more difficult to do when the relationships are recent. Although a person may have a large number of, for example, classificatory 'fathers' (men one's father would have called 'brother', usually), a person normally has only one recognised actual father, and stepfather/stepchild relationships are likewise distinguished as to being either actual or classificatory. (Where the actual paternity is a matter of dispute, a person may have more than one (partly-) recognised genitor.) I deal with this distinction between actual and classificatory kin by way of illustration below.

Step-kin include some other relations in addition to parents or offspring. In Wik society (Cape York Peninsula) the death of an actual grandparent may be followed by the recognition of an alternative person, already a classificatory grandparent of the same type as the deceased, as a substitute grandparent who fills some of the social roles of the one who has died. Such roles are 'special' or pseudo-actual replacement kin. The pseudo-actual role of genitor (*wuynpenh*, Wik-Ngathan) may also be assigned to a man who takes a non-Aboriginal person as their offspring. This term is quite distinct from the term that means 'upbringer-father' (*piipinh-thawan*), the latter being the usual means of referring to the male adoptive relationship, and also from the standard metaphoric locution for distinguishing father's younger brother (FB-) from father (F) or father's elder brother (FB+). Here again is a culturally significant piece of fine-tuning that locates certain relationships somewhere between actual and classificatory and makes the simple two-way distinction a very rough and somewhat misleading one. It also comes from a region where a form of the pater/genitor and mater/genetrix distinction has long been well-developed.[8]

At the opposite end of the spectrum, Western Desert people are widely reported as observing such distinctions with far less emphasis, placing even more stress than do others on biographical and spiritual history in determining which kin are 'real', which are 'siblings' and so on. There, as Laurent Dousset has observed, shared substance between people based on genealogical reckoning may be distinguished from other kinds of consubstantiality based, for example, on prolonged co-residence and shared Dreaming site affiliations, but the two kinds of sharing may still be distinguished. They are contrasted by Dousset in terms of 'a systemic foundation in actual kinship systems that are amenable to comparative approaches and typology', on the one hand, and elements of 'noise', including co-residence and shared localised Dreamings, which affect the reckoning of kin relationships and the terminology applied to them, on the other. He regards it as a mistake to think of such 'noise' factors as formal parts of the systemic kinship structure.[9]

Was kinship the polity?

Kinship is the cornerstone of classical Aboriginal social organisation. Kinship and social organisation also formed the backbone of the discipline of social or cultural anthropology from the early twentieth century until the 1970s. There is nothing particularly new or exotic about the complexities of Aboriginal kinship from an anthropological perspective, but they present a learning challenge, for example, to lawyers and bureaucrats involved in the native title regime. However, a serious decline in the teaching of kinship and social organisation at Australian universities after the 1970s has probably reduced the effectiveness of some anthropologists working in the field of indigenous land tenure.[10]

In a society which in the past did not employ specialist administrators or government structures separate from the conduct of daily life, and employed no occupationally separate judicial and policing system like that of an industrial state, culturally prescribed kin roles and kinship-based social organisation played a central role in Aboriginal systems of customary law. In an explicit sense, kinship-based institutions and authority roles were central to maintaining the reasonably orderly distribution of country as cultural and material property, and to providing regular methods for dealing with conflict and grievances. Thus the reckoning of land tenure interests, for example, on the basis of genealogical relationships is itself an implicit instance of customary law. That is, where they apply, the rules of descent and of other kinds of relatedness practised by a particular group are themselves part of customary Aboriginal land tenure law.

This kind of integration of the genealogical with the juro-political domain has tempted some to think of the classical Aboriginal social order as being almost equivalent to its kinship system. Eminent anthropologist Meyer Fortes referred to Aboriginal society as 'The Kinship Polity' in a paper which is a very useful, if technical, introduction to this question.[11] While his paper offers good insights into the encompassing role of kinship in classical Aboriginal society, and 'kinship polity' is an apt description in that case, forms of social organisation rooted in forms of genealogical relatedness are not simply reducible to kinship. Neither is kinship the only basis for the acquisition of territorial interests or inter-group political relations. Anthropologist Lauriston Sharp went so far as to describe the Yir-Yoront of Cape York Peninsula as 'People without Politics', emphasising the almost all-encompassing task of kinship-based structures and behaviours in classical Aboriginal governance.[12] Such accounts have, in my view, underplayed the importance of both the individual and the regional system.[13]

While it is not true that in Aboriginal societies 'everything is kinship', it is important to recognise that without a basic grasp of how Aboriginal kinship and kin-based social organisation operates in any given case, it is certainly not possible to claim to understand how local customary tenure of land and waters also operates. The subject is inherently difficult, for the simple reason that Aboriginal kinship systems and the social organisational structures and processes built on them are themselves often dauntingly complex.[14] Here I provide a very brief introduction to the subject before broaching some issues relevant to native title, beginning with conventions for the representation of genealogical relationships.

BASIC CONVENTIONS AND TERMINOLOGY

Visual symbols

Land claims in Australia, regardless of the jurisdiction concerned, usually involve the presentation of genealogical evidence, both orally and in the form of genealogical charts. It is important in this context to grasp the kind of shorthand notation anthropologists use for representing genealogical relationships, and here we begin by looking at the way kin relationships may be shown in genealogies, and then examine how they are normally abbreviated (Figures 4–7).

Genealogies may be shown vertically or horizontally. In the horizontal presentation, upper generations are on the left, descending to lower generations on the

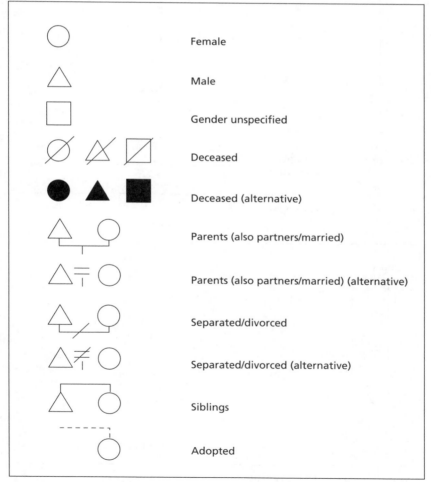

Figure 4: Basic genealogical symbols

right, and birth order among siblings runs from top (older) to bottom (younger) (Figure 5). In the vertical presentation, upper generations are at the top, descending to lower generations at the bottom, and birth order runs from left to right (Figure 6).

When anthropologists write about particular genealogical relationships, such as those between a person and their mother's mother's brother's daughter's daughter, in order to speed up the process they use some widely accepted conventions for abbreviating kinds of kin, gender, and relative age (Figure 4).

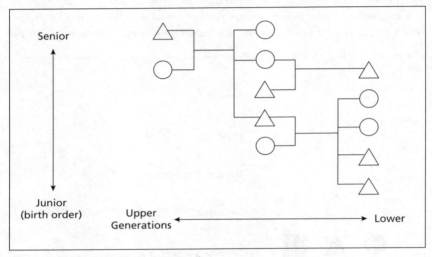

Figure 5: Presenting genealogies horizontally

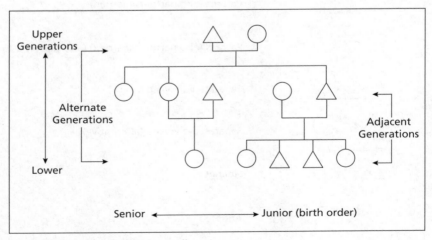

Figure 6: Presenting genealogies vertically

It is important not to confuse the eight basic *kintypes* (Figure 7) and all the others that can be generated from them (their 'relative products'), with *kin terms*; the latter are the different words used to refer to sets of kintypes in any particular language. Kintypes are the *denotata* of, or what are denoted by, kin terms. Kin terms also have connotata, or indexical characteristics, such as formality/ informality (compare *'Father'* with *'Pop'*), or vocative/referential distinctions ('Hey *Sis!*' versus 'That's my *sister'*).[15] One kin term typically covers several different kintypes.

The alternative convention for representing kintypes is to use Br, Si, Fa, Mo, So, Da, Wi, Hu and Ch, instead of the single-letter abbreviations below, but many of us prefer the shorter method, as most primary kin terms in English start with different letters and can be abbreviated by a single initial. Using Z for sister and S for son removes the problem of two terms starting with the same letter. Instead of m (man's) and w (woman's) many anthropological texts use the gender symbols ♂ and ♀ but m and w are more convenient as they are found on all keyboards with Roman letters.

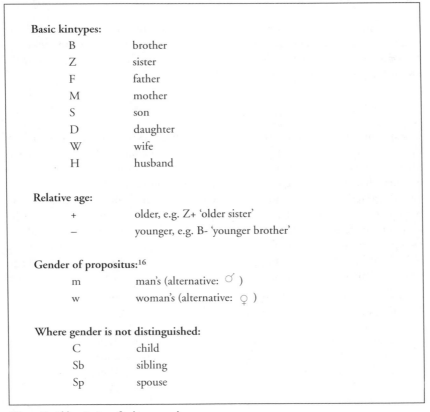

Basic kintypes:

B	brother
Z	sister
F	father
M	mother
S	son
D	daughter
W	wife
H	husband

Relative age:

+	older, e.g. Z+ 'older sister'
−	younger, e.g. B- 'younger brother'

Gender of propositus:[16]

m	man's (alternative: ♂)
w	woman's (alternative: ♀)

Where gender is not distinguished:

C	child
Sb	sibling
Sp	spouse

Figure 7: Abbreviations for kin term denotata

These abbreviations are all that are normally needed to specify any kin relation-ship. Anthropologists do not normally use U for 'uncle' or A for 'aunt', or other abbreviations for 'grandfather', 'great-great-great-grandfather', 'great aunt', 'mother-in-law' and so on; instead they normally specify these relationships by stating the component relationships underlying them, for example:

FB	father's brother
MB-	mother's younger brother
MF	mother's father
FZ+	father's older sister
FFFF	father's father's father's father
HM	husband's mother
WBWF	wife's brother's wife's father
MMBDD	mother's mother's brother's daughter's daughter
wC	woman's child
mC	man's child

Figure 8: Examples of combinatory use of symbols for basic kintypes

Thus only primary relationships (those based on parentage and partnering) are used in combination to generate all the others. This also gets rid of ambiguities – for example, is someone's 'uncle' a father's brother or mother's brother (FB or MB), and is the 'father-in-law' his or hers (WF or HF)?

Kin term semantics

In different cultures, kin terms can divide up the world of kintypes in very different ways. To people unfamiliar with the logic of a foreign kin terminology it may seem strange and 'unnatural'. For example, an English-speaker may feel it is 'natural' that the offspring of parents are divided on gender lines between 'sons' and 'daughters', and that both parents refer to their male offspring as 'sons' and both parents refer to their female offspring as 'daughters'. But in many cultures the semantics of terms for offspring may be quite different. In most Aboriginal kin terminologies there is a single term for both the sons and the daughters of any individual, but a man's offspring are commonly referred to by a different term from those of a woman. For example:

Kintype	Jawoyn	English
mD	*madak*	(man's) daughter
mS	*madak*	(man's) son
wD	*walk*	(woman's) daughter
wS	*walk*	(woman's) son

Figure 9: Jawoyn terms for offspring [17]

In such systems it is also typical that same-sex siblings of a parent (that is, FB, MZ) refer to that parent's offspring by the same terms that the parent does. Different-sex siblings of a parent, in many Aboriginal languages, use other terms, which in their basic form are also not differentiated as to gender. This is again in contrast with English, where any of a parent's siblings refers to that parent's offspring as 'nieces and nephews'. For example:

Kintype	Jawoyn	English
mBS	*madak*	nephew
mBD	*madak*	niece
wZS	*walk*	nephew
wZD	*walk*	niece

Figure 10: Jawoyn terms for siblings' offspring

In Jawoyn, unlike quite a few other Australian languages, both the sisters and the brothers of a parent refer to that parent's offspring by a single term, namely the one used by the parent in question:

Kintype	Jawoyn	English
wBS	*madak*	nephew
wBD	*madak*	niece
mZS	*walk*	nephew
mZD	*walk*	niece

Figure 11: Comparison of Jawoyn and English terms for siblings' offspring

It is rather more common for there to be a separate term or terms used to denote mZC or wBC, as in the following example from Wangkangurru:[18]

Kintype	Wangkangurru	English
wC, wZC	arluwa	daughter, son, niece, nephew
mC, mBC	atapiyaka	daughter, son, niece, nephew
mZC	thidnara[19]	niece, nephew
wBC	thidnara	niece, nephew

Figure 12: Comparison of Wangkangurru and English terms for offspring and siblings' offspring

Actual and classificatory kin

The distinction between actual and classificatory kin can be illustrated, in just one of its forms, by a diagram such as Figure 13.

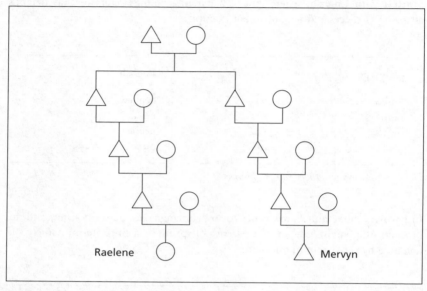

Figure 13: The actual/classificatory distinction: Raelene and Mervyn are classificatory siblings

What Figure 13 shows is that Raelene and Mervyn had FFFs who were actual brothers, that is, the two men had the same socially recognised natural or adopting parents. But over time this was forgotten and by the lifetime of their great grandchildren, maybe 100 years later, no actual genealogical connection between Raelene and Mervyn is any longer remembered. But they do know they should call each other by sibling terms (B and Z) and have been brought up to do so from earliest childhood. How do people know that Raelene and Mervyn should be classed as siblings? A typical answer to such a question would be: 'Because their fathers called each other 'brother' and were classed as 'cousin-brothers' (parallel cousins, see below)'. And why was this? 'Because in turn *their* fathers did the same'. The logic is: if Raelene and Mervyn's FFs called each other 'brother', these two men's sons would have called both of the men 'father', and thus would have been 'brothers'. Similarly, their children in turn would also have called each other by sibling terms.

In this particular case (an invented example, by the way), and unknown to Raelene and Mervyn, their two FFs called each other 'brother' because in turn *their* fathers not only called each other 'brother' but were regarded as *actual* (real, full, etc.) brothers.

In a very large number of cases, however, there is no remembered or traceable actual kin relationship involved in the deduction of who is related to whom and how. Where no ultimate consanguineal ('real' or perhaps 'blood'-related) or affinal (marital or in-law) relationship may be remembered or recorded, a classificatory kin relationship between two people is usually worked out by seeing what kin terms they apply to third persons whom they both know. In an area where kin class systems such as subsections or sections operate (see below), a stranger's class name may be used as a quick way to establish the kin connection. For example, a man of Jimija subsection (Mudbura language, northern Tanami Desert) would know that, in the absence of any known genealogical relationship, a woman of the same class (a Namija) must be his 'sister', while a woman of his preferred marrying class (a Nangala) must be his cousin. Classificatory kinship, not surprisingly, is sometimes referred to as a 'calculus'.

What is usually known as 'the sibling equivalence rule' governs the basic logic in many such cases. If my actual father calls Jimmy 'brother', then I must call Jimmy 'father' also; Jimmy is not my actual father, but 'a kind of father' because brothers are akin or structurally equivalent, the same **kin**d of relative. If Judy's mother calls my mother 'sister', then Judy must call my mother 'mother', as I do; and thus Judy and I must call each other 'sister' (assuming I am female) or 'sister' and 'brother' if we have different genders. This is because sisters are a**kin** or structurally equivalent, the same kind of relative. These examples are for illustration purposes only, and do not represent universals in Aboriginal kin term usage. In some languages, a FB+ is not called 'father' but is known by another term and MZ+ is not called 'mother', while their junior siblings are 'fathers' and 'mothers' respectively.

It is sometimes conventional in anthropological writings to distinguish classificatory kin from actual kin by enclosing the classificatory kin term in quotation marks, as in: 'Jeannie's mother was Topsy. Jeannie's close "mothers" are those parallel cousins of Topsy with whom Jeannie grew up.'

Primary and extended meanings

The fact that the same kin terms are used for both close, actual kin and people to whom one is not known to be related at all by consanguinity or marriage, does not mean that Aboriginal kin terms are vague or loose in meaning.

Such kin terms usually have both a *primary sense* and *extended senses*. Here I am adopting a particular position in what has been a rather long-standing debate in Australian kinship theory, namely the position which is argued for in detail by H.W. Scheffler.[20] Some theorists, particularly early in the twentieth century, argued that Aboriginal kin terms designate 'social categories' and are 'terms of relationship' between members of classes such as moieties, sections and subsections. The Schefflerian view is that in all well-documented systems, Aboriginal societies have systems of kin classification that rest on egocentric relations of genealogical connection.[21] These systems are remarkably similar Australia-wide in their basic logic, while there are substantial regions of the continent where there are no class systems at all and no record of their ever having existed.

The primary/extended distinction can be illustrated by examples from the Wik region (Cape York Peninsula). In Wik-Ngathan *kaathiy* is translated as 'mother'. Its primary sense of 'actual mother' can if necessary be made more explicit by substituting the expression *nganh-kelen,* literally 'the one who gave birth to me', in the case of one's own natural mother. Other pronouns are substituted for others' relationships. The first extension of reference of *kaathiy* is to the relationship of MZ-, one which can be made more explicit by the full idiom *kaathiy-ulkant,* literally 'mother of the cradle', translated as 'small mother' in English. From there, extensions of *kaathiy* run out in a theoretically unlimited way to cover relationships such as MFBD, MFFBSD, MFFFBSSD and so on, categories of women eligible to have married one's father under classical tradition. There are also some specialised usages, such as when a man calls his B+W *kaathiy* as a customary way of avoiding the real nature of their genealogical relationship (as cousins) and metaphorically representing the relationship as one in which sexual relations are taboo (mother–son). Another specialised use of *kaathiy* is when men, at least, address their MB- as 'mother' when in emotional distress, appealing to the nurturing side of the authority-role customarily assigned to such an uncle. It is clear that a kin term such as *kaathiy* is not a term of nebulous and scattered meanings but one whose various extensions of meaning radiate outwards from a core or prototype relationship that, as it were, drives the others, both structurally and in terms of emotional connotations.

Ego and propositus

Charts of kin terms usually have an 'EGO' at a central point so you can tell who you would call by what term if you were that person. Often upper case is a male *EGO* and lower case is female *ego*. In genealogical field notes the main informant from whose vantage point the family tree is being elicited is usually marked in some way by the researcher.

In any conversation between people who are referring to the kin of either participant, the junior person is normally taken as the vantage point for third person reference. That is, only one set of kin terms is used in the conversation to refer to third persons. For example, a woman would refer to her brother as 'uncle [MB]' when speaking to her daughter, but as 'brother' when speaking to her own mother or grandfather. The vantage point from whom the kin term is determined is called the *propositus*. This practice of taking the junior person as propositus is common worldwide, but it is more rigorously applied in Aboriginal communities of classical orientation than among most European Australians.

The practice becomes a problem when one is speaking to a gathering of different kin, some of whom are senior to ego, some of whom are junior. One solution is to refer to a third person from ego's point of view (for example, 'Uncle Arthur'), or, in contemporary circumstances, just to use a personal name, perhaps with an apology because of the perceived rudeness conveyed by the use of personal names among many kin under classical Aboriginal traditions. Especially if the context is one that originates in non-Aboriginal society, such as a meeting of an incorporated body or a land claim hearing, to varying degrees people are prepared to adopt a more European style of personal address and reference for the event. The offence that might otherwise have resulted is thus 'excused' because of the context.

In regions where subsections are used (see below), one can politely refer to (or address) anyone by their subsection name in such a context. One can also use other devices such as 'the mother of X' or 'the one whose father died at [placename]' to specify individuals without referring to one's own relationship to them. Totems are also a common way of obliquely referring to people in certain regions. A more unusual solution is the use, in the case of Wik-Ngathan, of a combination of kin terms each of which is appropriate to many addressees of consequence, such as when ego refers to a man who is younger brother to key senior men present, but father to many of the young people present, as *piip/thaak*, literally 'F/B-'.[22]

TECHNICAL TERMINOLOGY

Here I will lay out the senses in which I will be using some technical anthropological terminology in the rest of the chapter. All of the key concepts explored here have been subject to varying degrees of debate among anthropologists, and the reader should not imagine that what follows is a settled, canonical version of the anthropology of kin groups, as there is no such thing. Nevertheless, it is true to say that the twentieth century saw enormous advances in the clarification of these concepts among anthropologists, based on the explosion of ethnographic case material that became available after World War I and the interaction between this increasingly fine-grained ethnography and developments in anthropological theory.

Parentage and gender

The concept of *parentage* underlies elementary kinship categories in a most fundamental way. This is obvious in the case of the definition of a mother, a father, a son or a daughter, but it is true of other primary relationships as well. Siblings are people who share one or both parents. Cousins are people whose parentage includes at least two people who shared a parent. An aunt is a woman who shares a parent with one of one's parents. One's grandchild is someone who has a parent of whom one is oneself a parent, and so on.

Parentage may be of several different kinds, depending on how a particular culture deals with it. It is common for there to be a distinction between a parent considered to be one's 'birth' mother (*genetrix*) and one's adoptive, foster or 'social' mother (*mater*), on the one hand, and between one's 'begetting' father (*genitor*) and adoptive, foster or 'social' father (*pater*) on the other. There are wide differences between cultures as to the 'physical' role of fathers, especially, in procreation (see further below on Aboriginal traditions). Even within Aboriginal Australia, the 'physical' role of fathers in begetting children is construed with a good deal of local cultural variation, and in some areas may even be denied, and is in a variety of different relationships to the transmission of spiritual substance from father to child, depending on the region.

Clearly *gender* is another basic building-block of kin categories. In English kin terminology, one's 'daughter' is a female of whom one is a parent, regardless of one's own gender, and one's 'niece' is a female of whom one's sibling is a parent, regardless of one's own gender or that of one's sibling. That is, in this case we specify the gender of the offspring but disregard any differences of gender in the parenting and siblingship relations involved in the definition of the kin term for the offspring.

Filiation

Filiation refers to the fact of being the recognised or legitimate offspring of a parent. It is often used by anthropologists to go further than this, and to refer to the *jural status* of being someone's recognised offspring.[23] For example, among many Aboriginal groups in Australia, traditional country rights and group affiliations may come to a person principally through one or both parents. But as these rights and affiliations are important collective interests, the recognition of who one's parents are is not just a private, nuclear-family affair. It involves the *jural public*, those of one's community, peers and relations whose assent is very important to the establishment of one's entitlements to collective property and forms of religious identity under Aboriginal traditions. It is here that a distinction between natural parents and those who bring people up becomes especially relevant. It is sometimes the case that someone will say they acquire their principal country rights and group affiliations from the person or people who 'grew me up', rather than from natural parents.

It is useful to distinguish *one-step filiation* (for example, to one's M, or one's F) from *two-step filiation* (for example, directly to one's to MM, or to one's FM), and both of these from *serial filiation* (for example, to one's F, then he to his F, then the latter to his F and so on, or to one's M, then she to her M, the latter to her M and so on).

Patrifiliation is filiation to the father and certain of his group interests. *Matrifiliation* is filiation to the mother and certain of her group interests. Thus, in north-east Arnhem Land, the Yolngu people have what Ian Keen refers to as 'patrifilial groups', groups whose members acquire primary rights and interests in countries through patrifiliation.[24] Where people regularly acquire rights and interests through either or both parents, absent a rule specifying only one, their system may be said to be one of *parental filiation*.

Serial filiation, such as serial patrifiliation (to one's F, then he to his F, then the latter to his F and so on), results in *filiative strings* of connection back through time to one's forebears. But whether or not such filiative strings and those who belong to them also constitute *descent groups*, in the technical sense, has to be determined on further evidence.

Descent

In a technical anthropological sense, *descent* – particularly in the context of the customary handing down of identity and property interests – is commonly held to refer to 'a relationship defined by connection to an ancestor (or ancestress) through a culturally recognized sequence of parent-child links'.[25] That is, members of a descent group share a common, identifiable individual ancestor, or sometimes a set of ancestors such as two or three siblings, or a married couple, from whom they reckon their group membership. The field of descent theory, however, has long been characterised by academic debate.

A defining characteristic of descent groups, in the view of influential theorist Harold Scheffler, is that their members have *descent constructs* – culturally acquired understandings of the ancestor–descendant basis of group membership – and *descent-phrased rules* for group membership.[26] A typical descent-phrased rule is that the group recruits as members those who are fathered (or adopted) by a man whose patriline is normally identified as part of the group. This emphasises the way the people themselves construct such groups, as evidence for anthropological analysis. It also places estate group formation explicitly within the realm of customary law.

But in describing country group structure, for any particular region, the anthropologist must pay attention to more than the group members' own articulation of their constructs and rules. A rich anthropological account of such a system also requires evidence of the kind that ordinary people do not, perhaps cannot, bring to consciousness and make explicit in speech. This involves a careful study of genealogies in relation to who is said to belong to the group concerned, and the use of records of events such as group fission (splitting), amalgamation or incorporation. The way people in such groups understand their system and manage it is normally far more complex and period-bound than they are able, or willing, to make explicit to others.[27]

One of the limitations of ethnography that lacks any historical depth is that the anthropologist may have little to say about the nature of such groups over time.[28] While members of the society concerned may have the view that their land-based groups were established at the beginning of the world and do not change their characteristics or symbols, it is now well-nigh impossible, in the native title context, that an Australian court would accept such statements in the absence of evidence other than contemporary belief. Given the time depth of ethnographic studies in certain parts of Aboriginal Australia, it is now possible to construct histories of a number of land-holding groups and their estates over a period of century or more. This also means that descendants can find out what their antecedents told ethnographers fifty or a hundred years ago. This information may have some impact on how contemporary people understand the workings of their land tenure system. This impact may be different from that which longitudinal material has on the anthropologist attempting to make a technical analysis of groups. For example, a contemporary member of a group may be inclined to emphasise continuities in the record rather than discontinuities, and to focus on the history of their own group, not others. For an anthropologist, the relationship between patterns of regular cultural reproduction and cases of rupture or disjunction may be the focus of interest, and a sample of many groups is vastly preferable to evidence from just one group, in the establishment of generalisations. It may be that the groups of a particular area have a recognisable life-cycle, just as domestic groups do, moving towards a target of solidity, stability and consistency, and then from time to time undergoing fission, diminution, extinction and replacement. We do not yet have any published and detailed case studies of the histories of land-holding groups in Aboriginal Australia, although they could now be written for a number of areas.

Whether one is dealing with present-day oral accounts of groups, or these combined with archival material, it is useful in technical anthropological contexts to distinguish *descent* from *descendedness*. Descent here refers to a mechanism of the jural system by which being genealogically related to a certain ancestor provides the foundation for *constructs* (e.g. totemic groups) and *rules* (e.g. how the acquisition of property rights is properly done). Descendedness, by comparison, could be defined simply as the relationship of a person to a forebear regardless of whether or not they derive any particular jural standing, such as membership in a country-holding group, as a consequence of that relationship. It is helpful, in other words, to be able to discuss relationships between people and their forebears free of any particular implication for the nature of genealogically-defined groups or rights.

For the same reason it would be useful in such technical contexts to distinguish *ancestors* from *antecedents* or *forebears*. All the people to whom one is linked by parent-child relationships are one's forebears or antecedents, including one's own parents, regardless of whether or not one belongs to a society in which there are ancestor-focused descent groups. This is because ancestors, in a technical descent context, are particular antecedents who emerge to be recognised as founding figures for particular sets of their descendants who thus form a common identity and often hold, as a result of this identity, common cultural or other property.

An ancestor in this sense is not just a kin-relation slot, such as FF or FFF, regardless of who might have filled such a slot, but a remembered, usually named, individual. The land-holding groups of classical Aboriginal societies are widely reported as being based on descendedness, but they were most frequently formed on a basis of serial patrifiliation, not on descent from particular named, apical ancestors. Post-classical Aboriginal societies have moved towards the formation of groups of descendants based on common relationships to named individual ancestors (see Chapter 8). It is important to recall that relationships with forebears are not the exclusive pathway to membership of country-holding groups or sets of people. There are parts of Australia where neither descent groups nor groups formed by serial parental filiation play a privileged role or perhaps any role in the formation of such groups or sets. The Western Desert is the prime example of this.

Lineages, in some rather strict anthropological definitions, are descent groups based on either *patrilines* or *matrilines*, the memberships of which are thus reckoned by *unilineal descent* from an *apical ancestor*.[29] An apical ancestor is one who stands genealogically at the head, or apex, of a descent group consisting of their recognised descendants. They may have been dead for decades, even centuries, in some societies. A *patrilineage* reckons such descent through male parents only, but itself consists of both males and females. A *matrilineage* reckons such descent through female parents only, but likewise consists of both females and males. Patrilineages and matrilineages are the backbones of certain kinds of unilineal descent group, namely *patrilineal descent groups* and *matrilineal descent groups* (Figures 14 and 15).

When both patrilineal and matrilineal systems are present in the same society, the system may be said to be one of *double descent*, also known as *double unilineal descent*. There are no documented land-holding groups in Aboriginal tradition that are recruited by double descent (see further below).

Descent and filiation in Australian land claims

In spite of the technical distinction made by anthropologists between descent and filiation, it has become commonplace in anthropological writings on Aboriginal Australia, including reports prepared for land claims, to confound the two and refer to both as 'descent'. This was also true before the *Aboriginal Land Rights (Northern Territory) Act 1976 (Commonwealth)* required Aboriginal traditional owners to belong to a 'local descent group' (Section 3(1)).

This loose, vernacular definition of descent amounts to any systematic rule by which descendedness confers membership of a recognised group, in this case one that has rights and interests in property such as country. Under this loose definition, people who basically practise serial patrifiliation, for example, and who do not reckon descent from named apical ancestors, have been described as having

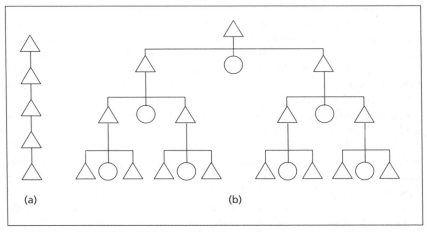

Figure 14: Patrilineal descent. (a) A patrilineal descent construct. (b) A patrilineal descent category. Note that it includes women, but not their children (after Keesing 1975:18)

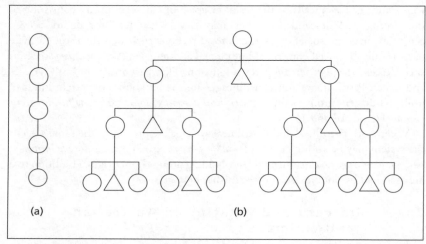

Figure 15: Matrilineal descent. (a) A matrilineal descent construct. (b) A matrilineal descent category. Note that it includes men, but not their children (after Keesing 1975:19)

systems of 'patrilineal descent', as in the *Murranji* land claim and a number of others.[30] In some cases, in the absence of a lineal descent ideology, the operation of a principle of filiation has been described instead, as in the *Malak Malak* land claim.[31] In that case it was accepted by the Aboriginal Land Commissioner as evidence for the existence of a 'local descent group' in the terms of the Land Rights Act, although not in the narrow technical sense in which the phrase was introduced by Edmund Leach in 1951.[32]

A simple one-step filiation to a parent, or a two-step filiation to a parent's parent, is a sufficient basis for acquiring rights in land in many parts of Australia, but this may take different forms in different regions.[33]

There are regions where people emphasise two-step filiations in reckoning landed interests. In the Victoria River region, in the case of the *Ngaliwurru and Nungali* land claim, the evidence indicated that people there 'took country' (acquired land and water interests) from both their father's father and mother's father. In some cases there were also people who claimed through their father's mother, and others who claimed through their mother's mother. The claimants as a whole, however, tended to restrict the taking of country to fewer than the four possible filiative relationships to grandparents.[34]

It is in the Western Desert that filiative links to country appear to be most free from restrictions on both the gender of linking antecedents and their generation level, and most likely to include links to affines (in-laws and their kin) as well as cognates. Among the Pintupi of the northern Western Desert, a person's conception site and thus Dreaming affiliations are the dominant bases of claims on land, but other bases include initiation at a place (for males), birthplace, or established residence at a place. A person may also claim a place on the basis that one of their parents or grandparents was conceived, initiated, born, resided or died there.[35] The Pintupi system thus allows for filiative connections of a shallow kind to form the basis of land interests, but they do not form chains of like filiations, such as serial patrifiliation; and descent, in the technical sense, is not the basis of land inheritance. On the other hand, conception may be regarded in this case, as a form of Dreaming-descent in the sense that the *Tjukurrpa* (Dreaming) with which conception identifies people are Dreaming ancestors. As Annette Hamilton said of the similar role of birthplace for Western Desert people further to the south-east: 'Symbolically, this is a sort of patrilineal descent, but the "father" is not the real father, but instead the totemic species whose essence is reincarnated in the individual born along his track.'[36]

A literalist might ask how one can have symbolic patrilineal descent from, for example, a Two Women Dreaming, known in the Lake Amadeus claim area of the Northern Territory as Kungka Kutjarra.[37] In the latter case, in fact, three men who claimed interests in the country of the Kungka Kutjarra legend did so on the basis of male human ancestors regarded as reincarnations of male Dreamings who figured in the Kungka Kutjarra story, namely a Lizard man and a Magpie man.[38] Only one of these reincarnations was a paternal antecedent. The other was the maternal uncle and 'brother', respectively, of two claimants. This particular evidence did not suggest a model of patrilineal descent from a Dreaming any more than it did from a person. In this case the Aboriginal Land Commissioner, Justice Michael Maurice, reached the conclusion 'that the *evidence* does not enable me to find that it is groups rather than individuals who have assumed a custodial role for the sites and track on the claim area'.[39]

This particular claim had been presented on the basis that the principle of descent involved was cognatic, there being eighteen cognatic units making up a 'one family' group of claimants.[40] Cognatic descent systems reckon descent through either or both parents. I discuss such systems in greater detail below. While pointing out the technical difference between descent and filiation to a parent, John Avery, the Aboriginal Land Commissioner's consultant anthropologist, posed the following: 'The question arises as to whether the distinction between descent and filiation has any significance for local descent groups within the meaning of the Act. In my view the distinction is not significant...'[41]

That is, he took the view that either mechanism could result in a set of people that would meet the legislative definition of a local descent group. Avery went on to justify his remark on the following grounds: Both 'rules of descent' and 'automatic inheritance by filiation', as mechanisms of group recruitment, offer the resultant group the kind of continuity over time that the legislative phrase 'local descent group' implies. So long as there are potential antecedents from a particular group, the continuity of such a group extends indefinitely into the future. Where a group's membership is primarily consequent on birth, and a child's entitlements are at least to some extent independent of the will of either parent, the symbolism of group identity is liable to be retrospective in character. In a descent group, ancestry is traced to a particular antecedent who lived at a particular point in time.

The symbolism focal to a filiative group, on the other hand, is liable to be indefinitely retrospective or have an 'eternal' character; the relationship between many groups and their Dreamings is of this kind. Both kinds of group share a common retrospectivity, however. Both kinds of rules (descent and filiation) make a distinction between the person and their ascribed status, and when such status is shared by a number of people the group attains a collective identity beyond the personalities of its individual members. Group membership based on birth rights is liable to be presented as something intrinsic to group members as persons, an aspect of their identity manifested in certain timeless symbols. The cultural and real property of such groups is thus often inalienable. These are not the ideas of groups whose property is alienable or which are unlocalised political associations. The legislation, Avery argued, was intended to reflect the communal and inalienable nature of traditional Aboriginal land-holding. The 'local descent group' of the legislation must be *corporate* for these reasons: 'That is, membership of the local descent group entails rights and responsibilities which transcend the individual, extending to others indefinitely in the future.'[42]

Avery concluded that the eighteen Western Desert groups presented in this case were, however, probably kindreds rather than descent groups in either the technical or non-technical sense. Although their personnel shared a sense of group identity recognised by their use of the name of a place identified with a key member, they were essentially groups of kin who tended to live together. Residential and marriage ties and personal alliances could change in unpredictable ways, however. The eighteen claimant subgroups were not corporate groups and it was doubtful that they had any importance to their members. The 'all one family' group, the collectivity of all Western Desert claimants, was not a descent group, but a segment of the regional population consisting of overlapping cognatic stocks.[43] Although witnesses said they could 'take' or 'be for' any or all of the countries of their grandparents, the transcript contained substantial evidence that, for men, patrifiliation had a particular significance for people's land relationships. Women's claims tended to be articulated cognatically and by kinship with other women, which suggested that the claims of men and women to country, in this case, should be treated on a different basis.[44]

The Aboriginal Land Commissioner was unable to find that these Western Desert claimants formed local descent groups and they were thus not traditional owners within the meaning of the Act. He noted that critics of the act's definition of traditional owners were numerous, but that they would do well to remember that the definition was 'probably entirely the work of two distinguished Australian anthropologists, Professor R.M. Berndt and the late Professor W.E.S. [*sic*: H.] Stanner'.[45]

Complementary filiation

In certain regions of Australia there is a ritual-based system of formalised *complementary filiation*. That is, as a crude simplification, individuals play one kind of role in relation to the sacred things and country of their fathers and fathers'

fathers, and a different kind of role in relation to the sacred things and country of their mothers and mothers' fathers.[46]

The patrifilial category, called *kirda, mangaya, gidjan, nimarringki*, etc, depending on the language, is often translated into English as 'owner' or 'boss'. The term for the complementary (and often, but not only, matrifilial) category of *kurdungurlu, kulyungkulyungpi, jungkayi* etc, is often translated as 'policeman', 'worker', or 'manager'.[47] *Kirda* and *nimarringki* (etc) are statuses conferred by one's patriline membership, or at least through patrifiliation, while *kurdungurlu* or *jungkayi* (etc) status is conferred through matrifiliation to one's mother's patrifilial ritual estate,[48] or to a connection she has to land through patrifiliation.

Since the advent of Northern Territory land claims in the 1970s, the tenure-related implications of these roles have been heavily stressed by claims of anthropologists in some contexts, while they seem to have mainly been focused on ritual matters in the past.[49] In land claims there has been a tendency to emphasise the 'manager' status of offspring of women of patrifilial groups rather than that of ritual 'managers' recruited on other grounds (marriage alliances, knowledge, proximity, willingness, kin-class status etc.). One can be a 'manager' for a country from which one's mother did not come, and indeed senior ritual specialists are often 'manager' for several different countries, so the role is not simply generated matrifilially. On the other hand, in order to have the right kinship status to be a 'manager' of an estate, one's kin-class identity (in terms of moieties, subsections, semimoieties etc. where these occur) has to be of the right sort, and this is something one does get primarily through one's mother – but kin-class identity is not of itself a specific country identity. Countries may be identified with a particular kin class, but a group of all people of the same kin class has no country as such.

Systems like *kirda/kurdungurlu*, however, while they stress the mutual dependence of two subsets of people with rights and interests in the one country, can definitely privilege patrifiliates in the long-term transmission of rights and interests in land, and in self-identification with the estate. That is, patrifilial links are often conceived of as going on 'forever' in the same pattern, passing from generation to generation through males, while matrifilial links leading to strong rights and interests in country are, under the classical systems, normally limited to only one or two generations of transmission through women. A woman's patrifilial interests may also be passed down to her son's sons, the latter being known as '*secondary kurdungurlu*' in land claim literature from the north-central Northern Territory. Furthermore, matrifiliates and patrifiliates may in some regions assert equivalent or 'level' degrees of responsibility for the one country, but they do not normally assert the *same* obligations, rights and interests. Their custodial roles and even many of their economic rights in country tend to be complementary rather than the same. Most importantly, patrifiliates are typically regarded as enjoying an identity with and *as* the spiritual substance of the ritual estate and the sacred sites of their countries. This relationship is sometimes called one of consubstantiality, or co-substantiality – the sharing of one substance. Justice Maurice in *Warumungu* said that: 'The kurtungurlus' responsibilities for their mothers' countries are frequently great, but these, by and large, do not arise from their intrinsic spiritual affiliations with the sites on their mothers' local group lands, but from their duties to their mothers and their mothers' patrilineal kin.[50]

This is not, however, to say that such complementary filiates do not have religious responsibilities towards the country that are equal to or, on occasion, even greater than those of patrifiliates and other holders of customary entitlements. The matrifilial 'manager' (*kurdungurlu, jungkayi* etc) statuses and roles rest on complementary filiation, but unlike many other instances of this pattern they complement the patrifiliation of *others* (those in the patri-group identifying with the country and its ritual substance), rather than the patrifiliation of ego.

Mother's side, father's side

In Aboriginal English and Aboriginal languages one often hears talk of 'the mother's side' and 'the father's side'. In a context of talk about the descent of rights in country, this usually refers to forebears traced through the mother and the father respectively. But it may also refer more broadly to any kin to whom one is related through the mother or through the father. The former are one's *matrilateral* ('mother's-side') kin, the latter one's *patrilateral* ('father's-side') kin. Relationships with just one 'side' are *unilateral* relationships. Relationships with both 'sides' are *bilateral*. It is important not to confuse these -*lateral* terms with the -*lineal* or -*filial* terms. One's patrilateral kin include some people who are not in one's patriline, and one's matrilateral kin include some people who are not in one's matriline. Your father's sister's husband, for example, is a patrilateral kinsman but he is normally not in your patriline.

In the *Uluru* case, anthropologist Robert Layton thought it could be argued that Western Desert conditions had so reduced the possibility of continuous patrilineal succession to estates that such succession could not be treated as the primary mode for transmission of rights. When a man was born outside his father's country and never visited it, patrilineal descent as a determinant of local affiliations became insignificant.[51] On the other hand, Layton considered there to be a bias toward patrilineality, given men's emphasis on keeping links with their fathers' estates.[52]

Layton referred to the identification of a person with either parent's country as a system of 'ambilineal descent'.[53] In an earlier publication I more or less equated Layton's 'ambilineal descent' with 'double descent'.[54] On further checking of various sources on these technical terms (helpfully supplied by Bruce Rigsby) it is now clear to me that most anthropological authorities would say that in an ambilineal system one may belong to either one's mother's or one's father's descent group but not both, while in a double descent system one belongs to a patrilineal descent group for some purposes and to a matrilineal descent group for others. In an ambilineal system the mother's and father's descent groups may be of the same type (for example, patrilineal), while in a double descent system two different kinds of descent group (matrilineal, patrilineal) are always involved. The term 'ambilineal' has been used now in several land claim anthropological submissions, beginning with *Uluru*, for systems that are better described as cases of 'parental filiation', as in this case, or as 'cognatic' in regions where descent groups can be demonstrated to exist and a person may belong to either or both descent groups of their parents.

In reconsidering his earlier evidence, Layton said in 1983 that his understanding of land relations in the region was still developing in 1979, and the evidence given after the submission of the *Uluru* claim book had shown that the 'ambilineal' model should have been extended to cover all four grandparental countries rather than just those of the parents, and also that the model did not account for all cases. He nevertheless defended the model in the sense that '89 per cent of individuals recorded joined the land-owning group of one or either parents'.[55] These figures were again published in Layton's *Uluru* book, where 69 per cent of 114 cases showed transmission of membership in land-owning groups to have been through the father, 20 per cent through the mother, 8 per cent through a parent's sibling, and three per cent through a grandparent. Layton concluded: 'Most people do, in fact, join their father's group.'[56]

It is likely that the strength of these figures in part reflects the land claim research context. If one starts by interviewing individuals who belong to a certain country, and then ask about their children and grandchildren, it is likely that people will put those offspring forward as having strong actual or potential rights in the countries of one or both parents and one or more grandparents, and in that sense may be described as 'belonging to the same group' as one or more antecedents. If, however, one starts by merely asking where is the main country for each individual child or adult in a person's universe of kin, the picture is likely to be much more heterogeneous. This does not vitiate the rights referred to, but it does affect the analysis of the 'group' holding a particular district. As discussed in Chapter 3 above, I prefer Myers' analysis of Western Desert (Pintupi) land-holding sets as 'descending kindreds'.

One of the widest of categories of relative is the *kindred*. A kindred in this sense is all the people recognised as the relations or kin of a particular individual, whether the kinship be 'real' or 'putative'. It is an egocentrically generated set, not a sociocentric one. Such a set is bilateral because it includes kin on both maternal and paternal sides.[57] 'Kindreds are not strictly speaking kin groups since they have neither a corporate character nor clear boundaries.'[58] A kindred is typically a unique set except in the case of those who are full siblings who have had no children. Myers' 'descending kindreds' is a reference to living individuals grouping themselves around places identified with shared kin of the past. He provides an example and diagram of a particular man and his father's mother's brother's son who were in such a relationship.[59]

The whole of a set of known actual relatives, past and present, make up a *cognatic stock*. Such a stock may be one recognised both by its own members and others of their community. In that sense it is *sociocentric* and a cultural construction by those of the relevant community. In another sense, where for example a scholar combines the knowledge of living community members with genealogical records of their ancestors' forgotten past, a cognatic stock may be much more an artefact of the research process, albeit one that includes an attempt to reflect community knowledge.

Cognatic stocks are the universes of which filiative groups and descent groups are subsets. A stock itself is not a descent group. Stocks overlap, such that even people as closely related as first cousins normally belong to more than one different stock.[60] People who have shared antecedents or forebears of any kind, whether unilineal or non-unilineal, are *cognates* (relatives by birth). These people may also be said to be *consanguineal* kin, literally '*blood relatives*', although this particular expression should not be assumed to refer to Aboriginal conceptions of blood relationships unless they can be demonstrated to exist in particular cases. Not all one's cognates are necessarily included in one's descent group. A descent group which consists of cognates, and is not restricted just to lineal (that is, patrilineal, matrilineal, or ambilineal) descendants, is a *cognatic descent group*. Again unlike a kindred, a cognatic descent group is essentially sociocentric, not egocentric, in its basis and definition – that is, it is much the same regardless of through which individual ego one traces the relationships, while each person's kindred is usually unique. Urban and rural Aboriginal cognatic descent groups identified by typifying surnames or other means are arguably sociocentric, although, like other similar kinds of sets of kin, their composition may be a matter of debate and different individuals may construe their composition differently because of their relative positions in networks of genealogical relationships. This variability does not reduce them to nothing but egocentric categories.[61]

One's patrilateral cognates are one's *agnatic* kin. Agnatic kin may be referred to as *agnates*. One's matrilateral cognates are one's *uterine* kin. People connected by marriage (or partnering), or at least by co-parenting, are *affinal* kin or *affines*. Co-parents vary from stable cohabiting pairs, to partners who do not necessarily ever live together but have children together, through to the recognised participants in a one-night stand that results in conception. Cases of the latter may still result in the child having recognised territorial identities that flow from those of both natural parents.[62]

One's affines include spouses, immediate in-laws, and – depending on the cultural context – may include even the larger numbers of people who are closely related to one's immediate affines. Anthropologists are not always careful to distinguish *emic* kin categories from *etic* ones. (The terms come from linguistics and refer to the distinction between the phonemic and the phonetic.) That is, a local cultural category roughly translatable into English as 'in-laws' or similar may, for example, include spouses of one's close consanguines but not siblings or other cognates of those spouses. This is the perspective of a member of the society concerned, known to anthropologists as an 'emic' perspective. By contrast, an anthropologist's analysis – even if the anthropologist were also a member of the community concerned – might class all known cognates of the spouses of a person's blood relatives as affines, but distinguish them into two categories on the basis of how they were culturally defined within the culture under study. This 'outsider perspective' is the 'etic' point of view.

It is perhaps not entirely inappropriate to say sweepingly that Aboriginal systems of land tenure are and have been moving from cognatic but heavily patrifilial systems to non-unilineal cognatic descent systems in the post-colonial period.[63]

Parallel versus cross kin and marriage

An important distinction is maintained, in many Aboriginal cultures, between *parallel* kin and *cross* kin. A parallel grandparent is a MM or FF, and a cross–grandparent is a MF or FM. That is, it often matters in generating terms for relationships traced via those people, whether or not the genders of two people are the same or different. In a number of Aboriginal languages, for example, there is a single grandparent term for FF and MM ('parallel grandparent'), and another, or two different others, for FM and MF. The Western Desert region is unusual in having grandparental terminology in which MF and FF share a single basic term, and MM and FM share another, as in European and many other systems.

The *parallel/cross* distinction mainly emerges in a land claims context when the distinction between *parallel cousins* and *cross-cousins* is made. Basically, a parallel cousin is one's FBC or MZC, while a cross-cousin is one's FZC or MBC. Cross-cousins and parallel cousins are indicated by different kin terms in most Aboriginal languages. The parallel cousin terms are usually the same as the sibling terms. Thus in Aboriginal English it is common, although not universal, for cross-cousins to be referred to as cousins and be addressed as 'cousin', 'cuz', 'cussie' etc, and for parallel cousins to be referred to as 'cousin-sister', 'cousin-brother', or simply as a sibling (brother, sister) and addressed as 'brother', 'sister', 'brud', 'bruz', 'sis', 'sissie', etc.

The structural features of the cross/parallel distinction can be made clearer by way of Figure 16.

Tamika and Dion are cross-cousins, whereas Raelene and Mervyn (Figure 13) are parallel cousins. That is, Tamika and Dion track their relationship by going up a generation level and a*cross* genders and then down again one level. Tamika's mother and Dion's father called each other brother and sister. This was ultimately because Tamika's MFF and Dion's FFF were full brothers, although this precise connection is now lost to living memory. Raelene and Mervyn trace their relationship by going up one level, jumping to a *parallel* kind of sibling (that is, one of the gender parallel to their own parent), and then coming down one level.

The most common marriage relationship preferred under Aboriginal traditions was one between couples who were classed as cross-cousins, although there are regional exceptions to this, and second-preference spouses are sometimes not even of the same generation level. In most regions, those classed as siblings – regardless of whether there was any genealogical link between them – were deemed to be in an incestuous relationship if they were to marry. This does not mean that distant classificatory siblings did not become lovers – 'distant sisters are good sweethearts'.[64]

Many small patrifilial land-holding groups of classical Aboriginal Australia have been described as *exogamous* – that is out-marrying, or practising *exogamy*. While

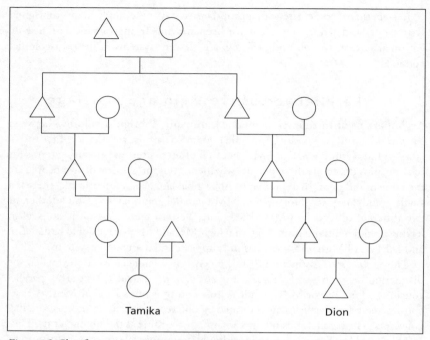

Figure 16: Classificatory cross-cousins (Tamika and Dion)

most such groups that are well documented do appear to have been exogamous, if not by customary-law rules then de facto, there are some reliable records in which they have been found to be just slightly *endogamous* (marrying-in) as well – that is, they practise occasional *endogamy*. These reports relate to the period of early contact or early colonial conditions, such that these marriages cannot simply be attributed to an alleged breakdown of the classical system. These cases include the 'tribes of the Kariera cluster' in north-western Western Australia, some Daly River groups in the Northern Territory, and certain Wik groups in Cape York Peninsula.[65]

Matriliny versus matrifiliation

Patrifiliation, serial or otherwise, is often the normative or privileged basis of recruitment to groups that are corporate with respect to land and waters as property in classical Aboriginal Australia.

Neither serial matrifiliation nor matrilineal descent, by contrast, forms the normative basis of any kind of country-holding group in classical or even post-classical Aboriginal Australia at all, as far as I am aware. Radcliffe-Brown, Elkin, the Berndts, Maddock, and Peterson came to this conclusion and there is no reliable evidence to call these views into question.[66] I have laboured the point here because in teaching in recent years I have encountered some resistance to the proposition that there is no evidence of 'matrilineal' country-holding groups in classical Aboriginal Australia. This resistance seems to be based on ideological rather than evidentiary grounds. The truly matrifilial or matrilineal institutions in Aboriginal Australia do not have territorial functions, but social ones, and in the major cases counter-territorial ones.

This is not to say that a subset of matrilateral kin may not have distinctive ceremonial and other roles in relation to land. Nor is it to say that matrifiliation does not form one of the commonest pathways to certain rights and interests in land. It does. But one-step matrifiliation is not serial matrifiliation, nor is it *matriliny*. In acquiring country through one's mother one is not, anywhere in Australia known to me, doing so as a member of a *matriline* or *matrilineage*, even where matrifiliation is, for a few generations, de facto repeated. In some urban and rural groups matrifiliation to a country-holding group may be repeated over several generations; as many as six are recorded in the case of the urban Larrakia of Darwin and Cox Peninsula.[67] This is not a consequence of a rule of matrifiliation, as such groups may be described as cognatic in composition and matrifiliates recognise patrifiliates of the same group as fellow members. These repetitions of matrifiliation form a series without being ideologically serial. The only people of whom I am aware who have an ideology of matriliny in relation to landed (for instance, tribal) identity are some contemporary people of western and northern New South Wales and south-east Queensland, but their ideology is not at all convincingly matched by the actual models of acceptable and regular practice of their communities.[68] This neo-traditional postulate seems to have arisen from the unlocalised matrilineal social totemism widely reported for that region in the nineteenth century and now largely defunct, and probably also reflects the matrifocal households that have emerged since colonisation.[69]

Through matrifiliation, in the classical land tenure systems, one is most often acquiring an interest in one's mother's patriline's country, or her conception country, or perhaps her mother's mother's patriline's country. (Here I use 'patriline' to refer to sets of people generated by serial patrifiliation, as well as those who might belong to a patrilineal descent group in the technical sense.) These are one-step matrifiliations but they do not form lineages, and they are not conceived of as generating matrilineal descent groups with descent-phrased rules of recruitment and perpetual interests in landed and other property.

Direct matrifilial classes

By contrast, in Aboriginal Australia matrilines (or serial matrifilial strings, if one prefers), are normally the basis of two distinct kinds of institutions. On the one hand there are in some regions *moieties* and *social totemic clans*, which are directly matrifilial in transmission. These may be called *matrimoieties* and *matriclans* respectively. In the Lake Eyre region Luise Hercus recorded the following matrimoieties (*Kararru* and *Mathari*) and the totemic matriclans (those of the same *mardu*, 'flavour') whose members are classed as belonging to one moiety or the other:

Kararru		Mathari	
arkapa	red ochre	*wadnhamara*	grub
wakarla	crow	*thantani*	shag [cormorant]
warrukathi	emu	*karrawara*	eaglehawk
		kukurla	golden bandicoot

Figure 17: Matrimoiety totems, Lake Eyre region (from Hercus 1994: 12)

A *moiety* is a 'half' of society – individuals normally belong to one or the other – and there are in some regions patrimoieties instead of, or as well as, matrimoieties. Matrilineal moieties were once widespread in southern Australia, especially. They were strictly exogamous, by customary law. In such a system one has the same moiety identity as one's mother. Women pass it on in turn to their children. Men do not. Moiety identities chain back through time, as also do matrifilial totemic clans and patrifilial ones, but the matrifilial ones are likely to be much more stable than patrifilial groups (here, for convenience, called patriclans). A.P. Elkin said this was because membership in them did not require knowledge or ritual participation. I think there are other factors at work, such as the absence of a direct link to the economy in the case of matriclans; the fact that matriclans are more linking than oppositional in character; the fact that their members were far less localised than patriclan members, and the fact that they could have thousands of members when patriclans typically have memberships in the range of 1–50. Matriclans also have a history of great historical endurance, certainly in the Lake Eyre region and New South Wales, where people may still identify with their matrifilial totem but many other classical religious and social institutions have long since disappeared.[70]

Direct matrifiliation is the basis on which people are recruited at birth to matrimoieties and matrilineal *semimoieties*, which as their names imply are divisions of society into two and four categories respectively. A child has the same matrimoiety and matri-semimoiety as its mother. Matrimoieties are far more widespread than matrilineal semimoieties.[71] Neither is used to characterise landed estates and neither confers land interests as such.

Direct matrifiliation is also the basis on which people acquire social totems, and thus matriclan membership, in several large regions.[72] In most of these systems all the people in one's own matriline have the same totem as ego, but there are also many other people, not consanguineally related to ego, who may have this same matrilineal totem also. In spite of this lack of a 'literal' genealogical connection, all may still be regarded as being of one 'blood' or 'flavour' or 'sweat-smell' or 'meat' – that is, they are often fictive consanguineal uterine kin with whom sexual intercourse would constitute incest. They form a strictly exogamous set, at least in the normative sense. They may come from far distant territorial groups, but all will recognise that they are 'one' totemically. In the many different languages of the north-central Northern Territory, the various names of plants, animals, cloud types and so on, which function as matrifilial totems, as well as the name for the matritotem institution itself (*ngurlu*, which also covers 'subsection'), widely take the same lexical form. But the same languages may have quite distinct ordinary terms for the same phenomena that constitute the totems. In other words the matri-totem terminology is linguistically internationalistic. I think this demonstrates even more strongly, if it were necessary, that the matriclans of the region are in no sense subdivisions of landed entities such as language groups, and that one of their roles is to balance and counter territorialism by promoting cross-territorial links between uterine (and fictive uterine) kin. That *ngurlu*, at least in several languages, refers to both matri-totem and subsection offers support for the view that subsections are felt to be essentially from the same matrifilial source.[73]

The totems that are passed down in this way are almost never uniquely allotted to one or other section in a section system, although each belongs strictly to one matrimoiety or the other, never to both. Even where, in a rare New South Wales case, totems apparently were allotted uniquely among the sections, they did not form even sets of one, two, four (and so on) totems per section. That is, they were not closed sets. R.H. Mathews documented an unusual Wiradjuri (NSW) subsystem whereby 'each section must have its own independent group of totems'. Since assignment of people to the sections is indirectly matrilineal, and thus a mother and child do not share the same section name, the totems cannot descend matrilineally, but the rule of totemic exogamy applied here just as it does with matrifilial totemic clans elsewhere.[74] Elkin thought it generally true that totemic exogamy is more strictly observed than section or moiety exogamy.[75] This does not accord with my own experience.

Indirect matrifilial classes

On the other hand, the matriline is the foundation of other important social–categorical systems that cross-cut recognised filiative groups to allocate all known members of one's social network to one or another of a series of categories, most of them dualistic at least in essence. That is, most of them generate kin superclasses which belong to even-numbered sets such as two (*patrimoieties*), four (*sections* and *patri-semimoieties*), six (sections, rare[76]) and eight (*subsections*). Unlike matrimoieties, matri-semimoieties and matriclans, these are not social categories that are handed down matrifilially in a direct sense, since while a child gets such a category through its mother, it does not belong to the same category as its mother.

These institutions are therefore *indirectly matrifilial*. This refers to the way people are assigned to their categories. These institutions rest on what are usually termed 'matricycles', rather than 'matrilines' as such. In the case of subsections, for example, there are two matricycles each consisting of four particular subsections. A child of either sex has the same subsection as that of its MMMM. The three intervening antecedents, the M, MM and MMM, have different subsection names. In the event of a preferred marriage between the parents, the child will also thus have the same subsection as that of its FF or FFZ, depending on gender. In an ideal patrifilial string, then, subsection identity will alternate each generation between only two subsections. For example:

FFF's subsection:	Japaljarri	FFFZ's subsection:	Napaljarri
FF's subsection:	Jungarrayi	FFZ's subsection:	Nungarrayi
F's subsection:	Japaljarri	FZ's subsection:	Napaljarri
Male **ego's** subsection:	Jungarrayi	Ego's sister's subsection:	Nungarrayi
mS's subsection:	Japaljarri	mD's subsection:	Napaljarri
mSS's subsection:	Jungarrayi	mSD's subsection:	Nungarrayi

Figure 18: Two Warlpiri subsections and their normative kintypes

In this case where Warlpiri terms are used (north-central Northern Territory), as in a number of other languages, males and females of the same subsection are distinguished by the fact that the male terms begin with /j/, and the female terms begin with /n/. For this reason, a single subsection is often referred to in an anthropological text by a combination of both, here N/Japaljarri.

Because in an ideal sense, and to a large extent in practice, the subsections alternate indefinitely down a patrifilial string, the pairs of subsections which do so are referred to as *subsection couples* or *patricouples*. Dreamings (Ancestral Beings of legend) in such a region have patricouple identities, and the places where they went and performed their legendary acts thus also have those patricouple identities. Ideally, the core human patrifilial holders of those places should each have a subsection that belongs to the same patricouple as the relevant Dreaming. This rests on a spiritual identification of these landholders with the Dreamings concerned. In the case of non-preferred marriages the child may end up with two subsections, one determined through the matricycle and used in everyday contexts, and another – that belonging to the father's patricouple (that is, the same as that of FF or FFZ depending on gender) – being invoked in ceremonial or land ownership contexts.

In a patrimoiety system the child has to have a moiety affiliation that is the opposite of its mother. In the case of a 'correct' marriage between the child's parents, the child has the same patrimoiety as the father. Where there is an incorrect marriage within the moiety, which is unusual, the father is usually 'thrown away' and the child takes a patrimoiety category calculated indirectly via the mother – that is, it must be in the moiety opposite to that of its mother.

Sections, subsections, patri-semimoieties and patrimoieties do not constitute 'descent groups' in the anthropological sense. They are kin superclass categories, or, more economically, kin classes. In most regions where they are found they are closely integrated with land tenure in complex ways which I do not enter into here.[77]

It is important to recognise that individuals in the same Aboriginal society may belong simultaneously to a patriclan, a matriclan, a set of 'managers' (e.g. matrifiliates acting as custodians of their mother's patrifilial country), a subsection, a semimoiety, a moiety, a cognatic descent group, and, of course, a kindred. That is to say, these kinds of structures and groupings are not in general mutually exclusive. There is therefore no basis for those nineteenth-century attempts to classify whole Aboriginal societies into 'matrilineal' versus 'patrilineal' tribes.

Sections, like subsections, are acquired indirectly through the matriline. But there are normally four named classes in a section system, in contrast with subsection systems in which there are eight named classes, often marked for gender so that there are sixteen distinct terms used in speech. In a four-section system, one's own section is that of neither parent, but the same as that of one's mother's mother. A marries B and the children are either C (if A is female) or D (if B is female), and C marries D, the children being A (if C is female) or B (if D is female).

Generation moieties

In addition to the two kinds of moieties discussed above, there are also what have been called 'generation moieties'[78] or, in stricter global anthropological language, a system of 'merged alternate generation levels'.[79] Unlike moieties which are socio-centric, these are egocentrically defined. They are of direct importance to ritual roles and the governing of sexual relationships rather than land tenure per se. They are exogamous by rule. Ego and ego's generation, plus their grandkin (and great-great-grandkin), belong to 'our side'. The parents and children of members of ego's generation, plus their great-grandkin, belong to 'their side'. These are not literal translations. The latter include 'we-bone' and 'they-flesh'. Generation moieties are characteristic of the Western Desert region. There are several other kinds of dual division relating to ritual which I do not discuss here.

8 Families of polity[1]

INTRODUCTION

ARE THE ABORIGINAL people from urban and rural Australia, whose lives in so many ways are like those of their non-indigenous neighbours, able to prove that they have a normative system of rights in country that is rooted in the pre-sovereignty past of their Aboriginal forebears? Are claimants from such backgrounds united in their common observance of a relevant body of laws and customs? Following on from the concerns of the previous chapter, I here address these questions principally through the lens of the links such people have maintained, or otherwise, between social organisation and the kind of belonging to country that gives rise to recognised customary rights capable of being recognised as native title rights. The evidentiary basis for this chapter is very much greater than space allows me to present here, but I refer readers to my earlier publication *Native Title and the Descent of Rights,* where that wider body of evidence is summarised.[2]

In a number of Australian Aboriginal land claims over the last fifteen years or more, and increasingly so in native title determination applications lodged since the passing of the *Native Title Act 1993,* urban and rural claimants, as compared with people from non-urban remote outback areas, have tended to define their relevant landed groups as language groups or regional groups rather than as a set of smaller entities such as clans. These wider groups nevertheless have internal structure, typically comprising a set of units usually referred to by the applicants as *'families'* identified by surnames in documents or oral evidence. In this discussion I will refer to indigenous use of the English words *'family'* and *'families'* in italics, to distinguish these usages from other references, for example, to sociological definitions of 'the family', or to other vernacular usage.

The internal structures of these land-affiliated groups show some remarkable commonalities across the continent. They also present certain technical difficulties. What are the *families* that typically constitute important internal subgroups of language groups or 'new tribes'? If membership of such a *family* is so often the primary pathway to customary entitlements to terrestrial and marine countries, what criteria determine this membership? If such a *family* is defined, as it often is, as 'descendants of ancestor X', yet not *all* descendants of X are regarded as being members, how do such groups delimit their memberships? Are these new structures, or are they transformations of classical structures that pre-dated the acquisition of Crown sovereignty? If they are transformations rather than new creations, are they nonetheless transformations so radical as to have effectively come into contradiction with the principles of Aboriginal land tenure that were present in the same regions in, say, 1788, 1825 or 1869? Does that matter? That is, even where the transformations have been graduated and 'organic' rather than abrupt, do they still vitiate a native title claim on the grounds that the normative system of the present simply no longer generally resembles that which obtained at pre-sovereignty? Is the character of such a gradually transformed system no longer 'traditional', even though historically rooted in and, at the level of principles, ultimately derived from the pre-sovereignty past?

As will be seen later in this chapter, several studies, most of them unpublished, have gone some way towards providing evidence that may be used in legal contexts where courts attempt to answer questions like these. It remains true, though, that there is a need for fuller and better ethnography on these and related subjects. While much of the ethnographic work carried out in rural and urban Australia has been of a high order, for various historical reasons only some of it has been directed towards exploring in detail the formal properties of contemporary kin groups, kin terminology and landed identity, for example. One reason for this, at least in the work of the 1940s–1960s, seems to have been that superficial patterns of cultural assimilation were often taken for granted as evidence that classical traditions of various kinds had simply disappeared. Indeed, in the assimilation era and its aftermath, many Aboriginal people were anxious to convince outsiders that their classical traditions had gone. But in many cases the older forms of relating to people and country had 'gone underground' or been so transformed as to be no longer readily recognisable as recast practices with classical foundations.

A stark example of this gap in the record is the paucity of information generally on how surnames have been assigned to individuals, what these surnames refer to when used as markers of collective identities, and what relationships there may be between these surnamed groups and 'tribal' and other landed identifications with certain places or areas. Another gap is the fragmentary record of personal address and reference systems used by those being studied. Although there are exceptions, anthropologists working in rural and urban Australia in the period prior to the 1970s applied their technical skills in the domains of kinship and social organisation more to salvaging remnant classical traditions than to characterising what was systematic about contemporary Aboriginal life. Deceptive similarities between the outward idiom of daily life in Aboriginal and non-Aboriginal rural communities may have decoyed anthropological curiosity in some cases. Both communities, after all, have 'families' and 'surnames', but this does not mean they are defined in the same way in both kinds of society and culture.

Families

Regardless of how it is locally defined, a human family is always a jural construct and never merely a biological or demographic datum. This is because it belongs to the realm of kinship, or recognised genealogical relationships, rather than merely to the reproductive history of some randomly selected set of individuals. The word itself, particularly in its various qualified usages ('close family', 'distant family', 'real family', 'just like family to us' and so on), implies a selection from a range of differentially recognised degrees of consanguinity, or actual relationship, and affinity or relationship through marriage. The motivation of such selection always entails judgments and expectations, amounting in this case to rules, about how such people do and/or should stand in relation to each other not simply in a genealogical sense but also in terms of social roles, statuses, obligations and affectual relationships. Kinship rather than 'mere biological connection' always implies the polity, especially in a society organised on the basis of kinship, as Aboriginal society was and still often is. Kinship also always has an underlying implication of amity,[3] and in a kinship-based society the absence or relative distance of a kin linkage may carry an underlying implication of animadversion. 'The *families*' are thus not only major forces of cohesion and mutual support in post-classical Aboriginal society, they also constitute an arena in which political conflict tends to be concentrated.

A further reason why the family is always a jural construct is because within any one culture its examples belong to a set, or a set of genealogically nested subsets, of like or parallel entities. That is, families are units of social organisation, and thus in any one society they are both structures of comparable or parallel internal makeup and at the same time they are units that together form a wider mesh or structure. In a kinship-based society relations between individuals almost always both entail and affect, sometimes quite comprehensively, relations between different families. The fact that such relationships are not neatly organised into hierarchical levels does not affect this.

The surnamed descent group stands to the household somewhat as the clan did to the band in classical systems. The former in each of these pairs is a social category, the latter a physical aggregation, so their memberships are rarely, if ever, the same, but they are conjoined in complex ways. In discourse Aboriginal people often appear to merge them, but in the case of surnamed descent groups this is because *family* surnames can be polysemous, being used in different contexts to refer to one or the other of:

- a cognatic descent group (see below); its members are normally distributed over several or many households;
- a minimal procreative family (parent(s) plus children), not all of whom have the surname by birth, and not all of whom may live together;
- a household with key defining residents from a particular *family*, but where the household contains people who are not members of *that family* by descent (they may be among its affines, for example, affines are relatives by marriage). A woman called Maggie Smith may be ' Not really a Smith', i.e., not a Smith by

descent; but she is married to a Smith, so she can be regarded as one of 'the Smiths' in certain contexts, at least so long as the marriage persists. However, a complicating factor is that her own children may be Smiths 'by blood', so she has a consanguineal *link* to the Smiths, which makes her connection to them more than one of mere affinity. In the event of conflict, if she is likely to side with her children then, again, she is more than 'one of the Smiths' by mere marriage.

- a wider group or 'mob' named after a focal descent group but containing members of other descent groups associated with them by a history of co-residence, territorial affiliation and so on.

In this chapter the focus is heavily on the surnamed *family* as cognatic group, although evidence concerning matrifocal households and wider 'mobs', for example, is relevant and will be discussed at certain points. The literature relating to these topics is not uniform, as anthropologists have usually carried out urban and rural studies with Aboriginal people of only one or two locations or regions.

Nevertheless the records available, when placed together, form a basis on which certain generalisations about social organisation relevant to the native title context become possible. I shall now lay out these generalisations.

POST-CLASSICAL ABORIGINAL SOCIAL ORGANISATION

A distinctive form of social organisation, centred on Aboriginal *family* identities and combining features of both classical Aboriginal and modern European societies, as well as a number of innovations, has emerged in urban and rural areas of most of Australia and is becoming increasingly manifest in a number of the remoter regions. Although they exhibit regional variations, systems of this kind exhibit a large amount of common content across the country. It is extremely unlikely that this distinctive form of social organisation developed in one region and then spread by diffusion to others. It is much more likely to have emerged among the various post-frontier populations more or less independently and for the same reasons.

Some of those reasons have to do with indigenous reactions to suddenly becoming a conquered and then subject people; others have to do with the continuation into the present of certain ancient principles for the conduct of relationships between people, places and things, albeit in a new technical and cultural environment; while others have to do with what Basil Sansom has called the 'expression of a recreated culture' and an 'emergent culture'.[4] These three underlying influences on the formation of post-classical Aboriginal society – reaction, continuity and re-creation – have nowhere formed exactly the same mix, but, as Elkin showed in his 1951 paper 'Reaction and interaction', there were strong historical similarities between the patterns of contact over much of the continent. As I think is borne out by the case material presented below, these similarities, combined with the persistence of distinctive pan-Aboriginal cultural values and shared underlying principles of social organisation, have generally led to remarkable commonalities among the '*families* of polity' of the various regions, and among the ways they organise their traditional land associations.

Sansom's 'Aboriginal commonality', however, is not the phenomenon I am describing here. The bundle of features he describes as being pan-Aboriginal, despite the lack of a pan-Aboriginal political or 'ethnic' unity, are common not only to urban and rural people but also to those who remain dominated by classical forms of thought, language, religion and social organisation in the remoter corners.

By 'social organisation' I refer to the anthropologist's modelling of social ordering and of the way that ordering is experienced in terms of values, expectations and rules. I thus refer to a combined description of both ideology and action, and of the mix of Aboriginal people's models with their observable behaviours, neither of which normally matches the other with complete exactitude, as in any other society. 'Social organisation' has become a rather old-fashioned term among anthropologists, but in a context where one has to be understood by non-anthropologists I prefer it to perhaps more accurate phrases such as 'sedimented social practice'. Anthropological jargon can have a very negative effect on some readers.

Aboriginal people may or may not identify with such anthropological analyses, but anthropologists do not claim to merely 'represent' an objective reality as experienced by their subjects. Any representation must acknowledge its limitations. One of these is that the 'insider view' of Aboriginal people is inevitably filtered and distilled during this process, and no claims are made for perfect accuracy in the anthropologist's account of it.

My focus here is on post-classical Aboriginal social organisation. Here I concentrate on the way a distinctive post-colonial Aboriginal social system, and in particular the cognatic descent group or surname-group system which is so central to it, is involved in the transmission and maintenance of traditional interests in country. (I refer to 'country' rather than 'land' as this is intended to cover marine as well as land interests.) In brief, a cognatic descent group is one formed by those who share recognised descent from a particular ancestor or set of closely-related ancestors, and who trace their links to such ancestors through either parent.

These cognatic groups are not 'extended families' of living people with a role confined to kinship and mutuality, nor are they households. They are kin groups of enduring and central importance to the conduct of Aboriginal business. They are *families* of polity in the sense that they form major structural elements of public life in Aboriginal society and do not belong merely to a domestic or private domain. They persist over long periods, and thus have many recognised deceased members who are not merely remembered but who continue to form powerful reference points in determining how their living descendants establish rights and interests in traditional forms of cultural property, including identification with country.

The surnames by which these *families* of polity are so often known constitute one of the main forms of currency in the discussion of internal Aboriginal political and economic life in much of contemporary Australia. These *family* identities confer a particular kind of rightful association with, for example, a mission, a pastoral station or a home town, but more than that they may also confer an identification with traditional land as a landholder. That is, they are usually the individual's key stepping-stone to tribal affiliation and the customary rights and duties of care that that affiliation entails. In that sense, to the extent that they confer some kind of proprietary interest and also enjoin certain obligations on their members, they are jural in nature. They can be descent groups whose corporate nature is definable in part in relation to customary relationships to property.

This is not to imply that people who are personally unaware of such specific *family* and tribal connections do not maintain a regional Aboriginal identity, such as being a 'Brisbane Murri' or an 'Adelaide Nunga', but this is a time of great flux in which many such people are seeking to re-establish a more specific traditional and landed identity. The large number of land claims mounted since the mid-1970s, especially the native title claims in rural regions of southern Australia, combined with a burgeoning interest in genealogies and ancestral history and the desire of the 'stolen generations' and their descendants to re-establish kin links obscured by the official institutionalisation of thousands of Aboriginal children, have resulted in a massive amount of research on the specific land links of Aboriginal ancestors in urban and rural Australia. Aboriginal people themselves are carrying out a good deal of this research. Iris Clayton and her sisters, for example, were sent to Cootamundra Girls Home and their brothers were sent to Kinchella Boys Home (in New South Wales). She described her genealogical and family history researches as in part based on the desire to have 'our identity returned. This is a need that is growing stronger every year. Our young people need their true identity returned to them with names and stories of their ancestors.'[5] Nevertheless, there will no doubt remain a number of individuals who identify as Aboriginal people and are accepted as such but who do not seek out their relatives or take part in the lives of the *families* of polity.

The persistence of the descent group as the primary customary land-holding group in post-classical Aboriginal society may have been a surprise to some. The Queensland *Aboriginal Land Act 1991*, for instance, provided for claims to be made on grounds either of traditional affiliation, historical association or needs. Thus far claims under that Act have proceeded either on traditional grounds, or on a combination of traditional and historical grounds. In the first case, that of *Cape Melville*, the claimants initially lodged their claim on both traditional and historical grounds, but after the hearing began they dramatically announced the withdrawal of the historical basis of claim.[6] They were the rightful claimants, in their view, not merely on the grounds of past associations of residence and land use, but above all because of their descent from former landowners. Those who initially claimed historical association in this case were not all the Aboriginal people who could trace an historical association to the land and sea concerned, but only those who could make proprietary claims over it under Aboriginal Law. In the second Queensland case, that of *Simpson Desert*, claimants used both traditional and historical bases of claim throughout the hearing process – but again the only people claiming historical association in this case were people descended from former landowners.[7]

The main features of post-classical Aboriginal social organisation that are relevant to country interests include those that now follow. This is not to be read as a list of the main features of post-classical Aboriginal societies in general, nor as a statement of pan-Aboriginal commonalities. The features discussed here are only those that, I argue, impinge most closely on the ways customary rights and interests in land and waters are transmitted and expressed, and which recur often enough to suggest they are widespread.

The families

The dominant social groupings are cognatic descent groups, usually referred to as 'the *families*'. These groups usually have remembered geographical origins and current landed affiliations, either in the form of a traditional homeland area, a mission, town or other settlement, or some combination of these. These hinterland origins and identities are frequently maintained in metropolitan contexts, and visiting between rural- and urban-based branches of *families* is often frequent and important, especially to attend funerals. Homeland and kin group identity can thus be maintained over generations of city living.

These *families* of polity are more enduring and stable than nuclear families or households, and now form the backbone of rural, urban and, in some cases, remote Aboriginal social organisation.

Cognatic descent groups are normally only subsets of the fuller cognatic stocks recognised by their members.[8] They restrict their memberships to such subsets by rather uniform mechanisms, principally a rule that unactivated membership hinders potential members from exercising group rights other than residual ones of identification. Over a long time, perhaps involving several generations, such unactivated membership may lead to divestment even of the right of certain of a group's descendants to identify with the group. Is this a case of a '*de facto* and not a *de jure* termination', to use Derek Freeman's description of the fact that 'it is merely the cessation of inter-communication, for whatever reasons, that tends to terminate kindred relations and the moral obligations associated with them'?[9] I am not sure. These Australian patterns of limiting recognition of active cognatic group membership are jural in character, but represent specific decisions in each case rather than a generalised rule based on, for example, degrees of consanguinity.

There is a dialectic interplay between the need to restrict these groups' memberships, and the desire of authoritative group members to keep as many potential newborn members within their own groups as possible. Loss of members through voluntary action, such as 'passing' into non-Aboriginal society, is often bitterly resented.[10]

Tribal membership

Membership of the cognatic descent groups I refer to here provides the core of a person's kin-group identity, and also forms the main legitimate pathway to identification with traditional lands and the higher-order groups associated with them in a 'country'-oriented context. That is, the individual's membership of a 'tribe' is normally required to be mediated by their membership of a recognised *family* of that tribal identity. These are not the 'tribes' of the Tindale-Birdsell type, which have been much questioned as an adequate modelling of classical local organisation. They are what is sometimes called 'the new tribes' or 'modern tribes'.[11]

Tribal units themselves are usually much larger than cognatic descent groups and are based on language affiliation, or occasionally on another type of regional affiliation, such as a nation (descendants of members of several language groups combined). Tribal identities of certain *families* may be disputed.

Families may thus be groups of social identity, land-holding or land-affiliated groups, and groups of polity. They are not political in the sense that pressure groups are, for they are not merely voluntary. Politically they are more like dynasties, parties and constituencies combined. They are often misleadingly referred to in administrative contexts simply as 'factions'. They may indeed constitute the core of local political factions, yet they are more than this. Their integration of politics, landed identity and kinship is part of what suggests these descent groups can be transformations of classical forms rather than a complete departure from those forms. This combination is typical of many acephalous societies. Writing of land-holding local groups in the Solomon Islands, H.W. Scheffler states: 'Though generally conceived as one or another kind of descent group, local groups were also elementary political factions.'[12]

Such Aboriginal *families* recruit members largely through the mechanism of parental filiation. Parental filiation provides an essential property qualification for engaging in custodial action with regard to traditional lands. Filiation is a recognised rights-conferring connection to a kin group based on the fact of being recognised as the offspring of a member of the group. In some cases the filiative link is formed primarily through the parent of a parent (e.g., the mother's mother). A filiative link may or may not be established by adoption.

Filiation to a parent, or through a parent to a grandparent, was the most widespread and privileged basis, although by no means the only basis, upon which tenurial rights and interests in country were bestowed within the classical Aboriginal systems. There is in this sense considerable continuity between classical and post-classical land tenure systems.

In the classical systems the individual personality and power of such an antecedent could affect the extent to which they were a primary reference point in reckoning interests in country; but this took place against the background of their formal roles as fillers of genealogical categories that themselves were regarded as the most powerful determinants in the system. For example, one could typically have primary interests in one's father's father's country, regardless of what kind of a person he was. Classically, roles of antecedents above the grandparental generation were not commonly at the forefront, or even in the background, of discourse about the derivation of rights among the living. In a post-classical system the individual antecedent, with their particular mix of knowledge, personality, longevity and fecundity, is much more important and only a few of them continue to be a primary reference point among those below the generation level of their grandchildren. Their names are perpetuated in a way that, in the classical systems, no human being's name normally was. But they resemble some of the functions of the Ancestral Beings, or founding clan Dreamings, of the older culture by becoming datum points from which living persons are joined by common descent and common country.

In most of the classical systems, however, filiations were strongly patterned by gender rather than broadly cognatic. That is, serial patrifiliation (if not patrilineal descent) was the most widespread privileged mechanism in assigning land rights. People also enjoyed rights in their mother's countries, and those of other kin.

Freedom of choice

In urban and rural Aboriginal communities, the primary *family* and country affiliations of children are often maintained as about equal between the mother's and father's sides while the children are still young, with the often stated expectation that 'they will decide if they want to go more one side than the other when they grow up'. This decision usually depends on their eventual choices of partners and places of main residence. At Hopevale (Queensland) in 1992 I found this in a number of cases, whilst in some others the 'side' with which children were clearly most affiliated was determined on their behalf by the senior adults of their *families*. This appeared to be a cultural characteristic of the *families* concerned, independent of closeness of residence to the home area of the respective parents, although the latter is usually a powerful consideration in assigning primary country affiliations to children in cognatic systems. The main factor governing this distinction between attitudes seemed to me to be one of closeness to classical traditions. Those who were culturally less drawn to European ways tended to allow young people less freedom of choice about their affiliations.[13] Regional politics may constrain choice, so that an individual simplifies life by having to 'stand up and be counted' as primarily a member of one parent's group and only secondarily as a member of the other's.[14]

Compared with the classical systems, in a post-classical system young people are afforded greatly increased freedom of choice over which of the descent groups into which they were born will become their primary group(s) of identification and hence of land interests. Kindred relationships in bilateral societies normally have an 'optative character' as against the more restricted range of choice available in unilineal societies.[15] This optation does not mean that cognatic group membership is purely voluntaristic. It is usually conceived of in a partly essentialistic way, being a choice among relationships of consanguineal ('blood') descent from antecedent landowners. In some widely-distributed regions the families of polity are accordingly called 'the bloodlines'.

Individuals belong to several cognatic stocks by reason of their ancestry but only one or a very few are normally their main *families* of orientation, and thus they are members of only those few descent groups. This is partly a matter of choice, but choice is constrained by residential history, active involvement in the relevant group's affairs and genealogical distance.

Thus while 'blood descent' is typically maintained as an essentialist core criterion of membership in such landed groups, sameness of gender in the persons transmitting primary descent group affiliations has by and large been abandoned and this has given 'tribal' or other landed identity a more flexible and optative character. This results, perhaps, in part from a shift in the cultural construction of the person occurring at this same historical phase when it occurred in different parts of Australia, albeit at different dates due to the slow movement of colonisation on the ground. That is, there is a general shift, during the culture-change processes under discussion here, from a thoroughgoing commitment to the doctrine of the essential equivalence of persons of certain kin/gender categories, towards greater possibilities for social individuation. There is also generally a decline or disappearance of belief in a perpetuable patri-spirit.

There is much in the cultural makeup of the classical Aboriginal past that suggests there were rather severe constraints on individuation. For example, the tradition of the laws of talion ('payback'), under which one's close kinsperson's life could be exacted in return for one's own misdeeds, reflects the strong version of this older tradition, a doctrine of the equivalence of persons whose structural identity is the same or very similar. So also does the levirate, the custom by which the younger brother of a recently deceased man became the husband of his widows. So also does the retrospective merging of parallel cousins into sets of full siblings, which so often occurs when their descendants construct genealogies for the anthropologist.

Classificatory kinship itself, one of the hallmarks of classical Aboriginal culture, rests on the capacity to recognise everyone in society as belonging to a finite number of kin categories, or kinds of people. This is possible through devices such as the rule of the equivalence of siblings, by which a mother's sister is a mother and a father's brother is a father, for example.

Cognatic descent groups enjoy a dominance in the social and political organisation of rural communities, especially those with majority Aboriginal populations such as the ex-missions, but may also be found in large cities such as Adelaide where communications between metropolitan and hinterland branches of descent groups are maintained. The classical principle of consociation leading to a degree of mutual trust and amity independent of genealogical closeness continues. But there is also in the history of colonisation an early emergence of personal friendship and 'marrying for love', and thus of dramatically increased choice in degrees of closeness of personal relationships, far beyond the degree possible under classical conditions.

At Aurukun (Cape York Peninsula) since at least the 1930s there has been the development of 'school-mate' relationships between children who went to school together, including pairs of children of opposite genders and different countries. The first of these were bush-born children and they were the first in their region to go to a school and live in a mission. I have seen such a relationship pulled into play to dampen down inter-clan rivalry and conflict. I think it was a cultural innovation. I am not aware of many Australian languages in which there is a word with anything like the sense of European terms meaning 'friend', although Western Desert *malpa* perhaps comes closest. Aboriginal words offered in translation of 'friend' during linguistic interviews are typically those that literally mean cross-cousin, co-initiate, companion (for example, sleeping partner) or some other relationship, often one of a non-voluntary kind. A shift in emphasis from kinship to friendship is characteristic of post-classical Aboriginal ways of relating.

In much of contemporary Aboriginal Australia, people make contextual choices between ways of relating to each other, and utilising kin address and reference systems, that move between the Aboriginal and European traditions. Most are able to use both, and to make the distinction between them. For example: 'She's my cousin Whitefella way but Blackfella way I call her sister', is a typical statement about parallel cousinship. Similarly, in a more Aboriginal context someone may prefer the use of their surname of cognatic descent group significance, while in other contexts (e.g. contacts with authorities, child maintenance matters) they may use their legal surname.

Following the main colonial impact and before the emergence of well-oiled legally-incorporated machinery such as participation in community administration, formal cultural organisations and the like, Aboriginal populations often went through a period of social atomisation. Distantly related *family* members who would formerly have kept in touch lost touch with – or were separated from – each other. Locally held traditions emerged, and some of these may be jealously guarded.

Some people have retreated from what they perceive as the claustrophobic pressures of their numerous kin, and prefer the relative anonymity of the city and relationships of choice. Others have found the emotional insecurity of being absent from their relatives brings a quick end to experiments with urban anonymity.

Under such post-colonial conditions, consensus and internal control within large cognatic and 'tribal' groups have become more difficult to achieve. This is especially so since the widespread demise of the sanction of execution for offenders against religious laws and classical marriage arrangements.[16] Under these conditions people may develop much more idiosyncratic views of things such as territorial boundaries, although they may share a common core view with those of others. For example, Jane Jacobs has published a map depicting some vastly differing conceptions of language group boundaries among Port Augusta Aboriginal people, albeit conceptions that share a heartland in each case.[17] New-old forms of cohesion and competition, as well as new forms of identity, may be built on a social combination of kinship and friendship and organised around sport, especially football.[18] The legal recognition of native title has brought pressures for many people in such communities to explore and emphasise their distinctively Aboriginal forms of social relationship, and to investigate their ancestry and kin links as never before.

Membership criteria

One becomes eligible for membership of a cognatic group by birth or adoption, and not merely by marriage to or co-residence with one of its members. Traditional land tenure interests of the first rank thus also cannot normally be acquired solely by marriage or co-residence. Marriage may, however, confer a quasi-identification with the spouse's cognatic group and possibly with a tribal group but this is not intrinsically permanent nor is it independently transmissable to offspring conceived with a later spouse of a different cognatic group.

All such groups ultimately exercise axiomatic principles of exclusion; for example, a person with no principled locally recognised basis for seeking recognition as a member is excluded.

Cognatic group structure

Cognatic descent groups may be nested, that is, they may have sub-branches. Cognatic groups may thus be distinguished as minimal (containing no structural subgroups), maximal (belonging to no larger cognatic descent group), or medial (located between minimal and maximal); there may be more than one medial level of sub-branching.

Cognatic descent groups may form parallel (non-nested) subgroups of land-holding entities such as tribes. That is, some 'branches' of a tribal group may not literally branch out from a common ancestor at all, but, as has often been recorded for estate groups in Australia, may still rightfully claim the same country on the shared basis of ancestry, but not on the basis of shared ancestry.

In different contexts individuals may identify differentially with minimal, medial or maximal groups (*minimal*: 'I'm a Smith.' *medial*: 'We Smiths and Joneses are all out of one grandmother, Old Topsy Brown (née Green).' *maximal*: 'I'm one of the Green mob really, because my grandmother Topsy 'Brown' was really a Green, and her brother's descendants, the Bendemeer Greens, are all my *family*.'). These macro-groups and their subgroups are distinguished in speech mainly by the use of surnames, or by reference to the nodal ancestors from whom their members are descended, or by reference to a focal living member, or a normal place of residence of core members, or some combination of these.

Women may use two surnames, either depending on context or in a hyphen-ated form. One of these will often be their birth surname, the other their married name. There is a recent tendency in some areas for women to relinquish the latter in favour of the former as they become more engaged in Aboriginal land and cultural heritage matters. In the classical systems women did not change their names on marriage, but retained their own names; in many cases these names reflected their landed identity, for example, by referring to place names, to song verses on certain Dreaming tracks, or to clan totems.

Many of the nodal ancestors and focal living members who are reference points in these *families* are women, but they may also be men. For many families the dominant pathway to the defining ancestor is via women. Group-defining ancestors may also be a recognised set of siblings rather than an individual.

Focal living members of *families* of polity are those most likely to become nodal, group-defining antecedents late in life or after death. Focal living members often make strenuous efforts to keep as many of their descendants as possible under their own descent group identity while they are alive. That is, there may be competition between grandmothers, and descent groups, as to 'which way the kids will go'. Such competition may long outlive the focal persons defining the groups. The idiom in which this choice between affiliations is stated may be '*mother's side or father's side*', but the reality may often be that it is the grandmothers, not the parents, whose '*sides*' are at stake and who work for the retaining of grandchildren and great-grandchildren within their own descendant groups.

The filiative steps by which the living trace connections to nodal ancestors may zigzag irregularly between maternal and paternal links, although a series of single-gender filiations often occurs within such strings (for example, FMMMF). Such single-gender strings of antecedents are not normally the result of descent-phrased rules[19] or cultural ideology and may terminate at any time.

Post-classical Aboriginal descent groups are thus rarely unilineal as such, although they may contain unilineal segments through adherence of some members to older rules. The contemporary ideology of landed descent in a particular region, especially among older men, may not for a time overtly recognise that non-unilineal descent has become in practice a legitimate pathway to group membership. For some groups the post-classical descent system may be 'presumptively patrilineal',[20] or it may even on occasion be asserted by them to be 'matrilineal', for example. In practice people may retain a patrilineal ideological bias while de facto acknowledging non-patrilineal group membership, or a recently introduced matrilineal ideology is present but non-matrilineal group membership is acknowledged, or groups may be simply and fully non-unilineal in the way they recruit. 'Non-unilineal' descent systems involve neither patrilines nor matrilines (that is, neither kind of unilineal group). 'Non-unilineal' is not a synonym for 'cognatic' as some cognatic systems may contain recognised unilineal segments. Examples of such systems are discussed below.

While a local and explicit or conscious ideology of landed group recruitment may be closer to the group's practices of the classical past, it is current practice that constitutes evidence for the actual principles espoused by the group. Such principles are rarely brought to consciousness in systematic detail and it normally requires anthropological analysis to lay out such implicit principles comprehensively and in an orderly way.

It is not only in the field of ideology but in that of current practice that evidence for or against the continuity of Aboriginal law and custom, dating from the establishment of Crown sovereignty to the present, is likely to be tested in a native title determination process. Continuity in this context does not mean absence of change. Change may be recognised as organic rather than abrupt and cataclysmic. Organic change is transformation rather than replacement. Transformed (post-classical) systems may thus be in continuity with the classical systems that preceded them, without seeming to be very similar to them.

MORE ON COGNATIC DESCENT GROUPS

A cognatic descent group is composed of people who share recognised descent from a particular ancestor or set of ancestral siblings, but only those who combine a certain kind of shared ancestry with a role as a body of people with some defined and shared purpose, identity, or property, for example.

While in the past some scholars have regarded cognatic kin sets as more or less equivalent to non-unilineal ones, it is clear that a set of cognatic descendants may actually include a unilineal set of descendants as well, such as an agnatic (patrifilial) set (Figure 19). (Here I am using the term 'unilineal' partly to avoid a barbarism such as 'monofilial'. That is, I am using it to cover patrifilial groups, although strictly speaking it refers to patrilineal or matrilineal groups.) Indeed the structure shown in Figure 19 closely resembles a number of Northern Territory land claimant groups, which include some people who are members by patrifilial membership and others who are members by matrifiliation.[21] While for older people such groups may be 'presumptively patrilineal' in regard to land tenure, it is likely that over time, once the cognatic principle is viable, the shift to a more broadly accepted cognatic principle of descent is hard to resist under contemporary social conditions.

Many Aboriginal people have non-Aboriginal cognates but do not include them in the groups that are defined as traditional landholders or members of a

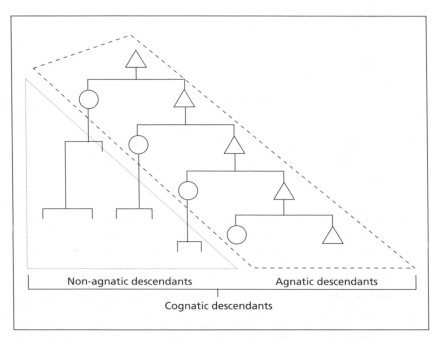

Figure 19: Agnatic, non-agnatic and cognatic descendants (after Keesing 1975:48)

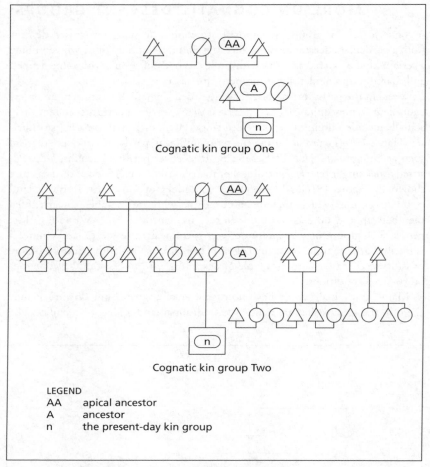

Figure 20: Two cognatic kin groups of south-western Western Australia (Birdsall 1988 Figures 8.1, 8.2)

particular tribal group. That is, the factor of wholly non-Aboriginal descendedness acts to exclude such people from the Aboriginal cognatic descent groups observed in land claims processes. It is only the Aboriginal ancestors of such groups who are eligible to be apical or nodal ancestors, the key persons from whom common descent is reckoned in defining group membership, when the cognatic group is one defined in relation to some Aboriginal matter and Aboriginal identity. This is not to say that non-Aboriginal ancestors are not important to their Aboriginal descendants – many are. And non-Aboriginal people may be adopted into Aboriginal country groups and enjoy customary country rights.

It may be useful to distinguish apical ancestors from nodal ancestors. Apical ancestors are founders of descent groups, but many such groups have subgroups branching off under other more recent ancestors at various nodes in a genealogical chart and, in modelling terms, in people's memories. People who are significant in the creation of sub-branches might be distinguished as nodal rather than apical, as they are not at the apex of the genealogy, either as a chart or as a set of memories.

A cognatic descent group that is a land-holding group under Aboriginal tradition may be individual-centred, in the sense of being focused upon a single dominant ancestral figure, such as a matriarch who had or has many descendants (Figure 20). She and her name may be definitional for the group of her descendants, and widely recognised by others as such. So it is not ego-centred in the sense that a kindred is. It is sociocentric. It has some kind of objective definition as an enduring corporation for those who recognise it within Aboriginal society, and an outside observer will usually find such groups to have unambiguous core memberships, even if memberships are unstable or subject to debate around the edges.

In classical systems people identify as a source of land interests one or more parental or grandparental kintypes rather than a named ancestor so often because it is the jural role of the parent or grandparent, their kin standing to ego as a type of antecedent, that really matters. The individual identity or personality of the forebear is not the foundational consideration. Or, rather, it usually is not, but in cases where a dominant person attracts descendants, perhaps a couple of generations after their death, acquiring filiations retrospectively as it were, the role of their eminence and personality is usually suppressed and by the time four or five generations have passed their personal identity will have been forgotten, or at least it would have been before modern times. Apical ancestors of cognatic descent groups may be thought of as specific individuals for many more generations, especially given the advent of records. In urban/rural systems, the powerful figure whose name is remembered for generations can be one's M, MM, FFM, MMF or MMMMM for example. This person is the reckoning point, and for a certain era goes on influencing the composition of country groups, often well after death. As noted above, a cognatic descent group is an ancestor-focused one, not one focused on particular kintypes such as FF or MM.

In sum, one might say that urban/rural Aboriginal cognatic descent groups are ancestor-focused, kindreds are ego-focused, and patrifilial and matrifilial classical groups are focused on certain antecedent kintypes as structural genealogical positions. This makes sense of the fact that the Wik of Cape York Peninsula use no genitives on grandparent terms when specifying a person's own country interests: for example, 'aak pepiy' (Wik-Ngathan) is literally 'FM country', not 'my FM's country'. The same applies to one's mother's country, which is 'aak kaath-kaal', literally 'M/MB- country'. This indicates the role of FM or M/MB- in a jural slot rather than as a specific remembered individual, and it may also imply inalienable possession, grammatically speaking. In Wik-Mungkan one's own clan estate is one's 'aak puul', literally 'FF' country'. Indeed, people often did not know their FFs because of the pattern of late male marriages, so the salience of FF in this case is not so much a matter of biography as of structured formal affiliations.[22]

Transformations in local organisation

Where the question is addressed in the older literature for regions such as coastal New South Wales, the core pattern of classical land tenure systems is often patrifilial, but for the more arid west and far west of that state there is evidence that 'birthplace' (possibly a reference to conception site) and ceremonial incorporation were as important as, or more important than, descendedness. South-central Queensland also appears to have been an area where pathways to tenure other than patrifilial ones applied.[23] But what is surprising, to put it mildly, is the extent to which ethnographers of the nineteenth century and in the south-east of the continent concentrated their attentions on non-landed institutions such as matrilineal social organisation, on ceremonies, on material culture, myths and languages, but seldom offered any detail at all on land tenure, especially in the vast region west of the Great Dividing Range.

The shift from patri-descent as the basis of enduring groups holding land in Aboriginal Australia in the post-contact period, in those areas where such traditions had been followed previously, could no doubt be ascribed to several factors. Sheer sudden loss of population, the arrival of children fathered by non-Aboriginal men, a decline of stability in marriage and of the very existence of marriage as an institution, a decline in the status and power of men, a rise in the role of personal choice in relationships, and a rise in the power and independence of women, for example, were probably major factors in the shift.

In the past some sociologists attributed this emergence of powerful women to the 'culture of poverty', a model roundly criticised by a number of scholars.[24] One of those so criticised was C.D. Rowley. Rowley tended to see contemporary post-classical Aboriginal society as locked in a cycle in which poverty reproduced the living conditions that generated the culture that reproduced poverty.[25] He did, however, acknowledge that anthropologists did not often share his views. In his team's major survey of urban and rural Aboriginal Australia in the 1960s, Rowley found

> many evidences of matri-focused authority. The dominant elderly woman who 'battles' to keep a home for dependent daughters and grandchildren on social service benefits (especially her pension) is not perhaps as common as often assumed, but she is in many ways the most impressive figure in the household. She is commonly the acknowledged holder of authority over the extended family beyond the household. ... By the anthropologist, her position may be traced back to the Aboriginal culture, and the effects on it of the loss of the spiritual role of the man... But her situation, and that of the younger woman who will also tend to conserve the frontier traditions, are also directly relevant to the current economic and social circumstances of Aboriginal society.[26]

In areas where cognatic descent groups prevail, the classical patrifilial group as a land-owning institution, if it existed prior to colonisation, is in decline or has already disappeared completely. However, descent from a former landowner typically continues to constitute the critical condition for recognition as a land-owner under contemporary Aboriginal tradition.

The initial arrival of children fathered by non-Aboriginal men created a need to adapt land tenure systems to the new circumstances. In those regions where the classical systems required people claiming primary estate affiliations to have the same patrimoiety, patrilineal semimoiety or subsection-couple identity as the country concerned, they placed a brake on the assignment of children to their mothers' countries, as a child should be in a category complementary to that of the mother in these regions. However, especially where such institutions were not present, children began in many cases to become identified as members of their mothers' land-holding groups. Where children were born whose genitors could not give them country (most often because they were non-Aboriginal), but the mother was in a stable relationship with an Aboriginal man, the child might be assigned to the latter's country, if he were willing. Some men, however, have not been willing to act as such a child's full pater and to accept the child of another genitor as his own for the purposes of land relationships. In a number of other cases a child born to a genitor other than the mother's husband, or born when the mother was single, has been assigned to the land-holding group of a man to whom the mother would have been married had she fitted in with older established practices such as promised marriage. That is, children with non-Aboriginal fathers have in such cases taken, not their mother's country, but that of a man they call 'father' who is neither their genitor nor their pater. I have observed cases of this among Mudbura people of the Murranji Track area and people of south-eastern Cape York Peninsula, and Françoise Dussart has observed it among Warlpiri people of the Yuendumu area.[27]

At about the same period, and in the main due to migration or removal from traditional living areas, old local estates became suddenly much more blurred in definition, or disappeared, or were effectively amalgamated into larger riverine drainage areas, or survived but with towns or major sites as their defining features, for example. The broadest form of landed identity became the 'new tribe'.[28] Recruitment to the tribe is now primarily via the cognatic descent group in many areas. Tribes are increasingly incorporated legally.

As local estates became vacated (that is, they no longer had living direct land-holders), succession to them, which formerly involved fission of large clans or recruitment of individuals to a revitalised small group through incorporation or conception, tended instead to be collective, carried out by the surviving families from the same region, but still defined geographically on a basis that arises from the classical cultural system (for example, drainage subdivision, language group area, regional alliance). Particular cognatic groups often continued to maintain a particular association with one part of the tribal land, based on the location of a former local estate, or on repeated foraging in the same area, say, but also commonly took the view that all the tribe's members collectively held all the tribe's lands.

This was made explicit in both the *Cape Melville* and *Kenbi* cases.[29] In some instances, forms of connection to traditional lands and certain classical practices, such as use of Aboriginal languages, became narrowed to '*family* traditions' as close interaction with others descended from the same original language group declined due to institutional separation, migration or other factors.

Aboriginal voluntary organisations and, more recently, Aboriginal branches of government and para-government bodies such as legal services and land councils, became a major domain in which families of polity and forces of localised landed identity are socially and culturally reproduced. The two cannot ultimately be treated in isolation from each other in many areas. This is a major point made by Jocelyn Davies.[30] Others have noted that 'Aboriginal families in urban and rural areas have developed a culture of their own through family, community and *organisational structures'.*[31] This remains, however, a poorly researched arena, with a few exceptions, even though it has a long history. Corporate organisations interact with, and may collide with, the informal 'local organisation' of their constituents. The same constituents are involved in, or impinged upon by, a range of organisations whose numbers have been growing rapidly for decades. The available studies tend to focus on such organisations piecemeal, and in the absence of detailed accounts of their integration (or otherwise) with genealogically-, historically- and geographically-based social groups. Aboriginal families have developed presences in the bureaucracy over a long period. Judy Inglis, for example, described Aborigines' involvement with public agencies in Adelaide in the late 1950s.[32]

Stratification

Members of particular cognatic groups may believe that they are of royal descent, or of a 'royal line', particularly if the record shows that they have ancestors on whom titles such as 'King' or 'Queen' were bestowed during the colonial era. This is consonant with the cultural emphasis on remembered, named, distant ancestry and recognised particular 'lines' of descent that are characteristic of post-classical Aboriginal cultures.

The first such titles were bestowed on King Bungaree and his wife Queen Gooseberry in Sydney in or before 1815.[33] The groups and areas of which such people were the colonially-inspired monarchs were often quite small and contained only a few hundred, perhaps only a few dozen, people. In south-east Cape York Peninsula in the 1920s there was a 'King' about every 50–100km along the coast.[34] Given this is an area where small clusters of patriclans owned quite different languages, and even the tiny clans themselves may be called 'nations' in regional English, this is perhaps apt. The recipients of these titles were typically used as go-betweens by colonial officials and others. A Russian visitor to Sydney in 1820 noted that inscribed gorgets ('king plates') were given to those 'who show most attachment to the English' in order to 'accustom the natives to submission' and encourage their assistance in tracking down escaped convicts.[35]

In some cases cognatic groups may be stratified by some form of class system.[36] In one Queensland case, documented in much detail, there was evidence of racial stratification.[37] In one region of New South Wales, there was evidence of stratification based on membership or non-membership of a fundamentalist sect.[38]

Surname groups

One of the characteristics of urban/rural cognatic groups is the very widespread practice of identifying them and their branches by surnames.

Bureaucratic considerations encouraged the use of surnames among Aboriginal people from quite early in the history of colonisation. Although Aborigines had – and in some areas still have – rather complicated naming practices of a classical kind, none of them could be regarded as being like the first name/surname combination of European traditions.

It is likely that missions and government stations were generally more consistent and meticulous in monitoring the assignment of surnames to children than were other record-keepers such as constables and squatters. I recall that even in the 1970s, when surnames at places such as Aurukun (Cape York Peninsula) had become regularised and more or less fixed in spelling on record cards, and at that time were being transmitted patrifilially, men in the open towns of the Gulf Country could still be known as [own first name] + [wife's first name], and women could be known in a similar way but vice versa. Their children would be called [own first name] + [father's first name], especially if the parents were in a stable relationship at the time. That is, there were couples whose members had names like Bobby Maisie and Maisie Bobby.[39] Their children tended to be called Freddy Bobby, Mona Bobby and so on, a patronymic system but not an enduring surname system, for such a Freddy Bobby might marry a Pearl and become Freddy Pearlie, and could in turn have children called Charlene Freddy, even Fred Freddy, given the tendency for names to be repeated down the generations. As a system for maintaining clarity as to who was being talked about, it worked brilliantly. But in time local clarity appears to have given way to the bureaucratic will, with or without the assistance of the decline of stable marriages, and many Aboriginal people now indeed bear an official European-type surname that was once a first name.

Aboriginal surname usage has often been taken to be evidence merely of assimilation to European culture. After all, superficially at least, the general tendency has been for Aboriginal people to adopt or be given surnames that are then acquired and perpetuated by children as a matter of parentage and by many women as a consequence of marriage or cohabitation. But even the earlier anthropological record on such matters suggests that surnames have long been used in distinctive ways by Aboriginal people.

It is best explained by way of a made-up illustration.[40] Let us say that the 200 descendants of Old Smith recognise that they are 'all Smiths'. One hundred of them are descendants of one of his daughters Bessie, who married a Mr Brown. These people are recognised as 'the Browns', that is, the Brown branch of the Smiths. The Browns are made up of six subgroups based on five recently incoming surnames acquired by marriage, namely the Joneses, Greens, Blaineys, Leftwiches, Davises – and some unchanged Browns. Thus 'Browns' has at least two distinct senses, the content of one being nested, along with five other parallel categories, within the content of the other. A Leftwich may say, when being introduced, 'My name is Leftwich but we're all part of the Browns'. A Brown woman married to a man called van der Post may say, 'I'm X van der Post but I'm really a Brown'.

The remaining 100 Smiths consist of three subgroups still bearing the surname Smith. Thus, again, we have a distinction between two kinds of surname group with an identical tag, but we could distinguish, perhaps, between 'macro-Smiths' and 'sub-Smiths'. All sub-Smiths are macro-Smiths, but not all macro-Smiths are sub-Smiths.

The three lots of sub-Smiths are distinguished genealogically – they each come from a different son of Old Smith himself. But they might also tend to live in different towns. They are thus, in local usage, 'the Koo-Wee-Rup Smiths', 'the Nar-Nar-Goon Smiths', and 'the Dargo Smiths'. In this case there is some relationship between genealogy and place of residence. This is not always true, however. The sub-Browns, who all come from one Brown and as yet have only a few children themselves, may be sprinkled through the same three towns. 'The Koo-Wee-Rup Browns', 'the Nar-Nar-Goon Browns' and 'the Dargo Browns' are residential categories rather than categories where common ancestry and co-residence coincide, unlike the three lots of sub-Smiths.

Post-classical kinship, personal address and reference

In contemporary rural Aboriginal society, kin remain extremely important to most people, much more so than for most non-Aborigines; and consanguineal relationships take precedence over affinal ones in many contexts. Elkin said:

> The positive side of kinship, however, is more important as a factor of social cohesion. The ideal marriage is based on it; so too are duties of mutual help and support, of making gifts and of performing prescribed parts in initiation and burial rites. This explains why civilized natives continue to place emphasis on kinship, especially if they retain any of the ceremonial life.[41]

There is much use of English kin terms but often with distinctively Aboriginal semantics.

Degrees of consanguinity may be carefully expressed in speech and other forms of communication. Certain key structural features of kin-relating and address/reference remain in line with classical practices. For example, the sibling equivalence rule often persists to a degree, the cross/parallel distinction between parents' siblings' children is often maintained, and certain grandkin and other terms may be used reciprocally (or quasi-reciprocally) as in classical systems (for example, 'Granny-girl' for granddaughter, 'Uncle-boy' for nephew).

The range of the kindred recognised by an individual generally continues to be much larger than among non-Aboriginal Australians (for example, wider than second cousins). Incest prohibitions extend further than in non-Aboriginal law (for example, to second and third cousins).

While these cognatic descent groups are typically exogamous, there is a tendency towards regional endogamy (see below). This raises the question of whether intra-kindred marriages are acceptable while intra-'*family*' (that is, intra-descent group) marriages are not, but we do not have the data to settle this question. Derek Freeman showed that in many bilateral societies marriage within the kindred was either permitted or even preferred, although as much could also be said of classical systems in Aboriginal Australia. Lineages, in contrast with kindreds, tend to be exogamous.[42] In some Aboriginal groups, however, a recent tendency is for the emergence of a rule of *tribal* (not just kin group) exogamy, based on the view that people of the same language group are 'too close' to marry, even if no blood link between them is known. In one urban area I have worked there has been great sensitivity over the issue between those who hold this view and those who have married members of their own language group. Marrying a non-Aboriginal person is often considered a much safer choice from this point of view.

The use of kin-based honorifics for high-status women (mainly Auntie, for example, 'Auntie Dodo', but also note 'Granny Moisey', 'Mum Shirl') reflects the use of the kinship idiom for a societal status; 'Auntie' is the dominant form. This system seems to be less frequently applied to men. 'Uncle' is also used as an honorific, but cases appear rarer. These particular uses of 'Auntie' and 'Uncle' are sociocentric not egocentric terms (that is, they are more like titles than actual kin terms) but their idiom is that of kinship, and in particular make reference to kin roles which, at least in the classical systems, are those that combine authority with nurturance.

Other kin terms may be used widely with non-kin; for instance, if people are close in years and friendly they may use 'sis' (sister), 'tidda' (sister), 'bruz' (brother) or 'cuz' (cousin) as terms of address with each other. Both the honorifics and these terms of solidarity may be described as fictive kinship. Fictive kinship systems are widely distributed around the world. In this case it seems clear that both respect and amity, in the classical cultures of Australia, were heavily tied to kinship relations and genealogical standing and something of this has been perpetuated in some post-classical forms. Loosened from actual genealogy, the idiom of both kinds of regard remains couched in kin archetypes.

There is a relatively high frequency of particular first names and surnames being repeated in a cognatic descent group. There can be a high degree of first-naming after senior kin. Numerical data on this practice are provided by Athol Chase for the Lockhart people of Cape York Peninsula. English first names repeated within families, on a sample of 32 cases, were about evenly distributed among those derived from fathers' and mothers' sides. Out of respect for those after whom they were named, such children's names were altered in address (e.g. 'Josiah' became 'J-boy', 'Donald' became 'D-boy', 'Nullum' became 'Lalla' and so on).[43] These kinds of names are often called 'nicknames'. There is a general practice of distinguishing an official first name from a nickname. Males especially have nicknames, often as the primary means by which they are known, now even in public life.

This brief summary is not intended as a description of every manifestation of social organisation in rural and urban Australia, but a survey of the evidence suggests that most if not all of the points made above are borne out in several or even many different parts of Australia. Brief summaries of much of the case material on which I base these observations are to be found elsewhere.[44]

The basic transformation

In areas of very arid terrain, bilateral parental filiation has long been a means of acquiring landed interests from an antecedent under Aboriginal tradition, and many other principles such as conception, burial place of a parent, long residence and ritual knowledge, also form viable pathways to land rights in that extreme case. In most of mainland Australia, however, patrifiliation has been the privileged pathway to land rights under classical Aboriginal tenure systems, notwithstanding the importance of complementary matrifiliation, and possibilities of succession to mother's (or MM's, FM's etc.) country.[45] Succession to the mother's country is quite common in the Wik region of Cape York Peninsula and occurs in similar areas where there are no kin class systems (no moieties, subsections, sections, semimoieties, etc.) standing in the way. Kin class systems usually require that people be of a different class from that of their mother and her country.

The transformational relationship between such a system and a simply cognatic one is relatively uncomplicated. It involves only two major steps. First, there was an expansion from groups made up only of patrifilially-related cognates (perhaps plus complementary matrifiliates), to groups made up of both these and certain other descendants of their female members including their grandchildren and beyond. Second, the privileging of patrifiliation dropped out, leaving the system simply cognatic. In slightly more detail, non-Aboriginal fathering of children created people whose Aboriginal ancestry, and thus their traditional land interests, could only be traced via women. For a time, and perhaps a long time, post-conquest landed groups consisted of a combination of agnates (patrifilial cognates) and non-patrifilial cognates (Figure 19). The non-unilineal cognatic principle gained acceptance, power relations between the genders altered radically, co-parenting partnerships went through a period of high instability, many Aboriginal children were born to non-Aboriginal genitors and, as a result, the patrifilial principle dropped out, leaving descent group composition simply cognatic in foundation (Figure 20).

However, the question arises whether such *families* of polity have come about through transformations of former practices in any strong sense in regions where serial filiations cannot be established as the mainspring of classical tenure. This topic requires further research.

Future directions

Demographically, the post-classical formation probably characterises the majority of the Aboriginal population of the country. Something like this formation may actually be present in remote communities more often than appears from the literature, even recent literature. Inquiries about land ownership in such places are usually met with a referral to the older men and women who are the senior custodians of tradition. What a group of women or men in their fifties or seventies say about current practice in the transmission of land interests may be expected to reflect their own life experience and their own views on the prescriptions of classical tradition.

But what, for example, does a twenty-year-old mother in the same community understand to be the way her children are being assigned interests in particular countries? Who now plays a definitive role in making such assignments? Does the mother object to such assignments when she realises the child may have a future in which personal choice plays a greater role than previously? How is country assigned to a child when the father is non-Aboriginal or unrecognised? Does the child take the mother's surname or the father's, or either in different contexts? How does surname assignment relate to country affiliations? Is there a range of variation in the way country assignments of children are carried out in the same community, depending on cultural differences between families, for example?

These and related questions have begun to be tackled by fresh fieldwork, largely as a result of the requirements of the native title regime. This new work should throw more light on the ways in which classical land tenure systems have been transformed into post-classical ones, where this has occurred, and why they seem to have done this in such convergent forms in different parts of the country.

The more we find out about such systems, it seems, the less casually can we resort to notions of 'fluidity', 'indeterminacy' and 'ambiguity' and reject out of hand the 'systems thinking' of past studies in Aboriginal kinship and social organisation.[46] The popularity of these freedom-connoting concepts perhaps does not rest entirely on their alleged postmodern intellectual virtues. They are from time to time a handy cover for our difficulty in reaching systematic accounts of phenomena that may turn out to be, as for example in the present context, whole tenure systems in rapid but mainly unidirectional flux, different tenure systems operating simultaneously in single populations but among different age brackets or kin groups with different social histories, or the emergence of new but hardly chaotic domains of optation. The ethnography required to describe such cases needs to be fine-grained and systematic, but it also needs to be informed by the rigour of anthropological theory, if areas of indeterminacy are to be demonstrated convincingly. Perhaps the most relevant body of theory in this instance is the now much-neglected domain of kinship and social organisation.

Social closure between Aboriginal and non-Aboriginal people in the same environment, either urban or rural, was widely reported for the post-war period. This relative closure may seem contradicted by the significant proportion of non-Aboriginal men married to Aboriginal women in these communities, but the survey evidence indicates that these men usually joined wholly or largely Aboriginal households, and did not import their non-Aboriginal kin or friends with them.[47] It was also reported that, after a much earlier initial contact period in which many children were born to women of full Aboriginal descent and genitors of non-Aboriginal descent, there was significant stabilisation such that a large proportion of subsequent unions were 'intra-caste', the fecundity of part-Aboriginal unions was higher than wholly Aboriginal ones, and health conditions improved.[48] The result was a population boom among people of mixed ancestry, after the devastating losses of the colonial and immediate post-colonial phase.

Thus while inter-racial attitudes, cultural differences and institutional and physical separation were often presented by post-war anthropologists as the major forces in explaining Aboriginal non-assimilation and non-integration with the majority of Australians, one must attribute at least equivalent power also to the now-burgeoning universe of kin to which people of Aboriginal descent belonged. Relationships with kin appear to have consistently outranked voluntary or accidental relationships such as those of work, church, friendship or neighbour-hood, in governing people's decisions, regardless of factors such as physical proximity or racial attitudes, in many parts of urban and rural Australia. Relationships with kin were of two main kinds; those based on descent and those based on marriage or, at least, co-parenting. Shared descent would typically outrank marriage as a form of relatedness, particularly if it were close. Basil Sansom, discussing the work of Jeremy Beckett on New South Wales Aboriginal people of the far west, also contrasts the 'enduring ties between mothers and their children' with what he called 'contingent fatherhood', a father's recognition being more contingent on his performance as a parent. Mother–child relationships, for many people of urban and rural Australia, thus stood at the apex of a relationship hierarchy and were central to social organisation.[49] The survival of the classical Aboriginal emphasis on kin, and ancestry, among the shattered and then later self-reconstructing groups of rural and urban regions, should not be surprising.

I have worked with a number of groups containing members who were separated from their parents and siblings in early childhood, and where those removed had even had their names changed by authorities upon institutionalis-ation, but who managed to overcome huge obstacles to reunite with their kin. In a few cases, where genealogical relationships could not be traced, they managed to re-establish relationships with people of the same traditional country. In these latter cases there seems to be a reasonable assumption that people from the same country must be, somehow, related.

The survival of an emphasis on relations of kinship and descent in post-classical Aboriginal society typically entails a parallel emphasis on home ties. For many, and perhaps most, rural hinterland people urban migration failed to erase links to the places they had come from, especially if they settled within a day's travel of them. The arrival of widespread car ownership in the 1950s and 1960s must have had an important impact on this mobility. It may also have been a factor in facilitating the original urban migrations themselves. Note, however, that Sydney, Adelaide and Melbourne in the 1950s–1970s differed considerably from Brisbane in 1973. In the latter case it was found that 90 per cent of Aboriginal people surveyed had never been to a mission, about three-quarters had spent little, if any, time on government reserves or missions; most had migrated to the city from rural towns and provincial centres, and a majority had remained at the same address for all of the previous year.[50] Ellen Biddle had earlier found that nearly 66 per cent of a sample of over 2,000 Brisbane Aborigines consisted of people who had never lived on an Aboriginal reserve or settlement. Most of those with such experience (60%) came from Cherbourg, the closest such settlement to Brisbane.[51] The great distances between Brisbane and most Queensland Aboriginal settlements may account for the differences between Brisbane and other metropolitan communities of eastern Australia.

While so often phrased in terms of ties to a mission, town or pastoral station, these links were also often remembered as those of a family to its 'tribal land', although a period in which such traditions were 'underground' seems to have restricted specific knowledge of tribal names and territorial details among those who were growing up in the cities.

The undergrounding of Aboriginal traditions and cultural practices, particularly during the assimilation era, deserves closer study than is possible here. Examples of concealment of traditions from non-Aborigines are given in several case studies.[52] Russell Hausfeld was also particularly struck by the phenomenon while resident manager of Woodenbong Aboriginal Station from 1956 to 1960. He referred to it as 'dissembled culture', a term that did not catch on.[53] Caroline Kelly gives another example, for Cherbourg settlement in Queensland: 'They fear the ridicule of the white man, but at the time of death one can observe how deep-rooted is this belief [in totemism] and in their grief mourners who previously seemed completely under mission influence, return to the older forms as if they had never ceased to practise them. ...'[54]

Kelly made another observation about the concealment of certain kinds of knowledge from young people brought up among non-Aborigines, one that has parallels elsewhere in the literature: 'The older people guard their religious secrets very jealously from the young men and women who have been reared since birth with white people.'[55]

Elkin wrote of how the Flinders Ranges people of South Australia

> shielded their culture with a reticence greater than I have elsewhere found, and did so just because, as a result of their partial civilization, they realized that white men, generally speaking, would not appreciate its significance, and might also use any information gained for journalistic purposes. Their very reticence and diffidence was an index of the value to them of what remained of their culture.[56]

With the end of this undergrounding period and the renaissance of traditional forms of identity, the *families* of polity have become the most visible customary organisational structures of post-classical Aboriginal society. Their characterising surnames, not surprisingly, feature prominently on applications forms for determinations of native title.

Notes

Abbreviations used below:

ALJR   *Australian Law Journal Reports*
FCR   *Federal Court Reports*
FLR   *Federal Law Report*
HCA   High Court of Australia

INTRODUCTION

1 The most comprehensive pathway through this material is via the website of the National Native Title Tribunal (www.nntt.gov.au). For a summary of important recent developments in native title law resulting from majority decisions in the High Court of Australia 1999–2002, see Wright (2003).

2 *Mathaman and Others v Nabalco Pty Ltd and Commonwealth of Australia.* Supreme Court of the Northern Territory, Blackburn J, (1969) 14 *FLR* 10, *ALR* 685.

3 *Milirrpum v Nabalco Pty Ltd and Commonwealth of Australia.* Supreme Court of the Northern Territory, Blackburn J, (1971) 17 *FLR* 141; (1972–73) *ALR* 65. For a detailed account of the case from an anthropological perspective see Williams (1986).

4 *Aboriginal Land Act 1991* (Queensland) Section 46.

5 *Mabo v Queensland [No 2]* (1992) 175 *CLR* 1.

6 *Native Title Act 1993* (Commonwealth); Bartlett (1993a).

7 *Members of the Yorta Yorta Aboriginal Community v Victoria* [2002] HCA 58. See further Chapter 6.

8 *Western Australia v Ward* [2002] HCA 28 (2002); 76 *ALJR* 1098.

9 *Macquarie Dictionary* (1991:1213).

10 Barnard and Spencer (1996:615).

11 Sutton (1995c).

12 This distinction was introduced in Sutton (ed. 1988). Although subject to some debate and also some misunderstanding, it has become widespread in Australianist anthropological writing since that time. 'Australianist' is a conventional term for Aboriginal studies.

13 On the 'jural' see e.g. Barnard and Spencer (1996:610). On my reflection of the jural paradigm in relation to the anthropology used in native title contexts see Mantziaris

and Martin (2000:33–35), Pannell and Vachon (2001), Sutton (2002), Avery (2002).
14 Sharp (1996).

1 KINDS OF RIGHTS IN COUNTRY

1 This chapter contains a revised version of material published in Sutton (2001b).
2 Pearson (1997: 154).
3 Wheeler (1910:27,38–45).
4 Meggitt (1964:174). For discussion of Meggitt's 'community' see Chapter 4.
5 Anderson (1989:82).
6 P. Sutton field notes (1974).
7 Hiatt (1962), and see Chapter 1.
8 Peterson *et al.* (1977:1005–1006).
9 Peterson *et al.* (1977:1006–1007).
10 Part of it appeared in a revised form in Peterson (1983).
11 For details of this process in the Arrernte area see Strehlow (1947).
12 Trigger (1992:110), French (1995:9–11), Tindale (1974:214).
13 For *Finniss River* and *Lake Amadeus* see Aboriginal Land Commissioner (1981, 1989);
   for *Kenbi* see Aboriginal Land Commissioner (1991b, 2000); for the Far West Coast
   see Macdonald *et al.* (1998), and for literature on southerly and south-easterly
   migration by Western Desert people from before the 1850s to the 1950s see Tindale
   (1974:213), Brady (1987).
14 Aboriginal Land Commissioner (1982, 1988a), Land Tribunal (Queensland) (1994,
   1996).
15 Morphy and Morphy (1981).
16 On atomism and collectivism see Chapter 4.
17 In the Western Desert it is also possible to use a spousal relationship as a reason to
   make claims on a district, although such a link alone does not often amount to much
   (Sutton and Vaarzon-Morel 2003).
18 See Warner (1958:33–35), Williams (1986:38,98,175), Keen (1994:73–75).
19 Williams's footnote here refers to the introduction of the notion of 'inchoate rights'
   by E.A.H. Laurie QC in the *Ayers Rock* land claim in 1979. 'The concept was subsequently taken up and developed by the Aboriginal Land Commissioner in his report
   on that claim [1979: 5, para. 27]' (Williams 1986:191).
20 Williams (1986:175).
21 Aboriginal Land Commissioner (1979: para. 27).
22 Williams (1986:189).
23 See Goddard (1996), Nash (1980), Aboriginal Land Commissioner (1988b:57).
24 Nash (1980:9).
25 Morel *et al.* (1992:30–31).
26 On easements see Doolan (1979), and on the remarkable distances some groups
   travelled through other countries, under strict conditions, to get red ochre, see e.g.
   Wheeler (1910:68–69), Jones (1984).
27 von Sturmer (1984:113–115), Anderson (1989:75–76).
28 Cf. Penner (1997:20–22) on contingent norms.
29 Anonymous reader 'A', who made this comment when assessing the present text.
30 QG 174 of 1997, Schedule – Determination of Native Title, Part G.
31 In pre-colonial terms, the Western Desert seems to have been the region of greatest
   degree of choice. See further Chapter 8.

32 These cases are most likely to occur in the Western Desert and in those rural and urban areas where colonial impacts have been greatest.

33 Gluckman (1965:36, 44–45).

34 John Avery (personal communication).

35 Strehlow (1947).

36 See Chapter 8 below.

37 See Chapter 8 below.

38 I thank Susan Woenne-Green for alerting me to the generic/specific distinction in the context of specifying customary rights.

39 On customary Aboriginal and Torres Strait Islander rights in marine species see Johannes and MacFarlane (1991), Sharp (1996, 2002) and the papers in e.g. Gray and Zann (eds.) (1988), Meyers *et al.* (1996), Peterson and Rigsby (eds.) (1998).

40 See further Chapter 4.

41 One of the more important books to have recently appeared is Hann (ed.) (1998). In relation to Aboriginal Australia see especially Rigsby's very useful survey of property theory (1998).

42 Hoebel (1966:424) quoted in Hann (ed.) (1998:4).

43 Radcliffe-Brown (1935(1952):32–33).

44 Hiatt (1965).

45 Rigsby (1998), Stanner (1969).

46 Myers (1988).

47 Myers (1982).

48 Sharp (1934b:23).

49 See especially Williams (1982, 1986, 1999a).

50 E.g. Hiatt (1962), Peterson and Long (1986:63), Kolig (1978:77).

51 *Macquarie Dictionary* (1991:1511).

52 The identification of trees with ancestral beings and mythic figures and their individual human descendants (or manifestations) has long been reported for the Northern Arrernte area (e.g. Pink 1933:186) and the neighbouring Western Arrernte (e.g. Strehlow 1947:68). This is a practice also found in the north-central Northern Territory (see e.g. Merlan (1982) and Sutton (1983) for the Roper–Elliott region). Trees under which Wik babies' afterbirth was buried have sacred associations for these particular individuals throughout their lives, but I know of only one case where such an individual tree-mediated connection gave rise to a claim on a Wik estate, and that was in the context of attempted (and failed) succession to an untenanted estate (my own fieldwork).

53 Vachon and Pannell (1995).

54 Altman (1987:176).

55 Wootten (1995:111).

56 For literature on Aboriginal burning rights and practices see e.g. Hallam (1975), Latz (1995:29–43), Rose (ed.) (1995c), Langton (1998) and further references therein.

57 Watson (1983).

58 On rights in minerals as an 'incident of native title' see Meyers *et al.* (1997).

59 On classical Aboriginal trade in Australia see e.g. McCarthy (1939), Thomson (1949), Micha (1970), Mulvaney (1976).

60 On the coexistence of interests in land under the common law see Tehan (1997). On coexistent interests held in common country or sites by Aboriginal groups, see e.g. Sutton (1995c:49–60) for an overview.

61 Stevens (1974:205).

62 Riddett (1990:83).

63 Quoted in Lyon and Parsons (1989:7).

64 Stanner (1938).

65 E.g. Reynolds (1981:169); similar statements abound in the pastoral historical literature.

66 See May (1994: Chapter 3), Reynolds (ed.) (1972: Chapter 3), Trigger (1992: Chapter 10).

67 Loos (1982:161).

68 E.g. Reynolds (1981:169); Reynolds (ed.) (1972: Chapter 3); Trigger (1992: Chapter 10, 'Coercion, resistance and accommodation in colonial social relations').

69 See Berndt and Berndt (1987: Chapter 10 'Traditional Continuities'); May (1994: Chapter 6 'Continuity and Change').

70 McGrath (1987:158).

71 Anderson (1983).

72 McGrath (1987:158).

73 Macdonald (1997).

74 Peterson and Long (1986:72).

2 LOCAL ORGANISATION BEFORE THE LAND CLAIMS ERA

1 This chapter contains a revised version of material published in Sutton (1999b).

2 Hiatt (1996:13–35).

3 Howitt (1878:300).

4 Fison and Howitt (1880:215–6, 225, 227–229; map facing half-title page entitled 'Sketch Map of Gippsland. Shewing approximately the Positions of the Clans of the Kurnai Tribe'; see also Howitt (1904:76–77).

5 Howitt and Fison (1883:34).

6 Howitt (1883b:800).

7 Howitt (1883b:809).

8 Howitt (1884:439). Fison carried out no fieldwork of his own among Australian Aboriginal people.

9 Howitt (1885:301). Emphasis added.

10 Howitt and Fison (1885:144–145), emphasis original.

11 Howitt (1883b:804,809).

12 Howitt (1883b:809).

13 Howitt and Fison (1885:144).

14 Howitt and Fison (1885:143), emphasis original.

15 Howitt and Fison (1885:145).

16 Howitt in Fison and Howitt (1880:226).

17 Howitt (1904:73–74).

18 Fison and Howitt (1880:224).

19 Meggitt (1962), Hiatt (1965).

20 Howitt (1888:320).

21 Howitt (1891a:344–345).

22 Howitt (1891b:35).

23 Howitt (1904:44).

24 Howitt (1904:47).

25 Fison and Howitt (1880:232), Howitt (1883b:799, 1904:41). Also: 'Some tribes are again spoken of by the name of their language'. (Howitt 1904:xii).

26 Fison and Howitt (1880:27). Emphasis added.

27 Fison and Howitt (1880:29).

28 Howitt and Fison (1883:33).
29 Howitt (1883a:185).
30 Howitt (1884:433).
31 Howitt (1884:433–434).
32 Howitt (1884:457–458).
33 Howitt and Fison (1885:154).
34 Howitt (1904:142–143, 173–174).
35 He was then plain Mr Brown. See [Radcliffe-]Brown (1913).
36 [Radcliffe-]Brown (1913:145).
37 [Radcliffe-]Brown (1913:146).
38 [Radcliffe-]Brown (1913:145).
39 [Radcliffe-]Brown (1913:146).
40 [Radcliffe-]Brown (1913:147).
41 [Radcliffe-]Brown (1913:146).
42 [Radcliffe-]Brown (1913:147).
43 [Radcliffe-]Brown (1913:147).
44 [Radcliffe-]Brown (1913:147).
45 Later (1969) he said some Kariera local group members did marry each other.
46 [Radcliffe-]Brown (1913:147).
47 [Radcliffe-]Brown (1913:147). Emphasis added.
48 [Radcliffe-]Brown (1913:146).
49 Radcliffe-Brown (1914:626).
50 Radcliffe-Brown (1918:222). Emphasis added.
51 On the distinction between owning and speaking a language, especially in relation to native title, see Walsh (2002).
52 Radcliffe-Brown (1918:222),
53 *Macquarie Dictionary* (1991:849).
54 E.g. Strehlow (1965:136).
55 *Macquarie Dictionary* (1991:849).
56 Emphasis added.
57 Radcliffe-Brown (1918:224). Emphasis added. Much of this is repeated and summarised also in Radcliffe-Brown (1952), especially at p120.
58 Radcliffe-Brown (1930–31:36,37).
59 Radcliffe-Brown (1930–31:34–35).
60 Radcliffe-Brown (1930–31:442; see also p59).
61 Radcliffe-Brown (1930–31:35–36).
62 Radcliffe-Brown (1930–31:59). Emphasis added.
63 Radcliffe-Brown (1930–31:59, fn8).
64 Radcliffe-Brown (1930–31:61).
65 Radcliffe-Brown (1930–31:214).
66 Radcliffe-Brown (1930–31:210).
67 E.g. 'These tribes have the normal organization into patrilineal hordes ...' (p333).
68 Radcliffe-Brown (1930–31:63).
69 Radcliffe-Brown (1930–31:333).
70 Radcliffe-Brown (1930–31:438).
71 Radcliffe-Brown (1930–31:435,438).
72 Radcliffe-Brown (1935 (1952):34).
73 Radcliffe-Brown (1954:105).
74 Radcliffe-Brown (1956:365).
75 Radcliffe-Brown (1930–31:445).

76 Radcliffe-Brown (1930–31:449).
77 Radcliffe-Brown (1930–31:445–455).
78 Stanner 1979 [reporting in 1934, cited in Elkin 1953:417]; Thomson (1939: 211–212); Kaberry (1939:30–31,136); Elkin (1953); Elkin (1954:44–48); Berndt (1959:95–96).
79 Hiatt (1962:271).
80 Hiatt (1962:272).
81 Hiatt (1962:274).
82 Cited in Hiatt (1962:275).
83 Hiatt (1962:276).
84 Hiatt (1962:277).
85 Hiatt (1962:278).
86 Cited in Hiatt (1962:278).
87 Hiatt (1962:281–282).
88 Hiatt (1962:283–284).
89 Hiatt (1962:284).
90 Hiatt (1962:286).
91 Barker (1976).
92 Stanner (1965).
93 E.g. Stanner (1965:13).
94 Peterson (1983:42), von Sturmer (1978).
95 Stanner (1965:21).
96 Tindale (1974).
97 Hiatt (1966:81–92).
98 Peterson and Long (1986).
99 [Radcliffe-]Brown (1913:160).
100 He virtually repeats this same statement in a later paper also (1930–31:437).
101 [Radcliff-]Brown (1913:160).
102 [Radcliffe-]Brown 1913: 160).
103 E.g. Radcliffe-Brown (1929).
104 Peterson and Long (1986: Chapter 5).
105 AL refers to Arnhem Land, CY to Cape York Peninsula.

3 ABORIGINAL COUNTRY GROUPS

1 This chapter contains a revised version of material published in Sutton (2001a).
2 *Ward v Western Australia* (1998) 145 *ALR* 512
3 *Native Title Act* 1993 (Cth), s 81.
4 Available at *http://www.fedcourt.gov.au/pracproc/practice_direct.html* as at May 2002.
5 *Native Title Act 1993* (Cth), ss67, 68.
6 McIntyre and Doohan (2002:195).
7 McIntyre and Doohan (2002:202).
8 See Mantziaris and Martin (1999:27–35).
9 See *Native Title Act 1993* (Cth) s233.
10 Anderson (1984:91).
11 Anderson (1984:92).
12 Calley (1959).
13 Schebeck (2001, a revised version of Schebeck 1968). In trying to understand group naming in the region one also needs to consult the other anthropological literature

such as Warner (1958) and Keen (1994), and other linguistic literature such as F. Morphy (1983), Zorc (1986).

14 An abbreviated version of Schebeck (2001:48–49). The scheme is based principally on observed use, Yolngu nomenclature theory, and etymology. For clarification of what these distinctions refer to, and for the highly detailed sociolinguistic basis for the classification, the reader will need to study the whole text.

15 Schebeck (2001:49). For this region, the anthropologist who has most confronted such 'indeterminacies' in theoretical and ethnographic terms has been Ian Keen (e.g. 1994, 1995a, 1997b, 2000); see further Chapter 6.

16 Williams (1986:73).

17 Holcombe (1998:35–46).

18 For a general introduction to the ethnography of speaking see Hymes (1974).

19 Turner (1974:11). Cf. Waddy (1988:158).

20 See Peterson and Long (1986:13–16).

21 Malinowski (1913 (1963):132–153).

22 Wheeler (1910:45).

23 Sharp (1937:241, 242).

24 Sharp (1937:238).

25 Sharp (1937:244).

26 Sharp (1937:248).

27 E.g., Eyre (1845 (1997) II:304); Fraser (1892:69).

28 Rigsby and Chase (1998:205–206). See also Thomson (1932:162–163).

29 Williams (1986:78).

30 Schebeck (1968:43).

31 Radcliffe-Brown (1952:34,36).

32 Stanner (1965:2).

33 Stanner (1965:2).

34 On developments in post-classical local organisation see Chapter 8.

35 Tindale (1925–26:64; the photographs are at pp74 and 94).

36 Rose (1960:206–207).

37 Rose (1960:207).

38 As Groote Eylandt has only one language, Anindilyakwa, there would be a relatively low likelihood of people of different languages being found in single bands except perhaps on the western and north-western side where people had more interaction with speakers of varieties of Yolngu Matha and Nunggubuyu (see Turner 1974).

39 These figures are from R. Lauriston Sharp's bush camp censuses of 1932–35. He wrote (1934b:32):

> The camps comprise fragments of many different clans, the individual members of which shift about from one camp and country to another, some being associated with one large portion of the tribal territory, which is considered their range, others with another. Even during the rainy season, when the community splits up into very small camps, the men of a clan are separated and do not live together in their own territory as a horde. This does not vitiate the sentimental ties which attach a clan to its own particular 'home' countries, which if not often or regularly lived in by a clan member, are frequently visited. In the arrangement of the larger dry season camps, tribes live separately if more than one are represented, but within the tribal grouping the clans are divided and mixed.

This last statement is problematic, given that inter-language marriages, here principally between Yir Yoront and Thaayorre, mean that many camps cannot be fitted into this scheme.

40 Data on languages absent, but elsewhere R.L. Sharp, the source of these figures, said (1958:3):

> During the years the author spent among the northern Yir Yoront he traced the peregrinations of a series of individuals and plotted their wet season camps when they were partially immobilized, each year with different camp mates. Throughout his entire stay in the bush he was never out of earshot of Kuk Taiori speakers.

This implies that a minimum of two linguistic affiliations would normally be found in such camps.

41 Here I omit the Rose/Tindale figures for Groote Eylandt as the available camp numbers there are only of adult men.

42 See Keen (1995a) for this North East Arnhem Land example.

43 See Warner (1958), Schebeck (1968, 2001), Williams (1986), Morphy (1991), Keen (1994).

44 For the former, see Keen (1995a); for the latter, see Sharp (1934b:20–21).

45 On semimoieties generally see Chapter 7. For semimoieties in this region see e.g. Reay (1962), Trigger (1982), Avery (1985).

46 Blundell (1980:113), Rumsey (1996).

47 Spencer and Gillen (1904:28); Blundell (1980:109–111).

48 Stanner (1979).

49 Derived from Chase (1984:110–111).

50 von Sturmer (1978).

51 Probably the lancewood *Acacia crassicarpa*.

52 Hale (1966:163).

53 For details see Sutton (1991).

54 Mark Harvey (personal communication).

55 Keen (1980:72).

56 Keen (1980:71–81), Ritchie and Bauman (1991).

57 Keen (1980:71–81).

58 Merlan (1998:81).

59 Merlan (1998:81).

60 For some recent history of the Gaagudju as incorporated see Levitus (1991). For the Jawoyn language group see Merlan and Rumsey (1982), Rumsey (1993), and Merlan (1998: Chapters 3 and 4, especially pp81,112,125); for the emergence of a 'Jawoyn Nation' that deals with native title interests among other things see Gibson (1999).

61 Bruce Rigsby (personal communication).

62 Cf. Keen (1980:76).

63 Berndt and Berndt (1970:54).

64 Berndt and Berndt (1970:237–239).

65 Wik region (my own notes). See also Falkenberg (1962) for the Port Keats region.

66 For details see Sutton (1978:142 & map 11).

67 Hiatt (1965:19,24); Bagshaw (1995:123).

68 For the original listing see Sutton and Palmer (1980:51–52). In Sutton (1999a) I referred to these names as 'estate names', and I now correct that. Also note that the entry '*Wani Wukwuk*' in both lists should be changed to *Dak Tinba*.

69 Sutton and Palmer (1980:46).

70 Sutton (1978:127).

71 See Henderson and Nash (eds) (2002) for papers on linguistic topics associated with native title cases.

72 Sharp (1934b:20).
73 Sharp (1958:233–234).
74 Sharp (1958:233).
75 See map in Sutton (1991:63).
76 On language groups and land rights in Australia there is a large literature, much of consisting of anthropological and judicial reports in the forensic domain, but see e.g. Sutton and Palmer (1980), Rigsby and Sutton (1980–82), Merlan (1981), Rumsey (1989, 1993), Walsh (2002).
77 Sharp (1937), Meggitt (1962).
78 Dixon (1976:212).
79 For a sophisticated example in an Aboriginal context see Hansen (1984).
80 Heath (1981:1).
81 See Dixon (1997, 2002).
82 E.g. compare figures 6.1, 6.3 and 6.9 of McBryde (1986).
83 Sutton (1973).
84 Sutton (1978).
85 Crowley (1997).
86 Nash (1990).
87 Nash (1990).
88 Merlan (1994:6–7).
89 Merlan (1983:vii).
90 McKay (2000:158–160).
91 Warner (1958:34), Schebeck (1968, 2001), Williams (1986:61–64), Keen (1994: 75–79)
92 Rigsby (1992:355).
93 Sutton (1993:29).
94 Sutton (1978:138), von Sturmer (1978:326–326), Smith and Johnson (2000: 365–368).
95 Radcliffe-Brown (1930:693), Krzywicki (1934), Birdsell (1953), Dixon (1980:18).
96 Sutton (2003).
97 For details behind this reconstruction see Sutton (2001c:460).
98 See Birdsell (1973).
99 Berndt *et al.* (1979:33).
100 Alan Dench (personal communication).
101 See e.g. Whitehurst (1992).
102 Tindale (1974: map).
103 Meggitt (1962:34–35).
104 Sharp (1937:219).
105 Merlan (1981:144).
106 Evans (2002:70).
107 Merlan (1981:145).
108 Myers (1986:135).
109 Myers (1986:138).
110 Myers (1986:128). On kindreds see Chapter 8.
111 Myers (1986:142). Emphasis added.
112 Myers (1986:144, 160–161).
113 Myers (1986:162).
114 Myers (1986:70).

115 Myers (1986:128–129).

116 Myers (1986:162).

117 Myers (1986:119).

118 Myers (1986:48–54).

4 ATOMISM VERSUS COLLECTIVISM

1 This chapter contains a revised version of material published in Sutton (1995a and 1995b).

2 The *Native Title Act* does, however, provide constraints on applications lacking sufficient authorisation from the group on whose behalf they are lodged (see ss61(2) and (4), 66B, 251B).

3 Hagen (1999).

4 Edmunds (1995).

5 *Native Title Act 1993* s94.

6 See Sutton (1995c:42) for more detail on this point.

7 See Chapter 5 below for the application of regional considerations to the question of underlying customary titles.

8 *Native Title Act* s223.

9 Peterson and Long (1986:151).

10 Mantziaris and Martin (2000:284).

11 Mantziaris and Martin (2000:286). Emphasis original.

12 See Chapter 6 below for more detail on the notion of systems of country relationships.

13 iii Peterson (1976:50).

14 See Mulvaney (1976) on 'the chain of connection' in Aboriginal trading in colonial-era Australia and earlier.

15 Roth (1897:41).

16 See Fraser (1892), and front endpaper to Threlkeld (1892).

17 Mathews (1898a).

18 Mathews (1898d:66–67). Elkin (1975–76:148) reproduced this map in his tribute to Mathews.

19 Mathews (1898b, c, and e respectively).

20 Mathews (1900b:91).

21 Tindale (1974: map), Berndt *et al.* (1979).

22 Mathews (1900a: opposite p574).

23 Mathews called moieties phratries, and both sections and subsections he called sections, in this case (1900a:575). On his map the Blue line A–B is the eastern limit of circumcision, and the yellow line C–D (and northern section of the A–B line) the eastern limit of subincision. The blue line E–F is the western limit of both rites (Mathews 1900a:577–578).

24 Howitt (1904:41).

25 Peterson (1976:60).

26 Keen (1997a).

27 Sharp (1958).

28 Keen (1997a:268).

29 Keen (1997a:273).

30 McConvell (1996).

31 See e.g., Tindale (1974:41,125,127,136,142,156,200,214).

32 Tindale (1974:79).

33 Sharp (1958).

34 E.g., Berndt and Berndt (1993:19).

35 Berndt and Berndt (1988:35).

36 Berndt and Berndt (1988:22, 1993:19,27).

37 Smith (1989).

38 There is a tradition of 'community studies' in anthropology. Examples from Aboriginal Australia include Chase (1980), Trigger (1992) and Holcombe (1998). For an insightful discussion of problematic and complex relationships between local polities and Aboriginal settlement communities see Rowse (1992:50–58).

39 See Chapter 2 above for the core/contingent rights distinction.

40 Meggitt (1962: 214).

41 Meggitt (1962:94).

42 Meggitt (1962:51).

43 Peterson (1969:30).

44 Elias (2001:172–175).

45 Meggitt (1962:249).

46 See further below, where I discuss Meggitt's distinction between the 'natal community' and the community of long-term residence.

47 Meggitt (1962:49–50).

48 Meggitt (1962:49,51; see also p244).

49 Meggitt (1962:5,51).

50 Meggitt (1962:47). Manganyarnpa = Yalpari (Elias 2001).

51 Jackson (1995:32–33).

52 Aboriginal Land Commissioner (1992:10), Bell (1993:112).

53 Meggitt (1962:49).

54 Meggitt (1962:57).

55 Meggitt (1962:54–55).

56 Meggitt (1962:51).

57 Meggitt (1962:54).

58 Meggitt (1962:47).

59 Meggitt (1962:72–74).

60 Meggitt (1962:48).

61 Meggitt (1962:48–49).

62 Meggitt (1962:214).

63 Meggitt (1962:288).

64 Meggitt (1962:243–244,245) Emphases added.

65 Meggitt (1962:211).

66 Cf. Meggitt (1962:xiii–xiv).

67 See Meggitt (1962:67) on the role of conception.

68 Meggitt (1962:249).

69 Morphy and Morphy (1984:52), referring to Meggitt (1962:69).

70 For a nice example of this feedback relationship, see Hiatt (1982:20).

71 Meggitt (1962:214).

72 Meggitt (1962:207).

73 Meggitt (1962:205,69).

74 Hiatt (1996:25).

75 Hiatt (1982:21).

76 Hiatt (1982:24–25).

77 Fison and Howitt (1880:226).
78 Sutton (1978:72).
79 Hiatt (1965:19).
80 Hiatt (1965:24).
81 Hiatt (1965:25).
82 Hiatt (1982:19).
83 Hiatt (1965:35).
84 Hiatt (1965:37).
85 Hiatt (1982:22).
86 Hiatt (1965:24).
87 Hiatt (1965:19).
88 Hiatt (1965:24).
89 Hiatt (1965:25).
90 Geoffrey Bagshaw (personal communication).
91 This is a correction to the 'in mangroves' of Bagshaw (1995:123), courtesy G. Bagshaw (personal communication).
92 Bagshaw (1995:122–123).
93 See Sutton (1978:126–128) on 'nickname' clusters.
94 Gumbert (1984:91).
95 Gumbert (1984:196).
96 Gumbert (1984:92).
97 Gumbert (1984:103).
98 For more detail on this see Sutton (1995c).
99 Povinelli (1993).
100 Povinelli (1993:3).
101 Povinelli (1993:30).
102 They have also done so formally, see the transcripts of the two hearings of the *Kenbi* Land Claim.

5 UNDERLYING AND PROXIMATE CUSTOMARY TITLES

1 This chapter contains a revised version of material published in Sutton (1996).
2 Emphases added.
3 *Mabo v Queensland (No 2)* (1992) 175 *CLR* 1 per Brennan CJ at pp61–62. Emphasis added.
4 *Mabo v Queensland (No 2)* (1992) 175 *CLR* 1 per Brennan CJ at p42.
5 Macdonald (1996: Chapter 6).
6 Schwab (1991:132).
7 Land Tribunal (Queensland) (1996: paras. 766–778).
8 Maddock (1984:212).
9 Maddock (1984:212–213).
10 Evans (1992:20–21).
11 Henderson and Dobson (1994:332). Compare also the range of meanings listed for *tjurunga* by Strehlow (1947:85–86).
12 My own unpublished fieldnotes 1973–78.
13 Macdonald (1986).
14 Anthropological discourse has generally abandoned the term 'custom' but it has continuing use in Australian law. See Rigsby (1996).
15 Cf. Wootten (1995:110) and see Wootten (1994a, 1994b).

16 On the problem of systems, see further Chapter 6.

17 Macdonald (1996).

18 My own field notes. For the Victoria River region see Daly Pulkara's statement 'The Earth got a culture inside', in Rose (1992:229).

19 *Macquarie Dictionary* (1991:1419).

20 Reay (n.d.:10).

21 Trigger (1989:15).

22 Williams (1982:141). Emphasis added.

23 Keen (1988b:277). Emphasis added.

24 See e.g. Keen (1994:12–15, 265–276).

25 *Macquarie Dictionary* (1991:1804).

26 Oxley-Oxland and Stein (1985:5); *Mabo v Queensland (No 2)* (1992) 175 *CLR* 1 per Brennan CJ at p53.

27 Sutton (1995c:53).

28 *Native Title Act 1993*: s223(1).

29 On the latter as a 'fiction' see *Mabo v Queensland (No 2)* (1992) 175 *CLR* 1 per Brennan J at pp46–49.

30 Keen (1989:38).

31 Myers (1980a,1980b).

32 Myers (1980b:312).

33 Keen (1989:19).

34 Sutton (1995c:59–60).

35 See e.g. Kolig (1978), Stanton (1983), Palmer (1983).

36 Sutton, Morel and Nash (1993:40). The men were recognised as traditional owners at Muckaty by the Land Commissioner (ALC 1997:42–43).

37 Sutton (1997a).

38 Berndt and Berndt (1993).

39 Stanner (1965:237).

40 *Aboriginal Land Act* 1991 (Qld) s1.03.

41 Peterson and Long (1986), Sutton (1995c).

42 E.g. Peterson, Keen and Sansom (1977), Kolig (1978), Akerman (1995), Sutton (1995c:53).

43 Sutton (1980: Appendix).

44 Pink (1936:283–4).

45 Cf. Peterson and Long (1986:53–54).

46 Wheeler (1910:40,44–45,62).

47 Sutton (1995d:48).

48 See Keen (1994:114) for a similar distinction that applies in North East Arnhem Land.

49 Sutton (1978:71 Fig. 5).

50 Aboriginal Land Commissioner (1981).

51 Keen (1989).

52 Strehlow (1947:156)

53 As in Keen (1988b).

54 E.g. Strehlow (1947: Chapter 3).

55 John Avery (personal communication).

56 I am grateful to John Avery (personal communication) for reminding me of this case and fleshing it out further for me.

57 Stanner (1965:230).

58 Deborah Bird Rose (personal communication).
59 Cf. Peterson (1976), Sutton (1995c:50–51).
60 Sutton and Vaarzon-Morel (2003: Chapters 5–7).
61 Sutton (1978:59–60).
62 Sutton (1993:31), Sutton, Chase and Rigsby (1993).
63 Kolig (1978:62–63).
64 Sutton (1978:82–83).
65 Keen (1994:102).
66 Keen (1994:105).
67 Ian Keen (personal communication). See further Chapter 7 on Keen's rejection of the term 'clan' for this region.
68 See Warner (1958).
69 Merlan (1981:144–145).
70 Peterson and Long (1986:147).
71 Peterson and Long (1986:58–59).
72 Aboriginal Land Commissioner (1982), Land Tribunal (Queensland) (1994a), and Sutton (1995b) respectively.
73 Goddard (1996:102,213).
74 Henderson and Dobson (1994:286–287 and see p455 under *kwertengerle*).
75 For a brief overview of the literature on this see Sutton (1995c:40,161).
76 Evans (1992:44).
77 Goddard (1996:102).
78 Sutton (1993).
79 Heath (1981:204).
80 Sutton (1995d:24,82 plus unpublished notes).
81 I changed the orthography between 1978 and 1995, unstressed vowels now being shown as /e/ instead of /a/, and all underlying stems are now shown as consonant-final.
82 Sutton (1978:57–58).
83 My field notes. Emphasis original.
84 Quoted in Kennedy *et al.* (1996).
85 Keen (1994:285).
86 Myers (1986:128).
87 Myers (1986:141).
88 Sutton, Morel and Nash (1993:46–47).
89 Strehlow (1965, 1970).
90 E.g., Strehlow (1970:123–128).
91 Strehlow (1970:116).
92 Sansom (1980b:259ff).
93 David Brooks (personal communication).
94 Land Tribunal (Queensland) (1995).
95 Merlan (1995).

6 THE SYSTEM QUESTION

1 This chapter contains a revised version of material published in Sutton (1999a).
2 *Members of the Yorta Yorta Aboriginal Community v Victoria* [2002] HCA 58, paras. 86–89 per Gleeson CJ, Gummow and Hayne JJ, emphasis original.
3 *Members of the Yorta Yorta Aboriginal Community v Victoria* [2002] HCA 58, paras. 44, 83 per Gleeson CJ, Gummow and Hayne JJ.

4 Neate (1996:254–257).

5 *Yorta Yorta v Victoria* (2001) 110 FCR 244 at para. 127 per Branson and Katz JJ.

6 Williams (1986:212–215).

7 See *Mabo v Queensland (No 2)* (1992) 175 CLR 1 at p42 per Brennan J, at 191 per Toohey J., and at p110 per Deane and Gaudron JJ. Emphasis added, P.S.

8 *Members of the Yorta Yorta Aboriginal Community v Victoria* [2002] HCA 58, paras. 39, 40 per Gleeson CJ, Gummow and Hayne JJ.

9 *Members of the Yorta Yorta Aboriginal Community v Victoria* [2002] HCA 58, para. 42 per Gleeson CJ, Gummow and Hayne JJ.

10 *Mary Yarmirr & Ors v The Northern Territory of Australia & Ors* [1998] 771 FCA, paras. 68–83.

11 See especially Myers (1986).

12 Keen (1997b:67).

13 Keen (1997b:73).

14 E.g., Keen (1997b:92).

15 Keen (1997b:91).

16 Keen (1997b:87).

17 Keen (1997b:91).

18 Aboriginal Land Commissioner (1991a: para 9.1).

19 Myers (1986:293–295).

20 Myers (1986:295–296).

21 McConvell (1996).

22 Hamilton (1982:103). Emphasis added.

23 Stanner (1963:36–37),

24 Keen (1988a:104–105). On structuration, see Giddens (1979).

25 And see above, this chapter, on the problem of subjective tests of tradition.

26 Silverstein (1985:795–796).

27 See Sansom (1980a) and, in particular, (1980b).

28 Sansom (1980b:257, 259, 260, 261, 269, 273, 278, 279).

29 See Sutton and Palmer (1980).

30 Sansom (1980a:11).

31 Sansom (1980a:11).

32 Sansom (1980a:10).

33 Maddock (1982:70).

34 Kaberry's figures (1939:115) are, in more detail: Lunga (1) 83.1%, Lunga (2) 83.7%, Djaru 80.7%, Kunian 91.6%, Punaba 85.0%, Wolmeri 95.5%. Other renderings of these language names include: Kitja (Lunga), Gooniyandi (Kunian), Bunuba (Punaba) and Walmatjarri (Wolmeri).

35 Maddock (1982:70).

36 Hiatt (1965:78).

37 Shapiro (1981:77).

38 Sharp (1934a:416–417).

39 Warner (1958:105).

40 Keen (1994:90).

41 Keen (1994:89). Emphases added.

42 Keen (1994:79).

43 Keen (1994:89–91).

44 Keen (1994:87).

45 David Nash (personal communication).

46 Keen (1994:63–64).

47 Shapiro (1981:101–102).
48 Keen (1994:65).
49 Keen (1994:73–74).
50 Keen (1994:75).
51 Keen (1994:64).
52 Keen (1994:66).
53 Keen (1994:68–71).
54 Keen (1994:164,293).
55 Keen (1994:167).
56 Keen (1994:105). See also Keen (1995b).
57 Morphy (1997:132–135).
58 See e.g., Williams (1986:94–98 and further index references).
59 See e.g., the relevant definitions of corporate groups in Barnard and Spencer (1996: 599), Barfield (1997:86).
60 Morphy (1997:132).
61 Morphy (1997:134).
62 See further Chapter 7.
63 Keen (1994:45) and see further below.
64 John Morton (personal communication).
65 Komei Hosokawa (personal communication)
66 Williams (1999b:127,134–135,137).
67 Williams (1999b:136).
68 Keesing, cited in Williams (1999b:136).
69 Sutton (1978:58).
70 Sutton (1978:59–60). Emphasis added.
71 Keen (2000).
72 Giddens (1979:61–62), emphasis original.
73 Morgan (1858:134).
74 Morgan (1858:132).
75 Davidson (1938:671).
76 Davidson (1938:671–672).
77 John Morton (personal communication).
78 E.g.. Mudbura, Sutton (1983:85).
79 Moore (1884(1978)).
80 See Land Tribunal (Queensland) (1994b:62,97).
81 Luise Hercus (personal communication).
82 See Breen (1970), Haviland (1974).
83 Alpher and Nash (1999).
84 O'Grady, Voegelin and Voegelin (1966:26).
85 Black (1997); Alpher and Nash (1999).
86 Dixon (1997:92).
87 For evidence regarding this in the upper Roper River region, see Merlan (1981).
88 Silver and Miller (1997:305).
89 Silver and Miller (1997: Chapter 13).
90 Campbell (1997:353–376).
91 E.g., Sterritt *et al.* (1998: Chapter 2).
92 Dixon (1997:92).
93 Chadwick (1997).
94 See Bell (1998:97–98,617), where she relies in part on unpublished linguistic work by Maryalyce McDonald.

95 Sutton (1991:63).
96 Sutton and Vaarzon-Morel (2003: Chapter 6). This cumulative, almost 'points-system' approach was first suggested by Jon Willis (pers. comm. to Robert Tonkinson).
97 Sharp (1968:159), emphasis original; and see Sutton (1978:116).
98 Edge (1998).
99 Sutton and Palmer (1980:47).
100 This was probably a reference to Scheffler (1966:543).
101 Letter from W.E.H. Stanner to Peter Sutton, Canberra 2/6/80.
102 The data are presented in a table at the end of Sutton (1999a).
103 See Sutton and Palmer (1980:47–48), Aboriginal Land Commissioner (1982:35).
104 Rose (1960:69,475,63,91).
105 Rose (1965:54,82).
106 Stanner (1933:14).
107 Of these eight, half were also the same in 1957.
108 Of these nine, three, possibly four, were also the same in 1957.
109 Howitt in Fison and Howitt (1880:186).
110 Howitt in Fison and Howitt (1880:255).
111 E.g., Dixon (1972:xix), Nordlinger (1998:xi).
112 Available at *http://fedcourt.gov.au/pracproc/practice_direct.html* as at May 2002.

7 KINSHIP, FILIATION AND ABORIGINAL LAND TENURE

1 This chapter contains a revised version of material published in Sutton (1998).
2 For a well-documented example see Thomson (1932).
3 See further Fortes (1969:56–57). There has been a major debate among anthropologists centring on this issue. For two vigorously argued and opposed views see Schneider (1984) and Scheffler (1986, 1991).
4 Wangkangurru is a language of the area between the north end of Lake Eyre and the central Simpson Desert. Examples here are from Hercus (1994:14).
5 This is a language of the area between Alice Springs and the north-west Simpson Desert. Examples here are from Henderson and Dobson (1994:477). 'Stomach' is presumably a euphemism. Open talk about the details of reproduction is generally prohibited under classical Aboriginal traditions.
6 See von Sturmer (1981).
7 See, e.g., Thomson (1935), Warner (1958), Meggitt (1962), Hiatt (1965), Berndt (1971), Heath, Merlan and Rumsey (eds). (1982), Merlan (1989).
8 Thomson (1936).
9 Dousset (2002:200–201).
10 For a review of Aboriginal kinship studies 1961–1986 see Keen (1988a). Prior to the native title era perhaps the last major efforts to publish in this domain were those of Shapiro (1979), Turner (1980), and Heath, Merlan and Rumsey (eds) (1982). A recent resurgence of interest in the subject, significantly stimulated by native title work, is reflected by papers in Finlayson, Rigsby and Bek (eds) (1999), and McConvell, Dousset and Powell (eds) (2002).
11 Fortes (1969).
12 Sharp (1958). For basic references on the question of the nature of classical Aboriginal governance, see Berndt (1965), Hiatt (1986), Keen (1989), Maddock (1984), Meggitt (1964), Williams (1985).

13 A shift involving greater recognition of the political roles of individuals occurred from the early 1970s on; for a review see Hiatt (1986). On regional systems see e.g. Sutton (1990), Keen (1997a).

14 There is no easy way into this material, although Maddock (1982:56–104), Williams (1981), Berndt and Berndt (1981:46–106) and Edwards (1993:42–54) are useful attempts to introduce Aboriginal kinship and social organisation to the general reader. For an introduction to the anthropology of kinship-based groups see Keesing (1975). For the standard technical text on Aboriginal kinship systems see Scheffler (1978), but note that Scheffler argues in favour of the Fortes position and against the finding that there are any descent groups in Aboriginal Australia, in terms of the technical definitions of anthropology (cf. also Scheffler 1986, 2001).

15 Bruce Rigsby (personal communication).

16 The *propositus* is the person from whose vantage point the relationship is being viewed. See further below on this.

17 Jawoyn is a language of the Katherine region, Northern Territory. Data on Jawoyn kin terminology (Figs. 9 and 10) are from Merlan (1989).

18 From Hercus (1994).

19 As usual, there are complications: in Wangkangurru, mZC is *kulakula* if of the same moiety as ego, but *thidnara* if of the opposite moiety (due to wrong marriages?) (see Hercus 1994:13–14). The concept of ego is explained in the next section of this chapter.

20 Scheffler (1978:1–38).

21 Scheffler (1978:15).

22 Sutton (1982:190).

23 See Fortes (1959:206).

24 Keen (1994, 1995a). I discuss below the debate over Keen's rejection of the term 'clan' for these groups.

25 Keesing (1975:148).

26 Scheffler (1966).

27 See further above, Introduction.

28 Cf. Nadel (1951:12–13).

29 E.g. Keesing (1975:150)

30 Sutton (1983:84–86).

31 Sutton and Palmer (1980:47).

32 Aboriginal Land Commissioner (1982: paras. 172–177); Leach (1951).

33 See, e.g., discussion of the lower Daly River area in Chapter 6 above.

34 Aboriginal Land Commissioner (1994:paras. 3.1–3.2.2).

35 Myers (1986:128).

36 Hamilton (1982:102).

37 See Aboriginal Land Commissioner (1989: paras. 109–114).

38 Aboriginal Land Commissioner (1989: para. 111).

39 Aboriginal Land Commissioner (1989: para. 293, emphasis original).

40 Avery (1989:72,74).

41 Avery (1989:73).

42 Avery (1989:74).

43 For the definition of cognatic stocks, see below.

44 Avery (1989:77).

45 Aboriginal Land Commissioner (1989: para. 100).

46 On complementary filiation, see, for example, Fortes (1953:33), Keesing (1975: 46–48).

47 See, e.g., Maddock (1983), Bell (1993: Appendix 2) for expositions of such formations.

48 See Barker (1976).

49 See, e.g., Meggitt (1962).

50 Aboriginal Land Commissioner (1988b:para. 30.1.16).

51 Layton and Rowell (1979:52, 54).

52 Layton (1983a:25).

53 Layton (1983a:24). Layton (1986b:232) states that the term 'ambilineal' emerged during the *Uluru* hearing and was not used in the claim book. However it did appear there, see Layton and Rowell (1979:50).

54 Sutton (1998:32).

55 Layton (1983b:233).

56 Layton (2001:47). This book's first edition was in 1986.

57 Barnard and Spencer (1996:611).

58 Barfield (1997:268).

59 Myers (1986:133).

60 See Freeman (1961:200).

61 Cf. Macdonald (1986:197).

62 Recorded from western New South Wales by Gaynor Macdonald (personal communication).

63 See Chapter 8 for detailed discussion.

64 Stanner (1963:36).

65 Radcliffe-Brown (1969:499), Stanner (1933:394), Sutton (field notes).

66 Radcliffe-Brown (1930–31:62), Elkin (1979:118–119), Berndt and Berndt (1981: 42), Maddock (1982:38) Peterson and Long (1986:14–17).

67 Sutton (1998:126).

68 Personal communications: Gaynor Macdonald (western NSW), Bruce Rigsby (northern NSW); also Macdonald (2003, south-east Queensland).

69 On matrilineal social totemism see next section. On matrifocal households widely reported in post-colonial Aboriginal Australia see further Sutton (1998:72–128).

70 Elkin (1979:119).

71 On the latter see Berndt and Berndt (1988:55–56, 1970:60–75) on western Arnhem Land. At one stage the Berndts called these matri-semimoieties phratries. This is not how the term 'phratry' is generally used.

72 For the conventional distinctions among types of totems see Elkin (1933). Social totems are those that do not have land-based ritual cults or sites.

73 See further Sutton (1983).

74 Mathews (1897:173–174).

75 Elkin (1933:86ff).

76 This arises in a region (Mount Margaret, Western Australia) where people using two different section systems have intermarried, see Elkin (1940:315–327), Christensen (1981:248–279).

77 For explanations of these complex structures see the introductory literature cited above, and also Shapiro (1979:31–82).

78 White (1981).

79 Tonkinson (1991:196).

8 FAMILIES OF POLITY

1 This chapter contains a revised version of material published in Sutton (1998).
2 Sutton (1998:72–128). A revised version of this material is available from the author (*PeterSutton1@compuserve.com*).
3 Fortes (1969).
4 See Sansom's 'The Aboriginal commonality' (1982:120).
5 Clayton (1988:53).
6 See Land Tribunal (Queensland) (1994a). The claimants were successful.
7 See Land Tribunal (Queensland) (1994b). The claimants succeeded on historical grounds but failed on traditional grounds.
8 On cognatic stocks see Freeman (1961).
9 Freeman (1961:210).
10 Barwick (1971a:19); Clarke (1994:310).
11 Rigsby (1995).
12 Scheffler (1971:274).
13 Field notes and see Sutton (1993).
14 I thank Marina Rigney, a student of mine whose parents came from Ngarrindjeri and Kaurna backgrounds respectively, for this observation.
15 Freeman (1961:209).
16 This sanction appears to have survived best in the Western Desert region, see Sutton and Vaarzon-Morel (2003: Chapter 7) for evidence that it continues in one sub-region at least.
17 Jacobs (1986).
18 See Calley (1959:105–106); Tatz (1996:180–183, 302, 318).
19 See Scheffler (1966).
20 Robert Layton's phrase, in the case of *Finniss River* (see Aboriginal Land Commissioner 1981).
21 See Aboriginal Land Commissioner (1981:paras. 152–164).
22 My own field notes.
23 See, e.g., cited material in Sutton (1998: 67,80,81).
24 E.g., in the Aboriginal case by Langton (1981).
25 Rowley (1972:150,308,317).
26 Rowley (1972:329).
27 Dussart (personal communication)
28 See Rigsby and Hafner (1994), Rigsby (1995); Sutton (1995c:47–48).
29 Land Tribunal (Queensland) (1994a); Sutton (1995b).
30 Davies (1995)
31 Bourke and Edwards (1994:95). Emphasis added.
32 Inglis (1961:204).
33 Troy (1993:6).
34 My own field notes 1974–78.
35 Bellingshausen in Barratt (1981:39). For general works on Aboriginal gorgets see Cleary (1993); Troy (1993). For the biography of an Aboriginal queen see Somerville *et al.* (1995), and for that of an Aboriginal princess see Gara (1990). On the role of Aboriginal kings as brokers in north-west Queensland see Trigger (1992:51–52). The surname 'Prince' in that region derives from names of men whose fathers were appointed kings, just as the well-known Larrakia man of the Darwin region, Prince of

Wales, was so named because his father was called King George. Implications of hereditary office are rare, however (cf. Trigger 1992:52).

36 For Moree (NSW) see Reay and Sitlington (1948). For Cherbourg (Queensland) see Guthrie (1975). For New South Wales generally see Bell (1965:409–414).

37 Terwiel-Powell (1975, 1989).

38 Calley (1964).

39 These are made-up names.

40 This imaginary case was inspired by the way Keesing illustrates kinds of kin groups (1975).

41 Elkin (1935:143).

42 Freeman (1961:208–209).

43 Chase (1980:335).

44 Sutton (1998).

45 Langton (1997).

46 Keen (1988a:104).

47 See especially the works by Barwick, Beasley, Beckett, Bell, Biddle, Gale, Kitaoji, Lickiss and Reay cited in Sutton (1998).

48 See Tindale (1941); Barwick (1971b); Fink (1965); Inglis (1964); Terwiel-Powell (1975).

49 Sansom (1982:125).

50 Brown, Hirschfeld and Smith (1974:20–21).

51 Biddle (1969:97, 126).

52 See Sutton (1998: 72–124); see also Calley (1957: 205–207).

53 Hausfeld (1960, 1963).

54 Kelly (1935:472); see also Kelly (1944:148–153).

55 Kelly (1935:472).

56 Elkin (1935:122–125).

References

Aboriginal and Torres Strait Islander Social Justice Commissioner 1995. *Native Title Report January–June 1994*. Sydney: Office of the Aboriginal and Torres Strait Islander Social Justice Commissioner.

Aboriginal Land Commissioner (Toohey J) 1979. *Uluru (Ayers Rock) National Park and Lake Amadeus/Luritja Land Claim, Report No. 4*. Canberra: Australian Government Publishing Service.

Aboriginal Land Commissioner (Toohey J) 1981. *Finniss River Land Claim, Report No. 9*. Canberra: Australian Government Publishing Service.

Aboriginal Land Commissioner (Toohey J) 1982. *Daly River (Malak Malak) Land Claim, Report No. 13*. Canberra: Australian Government Publishing Service.

Aboriginal Land Commissioner (Kearney J) 1988a. *Jawoyn (Katherine Area) Land Claim, Report No. 27*. Canberra: Australian Government Publishing Service.

Aboriginal Land Commissioner (Maurice J) 1988b. *Warumungu Land Claim, Report No. 31*. Canberra: Australian Government Publishing Service.

Aboriginal Land Commissioner (Maurice J) 1989. *Lake Amadeus Land Claim, Report No. 28*. Canberra: Australian Government Publishing Service.

Aboriginal Land Commissioner (Olney J) 1991a. *McLaren Creek Land Claim, Report No. 32*. Canberra: Australian Government Publishing Service.

Aboriginal Land Commissioner (Olney J) 1991b. *Kenbi (Cox Peninsula) Land Claim, Report No. 40*. Canberra: Australian Government Publishing Service.

Aboriginal Land Commissioner (Olney J) 1992. *Tanami Downs Land Claim, Report No. 42*. Canberra: Australian Government Publishing Service.

Aboriginal Land Commissioner (Gray J) 1994. *Ngaliwirru/Nungali (Fitzroy Pastoral Lease Land Claim No. 137, Victoria River (Bed and Banks) Land Claim No. 140, Report No. 47*. Canberra: Australian Government Publishing Service.

Aboriginal Land Commissioner (Gray J) 1996. *Jawoyn (Gimbat Area) Land Claim No. 111, Alligator Rivers Area III (Gimbat Resumption – Waterfall Creek) (No. 2) Repeat Land Claim No. 142, Report No. 48*. Canberra: Australian Government Publishing Service.

Aboriginal Land Commissioner (Gray J) 1997. *Warlmanpa (Muckaty Pastoral Lease) Land Claim No. 135, Report No. 51*. Canberra: Australian Government Printing Service.

Aboriginal Land Commissioner (Gray J) 2000. *Kenbi (Cox Peninsula) Land Claim No. 37*. Canberra: Australian Government Printing Service.

Akerman, Kim 1995. Kimberley and Dampier Land. In Appendix 2 of P. Sutton, *Country: Aboriginal Boundaries and Land Ownership in Australia*, p99. Canberra: Aboriginal History Monographs.

Alpher, Barry 1991. *Yir-Yoront Lexicon: Sketch and Dictionary of an Australian Language*. Berlin: Mouton de Gruyter.

Alpher, Barry, and David Nash 1999. Lexical replacement and cognate equilibrium in Australia. *Australian Journal of Linguistics* 19: 5–56.

Altman, J.C. 1987. *Hunter-gatherers Today: an Aboriginal Economy in North Australia*. Canberra: Australian Institute of Aboriginal Studies.

Anderson, Christopher 1984. The Political and Economic Basis of Kuku-Yalanji Social History. PhD thesis, University of Queensland.

Anderson, Christopher 1989. Centralisation and group inequalities in North Queensland. In J.C. Altman (ed.), *Emergent Inequalities in Aboriginal Australia*, pp67–83. Sydney: Oceania Monographs (University of Sydney).

Avery, John T. 1985. The Law People. History, Society and Iinitiation in the Borroloola Area of the Northern Territory. PhD thesis, University of Sydney.

Avery, John T. 1989. The Lake Amadeus Land Claim: Report on traditional ownership. Appendix in Aboriginal Land Commissioner, *Lake Amadeus Land Claim, Report No. 28*, pp70–87. Canberra: Australian Government Publishing Service.

Avery, John T. 2002. Review: *Native Title and the Descent of Rights* by Peter Sutton. *Anthropological Forum* 12: 78–80.

Bagshaw, Geoffrey 1995. Comments on north-central Arnhem Land section of map by Stephen Davis. In Peter Sutton, *Country: Aboriginal Boundaries and Land Ownership in Australia*, pp122–124. Canberra: Aboriginal History Monographs.

Bagshaw, Geoffrey 1998. *Gapu dhulway, gapu maramba:* conceptualisation and ownership of saltwater among the Burarra and Yan-nhangu peoples of Northeast Arnhem Land. In N. Peterson and B. Rigsby (eds.) *Customary Marine Tenure in Australia*, pp154–177. Sydney: Oceania.

Bagshaw, Geoffrey (forthcoming). *The Karajarri Claim: a Case Study in Native Title Anthropology*. Sydney: Oceania.

Barfield, Thomas (ed.) 1997. *Dictionary of Anthropology*. Oxford: Blackwell.

Barker, Graham 1976. The ritual estate and Aboriginal polity. *Mankind* 10: 225–239.

Barnard, Alan and Jonathan Spencer (eds) 1996. *Encyclopaedia of Social and Cultural Anthropology*. London: Routledge.

Barratt, Glynn 1981. *The Russians at Port Jackson 1814–1822*. Canberra: Australian Institute of Aboriginal Studies.

Bartlett, R. H. 1993a. *The Mabo Decision, and Full Text of the Decision in Mabo and Others v State of Queensland: Commentary*. Sydney: Butterworths.

Bartlett, R.H. 1993b. The source, content and proof of native title at common law. In Richard H. Bartlett (ed.), *Resource Development and Aboriginal Land Rights in Australia*. Perth: Centre for Commercial and Resources Law, University of Western Australia and Murdoch University.

Barwick, Diane E. 1971a. What it means to be an Aborigine. In B. Leach (ed.) *The Aborigines Today*, pp16–23. Melbourne: Paul Hamlyn.

Barwick, Diane E. 1971b. Changes in the Aboriginal population of Victoria, 1863–1966. In D.J. Mulvaney and J. Golson (eds.) *Aboriginal Man and Environment in Australia*, pp288–315. Canberra: Australian National University Press.

Barwick, Diane E. 1985. This most resolute lady: a biographical study. In Diane E. Barwick, Jeremy Beckett and Marie Reay (eds.) *Metaphors of Interpretation: Essays in Honour of W.E.H. Stanner* pp185–239. Canberra: Australian National University.

Bates, Daisy M. 1985. *The Native Tribes of Western Australia* (ed. I. White). Canberra: National Library of Australia.

Beckett, Jeremy 1988. Kinship, mobility and community in rural New South Wales. In Ian Keen (ed.) *Being Black: Aboriginal Cultures in 'Settled' Australia,* pp117–136. Canberra: Aboriginal Studies Press.

Bell, Diane 1985. *Report on the Warumungu Land Claim.* Alice Springs: Central Land Council.

Bell, Diane 1993. *Daughters of the Dreaming.* 2nd edition. Sydney: Allen & Unwin.

Bell, Diane 1998. *Ngarrindjeri Wurruwarrin: A World that Is, Was, and Will Be.* North Melbourne: Spinifex Press.

Bell, J.H. 1965. The part-Aborigines of New South Wales: Three contemporary social situations. In R.M. and C. H. Berndt (eds.) *Aboriginal Man in Australia: Essays in Honour of Emeritus Professor A.P. Elkin,* pp396–418. Sydney: Angus and Robertson.

Bern, John, Jan Larbalestier and Dehne McLaughlin 1980. *Limmen Bight Land Claim.* Darwin: Northern Land Council.

Berndt, Ronald M. 1959. The concept of 'the tribe' in the Western Desert of Australia. *Oceania* 30:81–107.

Berndt, Ronald M. 1965. Law and order in Aboriginal Australia. In R.M. Berndt and C.H. Berndt (eds.) *Aboriginal Man in Australia. Essays in Honour of Emeritus Professor A.P. Elkin,* pp167–206. Sydney: Angus and Robertson.

Berndt, Ronald M. 1971. Social relationships among two Australian Aboriginal societies of Arnhem Land: Gunwinggu and 'Murngin'. In F.L.K. Hsu (ed.) *Kinship and Culture,* pp158–254. Chicago: Aldine.

Berndt, Ronald and Catherine Berndt 1970. *Man, Land and Myth in North Australia. The Gunwinggu People.* Sydney: Ure Smith.

Berndt, Ronald and Catherine Berndt 1981. *The World of the First Australians.* Sydney: Lansdowne Press.

Berndt, Ronald and Catherine Berndt 1987. *End of an Era: Aboriginal Labour in the Northern Territory.* Canberra: Australian Institute of Aboriginal Studies.

Berndt, Ronald M. and Catherine H. Berndt 1988. *The World of the First Australians. Traditional Aboriginal Life: Past and Present.* Canberra: Aboriginal Studies Press.

Berndt, Ronald and Catherine Berndt (with J.E. Stanton) 1993. *A World that Was. The Yaraldi of the Murray River and the Lakes, South Australia.* Melbourne: Melbourne University Press at the Miegunyah Press.

Berndt, Ronald M., W. Douglas, S. Kaldor and S.J. Hallam 1979. The First Australians. In N.T. Jarvis (ed.) *Western Australia: an Atlas of Human Endeavour,* pp32–37. Perth: Government Printer.

Berry, J.P. 1970. Marginality, stress and ethnic identification in an acculturated Aboriginal community. *Journal of Cross Cultural Psychology* 1: 239–252.

Biddle, Ellen H. 1969. The Assimilation of Aborigines in Brisbane, Australia 1965. PhD dissertation, University of Missouri, Columbia.

Birdsall, Chris 1988. All one family. In Ian Keen (ed.) *Being Black: Aboriginal Cultures in 'Settled' Australia,* pp137–158. Canberra: Aboriginal Studies Press.

Birdsall, Christina L. 1990. All One Family: Family and Social Identity among Urban Aborigines in Western Australia. PhD thesis, University of Western Australia.

Birdsell, J.B. 1973. A basic demographic unit. *Current Anthropology* 14: 337–356.

Black, Paul 1997. Lexicostatistics and Australian languages: problems and prospects. In Darrell Tryon and Michael Walsh (eds.) *Boundary Rider: Essays in Honour of Geoffrey O'Grady*, pp51–69. Canberra: Pacific Linguistics.

Blundell, Valda 1980. Hunter-gatherer territoriality: ideology and behavior in north-west Australia. *Ethnohistory* 27: 103–117.

Bourke, Colin, and Bill Edwards 1994. Family and kin. In C. Bourke, E. Bourke and B. Edwards (eds.), *Aboriginal Australia: an Introductory Reader in Aboriginal Studies*, pp85–101. Brisbane: University of Queensland Press.

Brady, Maggie 1987. Leaving the spinifex: the impact of rations, missions, and the atomic tests on the southern Pitjantjatjara. *Records of the South Australian Museum* 20: 35–45.

Breen, Gavan 1970. A re-examination of Cook's Gogo Yimidjir word list. *Oceania* 41: 28–38.

Brown, J.W., R. Hirschfeld and D. Smith 1974. *Aboriginals and Islanders in Brisbane*. Canberra: Australian Government Publishing Service. Australian Government Commission of Inquiry into Poverty.

Calley, Malcolm 1957. Race relations on the north coast of New South Wales. *Oceania* 27: 190–209.

Calley, Malcolm 1959. Bandjalang Social Organization. PhD thesis, University of Sydney.

Calley, Malcolm 1964. Pentecostalism among the Bandjalang. In Marie Reay (ed.) *Aborigines Now: New Perspective in the Study of Aboriginal Communities*, pp.48–58. Sydney: Angus and Robertson.

Campbell, Lyle 1997. *American Indian Languages: The Historical Linguistics of Native America*. New York: Oxford University Press.

Capell, A. 1962. *Some Linguistic Types in Australia*. Sydney: Oceania Linguistic Monographs.

Chadwick, Neil 1997. The Barkly and Jaminjungan Languages: a non-contiguous genetic grouping in north Australia. In Darrell Tryon and Michael Walsh (eds.) *Boundary Rider: Essays in Honour of Geoffrey O'Grady*, pp95–106. Canberra: Pacific Linguistics.

Chase, Athol Kennedy 1980. Which Way Now? Tradition, Continuity and Change in a North Queensland Aboriginal Community. PhD thesis, University of Brisbane.

Chase, A.K. 1984. Belonging to country: territory, identity and environment in Cape York Peninsula, northern Australia. In L.R. Hiatt (ed.) *Aboriginal Landowners*, pp104–128. Sydney: Oceania.

Christensen, W.J.K. 1981. The Wangkayi Way: Tradition and Change in a Reserve Setting. PhD thesis, University of Western Australia.

Clarke, Philip A. 1994. Contact, Conflict and Regeneration. Aboriginal Cultural Geography of the Lower Murray. PhD thesis, University of Adelaide.

Clayton, Iris 1988. Wiradjuri identity. *Australian Aboriginal Studies* 1: 53–55.

Cleary, Tania 1993. *Poignant Regalia. 19ᵗʰ Century Aboriginal Breastplates & Images*. Sydney: Historic Houses Trust of New South Wales.

Crowley, Terry 1997. Chipping away at the past: a northern New South Wales perspective. In P. McConvell and N. Evans (eds.) *Archaeology and Linguistics: Aboriginal Australia in Global Perspective*, pp275–295. Melbourne: Oxford University Press.

Davidson, Daniel Sutherland 1928. *The Chronological Aspects of Certain Australian Social Institutions*. Philadelphia: Department of Anthropology, University of Pennsylvania.

Davidson, Daniel Sutherland 1938. An ethnic map of Australia. *Proceedings of the American Philosophical Society* 79: 649–679 + map.

Davies, Jocelyn 1995. The uncertainty of the political. In P. Sutton. *Country: Aboriginal Boundaries and Land Ownership in Australia,* pp75–79. Canberra: Aboriginal History Monographs.

Dixon, R.M.W. 1972. *The Dyirbal Language of North Queensland*. Cambridge: Cambridge University Press.

Dixon, R.M.W. 1976. Tribes, languages and other boundaries in northeast Queensland. In Nicolas Peterson (ed.) *Tribes and Boundaries in Australia*, pp207–238. Canberra: Australian Institute of Aboriginal Studies

Dixon, R.M.W. 1980. *The Languages of Australia*. Cambridge: Cambridge University Press.

Dixon, R.M.W. 1997. *The Rise and Fall of Languages*. Cambridge: Cambridge University Press.

Dixon, R.M.W. 2002. *Australian Languages. Their Nature and Development*. Cambridge: Cambridge University Press.

Doolan, J.K. 1979. Aboriginal concept of boundary. How do Aboriginals conceive 'easements' – how do they grant them? *Oceania* 49: 161–168.

Dousset, Laurent 2002. Accounting for context and substance: The Australian Western Desert kinship system. *Anthropological Forum* 12: 193–204.

Edge, Hoyt L. 1998. Individuality in a relational culture. A comparative study. In Helmut Wautischer (ed.), *Tribal Epistemologies: Essays in the Philosophy of Anthropology*. Aldershot (UK): Ashgate Publishers.

Edmunds, Mary 1995. Conflict in native title claims. *Land, Rights, Laws: Issues of Native Title,* Issues Paper No. 7.

Edwards, W.H. 1993. *An Introduction to Aboriginal Societies*. Wentworth Falls (NSW): Social Science Press Australia.

Elias, Derek 2001. Golden Dreams: People, Place and Mining in the Tanami Desert. PhD thesis, Australian National University.

Elkin, A.P. 1933. Studies in Australian totemism. *Oceania* 4: 65–90.

Elkin, A.P. 1934. Cult-totemism and mythology in Northern South Australia. *Oceania* 5:171–192.

Elkin, A.P. 1935. Civilized Aborigines and native culture. *Oceania* 6: 117–146.

Elkin, A. P. 1940. Kinship in South Australia. *Oceania* 10: 295–349.

Elkin, A.P. 1953. Murngin kinship re-examined, and some remarks on some generalizations. *American Anthropologist* 55: 412–419.

Elkin, A.P. 1954. *The Australian Aborigines* (3rd edition). Sydney: Angus and Robertson.

Elkin, A.P. 1975–6. R.H. Mathews: his contribution to Aboriginal studies. *Oceania* 46: 1–24, 126–152, 206–234.

Elkin, A.P. 1979. *The Australian Aborigines* (5th edition). Sydney: Angus and Robertson.

Evans, Nicholas 1992. *Kayardild Dictionary and Thesaurus. A Vocabulary of the Language of the Bentinck Islanders, North-west Queensland*. Melbourne: Department of Linguistics, University of Melbourne.

Evans, Nicholas 2002. Country and the word: linguistic evidence in the Croker sea claim. In J. Henderson and D. Nash (eds.), *Language in Native Title*, pp53–99. Canberra: Native Title Research Unit, Australian Institute of Aboriginal and Torres Strait Islander Studies.

Eyre, E. J. 1845 (1997) *Journals of Expeditions of Discovery into Central Australia and Overland from Adelaide to King Georges Sound, in the years 1840–1841.* (2 vols)

T. & W. Boone, London (facsimile: Adelaide: Friends of the State Library of South Australia).

Falkenberg, Johannes 1962. *Kin and Totem: Group Relations of Australian Aborigines in the Port Keats District*. Oslo: Oslo University Press.

Fink, Ruth A. 1965. The contemporary situation of change among part-Aborigines in Western Australia. In R.M. and C. H. Berndt (eds.) *Aboriginal Man in Australia: Essays in Honour of Emeritus Professor A.P. Elkin*, pp419–434. Sydney: Angus and Robertson.

Finlayson, J.D., B. Rigsby and H.J. Bek (eds.) 1999. *Connections in Native Title: Genealogies, Kinship and Groups*. Canberra: Centre for Aboriginal Economic Policy Research (Australian National University).

Firth, Raymond 1963. Bilateral descent groups: an operational viewpoint. In I. Schapera (ed.) *Studies in Kinship and Marriage. Royal Anthropological Institute Occasional Paper No. 16*, pp22–37. London: Royal Anthropological Institute.

Fison, Lorimer and A.W. Howitt 1880. *Kamilaroi and Kurnai*. Sydney and Melbourne: G. Robertson.

Flowers, W.H. 1881 (1910). Sketch map of the Rockhampton and surrounding Coast District, showing the main tribal boundaries. The numbers in circles refer to the component groups of the different tribes. Plate XXVI in W.E. Roth, *North Queensland Ethnography Bulletin* No. 18 (= *Records of the Australian Museum* 8(1): 79–106, 1910).

Fortes, Meyer 1953. The structure of unilineal descent groups. *American Anthropologist* 55:17–41.

Fortes, Meyer 1959. Descent, filiation and affinity: a rejoinder to Dr. Leach (Parts I and II). *Man* 59: 193–197, 206–212, 301,309.

Fortes, Meyer 1969. *Kinship and the Social Order. The Legacy of Lewis Henry Morgan*. London: Routledge and Kegan Paul.

Fraser, John 1882. The Aborigines of New South Wales. *Journal of the Royal Society of New South Wales* 16: 193–233.

Fraser, John 1892. *The Aborigines of New South Wales*. Sydney: Government Printer.

Freeman, Derek 1961. On the concept of the kindred. *Journal of the Royal Anthropological Institute* 91: 192–220.

French, Justice R. 1995. Reasons for ruling on acceptance of a Native Title determination application. Application No: QN94/9. In the matter of the *Native Title Act 1993* and in the matter of the Waanyi Peoples Native Title Determination Application.

Gale, Fay and Joy Wundersitz 1982a. Adelaide Aborigines: a case study of urban life 1966–1981. In E. Fisk (ed.) *The Aboriginal Component in the Australian Economy*. Canberra: Development Studies Centre, Australian National University.

Gale, Fay and Joy Wundersitz 1982b. *Adelaide Aborigines*. Canberra: Australian National University Press.

Gara, Tom 1990. The life of Ivaritji ('Princess Amelia') of the Adelaide Tribe. *Journal of the Anthropological Society of South Australia* 28: 64–104.

Gibson, Chris 1999. Rebuilding the Jawoyn Nation: regional agreements, spatial politics and Aboriginal self-determination in Katherine, Northern Territory. *Australian Aboriginal Studies* 1999/number 1: 10–25.

Giddens, Anthony 1979. *Central Problems in Social Theory: Action, Structure and Contradiction in Social Analysis*. London: Macmillan.

Gluckman, Max 1965. *Politics, Law and Ritual in Tribal Society*. Oxford: Basil Blackwell.

Goddard, Cliff 1996. *Pitjantjatjara/Yankunytjatjara to English Dictionary* (2nd edition). Alice Springs: Institute for Aboriginal Development.

Gray, F. and L. Zann (eds.) 1988. *Traditional Knowledge of the Marine Environment in Northern Australia*. Townsville: Great Barrier Reef Marine Park Authority.

Gumbert, Marc 1984. *Neither Justice nor Reason: a Legal and Anthropological Analysis of Aboriginal Land Rights*. Brisbane: University of Queensland Press.

Guthrie, Gerard 1977. *Cherbourg: A Queensland Aboriginal Reserve*. Armidale: University of New England Press.

Hagen, Rod 1996. *Yorta Yorta Claims to areas in the Murray and Lower Goulburn region of Victoria and New South Wales pursuant to the Native Title Act, 1993 (Cmth). Yorta Yorta Native Title Claim exhibit A17*. Melbourne: Arnold Bloch Liebler.

Hagen, Rod 1999. Lumpers, splitters and the middle range: groups, local and otherwise, in the mid-Murray region. In J.D. Finlayson, B. Rigsby and H.J. Bek (eds.) *Connections in Native Title: Genealogies, Kinship and Groups*, pp73–84. Canberra: Centre for Aboriginal Economic Policy Research (Australian National University).

Hale, Kenneth L. 1966. The Paman group of the Pama-Nyungan phylic family; appendix to XXIX. In G.N. O'Grady and C.F. and F.M. Voegelin (eds.) *Languages of the World: Indo-Pacific Fascicle 6 (= Anthropological Linguistics 8(2))*, pp162–197.

Hallam, Sylvia J. 1975. *Fire and Hearth. A Study of Aboriginal Usage and European Usurpation in South-Western Australia*. Canberra: Australian Institute of Aboriginal Studies.

Hamilton, Annette 1982. Descended from father, belonging to country: rights to land in the Australian Western Desert. In Eleanor Laycock and Richard Lee (eds.) *Politics and History in Band Societies*, pp85–108, Cambridge/Paris: Cambridge University Press/Editions de la Maison des Sciences de l'Homme.

Hann, C.M. (ed.). 1998. *Property Relations: Renewing the Anthropological Tradition*. Cambridge: Cambridge University Press.

Hansen, K.C. 1984. Communicability of some Western Desert communilects. In J. Hudson and N. Pym (eds.) *Language Survey* pp1–112 (Work Papers of SIL AAB, B 11). Darwin: Summer Institute of Linguistics.

Hausfeld, R.G. 1960. Aspects of Aboriginal Station Management. BA thesis, University of Sydney.

Hausfeld, R.G. 1963. Dissembled culture: an essay on method. *Mankind* 6:47–51.

Haviland, John B. 1974. A last look at Cook's Guugu Yimidhirr word list. *Oceania* 44:216–232.

Heath, Jeffrey 1981. *Basic Materials in Mara: Grammar, Texts and Dictionary*. Canberra: Pacific Linguistics.

Heath, Jeffrey 1982. *Nunggubuyu Dictionary*. Canberra: Australian Institute of Aboriginal Studies.

Heath, J., F. Merlan and A. Rumsey (eds.) 1982. *Languages of Kinship in Aboriginal Australia*. Sydney: Oceania.

Henderson, John and Veronica Dobson 1994. *Eastern and Central Arrernte to English Dictionary*. Alice Springs: Institute for Aboriginal Development.

Henderson, John and David Nash (eds) 2002. *Language in Native Title*. Canberra: Native Title Research Unit, Australian Institute of Aboriginal and Torres Strait Islander Studies.

Hercus, Luise A. 1994. *A Grammar of the Arabana-Wangkangurru Language, Lake Eyre Basin, South Australia*. Pacific Linguistics: Canberra.

Hercus, Luise, Philip Jones, Sarah Holcombe, Peter Sutton (collated and ed. P. Sutton) 1996. *Simpson Desert (Wangkangurru) Land Claim*. Alice Springs: Central Land Council.

Hiatt, L.R. 1962. Local organisation among the Australian Aborigines. *Oceania* 32: 267–86.

Hiatt, L.R. 1965. *Kinship and Conflict: a Study of an Aboriginal Community in Northern Arnhem Land.* Canberra: Australian National University.

Hiatt, L.R. 1966. The lost horde. *Oceania* 37: 81–92.

Hiatt, L.R. 1982. Traditional attitudes to land resources. In R.M. Berndt (ed.) *Aboriginal Sites, Rights and Resource Development*, pp13–26. Perth: University of Western Australia Press for the Academy of the Social Sciences in Australia.

Hiatt, L.R. 1986. Aboriginal Political Life. [The Wentworth Lecture 1984]. Canberra: Australian Institute of Aboriginal Studies.

Hiatt, L.R. 1996. *Arguments about Aborigines: Australia and the Evolution of Social Anthropology.* Cambridge: Cambridge University Press.

Hoebel, E.A. 1966. *Anthropology: The Study of Man.* New York: McGraw-Hill.

Holcombe, Sarah 1998. Amunturrngu: An Emergent Community in Central Australia. PhD thesis, University of Newcastle (New South Wales).

Howitt, A.W. 1878. Notes on the Aborigines of Cooper's Creek. In R. Brough Smyth (ed.), *The Aborigines of Victoria* (2 vols.), pp300–309. Melbourne: Government Printer

Howitt, A.W. 1883a. On some Australian beliefs. *Journal of the Anthropological Institute of Great Britain and Ireland* 13: 185–198.

Howitt, A.W. 1883b. Australian group relations. *Report of the Smithsonian Institution* pp797–824.

Howitt, A.W. 1884. On some Australian ceremonies of initiation. *Journal of the Anthropological Institute of Great Britain and Ireland* 13: 432–459.

Howitt, A.W. 1885. The Jeraeil, or initiation ceremonies of the Kurnai tribe. *Journal of the Anthropological Institute of Great Britain and Ireland* 14: 301–325.

Howitt, A.W. 1888. Notes on Australian message sticks and messengers. *Journal of the Anthropological Institute of Great Britain and Ireland* 18: 314–332.

Howitt, A.W. 1891a. Presidential address to section G (Anthropology), *Report of the Third Meeting of the Australian Association for the Advancement of Science*, pp342–351.

Howitt, A.W. 1891b. The Dieri and other kindred tribes of Central Australia. *Journal of the Royal Anthropological Institute of Great Britain and Ireland* 20: 30–104.

Howitt, A.W. 1904. *The Native Tribes of South-east Australia.* London: Macmillan.

Howitt, A.W. and Lorimer Fison 1883. From Mother-right to Father-right. *Journal of the Anthropological Institute of Great Britain and Ireland* 12: 30–46

Howitt, A.W. and Lorimer Fison 1885. On the deme and the horde. *Journal of the Anthropological Institute of Great Britain and Ireland* 14: 142–168.

Hymes, Dell 1974. *Foundations in Sociolinguistics: an Ethnographic Approach.* Philadelphia: University of Pennsylvania Press.

Inglis, Judy 1961. Aborigines in Adelaide. *Journal of the Polynesian Society* 70: 200–218.

Inglis, Judy 1964. Dispersal of Aboriginal families in South Australia (1860–1960). In Marie Reay (ed.) *Aborigines Now: New Perspectives in the Study of Aboriginal Communities*, pp115–132. Sydney: Angus and Robertson.

Jackson, Michael. 1995. *At Home in the World.* Sydney: Harper Perennial (Harper Collins).

Jacobs, Jane M. 1986. Understanding the limitations and cultural implications of Aboriginal tribal boundary maps. *The Globe* [Geography department, University of Adelaide] 25: 2–12.

Johannes, R.E. and J.W. MacFarlane 1991. *Traditional Fishing in the Torres Strait Islands.* Hobart: CSIRO Division of Fisheries.

Jones, P.G. 1984. Red ochre expeditions: an ethnographic and historical analysis of Aboriginal trade in the Lake Eyre Basin. Parts 1 & 2. *Journal of the Anthropological Society of South Australia*, 22(7), 3–11; 22(8), 4–10.

Kaberry, Phyllis M. 1939. *Aboriginal Women, Sacred and Profane*. London: George Routledge and Sons.

Kartinyeri, Doreen 1989. *The Kartinyeri Family Genealogy*. Adelaide: University of Adelaide.

Keen, Ian 1980. *Alligator Rivers Stage II Land Claim*. Darwin: Northern Land Council.

Keen, Ian 1984. A question of interpretation: the definition of 'traditional Aboriginal owners' in the Aboriginal Land Rights [N.T.] Act. In L.R. Hiatt (ed.) *Aboriginal Landowners: Contemporary Issues in the Determination of Traditional Aboriginal Land Ownership*, pp24–45. Sydney: Oceania.

Keen, Ian 1988a. Twenty-five years of Aboriginal kinship studies. In R.M. Berndt and R. Tonkinson (eds.) *Social Anthropology and Australian Aboriginal Studies: A Contemporary Overview*, pp77–124. Canberra: Aboriginal Studies Press.

Keen, Ian 1988b. Yolngu religious property. In T. Ingold, J. Woodburn and D. Riches (eds.) *Hunters and Gatherers: Property, Power and Ideology*, pp272–291. Oxford: Berg.

Keen, Ian 1989. Aboriginal governance. In J.C Altman (ed.) *Emergent Inequalities in Aboriginal Australia*, pp17–42, Sydney: Oceania.

Keen, Ian 1994. *Knowledge and Secrecy in an Aboriginal Religion*. Oxford: Clarendon Press.

Keen, Ian 1995a. Metaphor and the metalanguage: Groups in Northeast Arnhem Land. *American Ethnologist* 22: 502–527.

Keen, Ian 1995b. Comments on North-east Arnhem Land section of Davis's map. In Sutton, Peter, *Country: Aboriginal Boundaries and Land Ownership in Australia*, pp124–125. Canberra: Aboriginal History Monographs.

Keen, Ian 1997a. A continent of foragers: Aboriginal Australia as a 'regional system'. In P. McConvell and N. Evans (eds.) *Archaeology and Linguistics: Aboriginal Australia in Global Perspective*, pp261–274. Melbourne: Oxford University Press.

Keen, Ian 1997b. The Western Desert *vs* the rest. In F. Merlan, J. Morton and A. Rumsey (eds.) *Scholar and Sceptic: Australian Aboriginal Studies in Honour of L.R. Hiatt*, pp65–93, 257–266. Canberra: Aboriginal Studies Press.

Keen, Ian 2000. A bundle of sticks: the debate over Yolngu clans. *Journal of the Royal Anthropological Institute* 6: 419–436.

Keesing, Roger M. 1975. *Kin Groups and Social Structure*. Fort Worth: Harcourt Brace Jovanovich College Publishers.

Kelly, C. [Caroline Tennant] 1935. Tribes on Cherburg [*sic*] settlement, Queensland. *Oceania* 5: 461–473.

Kelly, C. [Caroline Tennant] 1944. Some aspects of culture contact in eastern Australia. *Oceania* 15: 142–153.

Kennedy, F., L. McLean and D. Nason 1996. God gave us the land, not the High Court: elders. *The Australian*, 11 June.

Kolig, Erich 1978. Dialectics of Aboriginal life-space. In M.C. Howard (ed.) *'Whitefella Business': Aborigines in Australian Politics*, pp49–80. Philadelphia: Institute for the Study of Human Issues.

Krzywicki, Ludwig 1934. *Primitive Society and Its Vital Statistics*. London: Macmillan.

Land Tribunal (Queensland) 1994a. *Aboriginal Land Claims to Cape Melville National Park, Flinders Group National Park, Clack Island National Park and Nearby Islands*. Brisbane: Goprint.

Land Tribunal (Queensland) 1994b. *Aboriginal Land Claim to Simpson Desert National Park*. Brisbane: Goprint.

Land Tribunal (Queensland) 1995. *Aboriginal Land Claims to Vacant Crown Land in the Vicinity of Birthday Mountain*. Brisbane: Land Tribunal.

Land Tribunal (Queensland) 1996. *Aboriginal Land Claim to Lakefield National Park*. Brisbane: Land Tribunal.

Langton, Marcia 1981 Urbanising Aborigines: The social scientists' great deception. *Social Alternatives* 2(2): 16–22.

Langton, Marcia 1997. Grandmothers, company business and succession in changing Aboriginal land tenure systems. In Galarrwuy Yunupingu (ed.) *Our Land is Our Life: Land Rights – Past, Present and Future*, pp84–116. Brisbane: University of Queensland Press..

Langton, Marcia 1998. *Burning Questions*. Darwin: Centre for Indigenous Natural and Cultural Resource Management, Northern Territory University.

Latz, Peter 1995. *Bushfires and Bushtucker: Aboriginal Plant Use in Central Australia*. Alice Springs: IAD Press.

Layton, Robert 1983a. Ambilineal descent and traditional Pitjantjatjara rights to land. In Nicolas Peterson and Marcia Langton (eds.) *Aborigines, Land and Land Rights*, pp15–32. Canberra: Australian Institute of Aboriginal Studies.

Layton, Robert 1983b. Pitjantjatjara processes and the structure of the Land Rights Act. In Nicolas Peterson and Marcia Langton (eds.) *Aborigines, Land and Land Rights*, pp226–237. Canberra: Australian Institute of Aboriginal Studies.

Layton, Robert 2001. *Uluru. An Aboriginal History of Ayers Rock*. Aboriginal Studies Press.

Layton, Robert, and Meredith Rowell, with assistance from Rod Hagen and Daniel Vachon 1979. *Ayers Rock – Mount Olga National Park and Lake Amadeus Traditional Land Claim*. Alice Springs: Central Land Council.

Leach, E.R. 1951. The structural implications of matrilateral cross-cousin marriage. *Journal of the Royal Anthropological Institute* 8: 23–55.

Levitus, Robert 1991. The boundaries of Gagudju Association membership: anthropology, law, and public policy. In John Connell and Richard Howitt (eds.) *Mining and Indigenous People in Australasia*, pp153–168. Sydney: Sydney University Press.

Loos, N. 1982. *Invasion and Resistance: Aboriginal-European Relations on the North Queensland Frontier 1861–1897*. Canberra: Australian National University.

Lyon, Pam, and Michael Parsons 1989. *We are Staying. The Alyawarre Struggle for Land at Lake Nash*. Alice Springs: IAD Press.

McBryde, Isobel 1986. Artefacts, language and social interaction: a case study from South-eastern Australia. In G.N. Bailey and P. Callow (eds.) *Stone Age Prehistory: Studies in Memory of Charles McBurney*, pp77–93. Cambridge: Cambridge University Press.

McCarthy, F.D. 1939. 'Trade' in Aboriginal Australia and 'trade' relationships with Torres Strait, New Guinea and Malaya. *Oceania* 9: 405–438; 10: 80–104, 171–195.

McConnel, U.H. 1930. The Wik-munkan tribe of Cape York Peninsula, Part I. *Oceania* 1: 97–104.

McConvell, Patrick 1996. Backtracking to Babel: the chronology of Pama-Nyungan expansion in Australia. *Archaeology in Oceania* 31: 125–144.

McConvell, Patrick, Laurent Dousset and Fiona Powell (eds.) 2002. *Kinship and Change in Aboriginal Australia*. Special issue of *Anthropological Forum* (vol. 12 no. 2).

Macdonald, Gaynor 1986. 'The Koori Way'. The Dynamics of Cultural Distinctiveness in Settled Australia. PhD thesis, University of Sydney.

Macdonald, Gaynor 1996. *Bogan River Wiradjuri Anthropological Report* (re: Federal Court NG 6001 of 1995). Sydney: New South Wales Aboriginal Land Council.

Macdonald, Gaynor 1997. 'Recognition and justice': the traditional/historical contradiction in New South Wales. In D.E. Smith and J. Finlayson (eds.) *Fighting Over Country: Anthropological Perspectives*, pp65–82. Canberra: Centre for Aboriginal Economic Policy Research, Australian National University.

Macdonald, Gaynor 2003. Membership of and recruitment to social groups in the Sunshine Coast region. Anthropological report in relation to native title claims Jinibara (QC98/45) and Gubbi Gubbi #2 (QC99/35). Toowoomba: Queensland South Representative Body Aboriginal Corporation.

Macdonald, Gaynor, Geoffrey Bagshaw and Peter Sutton 1998. Connections to country in the Far West Coast region of South Australia: an anthropological survey. Report for the Far West Coast Native Title Working Group and Aboriginal Legal Rights Movement, Adelaide.

Macquarie Dictionary, 1991. (2nd edition). Sydney: Macquarie Library.

McGrath, Ann 1987. *'Born in the Cattle': Aborigines in Cattle Country.* Sydney: Allen & Unwin.

McIntyre, Greg, and Kim Doohan 2002. Labels, language and native title groups: the Miriuwung-Gajerrong case. In J. Henderson and D. Nash (eds.) *Language in Native Title,* pp187–204. Canberra: Native Title Research Unit, Australian Institute of Aboriginal and Torres Strait Islander Studies.

McKay, Graham 2000. Ndjébbana. In R.M.W. Dixon and B.J. Blake (eds.) *Handbook of Australian Languages, Volume 5,* pp154–354. Melbourne: Oxford University Press.

McKnight, David 1997. *People, Countries, and the Rainbow Serpent.* Oxford: Oxford University Press.

Maddock, Kenneth 1982. *The Australian Aborigines: a Portrait of their Society.* Melbourne: Penguin Books.

Maddock, Kenneth 1983. 'Owners', 'managers' and the choice of statutory traditional owners by anthropologists and lawyers. In Nicolas Peterson and Marcia Langton (eds.) *Aborigines, Land and Land Rights,* pp211–225. Canberra: Australian Institute of Aboriginal Studies.

Maddock, Kenneth 1984. Aboriginal customary law. In P. Hanks and B. Keon-Cohen (eds.) *Aborigines and the Law. Essays in Memory of Elizabeth Eggleston,* pp212–237. Sydney: Allen & Unwin.

Malinowski, Bronislaw 1913 (1963). *The Family Among the Australian Aborigines. A Sociological Study.* New York: Schocken Books.

Mantziaris, Christos, and David Martin 1999. *Guide to the Design of Native Title Corporations. A companion volume to The Design of Native Title Corporations: a Legal and Anthropological Analysis.* Perth: National Native Title Tribunal.

Mantziaris, Christos, and David Martin 2000. *Native Title Corporations: A Legal and Anthropological Analysis.* Sydney: Federation Press in co-operation with the National Native Title Tribunal.

Mathews, R.H. 1897. The totemic divisions of Australian Tribes. *Journal of the Royal Society of New South Wales* 31: 154–176.

Mathews, R.H. 1900a. The origin, organization and ceremonies of the Australian Aborigines. *Proceedings of the American Philosophical Society* 39:556–78 + map (plate VIII) facing page 574.

Mathews, R.H. 1900b. Divisions of the South Australian Aborigines. *Proceedings of the American Philosophical Society* 39:78–93 and plate VIII opposite p574.

May, Dawn 1994. *Aboriginal Labour and the Cattle Industry. Queensland from White Settlement to the Present*. Cambridge: Cambridge University Press.

Meggitt, M.J. 1962. *Desert People: a Study of the Walbiri Aborigines of Central Australia*. Sydney: Angus and Robertson.

Meggitt, M.J. 1964. Indigenous forms of government among the Australian Aborigines. *Bijdragen tot der Taal-, Land- en Volkenkunde* 120: 163–180.

Merlan, Francesca 1981. Land, language and social identity in Aboriginal Australia. *Mankind* 13:133–48.

Merlan, Francesca 1982. A Mangarayi representational system: environment and cultural symbolization. *American Ethnologist* 9: 145–166.

Merlan, Francesca 1983. *Ngalakan Grammar, Texts and Vocabulary*. Canberra: Pacific Linguistics.

Merlan, Francesca 1989. Jawoyn relationship terms: interactional dimensions of Australian kin classification. *Anthropological Linguistics* 31: 227–263.

Merlan, Francesca 1994. *A Grammar of Wardaman: a Language of the Northern Territory of Australia*. Berlin: Mouton de Gruyter.

Merlan, Francesca 1995. The regimentation of customary practice: from Northern Territory land claims to Mabo. *Australian Journal of Anthropology* 6: 64–82.

Merlan, Francesca 1998. *Caging the Rainbow. Places, Politics, and Aborigines in a North Australian Town*. Honolulu: University of Hawai'i Press.

Merlan, Francesca and Alan Rumsey 1982. *The Jawoyn (Katherine area) Land Claim*. Darwin: Northern Land Council.

Meyers, G.D., C.M. Piper and H.E. Rumley 1997. Asking the minerals question: rights in minerals as an incident of Native Title. *Australian Indigenous Law Reporter* 2: 203–250.

Micha, Franz Josef 1970. Time and change in Australian Aboriginal cultures: Australian Aboriginal trade as an expression of close culture contact and as a mediator of culture change. In Arnold R. Pilling and Richard A. Waterman (eds.) *Diprotodon to Detribalization: Studies of Change among Australian Aborigines*, pp285–313. East Lansing: Michigan State University Press.

Miller, James 1985. *Koori: A Will to Win. The Heroic Resistance, Survival & Triumph of Black Australia*. Sydney: Angus and Robertson.

Milliken, E.P. 1976. Aboriginal language distribution in the Northern Territory. In N. Peterson (ed.) *Tribes and Boundaries in Australia*, pp239–42 and map. Canberra: Australian Institute of Aboriginal Studies.

Moore, G.F. 1884 (1978). *Diary of Ten Years Eventful Life of an Early Settler in Western Australia and also a Descriptive Vocabulary of the Language of the Aborigines*. London. [Facsimile edition Perth: University of Western Australia Press].

Morel, Petronella, Peter Sutton and David Alexander 1992. *The Kanturrpa-Kanttaji Land Claim: Anthropologists' Report*. Alice Springs: Central Land Council.

Morgan, Lewis Henry 1858. Laws of descent of the Iroquois. *Proceedings of the American Association for the Advancement of Science* 11(2):132–148.

Morphy, Frances 1983. Djapu, a Yolngu Dialect. In R.M.W. Dixon and Barry J Blake (eds.) *Handbook of Australian Languages Volume 3*, ppxxiv, 1–188. Australian National University Press, Canberra.

Morphy, Frances and Howard Morphy 1984. Owners, managers, and ideology: a comparative analysis. In L.R. Hiatt (ed.) *Aboriginal Landowners: Contemporary Issues in the Determination of Traditional Aboriginal Land Ownership*, pp46–66. Sydney: Oceania.

Morphy, Howard 1991. *Ancestral Connections: Art and an Aboriginal System of Knowledge*. Chicago: Chicago University Press.

Morphy, Howard 1997. Death, exchange and the reproduction of Yolngu society. In F. Merlan, J. Morton and A. Rumsey (eds.) *Scholar and Sceptic: Australian Aboriginal Studies in Honour of L.R. Hiatt*, pp123–150, 271–274. Canberra: Aboriginal Studies Press.

Morphy, Howard, and Frances Morphy 1981. *Yutpundji-Djindiwirritj Land Claim*. Darwin: Northern Land Council.

Morton, John 1992. *The Palm Valley Land Claim: Anthropologist's Report*. Alice Springs: Central Land Council.

Morton, John 1997. Arrernte (Aranda) land tenure: an evaluation of the Strehlow model. *Strehlow Research Centre Occasional Paper* 1: 107–125.

Mulvaney, D.J. 1976. 'The chain of connection': the material evidence. In N. Peterson (ed.) *Tribes and Boundaries in Australia*, pp72–94. Canberra: Australian Institute of Aboriginal Studies.

Myers, Fred R. 1980a. The cultural basis of politics in Pintupi life. *Mankind* 12: 197–214.

Myers, Fred R. 1980b. A broken code: Pintupi political theory and contemporary social life. *Mankind* 12:311–326.

Myers, Fred R. 1982. Always ask: resource use and land ownership among Pintupi Aborigines of the Australian Western Desert. In N. Williams and E. Hunn (eds.) *Resource Managers: North American and Australian Hunter-gatherers*, pp173–195. Colorado: Westview Press.

Myers, Fred R. 1986. *Pintupi Country, Pintupi Self: Sentiment, Place and Politics among Western Desert Aborigines*. Washington/Canberra: Smithsonian Institution Press/ Australian Institute of Aboriginal Studies.

Myers, Fred 1988. Burning the truck and holding the country: property, time and the negotiation of identity among Pintupi Aborigines. In T. Ingold, D. Riches and J. Woodburn (eds.) *Hunters and Gatherers, 2: Property, Power and Ideology*, pp52–74. New York: Berg.

Nash, David 1980. *A Traditional Land Claim by the Warlmanpa, Warlpiri, Mudbura and Warumungu Traditional Owners*. Alice Springs: Central Land Council.

Nash, David 1990. Patrilects of the Warumungu and Warlmanpa and their neighbours. In P. Austin, R.M.W. Dixon, T. Dutton and I. White (eds.) *Language and History: Essays in Honour of Luise A. Hercus*, pp209–220. Canberra: Pacific Linguistics.

Neate, Graeme 1996. Proof of Native Title. In Bryan Horrigan (ed.) *Commercial Implications of Native Title*, pp240–319. Sydney: Federation Press.

Nordlinger, Rachel 1998. *A Grammar of Wambaya, Northern Territory (Australia)*. Canberra: Pacific Linguistics.

Northern Land Council 1995. Kenbi Land Claim, Larrakia Group, Personal Particulars. Darwin: Northern Land Council.

O'Grady, G.N. and C.F. and F.M. Voegelin (eds.) 1966, *Languages of the World: Indo-Pacific Fascicle 6* (= *Anthropological Linguistics* 8[2]).

Oxley-Oxland, J. and R.T.J. Stein 1985. *Understanding Land Law*. Sydney: Law Book Company.

Palmer, Kingsley 1983. Migration and rights to land in the Pilbara. In N. Peterson and M. Langton (eds.) *Aborigines, Land and Land Rights*, pp. 172–179. Canberra: Australian Institute of Aboriginal Studies.

Palmer, Kingsley 1984. Aboriginal land ownership among the southern Pitjantjara of the Great Victoria Desert. In L.R. Hiatt (ed.) *Aboriginal Landowners*. Sydney: Oceania.

Pannell, S. and D. Vachon 2001. Notes and queries in the native title era. *The Australian Journal of Anthropology* 12: 238–244.

Pearson, Noel 2000. Principles of communal native title. *Indigenous Law Bulletin* 5(3): 4–7.

Penner, J.E. 1997. *The Idea of Property in Law*. Oxford: Clarendon Press.

Peterson, Nicolas 1969. Secular and ritual links: two basic and opposed principles of Australian social organisation as illustrated by Walbiri ethnography. *Mankind* 7: 27–35.

Peterson, Nicolas 1976. The natural and cultural areas of Aboriginal Australia: a preliminary analysis of population groupings with adaptive significance. In N. Peterson (ed.) *Tribes and Boundaries in Australia*, pp50–71. Canberra: Australian Institute of Aboriginal Studies.

Peterson, Nicolas 1983. Rights, residence and process in Australian territorial organisation. In N. Peterson and M. Langton (eds.) *Aborigines, Land and Land Rights*, pp134–145. Canberra: Australian Institute of Aboriginal Studies.

Peterson, Nicolas, in collaboration with Jeremy Long 1986. *Australian Territorial Organization: a Band Perspective*. Sydney: Oceania.

Peterson, Nicolas, Ian Keen and Basil Sansom 1977. Succession to land: primary and secondary rights to Aboriginal estates. (A submission to the Ranger Uranium Environmental Inquiry.) In Joint Select Committee on Aboriginal Land Rights in the Northern Territory, *Official Hansard Report*, pp1002–1014.

Peterson, Nicolas, and Bruce Rigsby (eds.) 1998. *Customary Marine Tenure in Australia*. Sydney: Oceania.

Pink, Olive 1933. Spirit ancestors in a northern Aranda horde country. *Oceania* 4: 176–86.

Pink, Olive 1936. The landowners in the northern division of the Aranda tribe, Central Australia. *Oceania* 6: 275–305.

Povinelli, Elizabeth A. 1993. *Labor's Lot: the Power, History, and Culture of Aboriginal Action*. Chicago: University of Chicago Press.

Povinelli, Elizabeth A. 1996. *Kenbi Land Claim: The Belyuen Group*. Submission to the Aboriginal Land Commissioner. Darwin: Northern Land Council.

Powell, Fiona 2002. Transformations in Guugu Yimithirr kinship terminology. *Anthropological Forum* 12: 177–192.

[Radcliffe-]Brown, A.R. 1913. Three tribes of Western Australia. *Journal of the Royal Anthropological Institute* 43:143–194.

[Radcliffe-]Brown, A.R. 1914. The definition of totemism. *Anthropos* 9: 622–630.

Radcliffe-Brown, A.R. 1918. Notes on the social organization of Australian tribes. *Journal of the Royal Anthropological Institute of Great Britain and Ireland* 48 222–253.

Radcliffe-Brown, A.R. 1930–31. The social organization of Australian tribes. *Oceania* 1: 34–63, 206–246, 322–341, 426–456.

Radcliffe-Brown A.R. 1935 (1952). Patrilineal and matrilineal succession. In A. R. Radcliffe-Brown, *Structure and Function in Primitive Society. Essays and Addresses*, pp32–48. London: Cohen & West.

Radcliffe-Brown A.R. 1954. Australian local organization. *American Anthropologist* 56: 105–106.

Radcliffe-Brown A.R. 1956. On Australian local organization. *American Anthropologist* 58: 363–367.

Radcliffe-Brown, A.R. 1969. Letter to Claude Lévi-Strauss. Appendix in Claude Lévi-Strauss, *The Elementary Structures of Kinship*. (Tr. J.H. Bell, J.R. von Sturmer and R. Needham), pp499–500. Boston: Beacon Press.

Reay, Marie 1962. Subsections at Borroloola. *Oceania* 33: 90–115.

Reay, Marie 1963. Aboriginal and white Australian family structure: an enquiry into assimilation trends. *Sociological Review* 11(1): 19–47.

Reay, Marie and Grace Sitlington 1948. Class and status in a mixed-blood community, (Moree, NSW). *Oceania* 18: 179–207.

Reay, Marie n.d. Comments on the Borroloola land claim. Ms. submitted to Aboriginal Land Commissioner (Northern Territory).

Register of Wards. Schedule: Welfare Ordinance. *Northern Territory Government Gazette* No. 19B, 13th May 1957.

Reynolds, Henry (ed.) 1972. *Aborigines and Settlers. The Australian Experience 1788–1939.* Melbourne: Cassell Australia.

Reynolds, Henry 1981. *The Other Side of the Frontier: Aboriginal Resistance to the European Invasion of Australia.* Melbourne: Penguin Books.

Riddett, L.A. 1990. *Kine, Kin and Country: The Victoria River District of the Northern Territory 1966–1966.* Darwin: Australian National University North Australia Research Unit.

Rigsby, Bruce 1992. The languages of the Princess Charlotte Bay region. In T. Dutton, M. Ross and D. Tryon (eds.) *The Language Game: Papers in Memory of Donald C. Laycock,* pp353–360. Canberra: Pacific Linguistics.

Rigsby, Bruce 1995. Tribes, diaspora people and the vitality of law and custom: some comments. In Jim Fingleton and Julie Finlayson (eds.) *Anthropology in the Native Title Era: Proceedings of a Workshop,* pp25–27. Canberra: Australian Institute of Aboriginal and Torres Strait Islander Studies.

Rigsby, Bruce 1996. 'Law' and 'custom' as anthropological and legal terms. In J. Finlayson and A. Jackson-Nakano (eds.) *Heritage and Native Title: Anthropological and Legal Perspectives,* pp230–254. Canberra: Australian Institute of Aboriginal and Torres Strait Islander Studies.

Rigsby, Bruce 1998. A survey of property theory and tenure types. In Nicolas Peterson and Bruce Rigsby (eds.) *Customary Marine Tenure in Australia* pp22–46. Sydney: Oceania.

Rigsby, Bruce and Athol Chase 1998. The sandbeach people and dugong hunters of eastern Cape York Peninsula: property in land and sea country. In Nicolas Peterson and Bruce Rigsby (eds.) *Customary Marine Tenure in Australia* pp192–218. Sydney: Oceania.

Rigsby, Bruce and Diane Hafner 1994. *Lakefield National Park Land Claim, Claim Book.* Cairns: Cape York Land Council.

Rigsby, Bruce and Peter Sutton 1980–82. Speech communities in Aboriginal Australia. *Anthropological Forum* 5: 8–23.

Ritchie, David and Toni Bauman 1991. *Limilngan-Wulna (Lower Adelaide and Mary Rivers) Land Claim.* Darwin: Northern Land Council.

Rose, Deborah Bird 1992. *Dingo Makes us Human: Life and Land in an Aboriginal Australian Culture.* Cambridge: Cambridge University Press.

Rose, Deborah Bird 1995a. Victoria River region. In Sutton, Peter *Country: Aboriginal Boundaries and Land Ownership in Australia,* p112. Canberra: Aboriginal History Monographs.

Rose, Deborah Bird 1995b. *Kenbi (Cox Peninsula) Land Claim: Anthropologist's Report on Behalf of the Danggalaba Clan.* Unpublished submission to the Aboriginal Land Commissioner. Darwin: Northern Land Council.

Rose, Deborah Bird (ed.) 1995c. *Country in Flames. Proceedings of the 1994 Symposium on Biodiversity and Fire in North Australia.* Canberra/Darwin: Biodiversity Unit/North Australia Research Unit (Australian National University).

Rose, Frederick G.G. 1960. *Classification of Kin, Age Structure and Marriage amongst the Groote Eylandt Aborigines. A Study in Method and a Theory of Australian Kinship.* Berlin: Akademie-Verlag.

Rose, Frederick G.G. 1965. *The Wind of Change in Central Australia: The Aborigines at Angas Downs, 1962.* Berlin: Akadamie-Verlag.

Roth, Walter E. 1897. *Ethnological Studies Among the North-west-central Queensland Aborigines.* Brisbane: Government Printer.

Rowley, C.D. 1972. *Outcasts in White Australia*. Melbourne: Penguin Books.

Rowse, Tim 1992. *Remote Possibilities: the Aboriginal Domain and the Administrative Imagination*. Darwin: North Australia Research Unit (Australian National University).

Rowse, Tim 1993. *After Mabo: Interpreting Indigenous Traditions*. Melbourne: Melbourne University Press.

Rumsey, Alan 1989. Language groups in Australian Aboriginal land claims. *Anthropological Forum* 6: 69–80.

Rumsey, Alan 1993. Language and territoriality in Aboriginal Australia. In Michael Walsh and Colin Yallop (eds.) *Language and Culture in Aboriginal Australia*, pp191–206. Canberra: Aboriginal Studies Press.

Sansom, Basil 1980a. *The Camp at Wallaby Cross: Aboriginal Fringe Dwellers in Darwin*. Canberra: Australian Institute of Aboriginal Studies.

Sansom, Basil 1980b. Processural modelling and aggregate groupings in northern Australia. In L. Holy and M. Stuchlik (eds.) *The Structure of Folk Models*, pp257–280. London: Academic Press (ASA Monograph No 20).

Sansom, Basil 1982. The Aboriginal commonality. In R. Berndt (ed.) *Aboriginal Sites, Rights and Resource Development*. Perth: University of Western Australia Press.

Schebeck, Bernhard 1968. Dialect and social groupings in North East Arnhem Land. Typescript, Australian Institute of Aboriginal and Torres Strait Islander Studies Library, Canberra.

Schebeck, Bernhard 2001. *Dialect and Social Groupings in Northeast Arnheim [sic] Land*. Munich: Lincom Europa.

Scheffler, Harold W. 1966. Ancestor worship in anthropology: or, observations on descent and descent groups. *Current Anthropology* 7: 541–551.

Scheffler, Harold W. 1971. The Solomon Islands: seeking a new land custom. In Ron Crocombe (ed.) *Land Tenure in the Pacific*, pp273–291. Melbourne: Oxford University Press.

Scheffler, Harold W. 1978. *Australian Kin Classification*. Cambridge University Press, Cambridge.

Scheffler, Harold W. 1986. The descent of rights and the descent of persons. *American Anthropologist* 88: 339–350.

Scheffler, Harold W. 2001. *Filiation and Affiliation*. Boulder, Colorado: Westview Press.

Schneider, David M. 1984. *A critique of the study of Kinship*. Ann Arbor: University of Michigan Press.

Schwab, Jerry 1988. Ambiguity, style and kinship in Adelaide Aboriginal identity. In I. Keen (ed.) *Being Black: Aboriginal Cultures in 'Settled' Australia*, pp77–96. Canberra: Aboriginal Studies Press.

Schwab, Jerry 1991. The 'Blackfella way'. Ideology and practice in an urban Aboriginal community. PhD thesis, Australian National University.

Shapiro, Warren 1979. *Social Organization in Aboriginal Australia*. Canberra: Australian National University Press.

Shapiro, Warren 1981. *Miwuyt Marriage. The Cultural Anthropology of Affinity in Northeast Arnhem Land*. Philadelphia: Institute for the Study of Human Issues.

Sharp, R. Lauriston 1934a. Ritual life and economics of the Yir-Yoront of Cape York Peninsula. *Oceania* 4: 404–431.

Sharp, R. Lauriston 1934b. The social organization of the Yir-Yoront tribe, Cape York Peninsula. *Oceania* 5: 19–42.

Sharp, R. Lauriston 1937. The Social Anthropology of a Totemic System in North Queensland, Australia. PhD thesis, Harvard University.

Sharp, R. Lauriston 1958. People without politics. In V.F. Ray (ed.) *Systems of Political Control and Bureaucracy*, pp1–8. Seattle: University of Washington Press.

Sharp, R. Lauriston 1968. Hunter social organization: some problems of method. In R.B. Lee and I. De Vore (eds.) *Man the Hunter*, pp158–161. Chicago: Aldine.

Sharp, Nonie 1996. *No Ordinary Judgement. Mabo, the Murray Islanders' Land Case*. Canberra: Aboriginal Studies Press.

Sharp, Nonie 2002. *Saltwater People. The Waves of Memory*. Sydney: Allen & Unwin.

Silver, Shirley and Wick R. Miller 1997. *American Indian Languages. Cultural and Social Contexts*. Tucson: University of Arizona Press.

Silverstein, Michael 1985. Review of D. Parkin (ed.) *Semantic Anthropology: ASA Monograph #22*. Orlando: Academic Press (1982). *American Ethnologist* 12: 795–796.

Smith, Barry 1989. The concept 'community' in Aboriginal policy and service delivery. *Occasional Paper No. 1*. Darwin: North Australia Development Unit, Department of Social Security.

Smith, Ian and Steve Johnson 2000. Kugu Nganhcara. In R.M.W. Dixon and B.J. Blake (eds.) *Handbook of Australian Languages, Volume 5*, pp355–489. Melbourne: Oxford University Press.

Somerville, Margaret, with Florrie Munro and Emily Connors 1995. In search of the Queen. In Linda Barwick, Allan Marett and Guy Tunstill (eds.) *The Essence of Singing and the Substance of Song. Recent Responses to the Aboriginal Performing Arts and other Essays in Honour of Catherine Ellis*, pp133–141. Sydney: Oceania Monographs.

Spencer, Baldwin and F.J. Gillen 1904. *The Northern Tribes of Central Australia*. London: Macmillan.

Stanner, W.E.H. 1933. The Daly River tribes. a report of field work in north Australia. *Oceania* 3: 377–305, 4: 10–29.

Stanner, W.E.H. 1938. Economic Change in North Australian Tribes. PhD thesis, University of London.

Stanner, W.E.H. 1963. *On Aboriginal Religion*. Sydney: Oceania.

Stanner, W.E.H. 1965. Religion, totemism and symbolism. In R.M. and C.H. Berndt (eds.) *Aboriginal Man in Australia*, pp207–237. Sydney: Angus and Robertson.

Stanner, W.E.H. 1969. The Yirrkala case: some general principles of Aboriginal land-holding. Unpublished manuscript, 12pp. Australian Institute of Aboriginal and Torres Strait Islander Studies Library, Canberra.

Stanner, W.E.H. 1979. *Report on Field Work in North Central and North Australia 1934–35*. Canberra: Australian Institute of Aboriginal Studies [Microfiche No 1].

Stanton, John E. 1983. Old business, new owners: succession and 'the Law' on the fringe of the Western Desert. In N. Peterson and M. Langton (eds.) *Aborigines, Land and Land Rights*, pp160–171. Canberra: Australian Institute of Aboriginal Studies.

Sterritt, Neil J., Susan Marsden, Robert Galois, Peter R. Grant and Richard Overstall 1998. *Tribal Boundaries in the Nass Watershed*. Vancouver: University of British Columbia Press.

Stevens, Frank 1974. *Aborigines in the Northern Territory Cattle Industry*. Canberra: Australian National University Press.

Strehlow, T.G.H. 1947. *Aranda Traditions*. Melbourne: Melbourne University Press.

Strehlow, T.G.H. 1965. Culture, social structure, and environment in Aboriginal Central Australia. In R.M. Berndt and C.H. Berndt (eds.) *Aboriginal Man in Australia. Essays in Honour of Emeritus Professor A.P. Elkin*, pp121–145. Sydney: Angus and Robertson.

Strehlow, T.G.H. 1970. Geography and the totemic landscape in Central Australia: a functional study. In R.M. Berndt (ed.) *Australian Aboriginal Anthropology*, pp92–140. Perth: University of Western Australia Press.

Sutton, Peter 1973. Gugu-Badhun and its Neighbours: a Linguistic Salvage Study. MA thesis, Macquarie University.

Sutton, Peter 1978. Wik: Aboriginal Society, Territory and Language at Cape Keerweer, Cape York Peninsula, Australia. PhD thesis, University of Queensland.

Sutton, Peter 1980. Notes on some aspects of traditional Aboriginal land takeovers marked by conflict. Unpublished typescript 17pp. For the Finniss River Land Claim. Darwin: Northern Land Council.

Sutton, Peter 1982. Personal power, kin classification and speech etiquette in Aboriginal Australia. In J. Heath, F. Merlan and A. Rumsey (eds.) *Languages of Kinship in Aboriginal Australia*, pp182–200. Sydney: Oceania Linguistic Monographs.

Sutton, Peter 1983. An Aboriginal claim to unalienated Crown land on the Murranji Track (Northern Territory). In P. Sutton, L. Coltheart and A. McGrath *The Murranji Land Claim*, pp51–156. Darwin: Northern Land Council.

Sutton, Peter 1985. Gaps and lapses. *Adelaide Review* 10: 17–18.

Sutton, Peter (ed.) 1988. *Dreamings: The Art of Aboriginal Australia*. New York: The Asia Society Galleries and George Braziller; Melbourne: Viking.

Sutton, Peter 1990. The pulsating heart: large scale cultural and demographic processes in Aboriginal Australia. In Betty Meehan and Neville White (eds.) *Hunter-gatherer Demography, Past and Present*, pp71–80. Sydney: Oceania.

Sutton, Peter 1991. Language in Aboriginal Australia: social dialects in a geographic idiom. In Suzanne Romaine (ed.) *Language in Australia*, pp49–66. Cambridge: Cambridge University Press.

Sutton, Peter 1993. *Flinders Islands & Melville National Parks Land Claim*. Cairns: Cape York Land Council.

Sutton, Peter 1995a. Atomism versus collectivism: the problem of group definition in native title cases. In Jim Fingleton and Julie Finlayson (eds.) *Anthropology in the Native Title Era: Proceedings of a Workshop*, pp1–10. Canberra: Australian Institute of Aboriginal and Torres Strait Islander Studies.

Sutton, Peter 1995b. *The Larrakia Group. Submission to Aboriginal Land Commissioner, re Kenbi (Cox Peninsula) Land Claim*. Darwin: Northern Land Council.

Sutton, Peter 1995c. *Country: Aboriginal Boundaries and Land Ownership in Australia*. Canberra: Aboriginal History Monographs.

Sutton, Peter 1995d. *Wik-Ngathan Dictionary*. Adelaide: Caitlin Press.

Sutton, Peter 1996. The robustness of Aboriginal land tenure systems: underlying and proximate customary titles. *Oceania* 67: 7–29.

Sutton, Peter 1997a. Materialism, sacred myth and pluralism: competing theories of the origin of Australian languages. In F. Merlan, J. Morton and A. Rumsey (eds.) *Scholar and Sceptic: Australian Aboriginal Studies in Honour of L.R. Hiatt*, pp211–242, 297–309. Canberra: Aboriginal Studies Press.

Sutton, Peter 1997b. *Wik Native Title: Anthropological Overview*. Cairns: Cape York Land Council.

Sutton, Peter 1998. *Native Title and the Descent of Rights*. Perth: National Native Title Tribunal.

Sutton, Peter 1999a. The system as it was straining to become – fluidity, stability and Aboriginal country groups. In J.D. Finlayson, B. Rigsby and H.J. Bek (eds.) *Connections in Native Title: Genealogies, Kinship and Groups*, pp13–57. Canberra: Centre for Aboriginal Economic Policy Research (Australian National University).

Sutton, Peter 1999b. Anthropological submission on the Reeves Review. *Supplement to Australian Anthropological Society Newsletter 75, March 1999*.

Sutton, Peter 2001a. Aboriginal country groups and 'the community of native title holders'. *National Native Title Tribunal Occasional Paper* 1/2001, *http://www.nntt.gov.au*.

Sutton, Peter 2001b. Kinds of rights in country: recognising customary rights as incidents of native title. *National Native Title Tribunal Occasional Paper* 2/2001, *http://www.nntt.gov.au*.

Sutton, Peter 2001c. Talking language. In Jane Simpson, David Nash, Mary Laughren, Peter Austin, Barry Alpher (eds.) *Forty Years On: Ken Hale and Australian Languages*, pp453–464. Canberra: Pacific Linguistics.

Sutton, Peter 2002. Rejoinder to Pannell and Vachon. *Australian Journal of Anthropology* 13: 45–50.

Sutton, Peter 2003. Estates and linguistic identities in Aboriginal Australia. Unpublished manuscript.

Sutton, Peter, Athol Chase and Bruce Rigsby 1993. *Flinders Islands & Melville National Parks Land Claim, Appendices (Restricted): Genealogies, Maps, Group Register, Site Register*. Cairns: Cape York Land Council.

Sutton, Peter, David Martin, John von Sturmer, Roger Cribb and Athol Chase 1990. *Aak: Aboriginal Estates and Clans between the Embley and Edward Rivers, Cape York Peninsula*. Adelaide: South Australian Museum.

Sutton, Peter, Petronella Morel and David Nash 1993. *The Muckaty Land Claim*. Darwin: Northern Land Council.

Sutton, Peter and Arthur B. Palmer 1980. *Daly River (Malak Malak) Land Claim*. Darwin: Northern Land Council.

Sutton, Peter and Petronella Vaarzon-Morel 2003. *Yulara Anthropology Report*. Alice Springs: Central Land Council.

Sutton, Peter and Kenneth Hale (in preparation). *Language, Time and Native Title: The Wik Case of North Australia*.

Tatz, Colin 1996. *Obstacle Race: Aborigines in Sport*. Sydney: University of New South Wales Press.

Tehan, Maureen 1997. Co-existence of interests in land: a dominant feature of the common law. *Land, Rights, Laws: Issues of Native Title*: Issues Paper no. 12. Native Titles Research Unit, Canberra: Australian Institute of Aboriginal and Torres Strait Islander Studies.

Terwiel-Powell, F.J. 1975. Developments in the Kinship System of the Hope Vale Aborigines. An Analysis of Changes in the Kinship Nomenclature and Social Structure of the Kuuku-Yimityirr Aborigines. PhD thesis, University of Queensland.

Thomson, Donald F. 1932. Ceremonial presentation of fire in north Queensland. a preliminary note on the place of fire in primitive ritual. *Man* 32: 1 62–166.

Thomson, D.F. 1934. Notes on a hero cult from the Gulf of Carpentaria, north Queensland. *Journal of the Royal Anthropological Institute* 64: 217–235.

Thomson, Donald F.1935. The joking relationship and organised obscenity in north Queensland. *American Anthropologist* 37: 460–490.

Thomson, Donald F. 1936. Fatherhood in the Wik Monkan tribe. *American Anthropologist* 38: 374–393.

Thomson, Donald F. 1939. The seasonal factor in human culture. *Proceedings of the Prehistoric Society* 5: 209–221.

Thomson, Donald F. 1949. *Economic Structure and the Ceremonial Exchange Cycle in Arnhem Land*. Melbourne: Macmillan.

Threlkeld, L.E. 1892. *An Australian Language as Spoken by the Awabakal, the People of Awaba of Lake Macquarie (Near Newcastle, New South Wales) Being an Account of their*

Language, Traditions, and Customs. Rearranged, Condensed, and Edited, with an Appendix, by John Fraser. Sydney: Government Printer.

Tindale, Norman B. 1925–26. Natives of Groote Eylandt and of the west coast of the Gulf of Carpentaria. *Records of the South Australian Museum* 3: 61–102, 103–134.

Tindale, Norman.B. 1941. Survey of the half-caste problem in South Australia. *Proceedings of the Royal Geographical Society of Australasia, South Australia Branch* 1940–41: 66–161.

Tindale, Norman B. 1974. *Aboriginal Tribes of Australia. Their Terrain, Environmental Controls, Distribution, Limits, and Proper Names.* Berkeley: University of California Press.

Tonkinson, Robert 1991. *The Mardu Aborigines.* New York: Holt, Rinehart and Winston.

Trigger, David S. 1982. *Nicholson River (Waanyi/Garawa) Land Claim.* Darwin: Northern Land Council.

Trigger, David S. 1989. *Garawa/Mugularrangu (Robinson River) Land Claim.* Darwin: Northern Land Council.

Trigger, David S. 1992. *Whitefella Comin'. Aboriginal Responses to Colonialism in Northern Australia.* Cambridge: Cambridge University Press.

Troy, Jakelin 1993. *King Plates: A History of Aboriginal Gorgets.* Canberra: Aboriginal Studies Press.

Turner, David H. 1974. *Tradition and Transformation: a Study of Aborigines in the Groote Eylandt Area, Northern Australia.* Canberra: Australian Institute of Aboriginal Studies.

Turner, David H., 1980. *Australian Aboriginal Social Organization.* Canberra: Australian Institute of Aboriginal Studies/ Atlantic Highlands: Humanities Press.

Vachon, Daniel A. and Sandra Pannell 1995. Relocating native title: situated perspectives and practices from the Kimberley. Paper presented at the Australian Anthropological Society conference, University of Adelaide, September 1995.

von Sturmer, John 1978. The Wik region: economy, territoriality and totemism in western Cape York Peninsula, north Queensland. PhD thesis, University of Queensland.

von Sturmer, John 1981. Talking with Aborigines. *Australian Institute of Aboriginal Studies Newsletter* 15:13–30.

von Sturmer, John 1984. The politics of residence. In Australian Institute of Aboriginal Studies, *Aborigines and Uranium: Consolidated Report to the Minister for Aboriginal Affairs on the Social Impact of Uranium Mining on the Aborigines of the Northern Territory,* pp104–118. Canberra: Australian Government Publishing Service.

Waddy, Julie A. 1988. *Classification of Plants and Animals from a Groote Eylandt Aboriginal Point of View.* 2 vols. Darwin: North Australia Research Unit (Australian National University).

Walsh, Michael (comp.) 1981–83. Map 20: Western part of Australia. In Wurm, S.A., S. Hattori (and T. Baumann, cartography). *Language Atlas of the Pacific Area. Part 1: New Guinea area, Oceania, Australia.* Canberra: Pacific Linguistics for the Australian Academy of the Humanities in collaboration with the Japan Academy.

Walsh, Michael 2002. Language ownership: a key issue for native title. In J. Henderson and D. Nash (eds.) *Language in Native Title,* pp231–244. Canberra: Native Title Research Unit, Australian Institute of Aboriginal and Torres Strait Islander Studies.

Walsh, Michael, with Frank McKeown and Elizabeth Povinelli 1989. *Ten Years On. A Supplement to the 1979 Kenbi Land Claim Book.* Darwin: Northern Land Council.

Warner, W. Lloyd 1958 (2nd edition). *A Black Civilization: a Social Study of an Australian Tribe.* New York: Harper and Brothers.

Waters, Bruce E. 1989. *Djinang and Djinba–a Grammatical and Historical Perspective*. Canberra: Pacific Linguistics.

Watson, Pamela 1983. *This Precious Foliage. A study of the Aboriginal Psycho-active Drug Pituri*. Sydney: Oceania

Wheeler, Gerald C. 1910. *The Tribe, and Intertribal Relations in Australia*. London: Murray.

White, Isobel 1981. Generation moieties in Australia: structural, social and ritual implications. *Oceania* 52: 6–27

Whitehurst, Rose (comp.) 1992. *Noongar Dictionary. Noongar to English and English to Noongar*. Bunbury, WA: Noongar Language and Culture Centre.

Williams, Don 1981. *Exploring Aboriginal Kinship*. Canberra: Curriculum Development Centre.

Williams, Nancy M. 1982. A boundary is to cross: observations on Yolngu boundaries and permission. In N.M. Williams and E.S. Hunn (eds.) *Resource Managers: North American and Australian Hunter-gatherers*, pp131–154. Boulder, Colorado: Westview Press for the American Association for the Advancement of Science.

Williams, Nancy M. 1985. Aboriginal decision-making. In Diane E. Barwick, Jeremy Beckett and Marie Reay (eds.) *Metaphors of Interpretation: Essays in Honour of W.E.H. Stanner* pp240–269. Canberra: Australian National University.

Williams, Nancy M. 1986. *The Yolngu and their Land: a System of Land Tenure and the Fight for its Recognition*. Canberra: Australian Institute of Aboriginal Studies.

Williams, Nancy M. 1999a. The nature of 'permission'. In J.C. Altman, F. Morphy and T. Rowse (eds.) *Land Rights at Risk? Evaluations of the Reeves Report*, pp53–64. Canberra: Centre for Aboriginal Economic Policy Research, Australian National University.

Williams, Nancy M. 1999b. The relationship of genealogical reckoning and group formation: Yolngu examples. In J.D. Finlayson, B. Rigsby and H.J. Bek (eds.) *Connections in Native Title: Genealogies, Kinship and Groups*, pp125–139. Canberra: Centre for Aboriginal Economic Policy Research, Australian National University.

Wootten, Hal 1994a. Mabo – issues and challenges. *The Judicial Review* 303:330–340.

Wootten, Hal 1994b. The Mabo decision and native title. In S. Woenne-Green, R. Johnston, R. Sultan and A. Wallis (eds) *Competing Interests. Aboriginal Participation in National Parks and Conservation Reserves in Australia*. Maroochydore, Qld: Corgi Printing.

Wootten, Hal 1995. The end of dispossession? Anthropologists and lawyers in the native title process. In J. Finlayson and D. Smith (eds.) *Native Title: Emerging Issues for Research, Policy and Practice*, pp101–118. Canberra: Centre for Aboriginal Economic Policy Research, Australian National University.

Wright, Lisa 2003. Themes emerging from the High Court's recent native title decisions. Perth: National Native Title Tribunal (Legal Services Section).

Zorc, R. David 1986. *Yolngu-Matha Dictionary*. Darwin: School of Australian Linguistics.

Index